The History of Foxhunting

The History of Foxhunting

Roger Longrigg

Clarkson N. Potter, Inc./Publisher   NEW YORK

DISTRIBUTED BY CROWN PUBLISHERS, INC.

House Editor: Peter Faure
Designer: Brian Paine
Indexer: Roger Longrigg

Text setting, monochrome printing and binding by
Cox & Wyman Ltd, Fakenham, Norfolk, England
Colour printing by Jolly & Barber Ltd,
Rugby, England

Inquiries should be addressed to
Clarkson N. Potter, Inc., 419 Park Avenue South,
New York, N.Y. 10016

Library of Congress Catalog Card Number 74–21747

Endpapers illustration:
KING GEORGE III RETURNING FROM HUNTING THROUGH ETON
by Thomas Rowlandson, *c.* 1790–5.

Frontispiece:
COMENT ON DOIT CHASCIER ET PRENDRE LE REGNART
The method of foxhunting taught by Gaston Phébus in 1387
is perfectly recognizable: the horsemen are galloping to
stay with hounds, and hounds are close to their fox's brush.
What is odd, as in contemporary staghunting and
wolfhunting pictures (see pp. 30 and 36), is the mixture
of breeds in the pack (there is no doubt that the different
breeds were depicted as faithfully as possible). It seems that
Gaston believed in complementing the qualities of some
breeds with others when drawing his pack for a particular
chase or day: as some huntsmen include, for example, a few
doghounds in a bitchpack in order to improve its cry. The
much smaller hounds probably go underground. It is odd
that neither horseman seems to be carrying a horn, as motes
special to foxhunting had existed for at least 50 years.
Manuscript illustration from the *Livre de la Chasse*
by Gaston Phébus, 1387.

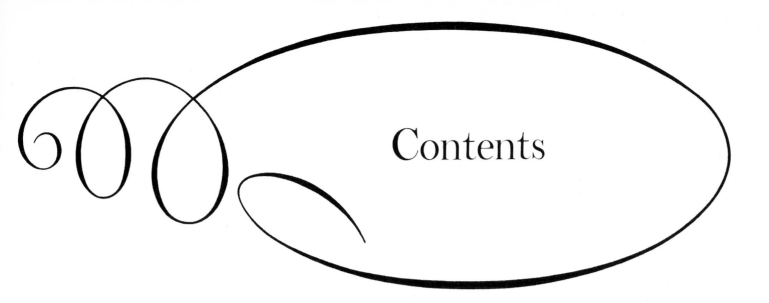

Contents

Contents

Contents

Acknowledgments

My greatest debt – and I wish there were any way I could repay it – is to the memory of the late Mr A. H. Higginson, a great Master of Hounds in two hemispheres and a great collector (and writer) of sporting books. Without his superb and almost comprehensive collection of British and American books now housed in the London Library, this one would have been very difficult to write and very superficial when written. I have had occasion before to thank the Librarian and staff of the London Library for their invariable kindness and helpfulness, and I do so again. Mr Alexander Mackay-Smith, most eminent of recent American hunting historians and himself a distinguished Master of Hounds, has been so kind as to read, and copiously and pungently annotate, my American chapters. He has put me right on a large number of points, and I am tremendously grateful to him. I should add that I have, after careful reconsideration and re-examination of the sources, adhered to some conclusions with which I know he strongly disagrees; any errors are therefore mine, not his. Of the many people who have lent me books, the most forbearing has been Mr H. Stewart Treviranus of Washington, D.C., who took the trouble to send me from America some precious (and very heavy) copies of rare limited editions. I must acknowledge the kindness of Mrs George Bambridge, Macmillan & Co. Ltd and Doubleday & Co. Inc. for permission to quote from *The Brushwood Boy* and *Little Foxes* by Rudyard Kipling; of John Farquharson Ltd for permission, on behalf of the estate, to quote from *Mount Music* by E. OE. Somerville and 'Martin Ross'; of Routledge & Kegan Paul Ltd for permission to quote from *The Foxhound of the 20th Century* by Cuthbert Bradley; and of Collins Ltd to quote from *Try Back: A Huntsman's Reminiscences* by A. H. Higginson. I have tried but failed to make contact with other publishers, who must either accept my apologies or answer my letters. By the staff of George Rainbird Ltd, and especially Mr Peter Faure, I have once again been shown almost superhuman patience and kindness.

List of Color Plates

[9]

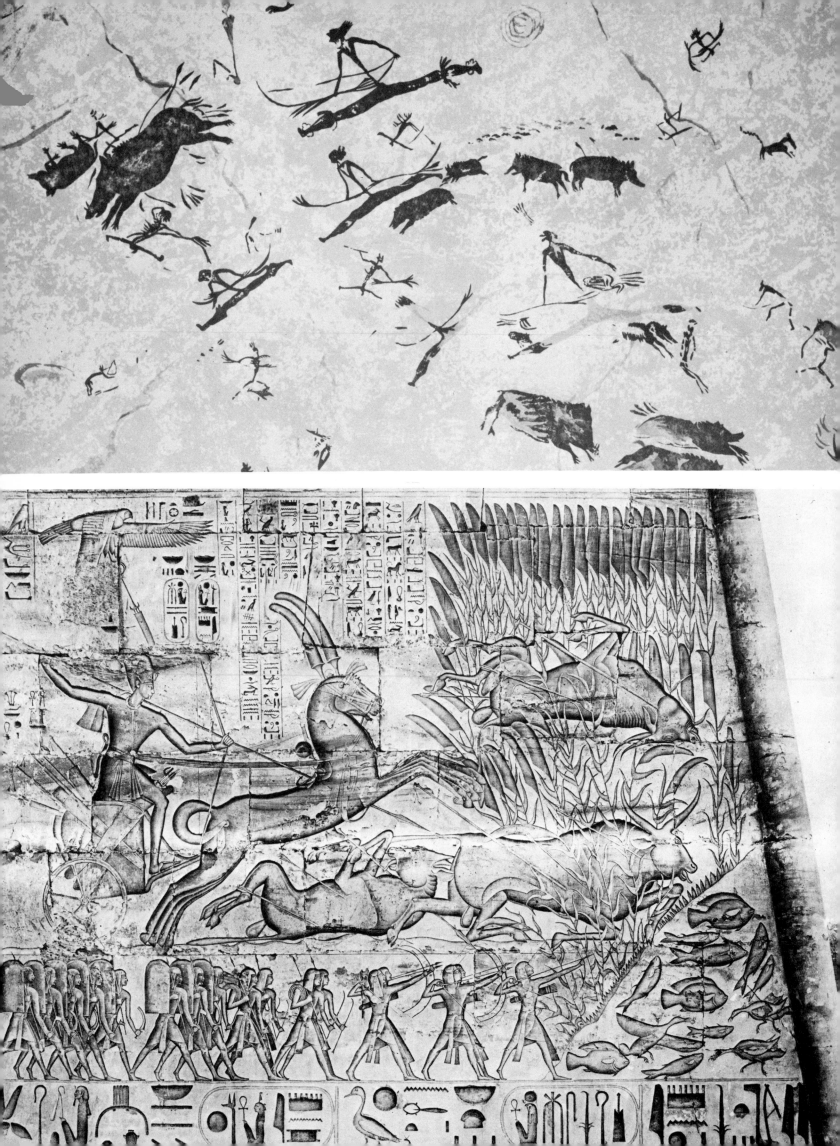

1 The Ancient World

Egypt, Assyria, Persia

In the austere and theocratic Egypt of the 15th and early 14th centuries BC, no pharaoh or noble could admit to enjoying his hunting, but by the mid 14th century the new 'heretical' atmosphere of Thebes allowed rich men to enjoy life. They hunted for sport; they were the first people to do so. They hoped to do so in the afterlife. Hunting became a part of polite education; it was also part of the royal mystique, copiously illustrated on ritualistic objects and clothes.[1]

Before about 1500 BC the Egyptians hunted on foot. Then the Hyksos arrived from the southern steppes with horse and chariot, and a noble's house had stables as well as kennels attached, in the charge of the huntsman.[2]

Most hunting was in the open desert, which had a lavish variety of game. A great man proceeded to the meet in his chariot, accompanied not only by the huntsman and his assistants but also by an extensive commissariat of men carrying food and drinks on yokes. The game was often driven into nets, often taken alive with a lasso, or induced into a cage, and brought back to the noble's gamepark where it was hunted with hounds. More elegantly, a noble sometimes hunted in the open desert by following hounds in his two-horse chariot.[3]

The Egyptians had scenting hounds, greyhounds, big fighting dogs of the mastiff type, and small dogs like terriers which they used for harehunting. They also coursed with cheetah and possibly lions.[4] Hunting dress was a mid-thigh tunic instead of the usual one to the knee; it was of a muted colour. Horses were divested of ornaments likely to scare away the game.

In Assyria, Nimrod 'was a mighty hunter before the Lord';[5] all Assyrian kings followed his precedent. The hunt was a kind of conquest; military conquest was a kind of hunt.

The game was lion and bull, stag, gazelle, ibex, onager, wild sheep and hare. They used javelin and bow, and for hare and partridge they had hawks. Like the Egyptians, the kings had parks in which game was preserved and sometimes hunted. They were much more addicted, however, to hunting in the hills to the north of Nineveh, and in the Tigris–Euphrates lowlands to the south. They had hounds and mastiffs; they also coursed hare and gazelle with greyhounds 'comely in going'.[6]

The great difference between Assyrian hunting and any before or contemporary lay in the size and quality of the horse. From the 9th century BC it was substantially larger than any other, which meant that it was ridden. The results were the

PREHISTORIC BOAR HUNTING
Man is a predator, but without the speed, strength or sensory equipment of his quarry. He overcame his physical deficiencies in four ways: by forming groups; by fashioning and using weapons; by using the nose and jaws of hounds; and ultimately by riding or driving horses. These prehistoric Iberians have achieved the first two stages; they have also learned to protect their legs against the undergrowth. The small animal on the right is hard to identify: it may be a fox; it may even be a hound. Silk-screen print by Douglas Masonowicz after a water colour by T.-B. Porcar from a Mesolithic cave in Castellón de la Plana, Spain.

RAMESES III HUNTING WILD BULL
The Egyptian horses of the early 12th century BC were evidently good; so were their drivers (the horses were still too small to ride). Rameses really did hunt (as the frail Tutenkhamun may never have done, for all the royal hunting mystique recorded in his tomb); unlike the contemporary Achaeans he drove himself while using bow and javelin. The bull was weakened with arrows, before being tackled with sword or spear. Rameses came out hunting with a great retinue of bowmen and barmen, but he must have left them far behind. Gazelle, hare, fox and ostrich were coursed with greyhounds. The hunting chariots were similar to war chariots but much lighter. Rock engraving at Medinet Habu.

world's first effective cavalry and the world's first hunting on horseback.

The bulk of the field as of the army rode their horses, but kings and notables both hunted and fought from chariots. By the late 7th century, however, King Assurbanipal hunted wild asses on horseback. This was considered impossible by Xenophon more than two centuries later, owing to the speed of the ass: a startling tribute to the Assyrian horse.

The Persians copied gameparks from Assyria; from the Medes they got horses even better than the Assyrian, and hunted entirely on horseback. They also learned from the Medes a cheerful, social, informal approach to hunting.[7] The horse was the celebrated Nisaean, which carried Alexander the Great on his conquests, and saved the Chinese Empire from the Huns.[8] This was the horse ridden by Darius, who hunted several times a month, taking half his guard. Often they missed their luncheon, which encouraged the king to consider hunting good training in hardship as well as horsemanship.[9]

Cyrus rode down stag and boar with a spear. Hunting stags in this way had become normal with the fast horses of the 7th century, but pig sticking was unique to this energetic king. He hunted on horseback all over his dominions. This enabled him to inspect the husbandry and security of all parts, a precedent followed in western Europe 1,500 years later.[10]

[12]

Greece

In the 10th and 9th centuries BC, Greece and coastal Asia Minor (Ionia and the Troad) still carried areas of dense forest, in which lived boar and stag. These conditions created a style of hunting quite unlike anything known to Egypt or the Middle East, being more like medieval sport. Odysseus, staying with Autolycus by Mount Parnassus, made a dawn start with his host's sons and their hounds after boar. They went up the hillside on foot through the woods, hounds in front slowly and meticulously hunting the line. The boar was surrounded in a thicket. Odysseus met it with his boar spear when it charged out.[11] The essence, in dense undergrowth, was a hound with a really good nose, a point made repeatedly by Homer. But above the forest there was bare hilltop; there the Homeric Greeks hunted ibex and hare, and sometimes coursed.[12]

Immediately after Homer's time, the Greek countryside began to change, and with it hunting. In Boeotia, farms had been carved out of the forest by 800 BC, and the countryman was not necessarily a huntsman. The only animal Hesiod's pupil was to have was a watchdog; there is no mention of a hound.[13] Where the forest receded, so did big game; as early as 750 BC the emphasis had begun to shift to the hare.[14]

By the 5th century there was intensive agriculture near all the cities. Flat land was under vines, figs, olives and corn. Big game fled to the mountains. Hares multiplied enormously. Horses, except on the roads, did expensive damage. The Greek sportsman became a beagler.

Xenophon was an expert horseman, and writing about 400 BC he warmly approved of hunting on horseback in suitable country.[15] But his own country of Elis was as tamed as that round Athens, and his horse was a covert hack. He went out hare-hunting alone with his hounds and his netkeeper (young, enthusiastic, not a slave). Hounds were brought out in couples, and the bitches had girths with spurs to protect the purity of the pack. They were tied to trees while the nets were placed. When they started the hare and began to hunt, it was disastrous to overrun them and unwise to holloa, which brought their heads up. If they checked, the huntsman cast back; if necessary he put a stick in the ground and cast all round it. The hare could easily outrun the hounds of the time; it was 'seldom caught in fair hunting', but by reason of its stupidity and panic. In spring the ground was stained by flowers, in autumn by fruit (which the huntsman was on no account to steal); a full moon was accused of drying up scent like a noonday sun. A keen man hunted every day except in a high wind. He and his netkeeper wore light, loose clothes and light shoes.

Harehounds were of two kinds: the Castorian, and a breed thought to be a cross of dog and fox. A good hound had a good nose, long ears, cat feet, strength, courage, speed, agility. A good pack hunted together, noses to the ground and going at a steady pace. Stallions were most carefully chosen. Puppies were given memorable names always of two syllables. Skirters and babblers were deplored (and grey eyes); it was recognized that such faults were often in the breeding. Xenophon held a view widely shared today, and as widely repudiated: the huntsman should always feed his hounds.[16]

Away from the cities and the lowlands there was still boar, here and there plentiful. The way it was hunted differed in no major respect from that of Homeric Asia Minor or medieval Europe. A tender-nosed Laconian bitch was used as a lymer; when she found, she was tied up and a net was carried round the thicket. Hounds were thrown in, and each man grasped spear and javelin. The hounds were Indian, Cretan or Locrian; there were also Molossians (mastiffs) and Spartans (big greyhounds).

The Greeks maintained, as strongly as the Assyrians and Persians, that hunting was training for war. Under the régime of the mysterious lawgiver Lycurgus, the Spartans, when not actually at war, spent their time in the next most profitable activities of dancing, feasting, hunting, physical training and debate. The uncomplaining boy whose vitals were eaten by the fox had poached that fox from someone's land; poaching and other forms of daring theft were part of his warlike education.[17] For hunting, the Spartans freely used each others' horses and hounds, as well as their slaves.[18]

But there was more to hunting that this, especially with the Athenians. To Plato relaxation in the ideal republic would be dancing, hunting, gymnastic contests and horse racing.[19] To Xenophon hunting was a necessary part of a well-rounded man's education. It was god-given and it could be justified on the strictest philosophical grounds. Nature, said Aristotle, made nothing in vain; having made animals suitable for hunting, it was plainly Nature's intention that they should be hunted.[20] The Sophists in the late 5th century formed the first vocal anti-bloodsports lobby, but their views were execrated by the writers quoted.

The Athenian gentleman, in fact, was an educated squire who took a full part in the political life of the city, and also in the rural life of his estate. The squire's experience, close to animals and to natural realities, improved the quality of his citizenship.[21] It is not at all grotesque to compare this ideal with that of England in the 17th to 19th centuries, or of men like Thomas Jefferson in America.

Italy and the Roman Empire

The ancient Etruscans hunted on horseback with spears, their horses being as good as the Greek and their country still wild. Then Rome tamed central Italy, and a land-based aristocracy established itself, which derived its inherited superiority specifically from inherited acres.[22] The Roman landowner was sporting; he had fast, strong horses and his own hounds. About 35 BC he was instructed: 'Look after your dogs; you will often course the shy wild asses, and hunt the hare and the doe with hounds; and often start the wild boar from their thickets with baying hounds; and over the high hills with the hunting-cry drive a great stag into the nets.'[23] These hounds, said the poet of sport as well as of love, had speed and power; they could 'sniff the wind with raised heads then lower their noses to the ground and speak to the line'.[24] A less sporting poet commiserated with the hunting widow: 'Out beneath the cold sky, forgetful of his tender wife, stays the hunter, whether a deer has been sighted by the trusty hounds, or a Marsian boar has broken the finely twisted nets.'[25]

Farming and overhunting made the larger game scarce by AD 100.[26] But by this time the Empire was cosmopolitan; it was Greek as well as Roman in language, Asian, Gaulish and African as well as Italian in territory. Hunting history moves to the provinces. In most respects, both quarry and methods were those of the Greeks, and writers on the subject produced supplements to Xenophon rather than wholly new approaches.

But there were major developments in both horse and hound.

The Persians, on their marvellous Nisaeans, had galloped fast enough to hunt the deer and wild ass on horseback; but the Greeks rode nothing of this class. The Romans in the last century BC not only had good enough horses to follow greyhounds after deer, but were also breeding and importing specialized horses for different purposes: in about AD 1 the cavalry horse was considered too heavy and awkward for hunting, for which a handier animal was required.[27] Specialization was, indeed, carried to a curious extreme about AD 180: 'For hunting spotted-footed deer, ride a dark-eyed horse; blue-eyed for bears; tawny-eyed for leopards; fiery and flaming for boar; and bright grey for the grey-eyed lion.'[28]

The improvement to hounds was still more startling, because it involved the importation of breeds completely unknown to the Greeks. There were two of these, quite different: the Celtic Segusius hound of Gaul, extremely fast; and the Agassaean breed from Britain. The British hound was small, lean, shaggy, barrel-bodied and remarkable for its powers of scenting. Very few years after the first Roman arrival in Britain, it was well known in Italy and considered the very best of all trackers,[29] and it kept this reputation for at least 200 years.[30] Although the Greek techniques of netting were still widely used, deer and hare could now be hunted without them. Where Xenophon was a beagler, Arrian and Oppian rode to harriers.

One other innovation deserves mention. The hunting horn was unknown to the Greeks or the early Empire. The later Romans had four-foot metal trumpets, straight, slightly upcurved, or in almost a full circle; they also had short curved natural horns. Their original purpose was for calling cattle. By AD 180 they were used, not for communicating with hounds or men, but for starting an animal out of covert by delivering a blast behind its ear.[31]

In Italy the game remained hare, deer and boar. But wider frontiers increased the variety of sport and the methods of catching it. Boar were lured into the nets by flute music.[32] The giraffe (believed a camel–leopard cross) was hunted as by the Ethiopians; the ostrich (believed a giraffe–sparrow cross) as by the Egyptians, with horses and hounds. Leopard was most easily caught by getting it drunk. Twenty jars of eleven-year-old sweet wine were poured into the waterhole; the leopard drank, danced madly like a Bacchante, and went to sleep. When hunting the gazelle you were on no account to give it time to stop and urinate; the breather, as well as the relief, gave it a phenomenal new burst of speed.[33]

Although Alexander the Great had enjoyed his foxhunting in Asia, from Xenophon to Arrian (400 BC to AD 100) the fox was almost always a pest which spoiled the harehunting. But as early as AD 80 Italians went foxhunting deliberately; the fox was netted at the end, and the effect on hounds was accepted as deplorable, but the chase itself was undoubtedly exciting.[34] In Thrace foxes were hunted for their pelts, of which the Thracians made caps. Elsewhere in AD 180 the hunt was usually got up because of the damage the foxes were doing, but the enemy was respected for his unique cunning. Ambush, noose and net were useless. The fox could only be hunted by a large pack of good hounds; and then the hunting was most enjoyable.[35] Fifty years later, in one man's view at least, the fox had joined the hare in esteem: autumn was the season of 'hounds, hares, and foxes'.[36]

ETRUSCAN HAREHUNTING

Nets were used by the Egyptians, and were normal in Greek hunting. The small ones were made of nine-ply string, of Carthaginian or Phasian flax, a yard high; they had a cord like a draw string, and were held up on stakes of varying height to cope with the unevenness of the ground. Road nets were twenty hands high and made of twelve-ply string. The large nets were as much as 180 feet long and made of sixteen-ply string. The great merit of the nets was that after a fair hunt the hare could be taken undamaged; this was possible because the hounds could be stopped, although these look bent on blood and, from their tails, resemble cheetahs. Flung hare-sticks assist the hounds to drive the hare into the net; the branch held by the horseman may be such a missile, or he may be 'thistle-whipping' the covert. Pontic Oinochoe attributed to the Paris painter, Etruscan, *c.* 520 BC.

North Africa was a sporting area with its own traditions. Dido had organized a hunt for Aeneas and his friends; a large party left the city as soon as it was light, taking nets, snares, broad-headed spears and keen-scented hounds. Dido herself was out, in unsuitable flowing garments. Then the storm broke, Dido and Aeneas sheltered in a cave, and it was the queen who was rolled over.[37]

By the time Virgil wrote this scandalous hunting story, Libyan huntsmen had abandoned most of the traditional equipment. They were able to do so because of their horses. The evidence not only of Roman writers, but also of the Roman racecourse, declares the Libyan the best horse in the world throughout the time of the Roman Empire. They also had very fast dogs, the so-called Ethiopian greyhounds, which suited the open desert where sight worked better than scent. With these they chased onagers, ridden down and taken alive, tamed, and used to breed admirable mules.[38]

Gaul meanwhile had both professional and amateur huntsmen; the former used nets, the latter went hunting and coursing for sport. They met at dawn on horseback, with hounds and greyhounds. For each hare caught, two obols were put in a votive moneybox; for each fox a drachma – three times as much, because the fox was much more difficult to catch; for a deer, altogether nobler, four drachmas. At the end of the season the money was used for a feast in honour of Artemis, the hounds all being garlanded and joining the revels.[39]

In the later Empire, more and more emperors were devoted to hunting. Hadrian and Trajan found relief from the cares of their office in the hunting field, and earned nothing but respect thereby; but Constans I was treacherously killed while hunting in AD 350, and Gratian was accused of neglecting his empire for hunting, and consequently assassinated in AD 383. Among soldiers, hunting retained its ancient reputation: Vegetius in AD 400 echoed the opinion of the previous 1,200 years when he said that hunting men were always welcome recruits. (Fisherman and falconers were invited to stay away.)[40]

HUNTING IN ROMAN BRITAIN
This mosaic, of *c.* AD 350, comes from Hinton St Mary, Dorset. Britain was one of the remote outposts where the later Empire hunted far more vigorously than at home. The island teemed with red deer, especially the areas, such as Dorset, covered with dense hardwood forest. The Romano–British owner of this hound undoubtedly hunted on horseback: the British horse, enlarged by blood from the Continent, had outgrown the chariot 300 years earlier. His huntsmen and bowmen followed on foot. The hound may be identified, though not with certainty, as the celebrated Agassaean, the probable ancestor of the Welsh and Breton breeds.

[16]

2 The Dark Ages

Arrival of the Barbarians

The Barbarian conquerors of Europe brought their own hunting with them, but in certain important respects they were the hunting heirs of the Empire. From Spain to the Rhineland, from England to Italy, the invaders rode, hunted and raced the Roman horse. The Franks also adopted the local scenting hound.

In Italy, barbarian vigour revitalized a decadent rural tradition. Odoacer and Theoderic, the first kings after the fall of the Empire, hunted the countryside as it had hardly been hunted for centuries. The Lombards brought not only a proto-feudal organization but an attitude to life in which 'war and the chase were their only pleasures, and their luxury knew no other objects'.[1] The Franks, the Burgundians, the Visigoths were all devoted to hunting, and a number of kings were killed by wild boars or by falling from their horses.

France

The strongest tradition developed in France. Dagobert's laws were the first which reserved the large game (stag and boar) for the king and his privileged nobles.

One of these fortunates was St Hubert (656–727), son of the Duke of Aquitaine. Hubert 'was fond of hunting, and followed the wild boar and the stag in the vast forests of the Ardennes' until one Good Friday he was converted by seeing a crucifix between the horns of a stag which he was hunting on horseback. He later retired to a hermitage, founded a monastery, miraculously cured a large number of people of hydrophobia, established his breed of black or black-and-tan hounds, and was consequently canonized as patron saint of hunters. In this office he replaced St Eustace, the circumstances of whose conversion were curiously enough identical.[2]

Charlemagne, who re-enacted Dagobert's laws, inherited like St Hubert both a family and a national hunting tradition: 'He practised equitation and the chase assiduously: which came to him from his breeding; for in the whole world could not be found a nation to equal the Franks in this.' He had his sons from an early age taught to ride horses and manage hounds.[3] Charlemagne made hunting a major state institution, not only preserving royal forests but also adding a kind of pomp which has remained peculiarly French.

In one isolated part of the country there was for centuries Celtic hunting, with Celtic hounds, unaffected either by St Hubert's breed or by royal instructions.

This was in the north west: ancient Armorica, which became Brittany when it was settled by refugees driven across the channel by the advancing Anglo–Saxons. They brought language, druidic religion, Arthurian legend, and a way of life unlike that of the rest of France; it seems certain that they brought also their special Agassaean hounds, and continued to breed and cherish them. It is not certain, but it is highly probable, that these Romano–British hounds were the principal ancestors of the *chiens fauves* (tawny or fallow) *de Bretagne*.

The Northmen meanwhile occupied the neighbouring part of France. They found excellent grazing and fine hunting country; they brought feudal organization and a notion of ducal power more absolute than anything else in Europe; they were active, greedy, lavish and 'given to hunting and hawking, delighting in horses and accoutrements'.[4] They acquired St Huberts, and from them developed their own breed of hound.

[18]

CONVERSION OF ST EUSTACE
OR ST HUBERT
It is not at all certain which saint is here shown: according to hagiography both were converted, while hunting, by the vision illustrated; both consequently retired from the chase to the cloister; both became patron saints of hunting. St Hubert retained this role, supplanting St Eustace; his day opens the season for most Continental hunting. The hounds, horse and clothes in the picture are not those of St Hubert's time but of the early 15th century. Painting by Pisanello.

Anglo–Saxons and Danes

The Anglo–Saxons were not horsemen when they arrived, but they rapidly became so. Bede many times mentions the English beginning to ride.[5] Then they began to hunt. Alfred the Great, before he was twelve years old, 'was a most expert and active hunter, and excelled in all the branches of that most noble art, to which he applied with incessant labour and amazing success'.[6] After his grandson Athelstan defeated King Constantine of Wales at the Battle of Brunanburgh, the annual tribute he imposed included 'hawks and sharp-scented dogs fit for hunting wild beasts'.[7] Edgar, like Cyrus, combined hunting expeditions with royal progresses of inspection. Ethelred forbade hunting on Sunday.

The hunting laws of the English kings did little more than affirm the right of property: a man could hunt on his own land but not on another's. The areas reserved for the king's sport were not disproportionate; nor were the penalties for poaching.

Cnut, like his Anglo–Saxon predecessors, loved hunting, and he 'reduced the laws of the forest in England to a system'. He did this at Winchester, at Christmas 1036. Of the laws there enacted, '"The *seventy-seventh* gives liberty to every man to hunt in his own Grounds, but forbids all men under a Penalty to meddle with the King's Game, especially in the places which he had fenced by Privilege." By those places thus privileged [comments Tyrrell in 1697] he means those which afterwards the *Normans* called *Forests*, being Ground Desart and Woody, lying open to the King's Deer.'[8]

The last English kings before the Norman Conquest hunted as enthusiastically as any of their predecessors. For Edward the Confessor, 'There was only one diversion in which he took the greatest possible delight, namely, to follow a pack of fleet hounds in pursuit of their game, and to cheer them on with his voice. Every day, after divine service, he took the field, and spent his life in these beloved sports.'[9]

Of Anglo–Saxon origin are the 'fence months', the close seasons in fawning and cubbing time. Cnut reduced this usage to law, forbidding all hunting for fifteen days each side of midsummer. This kind of prohibition was re-enacted throughout the Middle Ages, the 'periods of grace' varying and lengthening, whence derive the modern hunting seasons. The name for November was *Blot monath*, 'blood month', when serious hunting began.[10]

ANGLO–SAXON HUNTING
This picture of 'swine hunting' is said to show an English chieftain of the 9th century. The artist has included only one couple of what was undoubtedly a much larger pack – boar were found with scenting hounds and tackled with big alaunts, of which several were often injured or killed. The nobleman's boar-spear has the normal cross-piece (known to and described by Homer) which prevents the boar impaling itself and descending up the shaft on to the spearman; the huntsman has omitted this precaution. The horn is natural cow.

Ireland and Scotland

The Irish hunted with enthusiasm from unrecorded ages. According to legend, the first inhabitants lived entirely by hunting, fowling and fishing, the country being all forest and bog. Large gatherings of men were not profitable, owing to the quantity and bitterness of argument among the hunters.[11]

In AD I the horses were still too small to ride: Cuchulain and the Red Branch Knights of Ulster hunted on foot or in two-horse chariots.[12]

Two hundred and fifty years later there were large changes. The Fena of Erin were Finn's army in Kildare, all-powerful because they had large enough horses to ride. Clearly these were either imported or bred from imported stock; according to Irish tradition the important source was Spain.[13] Finn's men hunted all summer, all over Ireland, living off the chase. Finn himself on one occasion rested on the hill of Knockainy, in County Limerick, while his friends hunted in the plain below: 'and it was sweet music to Finn's ear the cry of the long-snouted dogs as they routed the deer from their covers and the badgers from their dens; the pleasant emulating shouts of the youths; the whistling and signalling of the huntsman; and the encouraging cheers of the heroes as they spread themselves through the glens and woods, and over the broad green plain of Cliach'.[14] Cailte and his friends heard the music of three different packs of hounds hunting round the head of Sliabh Lugda; they also heard a beagle pack giving tongue: 'heavy-sided, low-bellied' hounds.[15]

The methods of deercatching were set out in the Brehon Laws sometime before AD 800. The essence was a pit, with a spear stuck in a wooden socket at the bottom. The spear was of sharpened wood or had a metal point. Pit and spear were covered with a *brathlang*, a camouflaging layer of sods and brambles. This evil device was introduced by Coba, huntsman of King Heremon. The first trap that Coba set he fell into himself, breaking one leg and both arms and upsetting his drinking cup. He consequently died of his wounds and of thirst.[16] Thus alerted to the danger of the trap, the Irish made a law that verbal warning of any new pit must be given to all nine households nearest.[17]

When Maelfothartaig, son of Ronan King of Leinster, visited the King of Scotland, he found 'hounds for boars, hounds for deer, and hounds for hares'.[18] The boarhound was doubtless a kind of mastiff; the Scottish deerhound was virtually identical to the Irish wolfhound, enormous, rough-haired, long-nosed; the harehound may have been of the low-bellied breed we cautiously identify as the Irish ancestor of the English beagle.

CHINESE HUNTING, 5TH CENTURY
This painted ceiling of a 'fairy landscape' comes from the Tun-Huang Caves in Kansu Province: northern China, bordered by the Great Wall and in incessant conflict with the marauding Huns. The military successes of the latter were made possible by their horses and horsemanship; the empire therefore mounted immensely costly expeditions to get 'horses of supernatural birth' from Afghanistan: these were almost certainly descendants of the Nisaeans brought east by Alexander the Great and his successors. The Chinese then took to riding, learning Hun horsemanship and for it adopting Hun dress. Horses and horsemanship saved the Chinese northern frontier, and also made possible this vigorous hunting of antelope and lion. The stirrup was invented by the Huns at about this time; it was immediately copied by the Chinese and later by the Middle East and Europe.

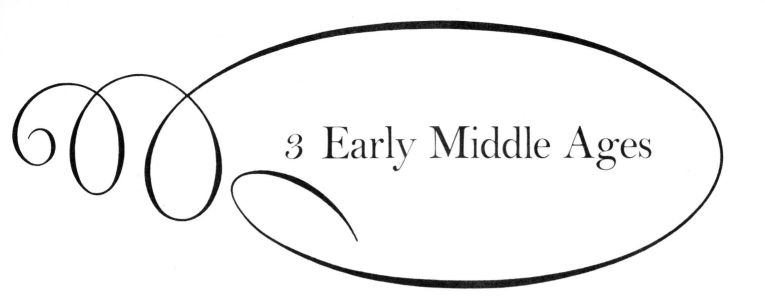

3 Early Middle Ages

France

In about AD 1000 'the first son of the lord is a fighter, the second a hunter, the third a farmer, and the fourth a stock-raiser'.[1] That second son helped to feed the household or garrison, and provide it with shoe and saddle leather, with wall and floor coverings.

The 11th-century huntsman chased boar, wolf, red and other deer, hare, and all the vermin beasts headed by fox and badger. He had big fighting dogs (alaunt or mastiff), sonorous-voiced scenting hounds more or less influenced by the blood of St Hubert's breed, greyhounds (*levriers*, light dogs), much smaller hounds of various local breeds ultimately derived from the Gaulish *Segusii*, and mongrel terriers for digging. He wore a belted tunic, and blew an 18-inch cow horn, the various calls of which were not yet subject to rule. Hunting was almost all in forests through which rides had not yet been cut. Much was therefore done on foot, and hounds often kept coupled, but a servant would be waiting in a cleared place, or by the forest's edge, with the horses.

These conditions put an immense premium on two hound qualities: cry and nose. Stamina would also have been desirable, but was not attained: consequently the French invented the system of hunting with relays of fresh hounds.

The St Hubert hounds went from the Ardennes into Normandy probably in the 10th century. Not much later they also went to the south west, there to develop, probably in the 11th century, into the Gascon hound. From some unknown source this derived its characteristic blue-mottled colour. Still in this early period, the British Agassaean was developed into the *chien fauve de Bretagne*, a totally different stamp of hound, rough-haired, tawny or grizzled-red, less distinguished for nose or cry but far superior in drive and courage, and extremely apt to riot. Probably at the same time, and almost certainly from the same stock, a grey hound (not to be confused with a greyhound) was developed. In appearance and all hunting qualities it was very like the tawny Breton.[2] In about 1250 and for 200 years it was the hound of the royal kennels, and became known as the *chien gris de Saint Louis*. Legend says that this king (Louis IX) brought the breed back from his Crusade, and even that it descended from Xenophon's hounds of the 5th century BC. Another legend declares that the Breton hounds came to Armorica from Troy after its fall.[3]

The development of these breeds of hounds made possible the science of French forest hunting, which was the product of peace, wealth, exclusivity and the decorative trappings of chivalry. In the 13th century, a great lord's castle, demilitarized, became a court to which everyone of social pretension looked, and in which boys of the knight class were brought up. Renault the Troubadour's Gallerent went to the court of Lorraine, and served there as 'squire, at table, in the chase, in the tourney, for two years'. Guillaume, in another romance, studied hawking and hunting as well as reading, writing, chess, backgammon, fencing, geometry, law and magic.[4] The noble household was thus huge, and so was the throng that made up the 13th-century hunting field. This was one reason for the rigid rules which began to control hunting. But it was not the only reason. Chivalry put a tremendous emphasis on forms, and a sport was not a sport, nor fit for noble persons, unless it was conducted with elegance and ceremony. This applied with as much force to hunting and hawking as it did to tourney and the game of courtly love.

While hunting grew complex as a ceremony, it also grew sophisticated as an art. It developed its own language – the Terms of Art of Venery – and there was more and more to describe. Each animal hunted had a different name at different ages, its own collective noun, its own laying-up place or refuge, footprint, excrement, copulation; the chasing of each out of its hiding place, the dismemberment of each after its death, had different names, not out of perversity, but because they were different processes.

Some of the terms first appear, and the techniques are first described, in a brief anonymous pamphlet of about 1250, *La Chace dou Serf*.[5] The huntsman is to take his lymer round the wood in the early morning, locate a deer, examine slot, fewmet and fray (footprint, dropping, marks on trees) in order to determine its quality, and report to his lord. The beast is then unharboured by the lymer and hunted by the pack. A variety of calls, of horn and voice, have become standardized. The stag when killed is undone according to a precise formula, this ceremony being accompanied by appropriate calls on the horn. This account begs large questions: but much of the technique and procedure of all forest deerhunting is firmly established by the mid 13th century.

England

After the Norman Conquest, England was divided into two quite different types of country: royal forest, and all else.

Cnut had organized and restated the Anglo–Saxon rules, and added some of his own; he had also fenced certain areas, probably modest, as gameparks; but, except on private property and during the fence months, hunting was free everywhere to everyone. So it remained over most of the countryside.

But between 1066 and 1100 a large minority of the face of the land was afforested. This does not mean that trees were planted, nor that farmers and villages were in all cases evicted: but simply that an area was, by a simple act of the royal prerogative, declared to be forest. It immediately came under the forest law, which had its own officers, courts and penalties, and was wholly outside the common law of the realm. Freeholders within the forest found their freehold severely qualified in respect of vert (anything green and growing) as well as venison (any animal); even farmers and freeholders anywhere near the forest were subject to stringent new regulations.

This was 'extremely unpopular with all classes of the English',[6] partly because of the immense scale of the afforestation, partly the hardship caused by it, partly the savagery of the penalties under the forest law and the latter's absolute novelty, and partly because valuable and ancient rights were being taken away. The English

KING JOHN STAGHUNTING
The black-and-white hounds are evidently crossbred Normans, like those being developed in Gascony, which often had this colour as well as the blue and the white. Their steadiness to riot is admirable: they are hunting right across a populous warren. The little brachets had a value in thick covert and sometimes, like beagles, were able to put the big hounds right. The grey horse is certain evidence of Eastern blood; greys appeared in England in numbers after the Crusades, and King John himself imported several presumed Arabs. He rides with breast-plate and crupper but without a nose band.

had enjoyed their hunting. 'The killing of a deer or boar, or even a hare, was punished with the loss of the delinquent's eyes; and that at a time when the killing of a man could be atoned for by paying a moderate fine or compensation.'[7] For killing a doe, Rufus increased the penalty to death.

Vert was defined as any leaf-bearing plant under which deer could shelter. It was as stringently protected as venison. 'Assart', the uprooting of covert, was a dreadful crime, for good reason: 'a Forest must be stored with great woods or coverts for the secret abode of wild beastes and also with fruitful pastures for their continual feed: for the want of either of these two, doth cause the exile of wild beastes from the forest to some other place'.[8]

The inconvenience suffered by freeholders within or near to a forest was extended by Henry I to their dogs. 'Every Farmer and Freeholder, dwelling in a Forest, may keep a *Mastiff* about his House; but such *Mastiff* must be lawfully *expediated* according to the laws of the Forest.' Expediation was performed as follows: 'Three claws of the Fore-feet shall be cut off by the Skin: And accordingly the same is now used, by setting one of his Fore-feet upon a piece of Wood eight inches thick, and a Foot square, and then setting a Chizel of two inches broad upon the three Claws of his Fore-foot, to strike them off at one Blow; and this is the manner of *expediating Mastiffs*.'[9] A dog thus prevented from running after the king's game was 'lawed'; the legal Latin was *mutilatus*.

Throughout the 12th century the royal forest continued to expand. Penalties also increased. Richard I added castration to blinding as the punishment for transgression.[10] Consequently the magnates extracted from King John general promises to reform the forest, contained in Magna Carta; and from the young Henry III in 1217 they extracted the *Charta de foresta*. This was intended less to change the law than to correct the many abuses by which foresters had been extorting money from freeholders. 'Richard de Neville', in whose family the office of Chief Forester was hereditary in the 12th century, 'is black and a bad man', wrote a clerk on the back of a roll.[11] Re-enacted in 1225, the Charter included the interesting article that wearing green in the forest was of itself an offence, because of the presumption, amounting to certainty, that the colour was worn for hunting.[12]

The excuse for the whole apparatus of the forest was that the king needed his relaxation: 'In the forests are the secret places of the kings and their great delight. To them they go for hunting, having put off their cares, so that they may enjoy a little quiet.'[13] All the kings of the period put off their cares avidly. The Conqueror and Rufus were 'passionately fond of hunting'. Henry II was upbraided by a Frenchman 'for spending too much time in hunting . . . Such a pursuit is not worthy of one who has been anointed with holy oil.'[14] But he was partly concerned with keeping his weight down.

Richard I had no time for hunting in England, spending only four months in the country in his ten-year reign. John more than made up for him. He had a corps of huntsman in his household under the command of the Marshal; like William I he often rewarded them with extravagant grants of land. His hunting establishment included knights for staghunting, paid eightpence a day with board and lodging, wildcat hunters and archers at fivepence a day, and four hornblowers paid threepence.[15] These were part of an immense peripatetic household; in spite of the venison they provided they were very expensive to house. The king and his retinue made a long stay at St Edmondsbury, in the time of Abbot Samson, principally for the hawking; when they all left at last, the king offered nothing for their entertainment, and only thirteen pence to pay for a mass for himself. He also left a silk cloak as a gift for St Edmund's shrine, but this was borrowed back by one of the retinue, and never seen by the brothers again.[16]

A subject could not, by definition, have a forest, but he could be given the franchise of a chase. Part of a chase, fenced, became a park. A lower order of grant, made far more freely, was a franchise of warren. These distinctions extended from the tracts of land to the beasts that were hunted over them. The beasts of forest or venery were the hart and hind, the boar, the wolf and the hare. The beasts of chase were the buck and doe (fallow deer), the roe deer, and sometimes the fox, badger, wildcat, marten and otter. (There is great inconsistency in these classifications, which vary from reign to reign and area to area.) The beasts and birds of warren were hare, coney, pheasant and partridge.

Forest hunting of the hart developed into the same complicated art as in France, although it was never attended by quite the same degree of elegant protocol. Outside the forest deer were often coursed, like hares, by the powerful greyhounds of the time.

Ownership of these dogs, and of the longbow, went right down society to the yeoman, a class into which the villein was already trying to turn himself. If this process was not unique to England in the early Middle Ages, it was certainly far more a feature of the English countryside than of any other. So was the life of the man next above, the holder of a knight's fee, a moderate manor. In Henry II's reign this class were newly-styled Knights of the Shire, and became a part of the government of the countryside. Most of them were far more interested in increasing the size of their estates (by marriage) and their value (by clearing and improvement) than in becoming officials, courtiers or soldiers, even though in theory they held their lands by dint of filling these roles. England therefore had a professional army instead of a feudal levy, and a country-loving squire class instead of a feudal knight class. The importance of squire and yeoman cannot be overstated. They made the life of the English countryside unlike any other.

The fox, meanwhile, was sometimes a beast of chase, and hunted from Christmas until Lady Day. It is hardly mentioned before the reign of Edward I. In 1278, in East Anglia: 'It is lawful for the Abbot of the Borough of St. *Peter* to hunt and to take Hares, Foxes and Martens within the Bounds of the Forest, and to have unlawed Dogs, because he hath sufficient Warrant thereto.'[17] In 1285, in the north-west Midlands, the Abbot of Chester had the right 'to run foxes and hares throughout all the forests of Cheshire'.

In 1299 we discern, in Edward I's Wardrobe Accounts, a royal pack of six couple of foxhounds *eo nomine*, with a huntsman and two kennelmen or whippers-in: 'Paid

LADY HUNTING A STAG
This illumination is from Queen Mary's Psalter of 1308. The sex of the archer is in fact quite uncertain, both robe and hair being feasibly male. Ladies did hunt in this period (as a few did in nearly all others) but a lady pulling a longbow is scarcely to be believed: they had special little crossbows, often highly decorated with inlaid wood, metal and mother-of-pearl. The technique shown is quite realistic: shooting over a single hound was a normal method of killing for the pot, as in 19th-century France and in New England.

UNEARTHING A FOX, ABOUT 1300
This picture is contemporary with the royal pack of foxhounds kept by William de Blatherwyck or de Foxhunte. Blatherwyck went out with six couple of hounds and two boys; the only hunt horse was used to carry the nets. The function of the royal pack was to get rid of destructive vermin; the persons illustrated are no doubt doing the same. It is interesting that one spade is square ended, one pointed. The horn blower is perhaps calling up the rest of his pack, or friends with various dogs, rather than playing a ritual fanfare.

to William de Foxhunte, the king's huntsman of foxes in divers forests and parks, for his own wages, and the wages of his two boys; and to the care of the dogs from November 20th to the 19th of November following, for 366 days, it being leap year, to each per day two pence ... £9.3.0.'[18]

Germany

German forest laws were more stringent, and their enforcement and penalties more savage, even than those of England, which the French regarded with shocked amazement. A German poacher was hunted by a pack of starving hounds which pulled him down within an hour and 'made quarry of him'.

Thirteenth-century Germany nevertheless produced two remarkable men who, among other accomplishments, are important in the history of hunting.

The first was the Emperor Frederick II, who loved his hawks as much as his conquests. His *De Arte Venandi cum Avibus* was written about 1254, and completed by his natural son Manfred; it was his own work, and quite original; it shows deep knowledge and real love of his birds.

About twenty years later Albertus Magnus wrote his *De Animalibus*. Albertus was a Suabian noble, who apparently spent his youth hunting vigorously. He entered the church, travelled widely, wrote at prodigious length on a bewildering variety of subjects, and was the teacher of Thomas Aquinas. His Natural History follows Aristotle in intention, but is original in content; its sections under *canis*, *equus* and *falco* constitute a hunting treatise. Dogs are classified as ignoble (watchdog) and noble (scenting hound and greyhound). The most noble has a *vox sonora*; its description matches the *chien noir de Saint Hubert*. There is detailed advice about entering hounds and greyhounds to various game, and about breeding, feeding and kennel management.[19]

The East

In the 12th and 13th centuries chivalrous Europe embarked on its Crusades, and learned a great deal from the East.

In Syria, Christians and Moslems hunted together in times of truce. With hawk and desert greyhound (Saluki) they hunted hare and gazelle; they rode down leopard and boar. The French learned also to course gazelle with cheetah, and the companions of St Louis hunted with the greatest enthusiasm in the unfamiliar open country of the desert. 'The knights of our troop chased a wild beast called a *gazel*, similar to a roebuck.'[20]

The Persians of the period adopted an approach to hunting sharply different from

Early Middle Ages

both their desert neighbours and their own more vigorous past. Kai Kaus ibn
Iskander advised his son, in the 12th century, to ride a big horse, and never an
ambler, in order to look dignified; but when hunting to go slowly and carefully, and
avoid pursuing any dangerous beasts. If there was any risk, it should be taken by a
servant, except when important persons were watching, in which case an appearance
of courage was desirable.[21]

Arabia in the 13th century was breeding an enormous surplus of horses, the largest
market for which was India. 'The reason why they want so many horses every year is
that by the end of the year there shall not be one hundred of them remaining, for
they all die off. They feed their horses with boiled rice and boiled meat.'[22]

Warfare, pageantry, racing and hunting were the function of these Arab horses
in India. Hunting was royal and noble; the principal game was tiger, pig, hare and
gazelle. Vijayanagar, in what became the Madras Presidency, was 'a typical example
of medieval town planning. The site of the capital was selected because a hare, which
was being coursed, turned on that spot and snapped at the hounds.' Not only cities
but states were founded as a result of hunting mishaps. The Raja of Kangra was
hunting pig when his horse fell into a deep well and it was assumed that the Raja
was dead. His widows were duly burnt and his successor took his place. Then someone
found him in the well. As he was officially dead and his successor to the principality
of Kangra had been duly appointed, all that could be done was to carve out a small
principality of Guler for him and his descendants.[23]

The hunting establishments of Eastern rulers were of scarcely credible size.
Bajazet had 7,000 falconers and 6,000 dogkeepers in the 13th century. Akbar had
1,000 cheetah; the most valuable was an animal called Semend-Manik, which was
carried to the meet in a palanquin, 'with a kettle-drum beaten before it'.[24]

Even these establishments were dwarfed by that of Kublai Khan, the Mongol
emperor of China. He once, according to Marco Polo's dazzled estimate, raised an
army of 360,000 horsemen at short notice, all of whom 'consisted merely of the
falconers and whippers-in that were about the court'. His two 'Keepers of the
Mastiff Dogs', Mongolian brothers named Baian and Mingan, each commanded
10,000 men, all dressed respectively in red or blue. Of each corps, 2,000 men had
charge of one or more mastiffs. Kublai thus went hunting with 20,000 men and
5,000 hounds, which drove huge areas of country inwards from the flanks. He also
used cheetah and lynx, and sometimes a trained lion, which hunted big game with
the help of a small hound, as a brachet helped an alaunt in contemporary Europe.

Kublai hunted from his new capital of Peking from December until February, 'to
the extent of some forty days' journey round the city'. On 1 March he started south
with 10,000 falconers, and hunted into May.

Two most interesting things about 13th-century Chinese hunting, both introduced
by the Mongols, were a close season and a total absence of exclusivity. 'Throughout
all the Emperor's territories, nobody however audacious dares to hunt any of these
four animals, to wit, hare, stag, buck, and roe, from the month of March to the
month of October. Anybody who should do so would rue it bitterly. Beyond the
term I have mentioned, however, everybody may take those animals as he list.'[25]

Kublai's successors, visited by Sir John Mandeville, enjoyed their sport with less
effort: in about 1325 'all about these ditches and vivaries is the great garden full of
wild beasts. So that when the great Cham will have any disport on that, to take any
of the wild beasts or of the fowls, he will let chase them and take them at the windows
without going out of his chamber.' But hart and boar were also hunted by hounds
'running with open mouth'.[26]

[26]

4 Later Middle Ages

France

The Hundred Years War was fought in France; much cleared land reverted to waste, and there was a large increase in poaching and in the destructive wild beasts.

Against this unpromising background, the art of venery received its first great original treatise since antiquity. *Le Livre du Roy Modus et de la Royne Racio* was written in Normandy about 1338; it is credibly ascribed to the comte de Tancarville, a great Norman noble, a soldier and a celebrated expert on hunting. He spent some time in England and there as well as at home was widely consulted on techniques and forms of the chase. King Modus is a figure from a legendary golden age; his name means 'Method', and that of his wife 'Reason'. They share the instruction.

Roy Modus names ten beasts of venery *que on prent à force* with running hounds. Five are sweet or 'red': hart and hind, fallow deer, roe and hare; five are foul or 'black': boar and sow, wolf, fox and otter. The bulk of the book concerns staghunting. The methods used are those briskly summarized in *La Chace dou Serf*, but the intervening century has brought a far more complex and exact procedure to the sport.

Humble men are not only allowed but encouraged to take all the *bêtes noires*, including the noble *sanglier*, the adult wild boar. The badger is specially desirable because its hide makes the most durable shoe leather. The hare, though a beast of noble sport when hunted *à force*, is to be taken as freely as the rabbit by humble folk for food.

The fox is cunning and thievish, and a model for lawyers and dishonest public officials. A farmer losing poultry is instructed to find the earth, and beat on it with sticks and make a great noise in order to drive the fox into nets; or the upwind holes are stopped and the fox is smoked out. But a full chapter is also devoted to catching the fox with running hounds and without nets. Once the fox is unkennelled and the hounds are on the line, the horsemen gallop after them doing nothing except encouraging them with appropriate calls on their horns; they may, if necessary, help them recover the line after a check. This is quite evidently foxhunting undertaken for its own sake, for interest and excitement; it has clearly become a noble amusement because several special horn calls now relate to the chase of the fox only.[1]

Ten years after *Roy Modus* was dictated to a clerk, Gace de la Buigne, another Norman noble, a churchman and royal chaplain, wrote his *Romans des Déduits* (1395). This poem instructs the king's son in falconry; it includes some advice on hunting. Its greatest importance is that it inspired Gaston Phébus to write one of the

greatest hunting books of all time, which continued to be read for centuries.

Gaston III, comte de Foix et de Béarn, was the greatest magnate of southern France, a man of the highest political and military importance until his death in 1391 after boarhunting. He was energetic, just, hospitable and passionately devoted to hounds and hunting. He fought all over Europe, including Scandinavia where he took part in a reindeer hunt. His lavishness and bright fair hair earned him the nickname (Phébus) by which he is known. He began his *Livre de la Chasse* in 1387.

To Gaston, harthunting is for nobles and great men; he describes the now-familiar sequence of harbouring, unharbouring, chase, bay, kill, undoing and quarry. But all other men, *de quelque estat qu'ilz soient*, ought to hunt all other beasts for sport, exercise, and to avoid the evil of idleness.

There are ten chapters on dogs, which Gaston loved. (He had 600 hounds of various breeds.) They include *chiens courans*, of the Gascon and other breeds, mastiff, alaunt and little greyhounds with short legs, sometimes rough-haired. Foxhunting *à force* is a very junior partner to staghunting, but it is conducted with enthusiasm in a perfectly recognizable way.[2]

England

Fourteenth-century England was peaceful, its wars being fought in Wales and Scotland and then in France. Its countryside was prosperous, especially when in about 1350 woollen cloth became an even more important export than raw wool; weaving was a cottage industry, and brought great new wealth to the villages. Trees continued to yield to sheep, and also to arable and dairyfarming and stockrearing. In the late 14th century the prosperous peasant could be prosperous indeed: the men of the Peasants' Revolt were not hungry, but angry because their economic position was not matched by their legal status (one of the things they demanded was the right to hunt). Social mobility extended up the ladder: Clement Paston, for example, was a yeoman in Richard II's reign; his son became William Paston of Paston Hall, a Justice and a gentleman.[3]

Prosperous townsmen had hunting establishments: the Wife of Bath complains that, before he commits himself, a man will always give a trial to household imple-

Above left
DEER STALKING, 14TH-CENTURY FRANCE
Although hunting in France in this period was usually thoroughly sporting, and aroused enormous enthusiasm, it was also utilitarian. Every animal hunted had a value, for pelt, leather or medicine if not for food. What is here demonstrated is an economical method of killing for the larder: quite feasible if the approach is made slowly and up wind. (It is today sometimes quite easy to get right up to a red deer in a car, which is how many are poached; the same is true of antelope and big game in Africa.) Manuscript illustration from the *Livre de la Chasse* by Gaston Phébus, 1387.

Above right
PURSUIT OF THE HARE, 14TH-CENTURY FRANCE
Gaston has made it easy for himself, by leaving strips of standing corn between the strips of stubble. The standing corn is beaten, and the hares emerge into the killing ground to be shot by longbow or crossbow. The arrowheads are special blunt ones, designed to knock the hare over without damaging its flesh. The horseman is using his height to spot hares for the bowmen. The greyhounds are probably kept in reserve: they will course a hare if the bowmen miss it. Their apathy contrasts with the charming and visible glee of the boarhounds waiting for their *fouail* (p. 30). Manuscript illustration from the *Livre de la Chasse* by Gaston Phébus, 1387.

ments, farm animals, and horses and hounds, but he never has a wife on approval.[4] Successful merchants also left the towns and became country gentlemen, demonstrating their new gentility by hunting: much of its literature between 1300 and 1500 taught these *arrivistes* not to commit solecisms.

The feudal system was in rapid decay in the 14th century, and was finally killed by the Wars of the Roses and strong Tudor government. One of the victims was the royal forest, which diminished steadily from Edward II's reign onwards. Against this, a number of great lords grew far more powerful than before. They were highly jealous of their hunting rights. And Parliament, which represented landowners, grew much more influential owing to the successive kings' need for money. The effect of all this was a system of gamelaws protecting private park and chase, rather than a forest law protecting the king's forest. This process went so far that the law refers to the forest of the king 'or any other person',[5] a usage impossible earlier.

An Italian contemporary remarked in astonishment: 'The nobles of England think themselves above residing in cities. They live in retirement on their country estates amid woods and pastures.'[6] But their rural retirement had in it a good deal of luxury and display, in imitation of the lavish court of Edward III, and in direct or indirect imitation of France.

Traditionally, this French influence was predominantly Norman, and Norman French remained the language of the court and of the chase. It was in this language (already archaic in France) that Edward II's huntsman William Twici wrote his little book, *Le Art de Vénerie le quel Mestre Guyllame Twici, venoeur le Roy d'Engletere fist.*

Twici (Twity, Twyti, Twety etc.) was paid sevenpence halfpenny a day in 1322, ninepence in 1326. He wrote his book about 1328. Like *La Chace dou Serf* it is a dialogue. It is probably not original. The hare is treated first (marvellous because it changes its sex); then, at greater length, the stag. It sets out such of the Terms of Art as had been determined in France and exported to England; and more space is devoted to naming the parts of the stag's attire (head) and explaining the recheat on the horn than to hunting methods. Twici was Englished almost at once by Gyfford or Giffarde, another royal huntsman.

About eighty years later Edward Plantagenet, 2nd Duke of York, wrote *The Master of Game*. He held this post for Henry IV; the book was written to instruct the future Henry V. It is almost wholly a translation of Gaston Phébus, with two interesting exceptions. First, the treatment of the hare precedes, as in Twici, that of the hart. Secondly, Gaston's accounts of nets and snares are omitted as irrelevant; the English hunted stags with hounds only.

A chapter is devoted to the fox: 'The hunting for a fox is fair for the good cry of the hounds.'[7] The fox is not, however, expected to be caught above ground in the open by Talbots, Gascons or brachets; he is forced from covert to covert, or back to his earth to be dug or netted. When coursed, he often evacuates dramatically into the greyhounds' faces.

At another level of foxhunting, villages all turned out to protect their poultry. Chaucer has a hunt followed by men with staves and women with distaffs; they had brass and boxwood trumpets and horns to call their cattle,

> . . . *in which they blewe and pouped*
> *And therewithal they shriked and they houped.*
> *It seemed as that hevene sholde falle.*

The noise even brought a swarm of bees out of their hive. The end of the hunt is not recorded.[8]

[29]

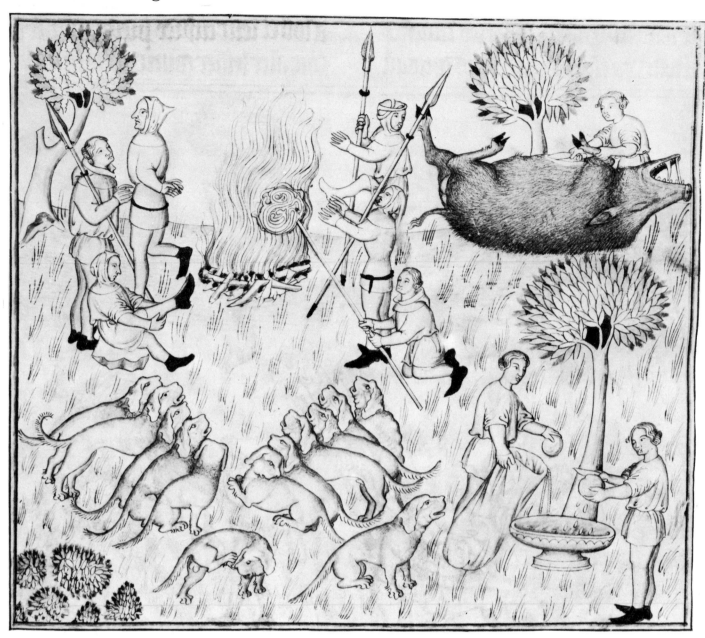

Although the royal forest diminished steadily, kings themselves still hunted lavishly and constantly. Edward II's hunting establishment, headed by Twici, was enormous, and Isabella, his queen, had her own pack of hounds; she left them at Canterbury for two years after a hunting visit, to the wounding of the monks. Edward III's court was modelled on Arthurian legend as well as French fact; it was a school of hunting and chivalry. In 1363 he entertained the kings of Scotland, France and Cyprus to a royal hunt as magnificent as a tournament. Campaigning in France, he always had with him, according to Froissart, sixty couple of staghounds (*forts chiens*) and sixty of harehounds.[9]

A century later, in July 1462, Edward IV 'rode on hunting into the forest of Waltham, whither he commanded the mayor with certain of his brethren to come and to give attendance upon him, with certain commoners of the city, where, when they were come, the king caused the game to be brought before them, so that they saw course after course, and many a deer, both red and fallow, to be slain before them.'[10]

At about this time Twici's little treatise was reworked as the anonymous *Craft of*

THE QUARRY
Coment on doit deffeir le sanglier (left):
not quarry, properly speaking, as the
flesh is not given to the hounds *sur le
cuir*: it is not *curée* but *fouail*. The 'black'
or 'stinking' meat of the boar is cooked
before hounds are given it, owing to
its nature. This is sometimes done in
the open at the place of the kill, often
in the courtyard of the castle. The
Devonshire Hunting Tapestry from
Tournai (*below*), a century later than
Gaston, shows no change from his time
or that of *Roy Modus* in the *curée* of a
deer. Hounds are encouraged to eat
part of the raw flesh immediately, *sur
le cuir*; entrails and blood are mixed
with bread which the *veneurs* and *valets*
have brought in their pouches. The
whole gory ritual was not only an
excuse for celebration and horn-blow-
ing: it was recognized as necessary for
the enthusiasm of hounds and especially young hounds. Manuscript illustration (*left*) from the *Livre de la Chasse*
by Gaston Phébus, 1387.

Venery (1450); and a generation later the 'schoolmaster–printer' included a hunting
treatise in his *Boke of St Albans* (1486), ascribed to Dame Juliana Berners, about whom
many guesses have been made but nothing is known. The *Boke* plagiarizes both
Twici and Edward Duke of York (themselves plagiarists); it follows both in its
admiration of the hare: 'That beest Kyng shall be calde of all venery. He is the
mervellest beest that is on ony londe.' This is because of the quality of his chase as
well as his sex change. Most of a caught hare is given to the hounds, having been
stripped (other beasts are flayed), but the loins are to be brought home 'to the kechyn
for the lordis meete'.

The *Boke of St Albans* was an immense success in various editions, and reprinted far
more often than any other English book of its time except the Bible. The reason was
that it instructed, like Twici, not so much in technique as in terms and forms, and
that mostly in doggerel for easy learning. Its readers were the yeomen and merchants
who wanted to be country gentlemen, and had to be taught to avoid humiliating
error. The Terms and Laws of Venery cover the precise words to be called to hounds
at different moments in different chases. These are without exception still in a sort
of French: *hors de couple avaunt le avaunt, sa fa cy avaunt, sweff mon amy sweff, illoques
illoques, venez venez so how fa.* These cries became English not by the substitution of
English words but by their further degeneration: *il est hault il est hault* turns, when
repeated quickly, into 'tallyho'.

Hounds listed in the *Boke* include 'Greyhound, Bastard, Mastyfe, Spanyell,
Rachys', and 'small ladies popis'.

Later Middle Ages

The *Boke* records the tradition that Sir Tristram, in the time of King Arthur, brought the Terms of Art to England; this tradition had just been set out at length by Sir Thomas Malory in *Le Morte d'Arthur*, written about 1470 and first printed by Caxton in 1485. Going to France for his education, Tristram 'laboured ever in hunting and hawking . . . And as the book saith, he began good measure of blowing of beasts of venery, and beasts of chase, and all manner of vermains; and all these terms we have yet of hunting and hawking.'

Malory describes English forest hunting at the very end of the medieval period (whatever period he may be pretending to describe) far more vividly than any other writer, providing a great many revealing details while using a good many perplexing words. It appears that a gentleman went out with a large pack of running hounds, a brachet and sometimes a few brace of greyhounds. The brachet was evidently still the little beagle: La Beale Isoud had one as a pet. One technique was that hounds hunted the stag until the greyhounds could finish him off: 'Then Gawaine and Galleris rode more than a pace after the white hart, and let slip at the hart three couple of greyhounds, and so they chased the hart', which the greyhounds killed. ('Couple of greyhounds' is in fact a solecism.)

More usual was the ordinary French method: relays were placed, and the stag shot or stabbed after it turned at bay.[11]

England was by this time in much closer touch with Gascony (which was English territory) than with Normandy; Edward II's detested favourite Piers Gaveston was a Gascon knight. This contact explains the importation of the blue-mottled Gascon hound to join the Talbot. These breeds were obviously crossed, and both crossed with the native brachet (whose name is spelled a dozen ways): but they were kept pure-bred as well, and their respective descendants are quite distinct. From the Talbot comes the black-and-tan bloodhound, from the Gascon the distinct Southern hound, which has no special association with southern England, and may well be Southern because Gascon.[12]

Italy, Germany, Portugal

The nobles of Italy continued to look inwards at the cultural and political life of their cities, rather than outwards at the life of their countryside. Italy's single late medieval hunting book is contained in the *De Omnibus Agriculturae Partibus* (1307) of Peter of Crescentia, also translated into French in 1373 by order of Charles V. After a distinguished legal career in various cities of Lombardy, Peter retired to Bologna and, most unusually, to the land, and compiled his treatise on agriculture mostly from classical sources. The thirty-nine chapters of Book X set out the methods of catching animals for food or pelts, or to prevent damage. Hounds are used for hare and ibex and sometimes stag, but nets and pits are the principal methods. There is no notion of sport and except in falconry there is no art or elegance.

Ferdinando I, King of the Romans, hunted energetically in Austria in the next century. He left before dawn and returned after dark, chasing boar, hart and bear. His sport was exclusive and his game strictly preserved.[13]

After France and England, the most sporting country of late medieval Europe was Portugal, especially in the reign of King John I, who married John of Gaunt's daughter Philippa and founded the ancient Anglo–Portuguese alliance. John was a successful and energetic king, and a hunting man and writer. His court was brilliant. We may imagine the hunting Mecca of the whole peninsula, comparable to the households of Edward III and Gaston Phébus.[14]

[32]

5 The Sixteenth Century

Effects of the Renaissance

Italy was as much the source of manners and ideals in the 16th century as Provence had been in the 13th. Baldassare Castiglione's *Il Corteggiano* (1528) was vastly influential all over Europe; it was translated into English in 1561 by Sir Thomas Hoby as *The Courtyer of Count Baldesar Castilio.*

The skills of hunting, hawking, riding and horsemastership were still, in Castiglione's world, an indispensable part of a polite man's attainments. Scientific horsemanship was indeed invented at this period by the Neapolitan Frederico Grisone, whose writings and pupils went everywhere. But Italian influence was not altogether happy on the hunting field. Its code of manners failed to travel; in France, Spain and Austria manners became elaborate, rigid and exclusive, in the hunting field as elsewhere, and elegance was confused with lavish ostentation. 'A yokel can butcher an ox, but it takes a noble to butcher a wild animal. Regard him, bareheaded, knees bent, holding the appropriate knife – the correct knife and no other – making the ritual gestures, and carving, according to the rites, certain limbs in a certain order.'[1]

LORENZO THE MAGNIFICENT AND HIS SUITE
Lorenzo de' Medici was a devious tyrant, a patron of arts and letters, the accomplished poet of 'grossly indecent' songs, and a hunting man: one of very few in the Italy of his day. His despotism in Florence had a firm base in the unprecedented prosperity of the Tuscan countryside, where he was consequently very popular; like Cyrus in Persia and Edgar in England he inspected his territories while hunting through them; like the Dukes of Beaufort and Rutland his hounds endeared him to his tenantry. A peculiarity, shown also by Ucello (p. 45), is the splendid width of the reins. The wild ass in the background is being coursed by very large greyhounds; the best of these were bred by the Gonzaga family of Mantua, and some are known to have gone to Florence. Fresco by Benozzo Gozzoli, Palazzo Medici Riccardi, Florence, 1459.

Royal Hunting in France

Louis XI made a vow to give up women, except for his wife. But she was 'not at all one of those in whom one could take great pleasure'. Consequently he devoted himself to hunting deer *à force.* He rose early, rode far, worked hard, returned late, and often, soaked to the skin, lodged in a labourer's cottage.

Louis XII maintained this level of enthusiasm, though not of exhausting effort. He started building the château of Blois in a royal forest eleven leagues by four, already dotted with simpler hunting lodges built by previous kings; it was full of various game. Blois was finished by his nephew François I, to whom Louis taught hunting at Chillon.

Louis XII introduced the characteristically 16th-century practice of hunting inside a toil, which adapted the classical technique of the long boar net and turned hunting into a spectator sport: the toil was a semicircular barrier on the edge of the forest up to which carriages could be driven, and in which boars and sometimes stags were killed. 'The king had a special hunting establishment which was called the *vénerie des toiles*, with 100 archers under the Captain of the Toils, whose only duty was to arrange the toils and carry the boar-spears on foot.'[2]

In François I's time neither the techniques nor the procedures of hunting changed in essence – the 150-year-old treatise of Gaston Phébus remained valid – but the king added an unprecedented amount of lavish pomp and exact protocol. 'Hunting has been elevated to its highest pitch of perfection.'[3] To make any mistake in speech or behaviour has become '*un blasme de sottise*'.[4]

François I and his court hunted constantly; they stayed a few days, hunted a few times, and moved on, which exhausted foreign ambassadors.[5] But his favourite hunting castle was Blois:

'These buildings are more than large – they are immense: yet I could not understand how they sufficed to house so many horses, so many huntsmen, so many hounds which, in the king's hunts, completely cover the ground; so many falcons, so many herons, which fill the sky.

'Sometimes the king takes with him not only his hundred pages and his two hundred horsemen – huntsmen or grooms – but also four or five hundred gentlemen; sometimes he is accompanied by the queen, or queens, attended by their many ladies in waiting and maids of honour. Then the whole château – all the apartments above, all the floors below, all the rooms between – the whole court is on horseback, all in red habits, trotting and galloping through the countryside behind the king also in a red coat, hunting the stag or the boar.'[6]

The two sorts of hunting which most engaged François I were killing boar in *la chasse dedans les toiles*, and staghunting *à force*; he also went beagling for hare with a pack of *petits chiens de la Loire*.

The first of these, a 'dangerous and royal pastime', was described by an Englishman to whom it was entirely new. The boar had been previously lodged at the edge of the forest. 'There was within the toil divers goodly gentlemen with the king, ready garnished to this high enterprise and dangerous hunting of the perilous wild swine. The king being in his doublet and hosen only, without any other garments, all of sheep's colour cloth.' They had 'in a slip a fair brace of great white greyhounds, armed, as the manner is to arm their greyhounds from the violence of the boar's tusks. And all the rest of the king's gentlemen, being appointed to hunt this boar, were likewise in their doublets and hosen, holding each of them in their hands a very sharp boar's spear.

'The king being thus furnished, commanded the huntsman to uncouch the boar, and that every person should go to a standing . . . and incontinent the boar issued out of his den, chased with an hound into the plain, and being there, stalked a while gazing upon the people, and incontinent being forced by the hound, he espied a little bush standing upon a bank over a ditch, under which lay two lusty gentlemen of France, and thither fled the boar, to defend him, thrusting his head snuffing into the same bush where these two gentlemen lay, who fled with such speed as men do from the danger of death.'[7]

Sometimes even the toil was too inconvenient for the ladies of the court. 'When this monarch was at Amboise, among other diversions for the ladies, he ordered an enormous wild boar, which he had caught in the forest, to be let loose in the court before the castle. The animal, enraged by the small darts thrown at him from the windows, ran furiously up the grand staircase, and burst open the door of the ladies' apartment. François ordered his officers not to attack him, and waited deliberately to receive him with the point of his sword, which he dexterously plunged between his eyes, and, with a forcible grasp, turned the boar upon his back.'[8]

[36]

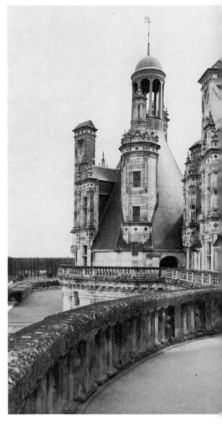

THE ROOF AT CHAMBORD
This château, like Anet, Blois, Chenonceaux, and later Versailles itself, combined the function of hunting box with that of palace and temporary seat of government. It was surrounded by royal forest, in which François I hunted stag and boar with immense corps of huntsmen and fields of gentlemen and often ladies. Stables, kennels, mews and heronries were on so vast a scale that it was amazing to visitors that even such huge establishments could house them.

The king's undoubted courage was put to better use in staghunting. He was a fine rider of the *cheval volant*, and went hard and dangerously over broken country. He hunted with relays of hounds, usually three, each of three couple held by two *valets*. The *valets* uncoupled the relays as the hunted stag passed. The first relay were the lightest and fastest hounds, the second the middling, and the third, expected to bay the stag, the most powerful and ferocious. To keep up with this succession of fresh hounds, the king had fresh horses held ready at each relay. He only hunted really good stags of ten points or more: but he often did so twice a day, having a *double equippage de vénerie*, a pack each for morning and afternoon.[9]

Henri II, who succeeded his father, was equally untiring in the chase. His queen, Catherine de' Medici, lost her husband to Diane de Poitiers when he was still dauphin; she hunted with her father-in-law to distract herself. Diane, with the architect Philibert Delorme, transformed the château d'Anet into *un véritable rendez-vous de chasse*, with magnificent stables, kennels, mews, and cages for cheetah. As dauphin and as king Henri stayed there constantly, for weeks at a time, hunting in his father's fashion. 'He goes hunting twice a week, and for six or seven hours follows the stag through the woods, regardful neither of fatigue nor of the safety of his life, his horse often rolling on him.'[10]

François II, his son, was as devoted to hunting as his father, grandfather and all other Valois. He was greatly encouraged by his Guise uncles, who were anxious to keep him hunting and out of politics. His wife Mary Queen of Scots hunted with him at Blois and Chenonceaux until, in December 1559, she was knocked out of the saddle by an overhanging branch while hunting at Blois. 'She is fully determined', wrote the English ambassador, 'to give up this kind of exercise.'[11]

Charles IX's reign is principally remembered for the massacre of St Bartholomew, memory of which drove the king mad, while 'the insupportable fatigues that he underwent while hunting' hastened his death, as they had his brother's.

In the first year of his reign, Charles had dedicated to him *La Vénerie*, by Jacques de Fouilloux, a book which enjoyed enormous and enduring success. The success is far more interesting than the book itself, as the latter depends almost wholly on Gaston Phébus; this shows how little hunting had changed in 200 years. As though in reproof, the king ten years later dictated his own *Traité de la chasse au cerf* to his secretary Nicholas de Neufville (or Villeroy), who published it in 1625, dedicated to Louis XIII, as *La Chasse Royale*. The king's book is most attractively dedicated to his principal hunting tutor, a simple huntsman called Mesnil.

Charles IX's successor Henri III was more interested in fancy dress and handsome lads than hunting. He was an accomplished horseman, and had a large hunting establishment, but he seldom used it, preferring more delicate amusements. Royal French hunting went briefly into abeyance. This was unimportant, as there were dozens of noble families for whom hunting was an equally strong tradition. Claude de Lorraine, father of the Guise, had been one of the greatest Nimrods of his time; his son François duc de Guise maintained his establishment and enthusiasm in the middle of the century. There were strong hunting traditions in Gascony, in Poitou and the other districts of the west, in Auvergne and Burgundy in the centre, in Lorraine in the east, and above all in Normandy. There families like the Montmorency, Le Veneur, Harcourt and Brézé chased stag, roe and hare generation after generation.

French Hounds

Fourteenth-century France had the black St Hubert hounds, and their Norman and Gascon descendants of various colours; and the rough-haired *chiens gris* and *chiens fauves* from Brittany. But Gaston Phébus also speaks of smooth-coated white hounds, and there is mention of 'white Talbots' going from Gascony to England. At some point – perhaps about 1400 – white hounds became especially associated with Poitou, and about 1470 one of these, called Souillard, was given to Louis XI. He was unimpressed, and passed it on to the seneschal Gaston, who gave it into the care of Jacques de Brézé on behalf of Anne de Bourbon. Souillard became a most important stallion hound, and his descendants began to fill the royal kennel.

One dog of this breed lined an Italian bitch, described as a pointer, which belonged to Louis XII's secretary Greffier. The result were the *chiens blancs Greffiers*, which had the noses of black St Hubert hounds and the speed of grey St Louis. They became in the time of François I the *chiens blancs du Roy*. A second outcross, about 1520, was with the *chiens fauves de Bretagne*, in the person of a stud hound called Miraud. The result were the very best hounds of all.

The hounds of Normandy continued in high esteem; Louis de Brézé, faithful to his family tradition, thought his black hounds far superior to the king's white.[12] They were undoubtedly wonderful line hunters, but too slow for Charles IX. He said they were best kept coupled, so it appears that he used them as lymers.

The *chiens gris de Saint Louis*, demoted from the royal kennels, were on the leg and very fast, but to Charles IX they were too apt to overrun their line, and their noses were not good enough to recover it. No horn, word or whip could stop them once they were on the scent of a straight-running deer.[13]

From the St Hubert were bred, in the north east of France, what seem to be two distinct miniatures: the *briquets* or *petits chiens d'Artois*, large beagles, evidently used for harehunting, and popular in England as well as in France;[14] and the *bassets d'Artois*. This short-legged version of the Norman staghound retained the nose and tongue of its noble ancestor, but was bred to go underground. It was the first French hound specifically intended for fox and badger. Fouilloux classifies foxhunting not as *la chasse des chiens courants* but *la chasse des chiens de terre*; the dogs he put down the earths were not terriers but basset hounds. He devotes four chapters to this chase, but despises it: '*Quant à la chasse des Renards, il y a peu de plaisir.*'[15]

English Kings, Queens and Countryside

Henry VII was never much of a sportsman, but Henry VIII hunted much like his contemporary François I. He was a man of great physical vigour, even after he grew fat; his harthounds were kept in Windsor Great Park (possibly at Ascot) and hunted in relays. The king often exhausted several horses. In order to hunt with the least inconvenience, he emparked large areas in and near London: St James's Park, previously marshy, was drained, fenced and stocked with deer; Hyde Park became royal in 1536 as a result of the dissolution of the monasteries, and was afforested by the king in both a legal and a literal sense; a tract which includes the modern Regent's Park was also part of his suburban hunting ground.

When Elizabeth went to Kenilworth in July 1575 there was 'a great hunting' on the 11th, 'another grand hunting' on the 13th, and 'a hunting in the afternoon' on the 18th. These 'huntings' were organized so that a great many people could see the sport in comfort in a limited area. In 1584 Leicester, the queen's host at

Kenilworth, organized a staghunt at Windsor. Sixty to eighty great harts were caught and put inside the toil. They ran backwards and forwards in front of the queen. Several were shot with crossbows; those only wounded were taken with hounds. The queen repaired to a hide on a hillock; the stags were let out of the toil in batches, and coursed with greyhounds where she could see and shoot them.[16]

Elizabeth also hunted more sportingly. When, in 1570, she was considering marriage to the duc d'Anjou, 'she talked much of the pleasure she and the Duke would find in hunting the stag in her forests'. In September 1600, when she was seventy-six, 'Her Majesty is well, and exceedingly disposed to hunting, for every second day she is on horseback, and continues the sport long.'[17]

Whereas, however, in France, a succession of kings were in the forefront of hunting skills and hound breeding, in England the whole forward movement of hunting became far less a royal than a private affair. Several related causes pushed English hunting into the sort of decentralized informality which made it so different from that of the Continent.

The 16th century saw a great reduction in the area of ancient forest: the Eliza-bethan sailors cut down oak trees for their ships; and many more were needed as fuel for smelting iron. More important, woodland, waste and arable all gave way to pasture.

With increased rural wealth went increased social mobility. Yeomen and mer-chants bought land, acquired coats of arms (the College of Heralds was kept busy throughout the 16th century) and joined the large, rich, ill-defined category of the gentry. The new gentry aped the old: 'It becomes a gentleman to be adept at blowing hunting-horns, to be skilful in the chase, and elegantly to train and carry a hawk. The study of letters should be left to the sons of rustics.'[18] Consequently

[39]

the *Boke of St Albans* went into edition after edition. 'Why you know,' said Ben Jonson, 'an a man have not skill in the hawking and hunting languages now-a-days, I'll not give a rush for him; they are more studied than the Greek or the Latin.'[19]

An immense thrust was given both to the wealth and the local importance of the hunting gentry by the dissolution of the monasteries in the 1530s. These had been, collectively, landowners on a huge scale; they were also the centres of local life and often of hunting. Almost all the land went into private hands. Some was absorbed into great estates, but much became the parks and farms of the gentry.

And the hunting squire was joined, as nowhere else, by the hunting yeoman. 'The middle people of England' could 'live in convenient plenty, and no servile condition.'[20] Many owned their own packs of hounds: a young man is urged, in 1591, 'to borrowe one couple of old Foxe hounds of some Gentleman, or Yoman, who useth to hunt the Foxe'.[21]

Deer and Hare

Harthunting about 1575 is:

A sport for Noble peeres, a sport for gentle bloods,
The paine I leaue for seruants such, as beate the bushie woods,
To make their masters sport.[22]

The procedure was that of France, though simpler. In Sir Philip Sidney's enchanting description: 'they came to the side of the wood, where the hounds were in couples, staying their coming, but with a whining accent craving liberty; many of them in colour and marks so resembling, that it showed they were of one kind. The huntsmen were handsomely attired in their green liveries, as though they were children of summer, with staves in their hands to beat the guiltless earth, when the hounds were at fault; and with horns about their necks, to sound an alarum upon a silly fugitive: the hounds were straight uncoupled, and ere long the stag thought it better to trust to the nimbleness of his feet than to the slender fortification of his lodging.'[23]

When Thomas Cockaine hunted with the Earl of Huntingdon and the Marquess of Northampton, twenty couple formed the main pack and another ten a relay four miles away. Hunting on his own estate in Derbyshire throughout the second half of the century, Cockaine laid on ten couple and had five for his single relay. (Cockaine, like Sidney, hunted a 'stag'; 'hart' as a term of venery was going out of use in their time.)

Cockaine was a well-connected gentleman, but by no means a great lord; yet he hunted the stag with his own pack. Simpler squires did so in the West Country. Charles Kingsley has Amyas Leigh and his friends hunting 'a hart of grease' about 1580, with skill but no formality, with Mr Coffin's hounds from Portledge, a private pack borrowed for the day.[24]

Roe were unlodged with a single lymer, like stags; half the pack was laid on, and the other half uncoupled after three or four hours. Fallow deer were hunted mostly in parks; Cockaine went out with uncoupled hounds at his stirrup (a completely unfamiliar plan) and tufted for a buck to rouse him. His is an early use of 'tufter', by which he clearly defines something different from bloodhound or lymer.

Parked deer were also shot and coursed, but although Elizabeth enjoyed coursing and shooting within the toil, it was not considered good sport: 'Kylling of dere with bowes or grehundes serveth well for the potte . . . But it contayneth therein no commendable solace or exercise in comparison to the other fourme of huntyng.'[25] Besides the toil, Elizabeth's reign saw the new, or newly codified, sport of paddock coursing. A mongrel drove a captured deer 160 yards to the lawpost; a brace of greyhounds was then slipped and coursed the deer towards the spectators, a mile away, down a wide railed avenue. The sport attracted heavy betting.

Hare coursing was for ladies and the frailer gentlemen: 'Huntyng of the hare with grehoundes is a righte good solace for men that be studiouse or them to whom nature hath nat gyven personage or courage apte for the warres. And also for gentilwomen, which fere neither sonne nor wynde for appairing their beautie. And peradventure they shal be thereat lasse idell than they shulde be at home in their chambres.'

Hunting hare as well as other game with hounds was much more highly esteemed. Venus urged Adonis to:

Uncouple at the timorous flying hare,
Or at the fox which lives by subtlety,
Or at the roe which no encounter dare:
   Pursue these fearful creatures o'er the downs,
   And on thy well-breath'd horse keep with thy hounds.

Shakespeare's hare, 'poor Wat', was faint-hearted and melancholic (and still masculine in sporting jargon), but he ran with baffling crosses and doubles, and used the foil of sheep 'to make the cunning hounds mistake their smell'.[26]

All this not only constitutes the charm and fascination of harehunting, which the Elizabethans appreciated as much as the ancient Greeks, but also makes it wonderful training for hounds: 'a hounde whiche is a perfect good Haryer, may be bolde to hunt any chace . . . of all chases, the Hare maketh greatest pastime and pleasure, and sheweth most cunning in hunting, and is meetest for gentlemen of all other huntings.'[27] Best of all, and most significantly for the future of British fieldsports, harehunting 'is not a privilege confined, like that of the buck, to great noblemen, but a sport easilie and equalie distributed, as well to the wealthie farmer as to the great gentleman'.

Foxhunting and Foxhounds

'Now for the hunting of the Fox or Badger,' says Gervase Markham, 'they are chases of a great deal less use, or cunning than any of the former, because they are of much hotter scent, as being intituled stinking scents & not sweet scents, & indeed very few dogs but will hunt them with all eagerness.' To Markham the best foxhound is apparently a Welsh or Breton: 'The grissl'd, which are ever most commonly shag-hair'd or any other colour, whether it be mixt or unmixt, so it be shag-hair'd are the best verminers, and therefore are chosen to hunt the Fox, Badger, or any other hot scents: they are exceeding good and cunning finders.'[28] Markham hunted the fox entirely in the woods, 'where a horse can neither conveniently make his way or tread without danger of stumbling'.[29]

Turberville used terriers, nets and traps. His terriers were of two sorts. One was the crooked-legged, smooth-coated breed from Flanders, Artois and the Low Countries; this is clearly the *basset d'Artois* being used below ground as its breeders intended. The other is shaggy-haired and straight-legged, able to hunt like a hound and then go into an earth.[30]

Turberville also hunted the fox above ground. He stopped the earths the previous midnight, then came out with both hounds and greyhounds. To this writer,

QUEEN ELIZABETH AFTER
A STAGHUNT
When a stag turned at bay, it was the
rule that the highest-ranking person
present gave it the *coup de grace* with
a hunting knife; failing this, he or she
made the initial ceremonial incision
which began the *curée*: a moment
described with furious derision by
Erasmus, *In Praise of Folly*. The hounds
here are going, with wonderful obedi-
ence, to horn instead of carcase. They
are the lemon-pie staghounds which
made up the royal kennel; some of
them were sent to Mr Hugh Pollard
at Simonsbath, Devon, who was ranger
of what was still the royal forest on
Exmoor; from this pack descended
the Devon and Somerset Staghounds.
The latter were dispersed, but some
went to Wales, nearly 300 years after
the date of this scene, to have a valuable influence on Welsh hound breeding (see p. 111).

foxhunting's principal merit was its season, January to March, when nothing else was hunted. This point had been made fifty years earlier by Sir Thomas Elyot: 'I dispraise nat the huntynge of the foxe with rennynge houndes: but it is nat to be compared to the other huntyng in commoditie of exercise. Therefore it wolde be used in the deepe wynter, whan the other game is unseasonable.'[31]

But one Elizabethan writer expresses a more positive attitude to foxhunting which is evidently not at all unique to him. Sir Thomas Cockaine succeeded to his estate at Ashbourne, Derbyshire, in 1538, after a boyhood spent in the household of the sporting Earl of Shrewsbury. His small book records fifty-two years of experience as 'a profess'd Hunter, and not a scholler'. He starts with foxhunting, only afterwards proceeding to hare, roe, stag, buck, otter and marten.

Having found in Edward I's reign a pack of foxhounds entered, if not bred, solely to fox, we now find the clearest possible evidence of purpose-bred packs of foxhounds. Here is 'A very good note for any yong Gentleman, who will breed Hounds to hunt the Foxe. You must breed fourteen or fifteen couple of small Ribble hounds, lowe and swift, and two couple of Terriars, which you may enter in one yeare.' Ribblesdale runs up into the Pennines in northern Lancashire. Cockaine, breeding

[42]

hounds sixty miles south in Derbyshire, is describing the small Northern hound.

Cockaine's whelps are to be 'chastized surely from sheape', and never permitted to hunt a hare or rabbit. They are entered at twelve months. One couple of old foxhounds, borrowed from a foxhunting neighbour, are put into covert, and the young entry uncoupled when they find. This is cubhunting, and they are to stay in covert. 'By that time you haue killed halfe a skore Cubbes in this sorte in seuerall Couerts or Woods, and haue taken two or three quicke Cubbes to make your Terriars withall, you will finde your Hounds well and perfect.'

When the season proper begins, two couple are chosen as 'trailers of an olde Foxe and finders of him'. The rest are kept in couples until the huntsman is certain that the finders have unkennelled a fox. Then the pack is uncoupled. 'And this tast I will giue you of the flying of this chase, that the Author hereof hath killed a Foxe distant from the Couert where hee was found, fourteene miles aloft the ground with Hounds.'

The Other Hounds

'Now of these hounds there are divers kinds, as the slow hound, which is a large, great dog, tall and heavy, and are bred for the most part in the West Counties of this Land, as also in *Cheshire* and *Lancashire*, and most woodland and mountainous Countries; then the middle siz'd dog, which is more fit for the Chase, being of a more nimble composure, and are bred in *Worcestershire, Bedfordshire*, and many other well mixt soyls, where the Champain and Covert are of equal largeness; then the light, nimble, swift, slender Dog, which is bred in the North parts of this Land, as *Yorkshire, Cumberland, Northumberland*, and many other plain Champion Countries: And lastly the little *Beagle*, which may be carried in a man's glove, and are bred in many Countries for delight only, being of curious scents and passing amusing in their hunting; for the most part trying, (but seldom killing) the prey, except at some strange advantage.'[32]

Many households had kennels like those of France. For their management the precepts of Gaston Phébus were still repeated almost word for word.[33]

Bitches were to be lined when the moon was in Aquarius or Gemini: 'for it is held amongst the best Hunts-men of this Land, that the Whelps which are ingendred under those two signs, will never run mad'.[34] Whelps, weaned at two months, should be sent 'abroad into Vyllages to keepe in some fayre place' – the place to be nowhere near a rabbit warren.

Staghounds were first entered to hare, and to hart at eighteen months. Young hounds joined older ones in the relays. They hunted harts 'in prime of grease' so that the game would not have the speed or stamina to eloign itself.

Rabbits were hunted with 'two or three Spanels or curres'. Smoke, ferrets and purse nets were also used. 'I accoumpt ferrettyng one of the coldest and vunpleasantest chaces that can be followed.'[35] But rabbiting could be a diversion for educated men. 'A company of scholars going together to catch conies, carried one scholar with them which had not much more wit than he was born with; and to him they gave in charge, that if he saw any, he should be silent, for fear of scaring of them. But he no sooner espied a company of rabbits, before the rest, but he cried aloud, "Ecce multi cuniculi," which in English signifies, "behold many conies," which he had not sooner said, but the conies ran to their burrows: and he being checked by them for it, answered, "Who the devil would have thought that the rabbits understood Latin?"'[36]

The Sixteenth Century

Horses and Horsemanship

'King Henrie the eight created a noble studderie and for a time had verie good success with them, till the officers waring wearie, produced a mixed brood of bastard races, whereby his good purpose came to little effect.'[37]

An inventory at the royal stud at Eltham early in the reign listed 'coursers, young horses, hunting geldings, hobbies, Barbary horses, stallions, geldings, mail, bottle, pack, Besage, and two stalking-horses'.[38] This may be matched with one of the greatest of private stables. The 'chequir roul of the nombre of all the horsys' of Algernon Percy, 5th Earl of Northumberland in 1512, listed 'gentell horsys, palfris, hobys, naggis, chariot horsys, trottynge horsys, and a proper amblynge little nag, when he goeth hunting and hawking'.[39] The nag was a small Scottish and Border bred horse. Though quite distinct from the Irish-bred hobby it was very similar. By the end of the century it was known as a Galloway, though not without confusion. Markham describes 'a certain race of little horses in Scotland called Galway nags, which he had seen hunt the buck exceedingly well, endured the chase with great courage, and the hard earth without lameness better than horses of greater puissance and strength'.

In 1565 Thomas Blundeville of Norfolk, quoting foreign authorities, said: 'Those horses that we commonly call Barbarians, do come out of the King of Tunnis land, out of Massilie Numidia, which for the most part be but little Horses, but therewith verie swift, and able to make a very long cariere, which is the cause why we esteeme them so much.'[40] In 1599 Gervase Markham urged gentlemen to use Eastern horses as sires. Both were speaking of the racecourse, but within a generation or two the hunter was beginning to benefit. This was one necessary advance in hunter breeding. The other – selectivity – started in the royal stud. In 1575 Leicester, inspecting the muddle at Eltham, invited the Neapolitan expert Prospero d'Osma to advise about its management. His principal instruction was that the various 'races' should no longer be haphazardly crossbred, but line-bred to their own kind so as to preserve their various excellences.[41] Both Eastern blood and selective breeding towards an objective became widespread in the next century.

Although there were still, at court and at Kenilworth, grandiose occasions suited by the collected trot and the massive Italian curb bit, the provincial gentry, informally and with small fields of horsemen out, were galloping over their country with snaffles. Here began a division which grew into a chasm between English and Continental horsemanship. There were English students of Grisone and later of Pluvinel: but the characteristic English style had nothing to do with collection, arched necks, curbs or straight legs astride *pique* saddles.

The English style was formed in the hunting field, and not least by the need to jump. Some areas had practically no fences or hedges until well into the 19th century, but conditions varied according to soil, husbandry, tenure and local custom. 'That I may lepe', says Wyatt, 'boeth hedge and dike full well.'[42] These were sheep and sometimes ox fences. A horse had to be trained to get over them, and Markham recommended following hounds hunting a drag, 'the chace of a traine scent . . . drawn either across ploughed lands, or athwart green fields, leaping ditches, hedges, payles, rails, or fences, or running through a warren'. 'Payles' surrounded parks, high enough to keep in deer. It is uncomfortable, even dangerous, to jump such obstacles when sitting 'on the fork' on a saddle with a six-inch pommel.

Hunting which included fourteen-mile runs, oxers and deer fences taxed the horses to the point that it was blamed for breaking them down. But 'Hunting horses

are never lamed through their immediate riding or labour, if they have a good keeper, but now and then through greediness of sport.' The important thing (a lesson forgotten in the early 19th century) was that horses must be got fit for hunting as well as for racing. Markham insisted that they must never be hunted fat and full of grass, but fed oats, horsebread (beans and flour) and good hay, and above all given regular work before the season. Thus, and only thus, a hunter became 'long-winded, tough, hard, and stout'.[43]

Spain, Italy, Germany, Flanders, Africa

Ferdinand of Aragon died of 'hunting and matrimony',[44] but 16th-century Spain was more interested in hawking. The misanthropic Philip II loved both hunting and hawking, but his hunting was not attractive. He, Don Carlos and the ladies of the court rode out to the toils, where they shot fallow deer from hides.

Renaissance Italy was more interested in politics, business and art than country life. According to Burckhardt, a very small proportion of the nobility was given to hunting.[45] Girolamo Riario and Ascanio Sforza organized luxurious hunting parties, with 400 and more mounted guests. In 1514 Lorenzo de' Medici asked Francesco Gonzaga of Mantua to send him greyhounds and falcons so that he could cut a dash at the papal court. The Pope himself, Leo X, issued a number of edicts and codes regulating hunting, and Leo XII published a hunting calendar of a kind which Italian governments have never found easy to enforce.

The Mantua family, like the Estes of Ferrara, were celebrated for their hounds as well as their horses. They hunted and bred with exceptional enthusiasm. In the middle of the century Ferdinando Gonzaga imported Scottish greyhounds for buck, and asked the French court for hounds to hunt fox and hare. Catherine de' Medici sent him nine couple of hounds and one of lymers.[46]

The inhabitants of Campanella's City of the Sun 'laugh at us who exhibit a studious care for our breed of horses and dogs', but do not attempt the selective breeding of people. Campanella spent all his life in Calabria, but it is not clear what, if anything, the south Italian dog breeders hunted. The ideal city, unlike real Italy, hunted with enthusiasm, and 'cavalry and infantry make use of hunting as the symbol of war'.

In Germany there was, by contrast, a traditional passion for hunting, personified by the Habsburg Emperor Maximilian I. His Flemish hunting was depicted in *Les Belles Chasses de Maximilien*, done a few years after his death in 1519. He had already dictated a treatise on hunting in the Tyrol, illuminated by the Tyrolese artist Jörg Kölderer about 1500; in this it appears that he hunted stag, not ibex or chamois, with hounds and without a bow. In Bavaria he held great *battues* in which every kind of game was shot.

This was the sport of the Emperor Charles V, whose *battues* were painted in 1544 by Cranach. A great herd of deer was driven to the edge of the forest, where the emperor and his retinue waited in elegant pavilions. Ladies and gentlemen all shot,

attended by 'loaders' with crossbows. The gun replaced the crossbow as soon as it was efficient.

A vigorous but only partly German tradition continued in Flanders. Maximilian's daughter, the Archduchess Margaret of Parma, was a huntress as celebrated as Catherine de' Medici. Margaret was surprised to learn that the queen mother and regent of France rode, like herself, '*la jambe par dessus l'arson*'; unlike Catherine's, Margaret's legs were decently concealed by long silk skirts.[47]

There was still a lively tradition of hunting in North Africa. Turberville claims to have met, at 'Rochell', an 'olde man named Alfonce' who had often been at the court of the Doucherib, the King of Barbary. There 'Raynedeare' were hunted at force by the white hounds of Barbary, which Turberville (following Gaston Phébus) believed to be the progenitors of the *chiens blancs* of France.[48] This is great nonsense. What the Moors and Berbers did was to course gazelle with greyhounds and probably cheetah.

Moral Opposition to Hunting

The Humanism of Erasmus and his friends was part of the Renaissance, but radically different from the mainstream of the Renaissance spirit. Hunting was cruel to animals and brutalizing to men, and had no place in Utopia. 'Among those foolish pursuers of pleasure, they reckon all that delight in hunting, in fowling, in gaming: of whose madness they have only heard, for they have no such things among them . . . What pleasure can one find in hearing the barking and howling of dogs, which seem rather odious than pleasant sounds? Nor can they comprehend the pleasure of seeing dogs run after a hare . . . If the pleasure lies in seeing the hare killed and torn by the dogs, this ought rather to stir pity, that a weak, harmless, and fearful hare should be devoured by strong, fierce and cruel dogs. Therefore all this business of hunting is, among the Utopians, turned over to their butchers; and those are all slaves; and they look on hunting as one of the basest parts of a butcher's work . . . They look on the desire of the bloodshed, even of beasts, as a mark of a mind that is already corrupt with cruelty.' The brutal Zapolets, by way of contrast, 'for the greatest part live either by hunting, or upon rapine'.[49]

No wonder *Utopia* was not published in England or in English in Henry VIII's lifetime; it was edited by Erasmus and printed in Louvain in 1516.

FLEMISH HUNTING, 16TH CENTURY
Simple countrymen are going out in midwinter, with all the dogs they can collect, to get any game they can find. The bobbery pack includes greyhounds, small terriers and bassets, the last of which were successfully bred throughout the Low Countries from ancient St Hubert stock. Hares and rabbits were probably the main objectives of these sportsmen. Painting by Pieter Brueghel the elder.

6 Europe
Seventeenth and Eighteenth Centuries

The Foxhunting of Louis the Just

In August 1603, Henri IV of France sent an expert huntsman, the sieur de Vitry, to visit James I of England, to demonstrate the French methods and learn the British.

It does not appear that the differences of technique which were developing in England had any influence in France, with two exceptions. One was the wider use of imported Scottish deerhounds for wolfhunting. Another was a new vogue, limited but undoubted, for foxhunting above ground with running hounds.

Robert de Salnove, in *La Vénerie Royale*, ascribed the invention of this novel sport to Louis XIII. Most of this book is yet another reworking of Gaston Phébus by way of Fouilloux, but the foxhunting chapters are original. According to Salnove, Louis XIII had two techniques; he unkennelled the fox with *limiers* and then coursed it with greyhounds (the method of Turberville); or, which he more enjoyed, laid on a pack of small running hounds as soon as the fox had been found (the method of Cockaine). He also introduced a new horn call, of his own devising, to signal that the fox had gone to ground. (Such a call had been familiar in England for at least two generations.)[1]

Louis XIII was the first but by no means the only foxhunting man in France in the early 17th century. Salnove says that many gentlemen greatly enjoy the sport, as a change after two or three days' harehunting. It is tempting to guess that Louis XIII's small hounds were English; certainly English hounds were well known in France at the end of the century, including small *chiens baubis* for hare and fox, and even smaller *bigles*.[2]

The *Chasse Royale* of Louis XIV and Louis XV

When Louis XIV took control of his country, the aristocracy was dangerously rich and dangerously powerful in the countryside. The king accordingly deprived it of all influence by concentrating all the nobles round himself to play meaningless roles in the massive ritual of the court at Versailles. The great aristocrats were not allowed to be countrymen. When they went hunting, it was simply as part of the interminable ceremony of *la chasse royale*, itself part of the devious machinery by which the king turned nobles into courtiers:

'When he hunted there was no hurry, no hallooing, no scampering. Roads were

[47]

made through the forest, that the trees might not presume to interfere with the ceremony. He arrived at the place in his coach, and mounted on horseback to a flourish of trumpets. The stag ran and the king followed, but both according to rule; the spot for the death was already appointed, and there the animal was brought to a stand and slain by the royal hand. Louis then returned to his palace without a curl of his hair discomposed, and ready to proceed with the other methodical and immutable grandeurs of the day.'[3]

In such ritual hunts, blowing the horn had become one of the more exhausting activities. The instrument had turned from the natural horn into a metal trumpet of gradually increasing length, which by this time was long enough to encircle the huntsman's body and play a range of notes. Forest hunting, with hounds and men invisible to each other, numbers of relays, widespread *veneurs* and *piqueurs*, and very big fields of horsemen, had always needed a more elaborate language of the horn than did an English squire hunting the hare in the open with a few friends: but from this necessity grew artistic but time-consuming concerts in the forest. Each eminent person was greeted on his arrival by the appropriate fanfare. Each stage of the hunt was marked by its special music. When a stag was sighted, calls announced the quality of its head. There were, by Louis XIV's time, no fewer than 500 different calls for staghunting alone, apart from those special to wolf, boar, hare and fox.[4]

The irony of all this is that Louis XIV himself was personally vigorous and extremely keen on hunting. When he was young he loved going out by himself, on foot, with a gun, 'like a simple country gentleman'.[5] Sometimes in later life he escaped from his own treadmill, and enjoyed a hunt from which he returned with by no means every curl in place. He was still riding to his hounds in 1712, when he was seventy-four. Sometimes, when he felt his age, he would drive himself in a little *calèche*; he went at full speed over bad ground and overturned at least once.[6] Some of his family and intimates shared this enthusiasm. In 1686 Monseigneur (Louis,

grand dauphin) hunted a wolf for ten hours in 'suffocating' heat.[7] In 1713, when the king was seventy-five and two years before he died, he was hunting in the forest of Rambouillet; 'a furious storm which rose at the beginning of the hunt spoiled somewhat their enjoyment. Madame la duchesse de Berry and the ladies on horseback with her were lamentably wet, but that did not at all put them off hunting.'[8]

It would appear that the stateliness of *la chasse royale* was part of political strategy, and not what Louis XIV really liked. The same may be true of Louis XV who, for all his reputation for slothful lechery, went out in the dawn with the *limiers*.

He rode English thoroughbreds. 'The French monarch', said Lord Bath in 1753, 'rides no other horses but ours in his favourite diversion of hunting. You may, at any time, see two or three hundred beautiful English geldings in those great and noble stables at Chantilli.'[9] He also had a fast pack: he crossed his *chiens blancs* with English foxhounds.

Marie-Antoinette went boarhunting in the next reign, in the forest of St-Germain-en-Laye, with the hounds of her brother-in-law Artois (later Charles X). A 'numerous and brilliant' field arrived in their *voitures de chasse*, elaborate and impractical vehicles. 'The Queen of France wore the uniform of the Hunt, with a profusion of gold lace, and as great a profusion of fine white ostrich feathers in her riding-hat.' Her coach was drawn by eight English bay horses; it does not appear that she left it.[10]

Hunting in the French Provinces; Hounds

Although the great magnates were compelled into the squirrel cage of Versailles, the lesser nobility continued to hunt their countries and breed their hounds. The country gentleman at the end of Louis XIV's reign enlivened his winters with boar-hunting and with drinking his own wine with his friends; but at other seasons, in most parts of France, harehunting was his main diversion. The fox was hunted all year round, there being no fear of his becoming extinct. Foxhounds were for preference small, but a brace of big greyhounds also came out.[11]

In Normandy, Artois, Lorraine, Poitou, Saintonge, Gascony, Franche Comté and every traditional area, hunting continued energetically throughout the 18th century. Hound breeding in particular developed. Everybody rode. In the Limousin, 'A friend of M. de Tocqueville's remembered a wedding amongst the *vieille noblesse* at which "many of the ladies arrived on horseback, followed by a servant leading a donkey which carried the ball-dresses in a band-box."'[12]

Unfortunately these sporting *gentilshommes* destroyed themselves, because only they, their friends and their servants were allowed to hunt.

Hounds were classified in 1714 into three sorts: the *race royale* for all larger game, the *race commune* for all except stag, and the *race mêlée* or *petite race* of harehounds. There were in addition bassets and greyhounds; and breeds of *chiens couchants*, pointers, of which the principal were *Espagnols* or *Epagneuls*, and Italian *griffons*, a name which then defined mute dogs for shooting and rabbiting.

Bassets, although true hounds and derived from the *races royales*, had originally been bred short-legged to go underground. In 1714 they were described as 'little dogs taught to recognize and hunt the line of the hare', and were shot over as well as being used for fox and badger. The best were still the *bassets d'Artois*, usually black.

The best greyhounds of the time were English and Turkish, the former outstanding for hare coursing. Irish and Scottish breeds (wolf- and deerhounds) were also imported for tackling wolf, boar and fox. Little rabbiting greyhounds came from Spain and Portugal. There was also a greyhound–running-hound cross, known as a *charnaigre*.[13]

During the 18th century increasing use was made of the speed of the English foxhound. Louis XV crossed his *chiens blancs* with foxhounds. More and more Norman breeders did likewise, so that a writer complained in 1778 that the pure Norman breed was becoming lost; the cross was faster, but losing its scenting powers.[14]

DEPARTURE FOR THE CHASE, HOLLAND 1666
The hounds here are local bassets, probably identical to the famous *bassets d'Artois* bred in the nearest part of France from the same St Hubert stock; there are also very big greyhounds. A gun accompanies the party. They are probably after hares, which will be pushed out of the long grass by the bassets and then shot or coursed. The lady will not be required to ride fast or negotiate obstacles. Painting by Adrian Van de Velde.

This was the period of Anglomania, during which thousands of the noble French made pilgrimages to England, trooped from country house to country house, and aped English dress and manners.[15] They imported English horses and English thoroughbred racing, to the scandal of the conservative elements.[16] Though they never imported English foxhunting as Louis XIII had done, they did import a lot of foxhounds, and few breeds of French hounds were quite the same again.

In this period the gentlemen of bas Poitou (later known as la Vendée) had a hunting club called the *Société de la Morelle*; this hunt bred a pack from old *poitevin* and *chien blanc* stock which was said to be the best in France – tall, fast, light-framed hounds, white or lemon-and-white (as their ancestry would suggest), with a quality of drive which, most unusually, owed nothing to the English foxhound.

Immediately south of this area, just above Gascony, the *saintongeois* hound was developed from Gascon stock: normally black-and-white instead of blue-mottled, but otherwise closely similar.

Poitevin and *saintongeois* hounds survived the Revolution in sufficient numbers to breed from, and all modern French hounds of the larger sort (*chiens d'ordre*) descend at least in part from one or both.

Germany, Austria and Italy

Royal and aristocratic German hunting continued, between 1600 and the time of Napoleon, to consist of large-scale slaughter. This was especially true in Saxony and Thuringia.

ROYAL HUNT OF LOUIS XV
In a characteristic French royal hunt of the mid 18th century, the rendezvous is at the junction of three rides, all railed because no one will leave them. The *veneurs* arrive with the fewmets in a sack, since their horns, once used for this purpose, are no longer of suitable shape; then come grooms with second horses; then *valets de chasse* with the hounds, both *limiers* and pack; then two dozen mounted *piqueurs*, magnificently liveried, all with horns encircling their chests; then more foot-servants and grooms; and at last the mounted field of sixty or seventy, surrounding the king's coach which is greeted by his fanfare. The fewmets are shown to the king and the day's Master of the Hunt. The king chooses one of the English thoroughbreds awaiting him. As the hunt gets under way, four to six horns are constantly blown in unison, making a splendid but often purposeless sound. The stag almost always soils, as the forests are full of water. *Prise, mort, curée* and the dispersal of the field take place to a nonstop *concerto grosso* of horn music. The hounds here are bigger than English foxhounds, but there is no doubt of the foxhound cross with which Louis XV increased the speed of his pack. Detail of painting by J. B. Oudry, 1730. By courtesy of Oscar and Peter Johnson Ltd.

The Electors John George I and John George II of Saxony, who cover the period 1611–88, killed between them 110,530 deer, 52,400 wild boar, and wolves and bears on an equivalent scale. Miles and miles of canvas screens were set up in the forest to hem in the deer, placed and operated by hundreds of peasants. Inside an inmost ring like a toil, there was an elaborate *al fresco* feast, after which the duke and his retinue shot the deer as they were driven in towards them by men and hounds. Mountains of carcases resulted. This butchery was accomplished with a ceremony as formal and elaborate as that of a French royal hunt. The hounds were afterwards led home by women.[17]

Later the sport of fox tossing became the favourite polite diversion. Captured foxes were put either within the toils of a deerhunt or in the courtyard of a castle, and induced to run over narrow slings of webbing. A gentleman held one end of each sling, a lady the other, and the fun was to toss the fox as it crossed the webbing. The fox was sometimes tossed twenty-four feet in the air. The ground where it fell was sanded so that it should not be killed too soon. The pleasure was enlived with other animals too. Augustus the Strong of Saxony had a passion for this sport; in one session he tossed to death 687 foxes, 533 hares, 34 badgers, 21 wildcats, 34 wild boars, and three wolves. In Brunswick society went in for masked fox tossing: ladies and gentlemen wore fantastic costumes, and the foxes and hares were also dressed up in cardboard, cloth and tinsel to caricature public persons of the day.

Austria's civilization was separate. There was a vigorously sporting Habsburg lead from the 16th century, which continued into the early 18th. The Emperor held royal and formal hunting parties, properly conducted, on the French pattern.[18] But Austrian society was snobbish, artificial and unsporting. Such parties ceased. All that the aristocracy could bring itself to enjoy was the effortless slaughter of the *battue*.

[53]

Italian sport was no more attractive than German. They imported the protocol of French hunting, but none of its spirit and not much of its skill.[19] Stags were sometimes stoned to death while standing at bay, in the presence of ladies in coaches and full court dress.[20]

The Duke of Parma was very fond of hunting: but after his death, reports Peter Beckford, 'I apprehend all hunting in the country ceased with him. The only sportsmen now remaining are gentlemen in green coats, who, taking their *couteaux de chasse* along with them, walk into the fields, to catch small birds.' In Florence and all Tuscany 'sports of the field are unknown'.

The exception was Turin, Piemonte being more French than Italian. At a royal staghunt 'the *coup d'oeil* is fine; *l'équipage de chasse, magnifique*; and the hunting the most interesting on this side of the Alps at least, for on leaving Turin you will not see another hound.' The feast before the unharbouring was 'a hot meal more resembling a dinner than a breakfast', but the Torinesi came into the field with 'their infinity of dogs, their numbers of huntsmen, their relays of horses, their great saddles, great bitts, and jack boots'. *Piqueurs* and hounds were equally ignorant of their business: 'the king bid them ask *Milord Anglois*.' When the stag, ignoring protocol, left the forest, only Beckford and a single *piqueur* followed; the *piqueur* declined to jump a ditch, and Beckford had hounds to himself.[21]

[54]

DUTCH STAGHUNT, 1650
The Low Countries were still very sporting at this period; the Orange family itself had a long and vigorous hunting tradition, which it retained, and which caused the death of William III the Dutch king of England. This painting resembles many others of the place and time, and it has an unreal look. Among many oddities, it is almost impossible to believe in a lady on a sidesaddle riding vigorously to hounds at this date. Painting by Johannes Hackaert and Nicolaes Berchem.

Above right
JAMES I AND VI, ABOUT 1575
James's mother, Mary Queen of Scots, hunted a great deal as a young princess in France with her mother-in-law Catherine de' Medici; she introduced Gallic forms and ceremonies when she came as a widow to Scotland, where there was already a strenuous hunting

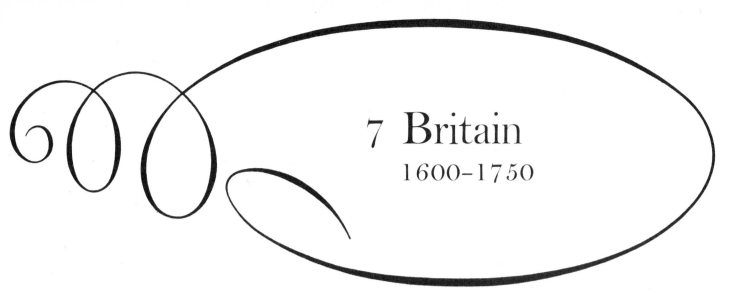

7 Britain
1600–1750

Kings and Courts

Robert Burton wrote, while surveying the court of James I, that hunting was 'the sole almost and ordinary sport of all our noblemen . . . 'tis all their study, their exercise, ordinary business, all their talk: and indeed some dote too much on it; they can do nothing else, discourse of nought else'.[1] James had been brought up to hunting in Scotland from early childhood. On his journey south to be crowned at Westminster he hunted all the way. Going from Belvoir to Burleigh: 'before his coming there were prepared train-scents; and live hares in baskets being carried to the heath, made excellent sport for his Majestie, all the way betwixt Sir John Harrington's and Stamford; Sir John's hounds with good mouths following the game, the king taking great leisure and pleasure in the same'.[2]

Bagged hares and train scents notwithstanding, James's attitude to hunting was one of the few admirable aspects of an otherwise odious personality. He urged on his son Prince Henry the merits of 'the hunting, namelie, with running hounds, whiche is the most honorable and noblest sort thereof; for it is a thievish forme of hunting to shoote with gunnes and bowes; and grey hound hunting is not so martial a game'.[3]

James's own favourite hunting country was round Newmarket. He spent so much time there that it became the seat of government for months of the year: this was why it became the headquarters of British racing. Both he and his son Charles I

tradition of a less ritualistic kind. Both under his mother's influence and when it was removed, James was brought up to hunting and hawking, as this childhood portrait shows. Hunting remained the passion of his life. Painting attributed to Bronckorst.

CHARLES I AND HENRIETTA MARIA
The king and queen, c. 1630, are departing for the chase. It is to be assumed that the dogs round them constitute their pack, in which case they are going rabbiting in the park. The spaniels are of the kind more generally associated with the king's gayer and more sporting son. Charles I was brought up to be a sportsman, and brought up his own sons likewise: but he has not himself left such a mark on sporting history as his father James I, his brother Prince Henry, his sons Charles II and James II, or his grandson the hapless Duke of Monmouth. Painting by Daniel Mytens.

tried to reverse the process of centuries by re-establishing royal forest, not to hunt in but for revenue; this was one of the activities that brought on the Civil War.

The war itself and the Cromwellian interregnum did a good deal of damage to the countryside (especially to stables and deer parks) but hunting was not apparently much affected. In 1643 a studious foreigner visiting England found a group of young people who took him hunting so often, and so enjoyably, that the winter had ended before he realized that it had begun.[4] In 1653 Izaak Walton's Venator said: 'I am a great lover of hounds; I have followed many a pack of dogs many a mile . . . What pleasure', even under Cromwell, 'doth man take in hunting the stately Stag, the generous Buck, the wild Boar, the cunning Otter, the crafty Fox, and the fearful Hare.'[5] The same year, a country neighbour of Dorothy Osborne's in Bedfordshire was 'drunk with joy that he had a wife and a pack of hounds'.[6]

Charles II hunted with energy and courage, but his great love (outside the bedroom) was the turf. His obsession with competitive riding extended to hunting: he enjoyed hunting matches, races behind hounds, of which the first recorded were at Newmarket in James I's reign. In 1661: 'This day, for a wager before the King, my lords of Castlehaven and Arran . . . did run down and kill a Stoute Bucke in St. James's Parke.'[7]

William III, like Charles II, was deeply interested in the turf; though 'wonderful serious and silent . . . very intent on affairs',[8] he was a deep plunger on both horse-races and cock matches. He was also a passionate hunting man all his life, though

THE ROYAL BUCKHOUNDS, 1734
Frederick Prince of Wales ('Poor Fred') is in the field for this day with the royal hounds, which were kept up by all the Hanoverian kings. But this was a bad period of the Buckhounds, which had damp kennels at Swinley and probably themselves badly needed an outcross. They were followed with far more enthusiasm, and probably looked after better, when George III and the Duke of Cumberland rode to them. Enormous numbers of red deer were kept in Windsor Forest; at this period they were tufted and killed; later they were carted and spared. Painting by John Wootton.

an ungraceful horseman; he died of an illness aggravated by too-strenuous hunting, and a bad fall, in Holland.

Queen Anne was equally devoted to the turf, and important in its history; she loved hunting too, and followed her hounds after the fat stags at Windsor. Like Louis XIV a few years earlier she drove herself in a light one-horse chariot 'furiously, like Jehu', and once covered forty-five miles after a stag before dinner.[9]

George I maintained the Staghounds or Buckhounds, though he made little personal use of them. (The pack had not been called the Harthounds since Queen Elizabeth's reign. It is not clear why they came to be called the Buckhounds.)

In George II's reign they hunted carted deer. In 1728 an elk was uncarted at Windsor and gave a 'brilliant run'; thereafter the staghounds chased deer uncarted at Hounslow, Sunbury and Richmond. George II himself followed his hounds, and his younger son the Duke of Cumberland was very keen. (This was the 'Butcher', execrated in Scottish history but immortal in that of the turf, since he bred Herod and Eclipse.) In 1734 the Princess Amelia, out with the duke and the Staghounds, had a fall and was dragged 200 yards, her petticoat caught on the pommel. She was sent home to be cupped.[10]

Countrymen and Countryside

'King James was wont to be very earnest with the country gentlemen to go from London to their country houses.'[11] Thus in the 17th century a medieval and Tudor tradition continued, in sharp contrast to the state of things in other countries and especially in France. And not only were landed proprietors usually resident on their estates, but their sport had a democratic instead of a socially divisive effect.

The sharpest difference was that the Continental aristocracies regarded themselves as busy in the city, idle in the country, while England saw things just the other way about. Richard Brathwaite in 1630 urged on the English gentleman the thousand useful occupations of country life, as against the extravagant idleness of London. But he also warned that too much hunting weakens the mind.[12] This warning sounded louder in the early 18th century. 'No Russian stupidity was ever more gross in its nature or half so pernicious in its consequences . . . Their business is to hunt the stag and the fox with their own hounds and among their own woods.'[13]

The supreme fictional example is Squire Western. This Somerset landowner lived in field, kennel and stable. Although he had been to the university he was uncouth and half-literate, and he spoke in a broad local accent. He was a High Tory, loathing courtiers, speaking of 'Hanover rats' and drinking 'the king over the water'; he was a foxhunter and a fox preserver.[14]

Squire Western, Sir Roger de Coverley and their like pursued their various chases in a countryside which was continuing to change. Wool had depopulated parts of the country for 300 years; early in the 17th century, as early in the 16th, there was freely voiced disapproval of the hardship this caused.[15] But the process accelerated in the 17th century, especially in the West Riding of Yorkshire and in Gloucestershire and Somerset. The effect was to make some country towns extremely rich: Frome, said Defoe, 'is very likely to be one of the greatest and wealthiest towns in England'.[16] This made the local gentry even less likely to trouble with London. Another effect was to make the rich owners of good grazing land richer still, able to breed better horses and better hounds, have both painted, and lead lives of solid luxury. A third was to create the most perfect country for hunting with running hounds.

Britain: 1600–1750

Early Foxhunting: Dorset, Yorkshire, Sussex

One of the Keepers of the New Forest in the reigns of James I and Charles I was Henry Hastings, second son of the Earl of Huntingdon, who lived in Dorset. 'His house was of the old fashion, in the midst of a large park, well stocked with deer, rabbits, and fish-ponds . . . He kept all sorts of hounds, that ran buck, fox, hare, otter, and badger; and had hawks of all kinds, both long, and short winged. His great hall was commonly strewn with marrow-bones; and full of hawk-perches, hounds, spaniels, and terriers. The upper end of it was hung with fox-skins of this, and the last year's killing. He lived to be an hundred; and never lost his eye-sight, nor used spectacles. He got on horse-back without help; and rode to the death of the stag, till he was past four-score.'[17]

The 2nd Duke of Buckingham, son of James I's assassinated favourite, left Charles II's exiled court, made his peace with Cromwell, came back to England, and married the daughter and heiress of Lord Fairfax, to whom Parliament had given most of Buckingham's Yorkshire estates. Fairfax was, before the Restoration and for some years after it, the most important single horsebreeder in England; he and his forebears hunted the Yorkshire dales. Buckingham did so too from 1657 until the Restoration of 1660 brought him back to London and Newmarket. He then hunted in Buckinghamshire from his house and kennel at Cliveden where he had, he said, 'the best pack of hounds that ever ran upon English soil'.[18] He later returned in disgrace to Yorkshire and devoted himself to the management of his Northern hounds. His country was large, and much of it very steep. It apparently had firm boundaries, since a hunt map existed (until burnt) dated 1678 and signed 'Villiers'.[19]

It is likely that he hunted hare, certain that he hunted fox, improbable that he found many stags: they were already very rare in Bilsdale and Ryedale early in the 17th century, mainly because of the 'moreyn'.[20]

His method was that of Cockaine a century earlier: a poem of about 1690 describes how a few hounds tufted the fox and the rest of the pack was uncoupled when they found.[21] The Buckingham Stone, near Chop Gate, commemorates the end of a three-hour run; only the duke and his huntsman Forster were up at the finish; the duke's horse died then and there, Forster's after two miles on the way home. Many other fine runs were recorded in Yorkshire tradition, and the duke's popularity among the sporting dalesmen would have astonished London and the court. He died of a chill caught digging out a fox in 1687. His horn survives: it was not the natural eighteen-inch curved horn, nor the melodious French trumpet, but the little, shrill, straight metal hunting horn which was an invention of his time.[22] He was a fine horseman and had a stud of magnificent horses; followers of his hounds were farmers and tenants.

Forster or Forester, of High Thorn, carried on the hounds after the duke's death. By 1714 a Mr John Such was hunting the Sinnington country: his drinking horn survives, engraved with a picture of a huntsman holding up a fox to his pack.[23] It thus appears that the country was divided among trencher-fed packs descended from the duke's.

At the other end of England lies Charlton Forest. In the 1660s Lord Grey of Uppark, nearby, established a pack of foxhounds. He was a friend of Charles II's natural son, the Duke of Monmouth, who was fond of hunting and of Sussex, and said that 'when he was King he would come and keep his Court at Charlton'.[24] He accordingly formed another pack and kennelled it at Charlton; his and Grey's were both in the care of a 'manager', Mr Roper, a Kentish gentleman and hunting expert. This arrangement dates from about 1675. It suffered a setback when Lord Grey ran off with his wife's eighteen-year-old sister, Lady Henrietta Berkeley. He was sent to the Tower after the Rye House Plot of 1683, but escaped by getting his guards drunk. In 1685 Monmouth rebelled against his uncle, now James II, with Grey as his general and Roper a principal lieutenant. For some reason Grey was only fined, but Roper fled to France where his skill earned him the privilege of hunting in the royal forest of Chantilly.

Roper came back to England, and Grey to full favour, with William III in 1688. Grey was created Earl of Tankerville. Roper went back to Charlton to manage what had been Monmouth's hounds and were now his own. He was extremely successful and popular, and in 1712 had 'the reputation of keeping the best pack of fox-hounds in the Kingdom'.[25] His fields were large and fashionable. This aroused the jealous rage of the 6th Duke of Somerset (Queen Anne's Master of Horse, who started Ascot races) who lived at Petworth. He asked Sir William Goring of Burton, 'Whose hounds they were so frequently coming near his house? And on being told that they were the Charlton Pack – Mr. Roper's, cried out, stammering with anger, "Who is he? Where is his estate? What right has he to hunt this country? I'll have hounds and horses of my own." And, in spite of Sir William's remonstrances, had kennels and stables built up on the Downs, near Waltham, called Twines (afterwards used by Lord Egremont as racing stables), and even condescended to send down first-rate cooks to tempt the Sussex gentlemen with a sumptuous breakfast; but they were faithful in their allegiance to Charlton, and, after a few years' vain endeavour to carry his point, his Grace gave away his hounds and left the field in disgust.'[26]

In 1721 Mr Roper was joined by the 3rd Duke of Bolton. From this year the first Charlton hound list survives; it reveals a large pack and the use of sires from a wide variety of sources, many remote.[27]

In February of the following year Roper died while out hunting, at the age of eighty-four, just after hounds had found at Findon. Bolton carried on alone, equally successful. He was given hounds by Sir Robert Walpole, and continued to get the best blood from all over England.

In 1729 the Duke of Bolton was beguiled away from Sussex by his second wife, the singer Lavinia Fenton (the original Polly Peachum in *The Beggar's Opera*). He gave his hounds to the 2nd Duke of Richmond.

The 1st Duke, another of Charles II's sons, had been born in 1671. Charlton Forest was granted to him by the king, and in 1720 he bought Goodwood House as a hunting box from the Compton family. The 2nd Duke succeeded in 1723, and in 1732 built Charlton House, more conveniently placed for eight o'clock meets now that he had accepted the hounds from Bolton. He 'maintained the hunt in a princely manner, and it soon assumed an importance and regularity unknown before, a hundred horses being led out every morning, each with his attendant groom in the Charlton livery – blue, with gold cord and tassels to the caps. The meets, although so early, attracted a great number of persons of all ranks and positions.'[28]

The duke was joined about 1730 by the Earl of Tankerville of Uppark, who had his own pack of foxhounds. (This was the 1st Earl of the second creation, previously Lord Ossulton and son-in-law of the 1st Earl.) He framed a set of rules of astonishing modernity: the whip was not to be used if a hound would come to his name; young hounds were to be rated gently for riot in covert; the second whipper-in's duty was to stay behind in covert to bring up the stragglers; when hounds were running on a good scent no voice was to be raised in case it brought up their heads; when they checked they were to make their first cast on their own, and only if they failed to

[59]

recover the line was the huntsman to help them; the field, meanwhile, was to keep well clear of the pack, and gentlemen were reminded that a 'confabulation' upwind of the fox was apt to head him.[29]

Still more closely associated with Charlton was Lord Delawarr (so spelled), who looked after the kennels and served as acting master. In 1733 he bred twenty-two couple of whelps, of which ten couple went out to walk with sixteen different farmers. By licence of the Lord Warden, the duke was allowed the New Forest for his cub-hunting, which Lord Delawarr conducted.

In 1733 Lord Tankerville became Master of the Buckhounds, which gave him special rights in the New Forest. He exercised these in 1734 by hunting with his own foxhounds there, which closed the forest to the duke for his cubhunting. 'This', said Lord Delawarr, 'is hard and I think your Friend Tanky uses you but very indifferently, for you will not have a whelp Enterd.'[30]

On 29 January 1737 the regular followers of the Charlton met at the Bedford Head Tavern in London, and at the Duke of Richmond's suggestion formed the Charlton Hunt Club (apparently the first such organization) with strictly limited membership and regular dinners.

The following year there was a truly remarkable run: 'It has long been a matter of controversy in the hunting world to what particular country or set of men the superiority belonged. But on Friday, the 26th of January, 1738, there was a decisive engagement on the plains of Sussex, which, after ten hours' struggle, has settled all further debates and given the brush to the gentlemen of Charlton.' They found at a quarter to eight in the East Dean wood, and ran in great circles round and round Sussex. There were many falls. Second and third horses were taken. They ran in the end 'to the wall of Arundel River, where the glorious twenty-three hounds put an end to the campaign, and killed an old bitch fox ten minutes before six'.[31]

Hound breeding continued, on Roper's and Bolton's lines, throughout this period. In the 1730s hounds came from, or bitches were sent to, the Duke of Rutland, Lord Cardigan, Lord Spencer, Lord Craven, Mr Noel and others; in the 1740s Mr Pelham, Lord Orford, Mr Bright.[32] The great huntsman Tom Johnson died in 1744, the duke in 1750. The Charlton pack was dispersed. One hound at least was immensely important – Charlton Ringwood (1741), which went to Brocklesby.

Other Early Packs

The Burton Hunt has a map of 'Parte of Lincolnshire showing the utmost bounderie for hunting ye Fox with our Hounds in the year of Grace 1672'.[33] On the same side of England, the le Strange family had had the duty of keeping foxes down in west Norfolk in the 16th century, and Nicholas le Strange continued to perform this office from 1641 to 1686. From 1696 to 1702 Mr Richard Mason kept a pack of foxhounds at Necton; he was succeeded by Sir Robert Walpole of Houghton, master for forty-three years. Sir Robert, even when Prime Minister, refused to read letters or dispatches when he had company for dinner, but 'when he saw the direction of his huntsman he said he would read it immediately'.[34]

North of the Burton country, foxhounds were kept at Brocklesby 'since 1700 certain; but they think considerably longer'.[35] (Hounds of some sort were there in 1623.[36]) In 1713 there were three packs in the area, those of Sir John Tyrwhitt, Charles Pelham and Robert Vyner. They combined their packs to form the modest establishment of 'sixteen couple of hounds, three horses, and a boy'; each owner was to be in charge for one third of the year.[37] Tyrwhitt and Vyner retired and Pelham continued alone; the hounds were thereafter branded with a 'P' and kennelled at his house.

The West had a tradition of staghunting and mixed hunting, but the Arundells of Wardour Castle, Wiltshire, 'kept a pack of fox-hounds hunting Wiltshire and Hampshire from the year 1696'. There were two separate countries, the one hunted from 'Wardover', the other from Brimmer, Hampshire, also Lord Arundell's property.[38]

Between these geographical extremes, a pack in Leicestershire was either started or carried on in 1697. A hunting horn is thus inscribed: 'Thomas Boothby, Esq., Tooley Park, Leics. With this Horn he hunted the *first pack* [i.e. best] of Fox Hounds then in England, 55 years. Born 1677, died 1752.' Tooley Park is now in the Atherstone country. Mr Boothby inherited it and, perhaps, a pack of hounds. He financed his hunting by marrying two Staffordshire heiresses; not content with them he kept a secret 'blossom'. The vicar found out and told the then Mrs Boothby, who was disgruntled; Mr Boothby took the vicar fishing and nearly drowned him.[39]

In Northamptonshire and Huntingdonshire, not far away, Mr Richard Orlebar of Hilnwick Hall formed a pack of foxhounds in 1702. His hounds seem to have been trencher-fed, as his bitches whelped at a variety of different farms.[40] He gave up his hounds in 1727. By way of the Duke of Richmond and Mr Pelham, his blood is in every kennel in England.

These foxhunters are remembered. It is impossible to guess how many there were, about or before 1700, of whom all record is lost. As early as 1689 there was a 'strict order of hunters, such as keep journals of every day's hunting and write long letters of fox-chases from one end of England to the other',[41] vigorous squires like Sir Roger de Coverley, whose 'stable-doors are patched with noses that belonged to foxes of the knight's own hunting down. Sir Roger showed me one of them that for distinction sake has a brass nail struck through it, which cost him about fifteen hours' riding, carried him through half a dozen counties, killed him a brace of geldings, and lost above half his dogs.' When the 'perverse widow' he was courting was cruel, he took it out on the foxes. These included bagmen. Sir Roger 'does not scruple to own among his most intimate friends, that in order to establish his reputation this way, he has secretly sent for great numbers of them out of other countries, which he used to turn loose about the country by night, that he might the better signalise himself in their destruction the next day.'[42]

And in some parts of England in 1714, 'fox hunters who have all day long tried in vain to break their necks, join at night on a second attempt on their lives by drinking'.[43]

England was thronged with other packs of hounds, some noble, some of ancient establishment: but the date of their entry to fox is quite unknown. The 3rd Earl of Lincoln, for example, hunted a large country in Nottinghamshire and South Yorkshire until his death in 1618; his son, the 4th Earl, until 1667; the latter's grandson, the 5th Earl, until 1692. About 1625 the 11th Lord Berkeley hunted both in Gloucestershire and from his mother's country house in Kentish Town. A deed refers to 'the considerable sporting retinue of this lord which he kept up to hunt the country of Gray's Inn Fields and Islington'. He had 150 hunt servants in livery – tawny in summer, white in winter.[44] The Coventry family kept hounds at Croome, in Worcestershire, from about 1600 to 1719, and the Lowthers had a pack in Westmorland from about 1650. In 1666 Sir John Lowther (later 1st Viscount) brought his hounds south to hunt the Cottesmore country. The Pryses in the

FOXHUNTING, ABOUT 1720
There was an unknown number of packs of foxhounds in England at this date; most were kept unostentatiously by private squires, whose sport would not have attracted the expensive brush of Tillemans. The most fashionable foxhunting establishment was the Duke of Bolton's at Charlton, but this landscape does not suggest his country in Sussex, nor Mr Pelham's or Lord Monson's in Lincolnshire, Sir Robert Walpole's in Norfolk, or Mr Boothby's in Leicestershire. Perhaps it is Wiltshire, and the pack Lord Arundell's: an identification no less speculative for being arrived at by the process of elimination. From the collection of Mr and Mrs Paul Mellon. Photo by courtesy of Arthur Ackermann & Son.

Gogerddan country, the Williamses in the Llangibby, the Arscotts in the Tetcott had packs of comparable antiquity, which they maintained; they probably killed a few foxes.

The Growth of Foxhunting 1710–50

In the Shires in 1730 the 3rd Duke of Rutland, the Earls of Cardigan (3rd) and Gainsborough (4th) and Lords Gower and Howe all had packs of hounds, though not all of foxhounds. They amalgamated their countries for foxhunting, formed a combined pack, and styled themselves the Confederate Hunt. The hunt's pack was kennelled at Croxton Park from mid October until the end of November, at Cottesmore in December and January, and at Thawston until the end of March. The Confederate pack had a standard of only twenty inches (they were fox beagles); larger hounds were drafted to the private packs which each Confederate still kept.

In 1732 Lord Gainsborough left the Confederacy and hunted part of the Cottesmore country on his own, side by side with his connection Mr Thomas Noel. Mr Noel had acquired his original hounds from the 3rd Viscount Lowther, who, following family tradition, brought the family pack annually from Lowther Castle to Fineshade Abbey, Northampton, until his death in 1721. From 1732 Noel's hound lists show litters by both Confederate and Lowther stallions.[45] He married Lord Gainsborough's widow and his country became very large. It is doubtful if any of his hounds, or those of Lord Spencer or the Duke of Rutland, were entered solely to fox.

The duke's neighbours to the north were ahead of the Shires, owing to a larger fox population or Mr Charles Pelham's example. The 1st Lord Monson inherited Burton in 1727 and entered the family pack to fox;[46] nearer Brocklesby the Skipwith or Skipworth family were sending foxhounds to Charlton by the late 1730s.[47]

The 5th Earl of Lincoln had died in 1692, and his large country was probably split up and the deer, hare and fox hunted by squires and farmers. The northernmost of

THE MEET, WOOTTON-UNDER-EDGE
This Gloucestershire scene was painted about the middle of the 18th century. Neither the Duke of Beaufort nor the Earl of Berkeley had yet entered his hounds to fox; it is doubtful if Lord Craven came so far. The hounds are very small; if they were modern one would call them harriers of the modern dwarf-foxhound type. But there were few harriers of that sort in the 18th century. The tentative conclusion is that these are fox-beagles, little sharp hounds like Cockaine's 'Ribbles', like those used by Sir Roger de Coverley before he got too old, like those of the 'Confederates' in the Shires at this period, and like the smallest of those which kept down the stout, destructive foxes of the Cumberland fells. Who had such a pack, in Gloucestershire at this time, is unknown. Painting by James Seymour. By courtesy of Arthur Ackermann & Son.

the three principal packs in Nottinghamshire in the early 18th century was Lord Castleton's at Sandbeck. He died in 1723 and was followed by the 3rd Earl of Scarborough, who hunted the modern Grove and Rufford countries until 1752. In South Notts Mr Chaworth and Lord Byron had contemporary packs. The latter had had staghounds in Sherwood Forest before turning to the fox; he sent a hound to Charlton in 1735.

About 1730, in Dorset, Mr Thomas Fownes started 'the first real steady pack of Fox-hounds in the western part of England', with kennels near Blandford. 'They were as handsome, and fully as complete in every respect, as any of the most celebrated packs of the present day [about 1810].'[48] (The historian of Cranborne Chase had not heard of Lord Arundell.) These hounds went to Yorkshire about 1745.

Foxes were rare in Devon in the 18th century, but Dartmoor was hunted from the 1730s by the packs of Amyas Child and Paul Orey Treby, who inherited his father's hounds and his huntsman John Roberts. They chased fox and deer, their largest problem being with poachers known as the Gubbins.

In Yorkshire, by contrast, foxes were plentiful to a fault. In the south of the West Riding, Mr Thomas Bright of Badsworth established a pack in 1720; he was exchanging hounds with the Duke of Richmond not long afterwards. A few miles to the east, sheepfarmers were plagued with foxes. To keep them down, Mr William Draper of Beswick got a pack together in 1726, and for twenty years hunted the Holderness country. He was very poor, very generous, and so successful that he was called 'the King's Huntsman of the East Riding'. On £700 a year he dressed and mounted beautifully his eleven sons and three daughters, while 'a leathern girdle round his drab coat and a rusty velvet cap were his royal insignia of office'.[49]

In 1746 Mr Draper's hounds went to Mr Henry Brewster Darley of Aldby.[50] He 'began to keep hounds in 1733. Kept foxhounds 32 years.'[51] Between Mr Draper and Mr Darley the 4th Earl of Carlisle hunted the Wolds from kennels at Londesborough. While other masters in the region preferred sharp little fox beagles, he bred exceptionally big hounds.[52] In 1730 Sir Robert Walpole offered him the post of Master of the Royal Foxhounds and Harriers 'with the salary of £2000 for yourself, deputy, and all charges attending the same';[53] but Lord Carlisle stayed in Yorkshire and there never was a pack of Royal Foxhounds.

MEMBERS OF THE DUKE OF BEAUFORT'S HUNT, 1744
The 3rd Duke of Beaufort succeeded in 1714 and died in 1746. He added deerhounds to his harriers in 1734, owing to the number of wild deer in Gloucestershire; by 1743 he had 32½ couple of deerhounds, one couple of foxhounds (Thunder and Giddy) and no harriers. The pack was entered to fox in 1762 by the 5th Duke. These gentlemen are deerhunting, in the uniform which, unusually, the hunt retained when it went from one chase to another; the uniform is itself surprising, as the 1st Duke, who adopted it, was a Tory so high that he never went near William III's court, and might have been expected to hunt rather in Tory scarlet than Whig blue. Painting by John Wootton.

To the west, both Sir Henry Slingsby of Scriven Park and Mr Francis Trapps of Niddsdale were hunting the modern York and Ainsty country, the former with 'small beagles' like those of the Confederates. In 1736 Mr Trapps reported to Sir Henry: 'Upon Monday last I found at Gibbet Whin Bed a brave old dog fox which made us a most shear and noble run, for the hounds went off with him at his very brush and had not one default in the whole chase which continued two hours upon extremity and killed him fairly above ground.' Mr Trapps's hounds were remarkable for their drive, which they owned, he said, to their being well blooded.

North of the Bilsdale country, the Turton family of Roxby established a pack of hounds soon after 1710. They were trencher-fed, the tenants of the estate being obliged by the terms of their leases to keep hounds. The hounds are said to have been harriers crossed with the Duke of Buckingham's sort; they were hunted mostly on foot. In the minutes of the Cleveland Friendly Society – a convivial body started in 1722 – it is made clear that all the members were fox- or harehunters, and were obliged (members in holy orders only excepted) to swear on a hunting horn that they favoured hunting.[54]

The Cumberland fox was a stout and expensive predator, and must have been hunted from time immemorial; hounds bred to catch it were used by Sir Thomas Cockaine in the reign of Elizabeth. Hunting on foot with a trencher-fed pack is recorded in the Melbreak country from about 1730. Similar farmers' packs were keeping foxes down at the same time in Liddesdale and in the country behind Cardigan in South Wales.

In 1722 the 2nd Duke of Grafton got a draft of fifteen couple from Mr Orlebar, which was the cream – perhaps the foundation – of his new kennel at Euston. He was given other hounds by Sir Robert Walpole. He hunted in East Anglia, and also took his hounds to kennels at Croydon from which he hunted in Surrey, Sussex and Kent. His Northamptonshire woodlands were used only for cubbing and spring hunting; they were also a source of foxes, which were turned down at Euston and in Surrey. The duke was a friend of the Duke of Bolton and a cousin of the Duke of Richmond, and by their invitation sometimes hunted parts of the Charlton country; his stallion hounds of Orlebar's breeding were of great value to the Charlton kennel. It is said that he became tired of the long hack from his London house north of the Thames to Croydon all the way round by London Bridge, and therefore led the parliamentary lobbying for the new Westminster Bridge. This opened in 1750, seven years before he died.

In Hertfordshire Mr John Calvert began hunting the fox over a large area about 1725; he had two packs, with kennels at Cheshunt and Redbourne; the hounds remained in his family for a century.[55]

At about the same time, the Fitzwilliam family, of Milton Park near Peterborough, started a pack of foxhounds to hunt a country in Huntingdonshire and Northamptonshire. The date is uncertain because a fire in the kennels destroyed the stud book before 1760.

The 5th Earl of Coventry re-established the family pack at Croome in 1738 and hunted his country in Worcestershire; Mr Selby began hunting a large area in the South Midlands – Bedfordshire and Buckinghamshire – in 1738; and the 4th Earl of Craven (of the first creation) began hunting his own vast estate at a date given as 1739.

The East Riding of Yorkshire and the extreme south of the West Riding, as well as the Duke of Buckingham's quondam country, were being vigorously hunted by foxhounds long before gentlemen in the rest of the county gave up their harriers.

Mr James Fox Lane of Bramham made the change about 1740. Farther north, Mr Bowes of Streatham Castle bought Mr Fownes's Dorset pack; the date was 1745 or earlier, as in that year Peter Beckford's father bought Mr Fownes's house. The hounds 'were taken to Yorkshire by their own attendants': to a region where the 'thistle-whipping' harehunters had never seen a covert drawn by foxhounds. 'When the huntsman came with his hounds in the morning, he discovered a great number of sportsmen who were riding in the cover, and whipping the furzes as for a hare; he therefore halted, and informed Mr. Bowes that he was unwilling to throw off his hounds until the gentlemen had retired and ceased the slapping of whips, to which his hounds were not accustomed, and he would engage to find a fox in a few minutes if there was one there. The gentlemen sportsmen having obeyed the orders given by Mr. Bowes, the huntsman, taking the wind of the cover, threw off his hounds, which immediately began to feather, and soon got upon a drag into the cover, and up to the fox's kennel, which went off close before them, and after a severe burst over a fence country, was killed to the great satisfaction of the whole party.'[56]

In the same year Mr Evelyn began hunting the northern half of Hampshire from kennels at Armsworth.

This list is nothing like comprehensive, as witness the many forgotten hound breeders whose names appear in the earliest kennel books. There were parts of England with unrecorded foxhunting: there were also, in 1750, many parts with no foxhunting at all.

LORD CRAVEN HUNTING AT ASHDOWN PARK, 1743
The 4th Earl of Craven began hunting in Berkshire at a date given as 1739; he was followed by the 5th and 6th Earls, who maintained the pack. Their large country included much river valley, much extensive forest, and a great deal of downland about Marlborough. Very little is on record about the hounds or hunt. These hounds are tricolour – black, white and tan – which makes it likely that they are, as described, indeed foxhounds and not harriers; they already influenced, and were influenced by, the Charlton Kennel. Painting by James Seymour.

Britain: 1600–1750

Deer, Hare and Otter

The 1st Duke of Beaufort established staghounds about 1690; he lived in retirement at Badminton owing to Tory principles as strong as Squire Western's. Following the taste of the time, the hounds were turned into harriers. But wild deer were so numerous in Gloucestershire that in 1734 six couple of deerhounds were added to the pack. Ten years later the kennel had only deerhounds, with one couple of foxhounds.[57] This was a most exceptional state of affairs. Red deer are too destructive to crops and trees to coexist with husbandry; except in preserved forest or wild moorland they became too rare to justify special packs of hounds. Parked fallow deer were hunted and coursed, and roe hunted with harriers in the few places where they were common: but in most of England harehunting was the pre-eminent country sport.

The laureate of harehunting is William Somerville, a Warwickshire squire with his own hounds for most of the first half of the 18th century (he died in 1742). His delightful blank verse is thoroughly informative about harehunting. His pack comes out in an April sunrise, or after the harvest is in; there is a merry and considerable mounted field; as the huntsman leads the pack out, uncoupled, the 'straggling cur that wildly roves' is soundly whipped 'till howling he returns, And whining creeps amid the trembling crowd'. Nobody beats ground or covert, but the huntsman is told:

> Throw off thy ready pack. See, where they spread
> And range around, and dash the glitt'ring dew.
> If some stanch hound, with his authentic voice,
> Avow the recent trail, the jostling tribe
> Attend his call, then with one mutual cry
> The welcome news confirm, and echoing hills
> Repeat the pleasing tale.

They hunt leisurely and carefully, casting themselves back when they check,

HAREHUNTING ABOUT 1680
'Hunting ye Hare with deep mouthed hounds' is Blome's caption to this page of the *Gentleman's Recreation*. The hounds are the Old Southern breed of Gascon origin, wonderful line-hunters with a great cry, slow, often so short of the killer instinct that they could be stopped just short of their hare by a stick or the voice. Hare-hunting with just such hounds was the pre-eminent English country sport in nearly all lowland places where red deer were not common: it remained so into the second half of the 18th century in spite of the growth and *réclame* of foxhunting.

following every turn of the hare when they recover the line. She lies in a clump of grass; the master sees her:

> *Now gently put her off; see how direct*
> *To her known mews she flies! Here, huntsman, bring*
> *(But without hurry) all thy jolly hounds,*
> *And calmly lay them on.*

When she runs, hopefully endways over unstained ground, there is plenty of jumping for the field. Shouts, hound music and horns – evidently several – empty the nearby village. Now she is sighted again:

> *See, how black she looks!*
> *The sweat that clogs th' obstructed pores, scarce leaves*
> *A languid scent. And now in open view*
> *See, see, she flies!*

The pack get to her and kill her almost immediately after they view.

Many individuals in the period – many whole countrysides – graduated from these comparatively gentle diversions to the rigours of foxhunting; but harehunting was always there to go back to. Sir Roger de Coverley, in the first years of the 18th century, grew too old to keep up with his fox beagles and got a pack of stophounds; he took them out 'encompassed by his tenants and servants'.[58]

The otter seems to have been hunted in this period with more enthusiasm than at any other time. To Izaak Walton, of course, the beast was 'villainous vermin . . . indeed so much, that, in my judgment all men that keep otter-dogs ought to have pensions from the King'. Venator says: 'I intend this day to do all my business, and then bestow another day or two in hunting the Otter, which a friend, that I go to meet, tells me is much pleasanter than any other chase whatsoever; howsoever, I mean to try it; for to-morrow morning we shall meet a pack of Otter-hounds of noble Mr. Sadler's, upon Amwell Hill, who will be there so early, that they intend to prevent the sun rising.'

They are on the river bank two days later: 'the sun is just rising . . . and the dogs have just now put down an Otter. Look! down at the bottom of the hill there, in that meadow, chequered with water-lilies and lady-smocks; there you may see what work they make; look! look! you may see all busy; men and dogs; dogs and men; all busy . . . Gentleman Huntsman, where found you this Otter? "Marry, Sir, we found her a mile from this place, a fishing . . . but we were here very early, we were here an hour before sunrise, and have given her no rest since we came; sure she will hardly escape all these dogs and men . . . Follow, therefore, my masters, follow; for Sweetlips was like to have him at his last vent."' Some of the field were on horseback.

The best otter hunting was in the far west: 'there is brave hunting this water-dog in Cornwall'.[59]

Cox a few years later suggests that hounds were only laid on if a first attempt at spearing failed: 'Remember in the Hunting of the Otter that you and your friends carry your otter spears to watch his vents: for that is the chief advantage and if you perceive where the otter swims under water, then strive to get a stand before him where he would vent and then endeavour to strike him with your spear: but if you miss, pursue him with the hounds which, if they be good otter hounds and perfectly entered will come chauntering and trailing along by the Riverside and will beat every tree-root, every osier bed and tuft of Bull rushes: nay, some times they will take the water and beat it like a spaniel. And by these means the otter can hardly escape you.'[60]

Somerville two generations later had a 'busy-questing pack' to hunt 'This subtle spoiler of the beaver kind'. But Somerville was not sporting in the river; he had nets and a great many spearmen, and took a slightly odious glee in the otter's death agonies:

> *Pierc'd thro' and thro'*
> *On pointed spears they lift him high in air;*
> *Wriggling he hangs, and grins, and bites in vain:*
> *Bid the loud horns, in gaily-warbling strains,*
> *Proclaim the felon's fate; he dies, he dies.*

Hounds

In 1600 the Talbot (bloodhound) was used as a lymer or tufter, and exceptionally, here and there in the north, as a packhound. The tall Southern and the small vixenish Northern were the principal packhounds, the former for hare, buck and roe, the latter for hare and fox. The principal staghound was the old lemon-pie of French royal origin. There were little beagles – some tiny – for hare- and rabbit hunting on foot. The rough-coated Welsh hound hunted all game. The Scottish sleuthhound hunted men.

It appears that many working hounds were a first cross between Southern (or Talbot) and Northern, the former contributing nose, cry and substance and the latter drive. There is no evidence that these crossbreds were successfully bred from. Well into the 18th century there is an evident distinction between the twenty-inch fox beagles which some masters entered to fox and the larger and slower hounds preferred by others. But large changes clearly happened in the very early 18th century. The owners of kennels responded to the requirements of foxhunting. The 'small Ribble hound' of the late 16th century did not answer without an outcross; it may have been short of cry, it may have been wild, it may have lacked substance and stamina. It may even have gone too fast. The Old Southern hound was incapable of catching a fox above ground. The solution of a first-cross working hound was both inconvenient and unreliable. Mr Roper, Mr Orlebar, Mr Noel, Mr Bright and others therefore developed a crossbred from which they bred. They communicated with each other, exchanging both information and hounds. Mr Bright's Badsworth Luther combined the blood of a large number of kennels,[61] and went himself as a stallion all the way from Yorkshire to Goodwood.

A more important example illustrates both the importance of the interchange between kennels and the antiquity of the process: the Duke of Richmond's Ringwood (1741). He was descended from Mr Orlebar's Tippler (1717) and Shifter (1719), both of which were in the draft which the Duke of Grafton got in 1722, and both of

'SOUTHERN MOUTHED HOUNDS', ABOUT 1660
This picture comes from Clandon Park, Surrey, from which the Onslow family hunted for many generations. Hounds like these were known by many names – Old Southern, Sussex harriers, Lancashire harriers: and in America, to which a pack of them was taken in 1650, old New England, old Pennsylvania, Eastern Shore (Maryland) and Delaware. In the latter places they could kill the grey fox, which runs like a hare, but not the red; in Britain they were useless for foxhunting. But they were wonderful harriers. They are long extinct in a pure form in Britain, but survive in America (Penn-Marydel). The blue-mottled colour is one of many, but it is special to the breed and characteristic of it. Painting by Francis Barlow.

which were freely used at Charlton. Charlton Ringwood (1741) went to Brocklesby, where he sired an enormous number of litters between 1746 and 1748. Mr Pelham inbred to him freely. Brocklesby Ringwood (1788), a great stallion hound painted by Stubbs, had at least forty lines to Charlton Ringwood, which was typical of all Brocklesby stallions over the previous thirty years. The blood filled the Belvoir kennel from the early 1750s, and was diffused all over Britain.

But the process of creating the foxhound was, by 1750, primitive and tentative. Foxhounds varied enormously in size, conformation, temperament and everything else. All sorts of outcrosses were still being tried. Hounds were still very slow. A generally admired type did not exist until Mr Hugo Meynell and his contemporaries invented it in the second half of the century.

Horses

This period is the most important in the whole history of the English horse, since it saw the creation of the thoroughbred and of the halfbred hunter of thoroughbred character.

In James I's reign began the change that was later so dramatic; it started in two ways. First, many more 'Eastern' horses arrived – Barbs and Andalusians to the royal stables and those of the 1st Duke of Buckingham, and Barbs bought at Marseille by private men. Racing was part of the reason, but only part. Secondly, there was a keen and widespread awareness, well documented, of the merit of careful breeding: this included breeding from the best strains available, and avoiding perpetuating defects; breeding towards defined objectives of speed, stamina, conformation and temperament; and keeping full records. Again, the turf was only one of many purposes.

In 1618 the transformation of the English horse could hardly have had time to begin. But an account in that year of the ideal hunter describes a good sixteen-hand halfbred of thoroughbred character. This horse is not much different from the racehorse, but they are trained quite differently, 'for the hunting-horse must endure long and laboursome toyle, with heates and cold, but the running-horse must dispatch his business in a moment of time'.

In the second half of the century two almost diametrically conflicting ideals dominated horsebreeding, with the hunter somewhere in the middle.

French scientific horsemanship was a minority interest, because of the price of the horses needed and the practical uselessness of the *manège*, for all its theoretical relevance to warfare; but the minority was rich, influential, vocal and included important horsebreeders. The most distinguished was the Duke of Newcastle, teacher, breeder and writer.[62] His seat and stud at Welbeck were in the country hunted by Lord Lincoln, but the high-school horsemanship he taught and the ideal horse he bred for it were remote from the needs of hunting.

In 1684 Thomas de Grey deplored 'the neglect of the Horse of menage, since the applying our Breed only to Racing'. To him the 'Noble Science' was the horseman-ship of Pluvinel, not hunting.[63] And it is true that since 1660 racing had grown immensely, partly as the whole country reacted against Cromwellian austerities, partly following the lead of Charles II himself: and breeding was consequently more and more directed at the turf.

Towards the end of the 17th century, however, two factors had the effect of bringing the widely disparate ideals of *manège* horse and racehorse together. One was the use by both schools of the Arab or Barb as a sire; although the mares differed

– Friesland or courser in the one case, Galloway or light saddle mare in the other – the prepotence of the Eastern stallions was such that the two types more and more resembled each other. At the same time, there was a deliberate and successful royal attempt to give the racehorse more strength and bottom: Charles II's Twelve-Stone Plates, which developed into the Kings' and Queens' Plates and Gold Cups of later reigns. These required six-year-olds carrying 168 pounds to run four four-mile heats and a final. Thoroughbred breeders directed their efforts to producing animals which could win these searching tests.

It was appreciated on the racecourse that courage and stamina derived from blood. It was also learned in the hunting field. As early as 1738 General Hawley (who rode seventeen stone) changed to a 'true blue that staid up the hills' during the great East Dean run with the Duke of Richmond's hounds.[64] Blood was more and more used for hunters. This is evident from the stud careers of the imported stallions. For example, Captain Byerley's Turk stood for many years in the North from 1690; in spite of his ultimate importance, he covered very few well-bred mares, and got hardly half-a-dozen good-class racehorses. General Honeywood's Arabian is only on record as having sired the two True Blues, out of a mare known only as their dam. Both must have had an enormous halfbred progeny. The Darley Arabian himself stood at Aldby, Yorkshire, from 1704 until 1730. Out of Colonel Childers's Betty Leedes he got the two Childers; he got Bulle Rock, the first thoroughbred in America; he got a very few other remembered racehorses. But for Richard and John Brewster Darley, in all those years, he may have got as many as 1,000 foals.

Hunting Ladies; Hunting Dress

The historian of Goodwood says that ladies came out in large numbers with the Charlton hounds. We do not know what ladies. On the day of the East Dean run the Duchess of Richmond was the only horsewoman at the meet; she seems to have been content with the meet.

But early in the 18th century we discover at least one of the heartiest and most outspoken kind of hunting ladies: 'I have very frequently the opportunity of seeing a rural Andromache, who came up to town last winter, and is one of the greatest fox-hunters in the country; she talks of hounds and horses, and makes nothing of leaping over a six-bar gate. If a man tells her a waggish story, she gives him a push with her hand in jest, and calls him an impudent dog; and, if her servant neglect his business, threatens to kick him out of the house; I have heard her in her wrath call a substantial tradesman a lousie cur.'[65]

Squire Western in Somerset encouraged his daughter to hunt with him: she rode a five-year-old sorrel mare that cost the squire sixty guineas.[66]

Hunting dress was far from standardized. In the grander hunts (the Charlton, Lord Berkeley's, the Duke of Grafton's) gentlemen wore boots and breeches, stiff long-skirted coats, and three-cornered hats like the French. From the French also came the occasional insistence on uniform colours of coat, though the colour was seldom scarlet. The long circular French horn was quite widespread, and curved cows' horns were still used as well as the new short copper or silver horn of the modern type.

Red was the Tory colour, blue the Whig. The Catholic Duke of York (James II) was a foxhunter; Squire Western, the archetypal Tory, is also the archetypal fox-hunter. The association of scarlet with foxhunting has been ascribed to this historical coincidence.

8 Britain
The Meynellian Period
1750–1800

Hugo Meynell and Quorndon

Hugo Meynell was born in 1735 at Bradley Hall, near Ashbourne, Derbyshire, in the country where Sir Thomas Cockaine hunted the fox 150 years earlier. Though a second son he was very rich because his elder brother was disinherited. In his boyhood he hunted with his own hounds in Staffordshire; 'he was then', said someone who knew him, 'the worst sportsman and wildest huntsman that I ever saw out with hounds.'[1]

In 1752 Thomas Boothby died, and that year or the next Meynell moved to Leicestershire, at the age of eighteen, to buy his hounds (probably) and hunt his country. He shortly moved his hounds and himself to Quorndon Hall, a house of moderate size to the north west of his first headquarters.

In his first years in Leicestershire he was remarkably unsuccessful, although he disciplined his youthful wildness into an eager energy which never left him. His methods were unorthodox and self-defeating. He never went out, according to an eye witness, with fewer than 100 couple. If the meet was as little as five miles away the pack was sent over the night before.[2] 'In the spring of the year, he broke in his Hounds at Hare.' 'Blood was a thing Mr. Meynell was more indifferent about than most owners of Hounds.' There was some sense in this at a time when foxes were much rarer than careful preserving subsequently made them: 'Murder of foxes', he said, 'is a most absurd prodigality.'[3]

During the 1760s and 1770s, however, his methods and his pack were transformed. By 1780 he was easily the most celebrated Master of Hounds in Britain. Several things contributed to his pre-eminence: his personal qualities; his science in the field; his country; his hounds; his followers.

'Mr. Meynell is of the middle height, of a compact and well-proportioned form; with a highly expressive countenance, and a very intellectual eye. His manners and general deportment are those of a man of the highest fashion, and he combines zeal with talent, which would render him distinguished in any pursuit that might be congenial to his inclination and taste. Fortunately for fox-hunting, he made that his election.'[4]

He liked a fox to be hunted in covert for a few minutes: 'a good rummaging in cover will do the Hounds service'. Like Lord Tankerville he demanded silence: 'When a Fox was found in a Gorse covert, very little noise or encouragement was made; and when he went away, as soon as the Hounds were apprised of it, they did not come headlong after; but commenced very quietly, and settled and collected together gradually, mending their pace, and, accumulating their force as they went along, completing what was emphatically termed – a terrible Burst. . . . It was Mr. Meynell's opinion, that a great noise, and scolding of Hounds, made them wild. Correcting them in a quiet way, was the most judicious method. Whippers-in are too apt to think their own importance and consequence consists in shouting, holloing, and unnecessary activity.'

When they checked: 'Mr. Meynell was not fond of casting Hounds, when once they were laid upon the line of scent; he left it to them.' He never lifted them through sheep.[5]

His personality, his science and his country attracted followers; so, most of all, did his hounds. 'The first qualities he considered, were, fine noses, and stout runners . . . Perfection consisted of true guiders, in hard running, and close patient hunters, in a cold scent, together with stoutness . . . Skirting, over-running the scent, and babbling, were the greatest faults.'[6]

An important event was the addition to his followers, about 1780, of Mr Childe of Kinlet, Shropshire, who had been hunting the Ludlow country – 'Flying Childe', a happy pun of his name with that of the first great thoroughbred racehorse. A French writer said in 1751 that Englishmen were 'out all day, always on the tail of hounds in their fox-hunting, jumping hedges and ditches';[7] but this description is thirty years ahead of reality. Childe, on the fine halfbreds for which his county became famous, did in fact what had hardly been attempted before, 'riding up to the hounds, and flying the fences as they came'.[8] He was at once imitated by Lord Jersey and Mr Cecil Forester (later Lord Forester), 'the very best rider we have amongst us'.[9] Mr Meynell said bitterly that he became accustomed to seeing a fox break covert, followed by Mr Forester and then the hounds, and that 'he had not enjoyed a day's happiness since they developed their racing ideas'.[10] He was, himself, 'like a regular little apple dumpling on horseback'.[11]

These men who thrust all day drank much of the night. In 1787 they were joined by Mr Ralph Lambton. After two years at Loughborough he found the Quorndon Club too boisterous, and in 1789 he took a house in the quiet little town of Melton Mowbray, the first hunting man to do so. Melton had 'but one inn, and that a very bad one; no bank, and very few good houses'.[12] But it was happily placed at the junction of the Belvoir, Cottesmore and Quorn (as both house and hunt were, for unexplained reasons, beginning to be called). Lambton was therefore joined there by Cecil Forester, Mr Cholmondeley (later Lord Delamere) and Mr Smyth-Owen; they took a house with only four 'best bedrooms', and constituted the original Old Club at Melton. They invented the scarlet evening coat. By the time Mr Meynell retired from active mastership Melton had decisively taken over from Loughborough as the Mecca of foxhunting.

Shires and East Midlands

Mr Tom Noel, 'Old Noel', continued to hunt his country to the east of Mr Meynell's until his death in 1788. His huntsman latterly was Arthur Abbey, who carried the horn into the next century; his hounds were said to be better than the Quorndon's.[13] Sir William Lowther (later 1st Earl of Lonsdale of the 2nd creation) bought the pack in 1799 from Mr Noel's heirs and successors.[14]

Lord Spencer divided his territory into the Pytchley and Althorp countries, hunting them alternately; this was socially successful with the gentlemen of each

DICK KNIGHT ON 'CONTRACT'

Dick Knight became the 2nd Earl Spencer's Pytchley and Althorp huntsman in 1782, and retired with his master in 1796 or 1797. He was one of the first of the really celebrated professionals, known far beyond Northamptonshire, with an electrifying holloa and a galloping style which was loved by the increasing numbers of gentlemen who hunted for the ride. The pack he bred was joined to, and effectively swamped by, Mr John Warde's in about 1798: but it is probable that in returning from Warde's 'jackasses' to small hounds, Lord Althorp and Sir Charles Knightley returned to Dick Knight's ideas. Contract was the horse Knight was riding when he jumped over a swimming parson. The artist of this and many other sporting pictures was Mr Claude Loraine Smith of Enderby, an intimate friend of Mr Hugo Meynell's and a famous man to hounds throughout the shires.

Painting by Claude Loraine Smith. By courtesy of Arthur Ackermann & Son.

area, although both countries were really too small. Dick Knight was huntsman from 1782; his holloa could be heard three miles away in frosty weather,[15] but he was quick and impatient, continually lifting his hounds and changing foxes.[16] This was probably the result of fields riding in the new Leicestershire style. A parson who habitually pressed hounds went into a brook one day, and was floundering in terror and chagrin. Dick Knight, on his famous horse Contract, jumped over him. 'His reverence', he said, 'swims like a cork; but never mind him; this is only Friday, and he won't be wanted till Sunday.'[17]

The Belvoir's earliest hound list starts with the 1757 entry, in the time of the 3rd Duke, 'John of the Hill'. In that year 290 horses were kept and regularly hunted with the duke's hounds, which were entered solely to fox in 1762.

John Marquess of Granby was effective master in the 1760s. He bred his hounds exceptionally small, which was feasible in a country almost wholly unfenced. The 5th Duke succeeded in 1787, at the age of nine. A committee ran things; the hunt remained popular but the kennel deteriorated. In 1791 Mr Percival (brother of the murdered Prime Minister) took charge of hunt and kennel, and engaged Newman as huntsman. In their charge the pack improved immediately and immensely, getting infusions of blood from Lord Spencer, Lord Fitzwilliam and the Duke of Beaufort. When the 5th Duke came of age in 1799 Belvoir had a first-rate pack again.

In the Burton country immediately to the north, the 3rd Lord Monson re-established the family pack in about 1774, when he attained his majority. He got drafts from Mr Pelham, Lord Spencer, Mr Meynell, Mr Noel and Lord Fitzwilliam. He was a notable hound breeder, using principally Brocklesby stallions (as had the Duke of Rutland) from 1781; his hounds, 'approximated nearer to Meynell's than any others of the day'.[18]

North Lincolnshire continued to be hunted by the Brocklesby hounds, throughout this period the most influential in improving and standardizing the breed. This is to be explained not only by their absolute quality, but also by the Pelhams' long-continued practice of inbreeding and line breeding – as to Charlton Richmond (1741) – which fixed the type and created the prepotence to transmit it.

There is wide disagreement as to when, and whence, the 4th Earl Fitzwilliam got his foxhounds and his huntsman Will Dean.[19] From the middle 1770s they hunted the Milton country, with the Wentworth for cubhunting. The establishment was extremely grand but also inept. The trouble was the huntsman's 'utter want of knowledge'. 'Foxes were dying an honourable death of old age in Bedford Purlieus, despite all the talent of Will Dean.' His hounds were fat and they were babblers; 'perhaps there never was a pack so thoroughly wild . . . They never were known to hold a scent for half a mile.'[20]

After the time of Lord Byron and Mr Chaworth, South Notts was hunted by unknown packs. Then Mr John Musters of Colwick Park established a pack in 1775. He hunted all south Nottinghamshire until, in 1798, he turned over part of the country to his son, who had just come of age. John Musters Jr was given ten couple of hounds by Hugo Meynell; in 1805, having married Miss Chaworth, he began to hunt the whole country.

In the north of the county, the 3rd Earl of Scarborough was succeeded in 1752 by the 4th, he in 1782 by the 5th. Contemporaneously with the 4th Earl Mr Francis Foljambe of Osberton hunted the Grove country. In 1772 the 6th Earl of Thanet rented Osberton and bought Mr Foljambe's pack, which was principally of Brocklesby blood. Mr Richard Lumley Savile had another pack at Rufford Abbey, from about 1770, until he succeeded his brother as 6th Earl of Scarborough in 1811.

Britain: 1750–1800

West Midlands

At an unknown date Mr John Smith Barry, younger son of the 4th Earl of Barrymore, began keeping hounds in Cheshire; by 1762 they were known as the Cheshire Hounds.

His hounds were celebrated for their speed, which in the following year led to the famous match on 30 September 1763: 'The Hon. Mr. *Smith Barry* and Mr. *Pochin* run each a Couple of Foxhounds on the *Beacon Course*, for 400 Gs. The first Hound to take 300 Gs., the second a hundred, which was won by Mr. *Barry*'s coming in first and second.'[21] 'Mr Pochin' was actually Mr Meynell. Mr Smith Barry's hounds, which won very easily, were Bluecap (an important sire) and his daughter Wanton.

The year before the match, on 7 November 1762, several harrier owners formed the Tarporley Hunt Club, to meet twice a year: 'each meeting to last seven days. The harriers never to wait for any member after eight o'clock in the morning. Every member must have a blue frock, with plain yellow metal buttons, scarlet velvet cape, double-breasted scarlet flannel waistcoat, the coat sleeve to be cut and turned up.'

In 1769 there was a change in the direction of sobriety, and a change from hare- to foxhunting. It was agreed that 'instead of three collar glasses, only one shall be drunk after dinner, except a fox is killed above ground'.[22]

John Smith Barry was succeeded by his nephew James in 1784; in 1798 the Cheshire Hunt Club (overlapping with, but distinct from, the Tarporley Club) quarrelled with James for reasons now forgotten; the members warned him off their coverts. The Cheshire County Subscription Hounds were consequently formed to hunt the country. Their basis was the existing private pack of Sir Peter Warburton, who was first master of the new hunt.

The northern part of the country was at this date hunted by Mr Leche of Carden Hall, Chester, a very jolly man who acquired a strong local accent from his friends, and was far too easy-going to control either his field or his hounds.[23] His father had hunted the country; his son later did so. They hunted their own hounds, which was almost unique in the 18th century.

In central Shropshire, the 'Shropshire Old Hunt' succeeded, or formed itself round, the earlier Shrewsbury Hunt Club by 1753; it met for a week with a pack of foxhounds. The members retained blue coats and the name True Blues; they gave a dinner and a ball, to which ladies wore scarlet habits.

Contemporary private packs included those of Mr Thomas Wall of Neen Sollers, who hunted fox, hare and otter probably with Welsh hounds, and Mr Noel Hill (later Lord Berwick).

Mr George Forester of Willey Park (usually then Wiley) was hunting what was roughly the modern Wheatland country by 1773. His whipper-in for thirty years was Tom Moody, 'a little eight stone man, decidedly dirty; he would wear his boots without taking them off from Monday to Saturday. His whole existence centred on hunting; he could not read a word; his spare time in Summer was spent in fishing for eels.'[24] As well as hunting Tom Moody liked grog and women. His death, from all three, was celebrated in a ballad sung by Charles Incledon at the Theatre Royal.[25]

Although he never married, Mr Forester was partial to ladies, and kept a number in cottages on his estate who bore him quantities of bastards. One such lady was Phoebe Higgs, 'a complete Diana', who regularly rode to hounds, taking vast leaps, and often giving the master a lead. When Mr Forester was old he resigned his coverts

to 'a pack of fox-hounds set up in his neighbourhood by some farmers'.[26] His own hounds became the trencher-fed Aldenham Harriers.[27]

To the south west, Mr William Childe of Kinlet Hall hunted the Ludlow country for a few years, until he went to Leicestershire; he was accompanied there by Cecil Forester (1st Lord), nephew and heir of the Squire of Willey.

Mr John Corbet of Sundorne Castle hunted the Shifnal country from about 1780 with his heavyweight huntsman Stephen Goodall. From 1778 he also went to the Meriden (Coventry) side of north Warwickshire.

The south of Warwickshire was hunted by Mr Wrightson from about 1780, with kennels at Swalcliffe Grange and at Stratford. In 1791 Mr Corbet took over the whole country, until 1811, hunting this large area four or five days a week, entirely at his own expense, with kennels at Meriden and Stratford.

'Warwickshire never before, nor since, witnessed such glorious days.'[28] 'A more popular master of hounds never hunted';[29] he had 'the manners and deportment of the highly-finished gentleman, although of a school of a somewhat earlier date'.[30]

Mr Corbet is remembered above all for 'the blood of the Trojans' – a toast drunk by generations of Shropshire hunting men. Trojan (1780) was a black-and-white hound, probably by Lord Spencer's Blueboy out of a harrier bitch called Tidings.[31] He was first entered to hare, then joined the foxhounds. His nose was marvellous, and Mr Corbet bred to him probably too much.[32] But as an influence he ranks even above the very different Cheshire Bluecap.

In east Shropshire and south-west Staffordshire the 5th Earl of Stamford hunted the Enville country; Beckford admired his pack.[33]

Cannock Chase, adjoining the Enville, was hunted by Sir Walter Bagot of Blithfield until his death in 1768, then by Sir Edward Littleton of Teddesley Park from 1774 to 1789. He was 'the last foxhunter of the old school'. He used to meet at dawn; you could hunt with him, go home to breakfast, and then go to the normal meet of another pack.[34]

Other packs in this crowded area belonged to Mr Harry Vernon of Hilton, one of the few Masters of Hounds to wear earrings, Lord Donegal and Lord Talbot of Ingestre.

North-west Staffordshire, known as the Woore country, was intermittently hunted by various private packs; one of them, in the last years of the century, was that of Sir Thomas Mostyn.

Herefordshire was hunted in the last quarter of the century by the Rev. Robert Symonds and his brother Edward. They had kennels at Ross, to which they brought the pack of their father, Thomas Symonds of Pengelly, when he died in 1774. Their pack and country grew steadily during the 1880s, and by the early 1890s they were hunting most of Herefordshire, crossing the Severn to hunt in the Cotswolds, and reaching as far as the Vale of White Horse side of the Rev. John Loder's Old Berkshire.

Gloucestershire and Oxfordshire

The 4th Duke of Beaufort (succeeded 1745) was not a great sportsman, but he kept the family staghounds. The pack was also maintained during the minority of the 5th Duke (succeeded 1756). In 1762 he was coming back from an unsuccessful staghunt when his hounds had a tremendous run after a fox; this converted him to foxhunting. His huntsman was Will Crane, 'considered by all the very best of his day', but drunken. He was dismissed, went to Newmarket, and trained Mr Smith Barry's hounds for the match of 1763.[35]

In 1776 the duke took over Lord Foley's Oxfordshire country additionally to his own at Badminton. The purchase of the Foley–Crewe hounds by Lord Fitzwilliam 'made an opening in that part of Oxfordshire which the Duke now hunts'.[36]

The 5th Duke was a careful and successful hound breeder, and his stallions began to be used by many other kennels. But the hunting seems to have been ill-managed. In 1780 Charles Warde recorded 'Hollowing and Mobbing beyond all description . . . had this been well managed the hounds would have shewn a fine day's sport having a Gallant Fox before them and hounds inclined to do well but for Huntsman and two Whippers-in; the world never produced their fellows: John Dilworth Huntsman, Thos. Alderton 1st Whipper, *Job the Devil*, the other.' Things went well only if hounds outran the hunt servants' horses. In 1789 it was no better: 'they tryed to mob their fox, and lost him by Hollowing and confusion, *very very bad*.'[37]

To the north, the Cotswolds were hunted by Lord Chedworth, of Stowell, from an unknown date until his death in 1762, then by Mr Bulkeley Fretwell, a very rich retired Nabob who knew all the leading breeders and created a wonderful pack.[38] The pack was dispersed in 1796 and the country was absorbed by his neighbours.

Lord Berkeley had four kennels, from which he hunted in effect four separate countries: Cranford, Middlesex; Gerrard's Cross, Buckinghamshire; Nettlebed, Oxfordshire; and Berkeley Castle. The picture of him hunting a continuous country stretching from Charing Cross to the mouth of the Severn is grand but inaccurate. One pack moved from kennel to kennel.

Mr John Warde had his own hounds at home in Kent in the 1770s. In 1776 he took them to Yattendon, Berkshire. In 1778 he bought Captain Peregrine Bertie's Abingdon pack. In 1780 he moved to Bicester, before going to Pytchley in 1798.[39] By this time his personality and his pack were famous. 'Rough as was his exterior, Mr. Warde was accomplished and well informed, and capable of adapting his conversation to any society into which he might be thrown.' He had 'gaiety of heart and lightness of spirit'.[40]

The hounds were already 'Warde's jackasses', the biggest in Britain, 'combining gigantic limbs, and extraordinary height and strength, with high form and symmetry'.[41] He never bred from Hugo Meynell's sort, despising their puniness. Years later, in the New Forest, he had a couple of Meynell's breeding which he called Queer'em and Quornite; he never entered them, but kept them to laugh at.[42]

Hampshire and Berkshire

Mr Thomas Ridge succeeded Mr Evelyn in Hampshire in 1748 or 1749; until 1795 his hounds hunted from Farnham to Romsey. Latterly he took a considerable subscription, made necessary by his twenty-one children; the organization formed by himself and his subscribers was called the Kilmston or Kilmiston Hunt. Bordering or invading his country were half a dozen private packs, mostly hunting foxes with harriers.[43] In 1795 Mr Ridge resigned. The hunt was dissolved, and immediately re-formed as the Hampshire Hunt.

From 1788 the Prince of Wales lived part of the year at Kempshot, in Mr Ridge's country, keeping a pack of staghounds. Mrs Fitzherbert stayed with him there; so did Charles James Fox, who appeared at breakfast dressed for hunting but was too gouty to ride.

Mr Poyntz of Midgham had another pack, which he used to bring to Overton. He was a character eccentric to the point of perversity. In 1793 the Prince of Wales turned from stag- to foxhunting, and Mr Poyntz became manager of his hounds. The royal pack only lasted for two years; many of the hounds went to Mr Chute.

Mr William Chute of The Vine or Vyne had harriers in the late 1780s with which he hunted a fox whenever possible. He had foxhounds from 1791, but gave them up, with an ill grace, in favour of the Prince. In 1795 'He procured fresh drafts of foxhounds, and declared, with a strong asseveration, that he would never again give up his country to prince, or peer, or peasant.'[44] His hounds, mostly from Goodwood, were 'very small, but very neat, very fast, very quick in their turns, and very stout'. He called them *multum in parvo*. Their owner had 'the appearance of anything rather than a master of foxhounds, streaming across the country with a long pig-tail down his back'.[45] His method of getting over fences was to dismount, hold on to his horse's tail and be towed.

The New Forest was hunted by various packs licensed by the Lord Warden. In 1781 Mr Vincent Hawkins Gilbert of Lamb's Corner established a pack and in 1783 a hunt club. 'He had a natural genius particular to himself: I have seen him often recover a fox in a wonderful way, when all chance of hitting him again appeared hopeless.'[46] 'Though a real gentleman in his general bearing [he] would sometimes suffer the zeal of the chase to swallow up his usual good manners.' It swallowed them up on one occasion recorded in his own diary: 'Horsewhipped one White for being impertinent and beating the hounds.'[47] He entered New Forest Justice, a hound with tremendous bone and 'as big as a deer',[48] sire of the Duke of Beaufort's Justice. His huntsman latterly was Tom Sebright.

There were several private packs in the modern Hambledon country; Mr Land of Park House effectively founded the modern hunt. He used to go out very early in the morning and draw both the Duke of Richmond's and Lord Egremont's westernmost coverts before they got there, which greatly annoyed both.[49]

The 5th and 6th Earls of Craven followed the 4th in their country between Newbury and Wantage. Their own estate was so large that they drew few other coverts. To the east, Mr Ellis St John kept a pack of harriers at Finchampstead,

hounds of the 'Old Dorset type', hunted by Thomas Tocock, chasing 'hare and buck'.[50] In 1790 Mr St John sold his harriers and bought a pack of foxhounds.

North of Lord Craven's, north west of Mr St John's, the Rev. John Loder, rector of Hinton Waldrist, established a pack about 1760 in north Berkshire and part of Oxfordshire. To his west, Mr Naper Dutton was already hunting a country of unknown size from Fairford, in which he was succeeded in 1776 by his son James. This pack was dispersed about 1780, and Mr Loder added the country to his own. The Rev. Robert Symonds, raiding all the way from Herefordshire, met Mr Loder and his daughter, a young widow, about 1795. Mr Symonds overcame Mr Loder's objections to the marriage by the gift of a stallion hound.[51] The two packs joined, the 'Welsh' (not Welsh at all) nicking well with the Berkshire.

The South West

In 1745 Mr Thomas Fownes's house, Stapleton Iwerne, near Blandford, was bought by Julines Beckford, whose fortune came from the family's plantation in Jamaica. His son Peter was born in 1740 and had his own pack of beagles at the age of thirteen. He was a schoolmate of Gibbon at Westminster and went on to Oxford, becoming a gifted linguist and learned historian. During vacations he bred his beagles with big old-fashioned harriers, and with these faster and lighter harriers hunted hare and fallow deer in Cranborne Chase. In 1766, home from his first tour in Italy, he acquired a pack of foxhounds.

By 1883, when he sold it, Beckford's pack was very good. Like other hound breeders of his time he was experimental, trying pointer, greyhound and Old Southern hound crosses.

In 1779, convalescing after a bad fall, he occupied his time writing a book in the form of a series of letters of advice to a young man. It was published anonymously in 1781, being advertised in West Country newspapers in August. It was given a ferocious notice in the *Weekly Review*, by a person who disliked bloodsports and suspected the author of being a hunting cleric. This prompted a second edition with Beckford's name and with notes rebutting the critic.

Two years later he went back to Italy, selling his pack to Thomas Grove.

[78]

FOX CHACE AT CASTLE COMBE
This shocking episode was used by Beckford as the frontispiece of his *Thoughts* in 1781. Castle Combe, at the Gloucestershire end of Wiltshire, is nearly in the middle of the modern Beaufort country, and was in much the same position in the home country of the 5th Duke. The latter had entered his hounds to fox in 1762. By 1780 he had bred a first-rate pack, hunted by John Dilworth, who succeeded the brilliant but drunken Will Crane. By Charles Warde's account in his diary, Dilworth, and both his whippers-in, were disastrous. Given the time and place, it must be assumed that these are the duke's hounds and that it is Dilworth's anxious face at the door.

In south Dorset the Drax family hunted their enormous Charborough estate from about 1760; Beckford took part of their country. He was followed there by Mr Sturt of Crichel (then usually Critchell). On the west bank of the Stour (Blackmore Vale) Mr Calcraft had a pack. The Prince of Wales took Crichel and bought Mr Sturt's and Mr Calcraft's packs; this was before he went staghunting in Hampshire. The Charborough country was resumed by Mr Drax Grosvenor.

Further west, the Rev. W. Phelips (Phelps, Philips) had a True Blue Hunt, with foxhounds, in the Cattistock country.

The Portman family kept hounds, hunting not the country which now bears their name but north-west Dorset and up into Somerset. 'A tame fox at the White Hart, Bridgewater, was brought up from a cub to run in the wheel as a turnspit.' One day it escaped and made 'wild work among the geese. The writer of this was out the next morning with Mr Portman's dogs', which found the fox and hunted him for thirty miles. At the end of this enormous ring, the fox jumped back into the inn garden, 'immediately entered the kitchen, darted into the spit-wheel, and began to perform his domestic office with as much unconcern as if he had been placed there for that purpose. The fat cook, with whom he was a great favourite, spread the place of his retreat with her petticoats, at the same time beating off the eager hounds with all her might and main.'[52]

After the Wardour pack's departure to Quorndon, Wiltshire was apparently unhunted for a dozen years. Then Mr Wyndham of Dinton established a pack in 1795.

In Devon, the Bragg family still hunted fox and hare over north Dartmoor with a pack established about 1604. Adjoining theirs was the country of Mr Paul Treby, who gave his pack to Mr John Bulteel of Flete. The latter's son, Mr John Crocker Bulteel, inherited the hounds in 1801.

In Cornwall, a hunt club was established on 1 January 1780 at Truro, each member keeping trencher-fed hounds, subscribing £25 a year, and giving a fortnightly dinner to the others. This club became the Four Burrow.

Yorkshire and the North

Mr Henry Brewster Darley's Aldby hounds continued to hunt most of the East Riding until 1764. The huntsman from 1750 was Moses Wing, who got 'Ten Pounds a year, half the Vales of the Stables & the Livery'. James Wright, whipper-in, got 'Five pounds a year, a Velvet Cap, Coat, Waistcoat, and Breeches'. (These terms were about usual for the time.) May Day was already, by custom apparently widespread, the date at which hunt servants' appointments started or terminated.[53]

The country was divided between Mr William Bethell and Mr Humphrey Osbaldeston (Holderness side), Sir Thomas Gascoigne, Mr Watson of Old Malton, the East Yorkshire or Driffield Hunt Club,[54] Mr Henry Bumper Savile, and Lord Carlisle of Castle Howard, with whose hounds a guineahen always ran or flew.[55]

The elder and younger Sir Rowland Winn were followed in the Badsworth country by the 2nd Earl of Darlington, who already had hounds at Raby Castle. His son, as Lord Barnard, began hunting his own hounds at the age of twenty-one in 1787.

In the Bramham Moor country, Mr Fox Lane retired in 1761; Mr James Lane Fox arrived about 1778. The hunt began its perennial alternation between the Lane Fox and Lascelles families.

East of this country was the outrageous Colonel Thornton. When he went hunting, 'Fourteen servants with hawks on their wrists, ten hunters, a pack of stag hounds and lap-dog beagles, and a brace of wolves formed the advance guard. Two brace of pointers, and thrice as many greyhounds in rich buff and blue sheets, with armorial bearings, followed in their train.'[56]

In 1795 Colonel Thornton offered to run his hound Merkin against any hound in England, five miles 'over Newmarket', the challenger to have a start of a furlong, for the scarcely credible wager of 10,000 guineas. There were no takers. In a private trial Merkin is supposed to have run the five miles in seven-and-a-half minutes – a large advance on Bluecap. Merkin had a head like a greyhound.

The Yorkshire side of the Tees was hunted in the 1770s by Mr (later Sir) Charles Turner; on 1 December 1775 they had a fifty-mile run after 'the noted old fox Caesar'.[57] Mr William Challoner's Guisborough hounds, or Cleveland Staunch Pack, had a sixty-three-mile run on 29 January 1785.[58] The Bilsdale went on as it always had; the Sinnington, under Mr John Kendall of Pickering, had a hunt club with a subscription of ten shillings a year. From about 1790 the 'gentlemen farmers of Clowton, Hackness and Staunton Dale' hunted between Pickering and Scarborough. Mr Hopper of Wykeham Grange, one of the owners, once heard a fox near his geese in the middle of the night. He let out two or three couple, ran five miles on foot in his nightshirt, and marked the fox to ground. The Vale of Cleveland had several small packs. The best known was the Roxby, still trencher-fed; after a good run the whole field went to an inn and stayed there for two or three days.

In north-western County Durham, Mr Anthony Humble of Prudhoe had a pack deriving from Mr Robert Surtees of Milkwell Burn. 'Humble's Hounds' may have existed before 1743.[59] They were inherited by his son Thomas, of Ettringham, about 1790, and became known as the Prudhoe. The 'Gentlemen of Sunderland' had a subscription pack hunting bag foxes by 1770. They once turned down a fox near Houghton-le-Spring; hounds changed to a wild fox which stood up for twenty miles, boarded a ship at Sunderland, and was saved by the crew.

Northumberland was hunted by a number of private packs, which included the Duke of Northumberland's at Alnwick. The duke once ate a fox's head, devilled, for dinner, after it had given them a good run.

In Cumberland an estate pack at Greystoke became a farmers' pack in 1759, partly kennelled at Keswick; it was known as the Cumberland Hunt by 1794, in which year it gave a hunt ball.[60] There were trencher-fed hounds at Threlkeld (Blencathra) before 1760.

South-east Midlands and East Anglia

The 4th Duke of Grafton was a hunting man (like the 2nd but not the 3rd); from about 1795 his woodland pack in Northamptonshire was hunted by Joe Smith; the tubby-barrelled hounds were 'as wild as hawks'.[61]

Most of Hertfordshire was hunted from 1775 by the Marchioness of Salisbury's Hatfield Hunt. Her hounds were exceptionally steady, and had the fine noses needed for that cold-scenting country. The fields, of forty or fifty, were almost all gentlemen who dined or stayed at Hatfield House; there were also a very few respected farmers and horsedealers.[62] Lady Salisbury 'constantly hunted with the Hatfield Hounds, in a sky-blue habit, with black velvet collar and a jockey cap, riding as hard as any sportsman in the field.'[63]

To her east, the Calverts hunted until 1799 and Mr Selby Lowndes until 1772. Part of his country was taken over by the 4th Duke of Bedford, who built kennels at Woburn with fountains and central heating.[64]

Much of Essex was hunted from about 1795 by J. and D. Rounding, jolly brothers who owned no land but showed good sport to fields of farmers. Tom Rounding was a 'facetious prime old huntsman . . . He never deserts his friend – nor flinches from the bowl.'[65] Other packs were 'The Talents' and 'The Invincibles', very sporting but a nuisance to Mr James Panton, who took over the Thurlow side of the Duke of Grafton's country in 1770. Adjoining him was 'Miser' Elwes, who hunted economically in Suffolk from about 1780. The Essex and Suffolk country was hunted by Sir William Rowley from about 1777. Mr Harding Newman managed the Essex Subscription Foxhounds from 1785; he and Sir William constantly disputed their coverts. East Essex was another distinct country.

West Norfolk was hunted by the Marquess Townshend and then by Mr Coke of Norfolk (later Earl of Leicester), whose pack roved as far as Epping and whose tenants hunted in scarlet.

Sussex, Surrey, Kent

The 3rd Duke of Richmond re-established the Charlton, as the Goodwood, when he came of age in 1757. He collected a great pack of hounds[66] and had two great huntsmen in Tom Johnson and Tom Grant.

Great care was lavished on these hounds. 'His Grace employed two men, one during the day and one during the night, for six weeks, in order that a fractured leg might be perfectly united, the dog having been ridden over when out with the pack. This attention was so successful that the hound ultimately joined the chase, to the great delight of the Duke.' In 1790 the duke built new kennels at Goodwood, very large and high; 'on one side they were partly lined with great iron plates, which were heated at the back by huge fires when required.'[67]

In 1773 Lord Egremont bought hounds from Yorkshire and took the country the Duke of Somerset had tried to hunt. Luke Freeman came with the hounds; he and they were an enormous success. The pack went to Goodwood when Lord Egremont gave up.

About 1760[68] a pack was kept at Bermondsey to hunt bagmen in the suburbs; about 1780 the Surrey hounds were established at Godstone and another pack to the west: the two combined as the Surrey Union in 1799. The Duke of York had a pack at Weybridge: 'they are worse than you can possibly imagine; they can neither draw, nor run, nor hunt; they all stink, and want brimstone.'[69]

Mr John Warde of Squerries, West Kent, hunted the fox there until he went to Yattendon. Afterwards Sir John and Sir Thomas Dyke of Lullingstone Castle established the West Kent.

Wales

Of much undoubted hunting there is little record.

In the far north, Mr Richard Puleston of Emral, Flintshire, hunted his own hounds (probably the first well-known owner to do so) in Flint and Denbigh as well as later in Shropshire. There may have been hounds at Wynnstay before 1749 and again about 1790.

To the west, in 1765, the Jones family began hunting the fox on foot in a wild, high country in Caernarvon and Merioneth. Their pack, the Ynysfor, continues in the family. The Pryses kept up their pack in the Gogerddan country in Cardiganshire; and it may be assumed that the farmers in the hills behind Cardigan itself still

MR PERRYMAN OF BEVERLEY, 1769
Beverley is in the middle of the modern Holderness country – the southern part of the East Riding – most of which was taken by Mr William Bethell in 1765, after the retirement of Mr Darley of Aldby. Mr Bethell's pack was described as extremely good; his country was considered the best-scenting and lightest-riding plough in England. A very good horse was therefore required (it still is); and some of the best hunters in England were bred locally. Mr Perryman's grey Driffield, his favourite, is a typical quality Yorkshire halfbred. Caps like this were generally worn by the members of the field, following the example of George III, until the tall hat became usual; the boots differed from the modern in being attached to the breeches by a large number of ribbons; the capacious coat was abruptly supplanted in the flying countries, more slowly in the provinces, by George Brummel's tight swallowtail. Painting by Francis Sartorius. By courtesy of Arthur Ackermann & Son.

hunted their Tivyside country. In south Pembrokeshire by 1789 Mr John Bartlett Allen hunted a country known from his house as the Cresselly. So much and no more is known of this hunt. In Monmouthshire, the Williams family maintained their Llangibby hounds. Mr William Addams Williams became master in 1790. The Chepstow Hunt existed by 1760, hunting fox, hare and otter with Welsh hounds.[70]

Scotland

Mr George Baillie of Mellerstain inherited a pack of hounds from his father, as well as an enormous house and a quantity of ancient Syracusan wine. He began to hunt an immense country about 1787. From 1792 his hounds were entered solely to fox.

An Edinburgh Hunt existed in about 1760 under the Earl of Errol; moving somewhat farther west it became the Linlithgow and Stirlingshire in 1775.

Lanarkshire, Renfrewshire and Dunbartonshire were hunted before 1771 by a Glasgow Hunt, the amalgamation of two packs. Kennels were built of materials given by Captain Roberton;[71] perhaps to honour this generosity a hunt within a hunt was formed: the Roberton Hunt, established on 8 April 1771, meeting twice a year with the members in brown coats and the earth stopper in a green one. At other times of the year the same hounds were the Glasgow:[72] an arrangement which may have seemed simple at the time but has been confusing ever since.

In Fife, Mr Alexander Wedderburn kept foxhounds at Birkhill before 1786. General Wemyss was master from 1789 to 1800; he had twenty couple of undoubted foxhounds in his first season.[73]

Far to the north, the Turriff country in Aberdeenshire was hunted from about 1755 by the Duke of Gordon.

In 1777 the Royal Caledonian Hunt Club was founded. Although its principal objects were racing and parties, its name was initially not wholly misleading: one of the few existing packs of hounds was brought to the venue of the meeting and hunted in the area.

Deer and Hare; Coursing; Otter and Badger; Matches

Red deer was by the end of the century very rare, except on the Devon and Somerset hills. In that area the Acland family kept the hounds descended from Mr Pollard's.

Yellow-pie hounds of the same breed still formed most of the royal pack, hunting tame stags in Windsor Forest or wherever they were let out. There were forty couple, about twenty-six inches high, with 'big heads, immense ears, and voices deep as the tolling bell of St. Paul's Cathedral. Unlike the fox-hounds now used, they flagged after the first burst, and did not run into a sinking deer; indeed, like blood-hounds, they scarcely lifted their noses from the ground until the stag was driven to bay.'[74] They were kennelled at Swinley, Ascot, a damp place which caused constant kennel lameness.

George III was very keen. He hunted twice a week when he was at Windsor with Lord Sandwich the master, Johnson the huntsman, and six yeoman prickers in scarlet and gold liveries and all with French horns. The king rode 'clad in his light-blue coat, with black velvet cuffs and top-boots buckled up behind; but as he rode nearly nineteen stone, the hounds were very often stopped to bring him onto terms'.[75] This often prolonged the hunt until late in the evening, to the chagrin of courtiers and hunt servants.[76] Sometimes the king himself was chagrined: 'when we hunt together, neither my brother [Duke of Cumberland] nor my son [Prince of Wales]

CHASE OF THE BADGER
Place, date and artist are all unknown; the scene is unusual but by no means unheard of. Badgers were normally taken underground by terriers, rather than hunted at force, but they were sometimes chased like this. They were very common in some foxhunting countries, including the Pytchley and the Dukeries, and sometimes fox-hounds – not always good ones – became accomplished badger hounds. The skins were valued, as they made warm waistcoats for the elderly. Painting by an unknown artist.

will speak to me; and one day lately, when the chase ended in a little village where there was only one post-chaise, my son and brother got into it and drove away to London, leaving me to ride to Windsor in a cart, if I could get one'.[77]

In 1794 Bill Bean, 'the arch trespasser of England', started hunting carted stags near London with five couple of hounds. His kennel was constantly moving round the suburbs; he was the scourge of farmers and market gardeners. The 'Epping Forest lemon pyes' were also hunting carted deer late in the 18th century.[78] This was the 'Common Hunt' of the City of London, followed by tradesmen; it was the only one of the many municipal packs which hunted deer, those of York, Scarborough, Norwich and other cities being harriers.

Throughout the period there were unguessable numbers of harehound packs in almost every part of Britain. The hounds were beagles, dwarf foxhounds, or, still commonest in 1750, Southern hounds. A typical establishment of about 1770 was

[83]

that of 'Andrew Raby', a prosperous gentleman but not hugely rich, who kept forty couple of a fifty-year-old strain which had been his father's. This fictional squire preserved foxes for the amusement of his neighbours, but was too nervous to go fox-hunting himself. His son thought the whole thing dead slow, and said so to the old professional huntsman, with 'Nimrod's' entire approval, in a most unattractive way.[79]

A lot of hares were coursed. In 1778, 'Coursing with Grey-Hounds, is a recreation in great esteem with many gentlemen. It affords greater pleasure than hunting in some respects. As, First, because it is sooner ended. Secondly, it does not require so much toil. Thirdly, the game is for the most part always in sight. Fourthly, in regard to the delicate qualities and shape of the greyhound.'[80]

The Elizabethan sport of paddock coursing for wagers seems to have died; instead, match coursing after hare became popular. Lord Orford of Houghton Hall, Norfolk, founded the Swaffham Coursing Society in 1776, in which the sport was regularized.

Lord Orford is said to have pioneered the scientific breeding of greyhounds just at the time that Hugo Meynell and his friends were developing the modern fox-hound; he tried lurcher, foxhound, and finally bulldog crosses.[81] After seven removes his bulldog cross was a success; 'one defect', however, 'this cross is admitted to have, which is a tendency to run by the nose.'[82]

Otter hunting remained a popular sport in Wales and the south west, owing partly to the numbers of otters and partly to the excellence of Welsh foxhounds for otter hunting. 'Nimrod' describes a poor man's pack of the period – three couple of hounds and a threequarter-bred bullterrier, the meet at five in the morning, and the otter spears doubling as leaping poles.[83] A normal method was for the pack to be divided, half with a man on each bank. Special otterhounds were already capable of owning a line in the water.[84]

Badger hunting was sometimes done with foxhounds, but usually with terriers with bells round their necks. The fun of the sport lay in the fighting qualities of the badger, which was also as valuable as in the 14th century: 'the skin being well dressed, is very warm and good for antient people, who are troubled with paralytic distempers'.[85]

Hunting matches were no longer after live game, as in the 17th century, but on a train scent in order that better ground could be chosen and the horses less abused. There were still wild-goose chases and hunting matches, but by the end of the century not many. Men were beginning to prefer to match their hunters on a racecourse, or in the new sport of cross-country steeplechasing.[86]

Hounds

In the late 16th century, small Northern hounds were entered solely to fox, but exceptionally. Early in the 17th it was normal to cross the Northern and Southern breeds to produce the middle-sized hound thought right for foxhunting: but this cross was not bred from in any careful or systematic way, or any type developed. In 1700, therefore, there were Northern and Southern hounds, a few Talbots, beagles, greyhounds, and lurcher and terrier crosses, but no distinct foxhounds. In the very early 18th century William Roper, Richard Orlebar, Charles Pelham and a few others began to produce a kind of hound which was recognizable, and recognized, as a foxhound. It was far from standard and very far from perfect. For two main reasons, however, large advances were made by 1750. One was the enthusiasm for

MR DELMÉ'S HOUNDS ON THE HAMPSHIRE DOWNS, 1738
The Delmé family lived at Cams Hall, Fareham, in the modern Hambledon country. There were several private packs in south Hampshire, but it is doubtful if any of them were entered to fox at this date. The green coats suggest harriers. John Delmé of Cams, a descendant, did keep foxhounds for one season (1813–14) but his master-ship was cut short by death. Other members of the family hunted, for some reason, not with the Hambledon but the H.H., their membership of the latter club being recorded by 'Aesop'. Detail of painting by James Seymour. From the collection of Mr and Mrs Paul Mellon.

foxhunting of men of education and wealth, which meant a sophisticated approach to selective breeding backed by copious means. The other was the interchange of blood and ideas between kennels at opposite ends of England.

The period 1750–1800 saw the development of hounds with far more speed and drive: but, at best, hunt was not sacrificed to chase. In conformation, good hounds at the beginning of the period had breadth of breast, depth of chest, well-sprung ribs, sloping shoulders, muscled forearms and running and jumping quarters; the second half of the 18th century gave them bone, straightness, clean necks and round cat feet. John Lawrence, observing the whole half-century, dated about 1770 'the definite change in the breed of foxhounds',[87] which is probably a fair central mark.

It is broadly true to say that when Hugo Meynell started hunting Leicestershire the modern foxhound did not exist, and that when he retired it did. Beckford's experiments of the 1770s with pointers and beagles, Thornton's with greyhounds, became less and less sensible or relevant; by 1800 if a man wanted foxhounds he bred from foxhounds.

It was fortunate for the development of the hound that the owners of the most influential packs operated in two quite different ways. On the one hand, the family packs were line-bred over a long period, creating type and prepotency on which other breeders could rely. On the other hand, individuals built up new packs, by purchase and breeding, working towards whatever objectives their hunting experience inclined them to favour. Of the former the most important was the 1st Lord Yarborough, of the latter Hugo Meynell. The Brocklesby hounds were throatier than Quorndon liked, but by the same token they had the cry which many hounds of the snaky-necked Meynell type lacked; and they had the prepotence to transmit it because they were inbred. What is important in this context is that the communication between such breeders grew continuously, in geographical range and breeding value. Information was more than ever exchanged as well as blood: from what Masters of Hounds and huntsmen told each other, they could breed to working qualities as well as to looks and pedigree.

Kennels and feeding were on fairly modern lines, which is hardly surprising since medieval writers are sound on these subjects.

Puppy walking and summer exercise were thoroughly understood, and well before 1800 young foxhounds were almost invariably entered to fox in early-morning woodland cubhunting in the early autumn, in the modern fashion.

Rounding of ears was unusual – perhaps unknown – in 1700, frequent but not invariable in 1750,[88] and accepted as invariable by Peter Beckford.[89]

Although the Northern hound was a major ingredient in the new hybrid, it continued to exist in a purer form as the fellhound. This retained its self-reliance and wildness – intensified because it was usually trencher-fed – and its nose and cry.

THE ALNWICK HOUNDS
This is the pack of the 2nd Duke of Northumberland, who succeeded in 1786 and died in 1817. It was only the best known of several in Northumberland, and its country may not in consequence have been much larger than the modern Percy. The hounds are excessively on the leg, but Sartorius was no Stubbs and his notions of conformation are not to be trusted. The duke is the one who once honoured a gallant fox by eating it. Detail of painting by Francis Sartorius. By courtesy of Roy Miles Fine Paintings.

Horses

'The old ENGLISH HUNTER was a strong bred horse, being bred between the racer and the lighter kind of cart mare. The hounds being slow, in course, speed was not the prime qualification in the horse.'[90] It was often ridden with a demi-pique saddle and straight legs, and always in a snaffle. The hunter was well schooled by methods still owing something to Pluvinel and the Duke of Newcastle: 'very great pains were taken in his mouth with the bitting, and an excellent education in the school or at the bar'.[91]

The foxhounds of the last quarter of the century left such horses out of sight. By about 1775, at least in the Shires, 'no eminent hunt was at that period without its share of thorough bred, seven eighths and three parts bred horses'.[92]

Certain far-seeing squires were virtually creating a new industry: 'a great many landed gentlemen, as far apart as Mr. Pelham, at Brocklesby Park, in Lincolnshire and Sir William Morgan, of Tredegar, in South Wales, were, between the years 1700 and 1800, improving the horses of their district by encouraging their tenants and neighbours to cross the horses of the district with sires of racing blood'.[93]

The development of the horse was not matched by any improvement in its training. Indeed methods were in general less wise than those of Gervase Markham. Hunters were put out to grass all summer, brought in just before the beginning of the season, purged and sweated (like racehorses) to get their flesh off, and given a quite inadequate amount of work, two weeks being thought enough;[94] they were then expected to carry a heavy man up to the Quorndon hounds.

Most horses lost most of their tails throughout the period: 'Such', complained George III's Gentleman of the Horse in 1771, 'is the cruelty and absurdity of our notions and customs in "cropping", as it is called, the ears of our horses, "docking" and "nicking" their tails, that we every day fly in the face of reason, nature, and humanity.'[95]

Clothes; Ladies

'We have discarded the heavy, cumbrous, and *slow*, in all things appertaining to the hunt whether as to customs, animals, furniture, and *toggery*, costume for the field, adopting every measure in almost an opposite extreme.'[96] Toggery was in fact the last to change. To the end of the 18th century hunting dress was 'large roomy horsemen's coats, long deep-flapped waistcoats, stout and capacious buckskin breeches, and boots which came well over the breeches'.[97] The coat was single-breasted. The boots were tied with a lot of ribbons to the breeches; they were always brown because a satisfactory blacking had not yet been invented. Round the neck a large, loose cravat 'like a pudding bag' hung over a laced or frilled shirt. The three-cornered hat was discarded by George III in 1786 in favour of a velvet cap; gradually but completely all hunting men followed the king's example. This caused confusion, as hunt servants became indistinguishable at a distance from the members of the field, except in those hunts which put them in special livery. The cap did not protect the back of the neck against rain, but its convenience and safety made it almost universal until the top hat became fashionable.

About 1750 two young Suffolk ladies rode astride in 'smart doeskins, great coats, and flapped beaver hats'. They were the last ladies to ride astride in England; they had been educated abroad. Very few women hunted in the next fifty years: 'as I recollect, Lady Craven, upon Pastime, never shrank from either fence or timber.'[98] There was Lady Salisbury in her sky-blue habit at Hatfield. Lord William Lennox saw one or two at Goodwood when he was a child.[99] Apart from the *mores* of the time, the reason was the sidesaddle; for cross-country riding it was uncomfortable and dangerous because the third pommel had not been invented.

The Countryside

In 1778 there were 69 forests, 13 chases and 800 parks in England. The biggest forests were the New Forest, Sherwood Forest, the Forest of Dean, and Windsor.[100] The area actually covered in trees continued its steady shrinkage; in 1800 the Forest

THE RETURN, 1787
Thomas Rowlandson evoked and commented rather than faithfully described: but there is no reason to suppose that any detail here is wholly imaginary. We may guess that this is the private pack of a gentleman, brought home after hunting to the kennels at his house. The lady being helped to the ground is almost certainly a member of the pack-owner's household, since, with few and disreputable exceptions, only such ladies rode to hounds.

of Dean 'is, at this time, much diminished; owing chiefly to the neighbourhood of several iron forges, which it has long supplied with fuel'.[101] For foxhunting, however, there were still far too many large woods and not enough small coverts.

Between 1760 and 1797 there were 1,539 private Enclosure Acts, by which private estates gobbled common land. The Leicestershire villages of Wiston and Foston each had about thirty-five houses; in the former, after an enclosure, every house disappeared except the squire's; in the latter, all except the parsonage and two herdsmen's cottages.[102] This caused widespread and intense hardship: 'Time was, when an abundant yeomanry, with cottage rights well maintained, could support the numerous poor; but, now, debauched, impoverished, and oppressed, they think only of the present day.'[103] 'Time was, when these commons enabled the poor man to support his family, and bring up his children. Here he could turn out his cow and pony, feed his flock of geese, and keep his pig. But the enclosures have deprived him of these advantages.'[104] At the same time, the Industrial Revolution was destroying the cottage industries, especially weaving. The dispossessed and pauperized yeoman and his children went to the towns to work in the mills.

The effect of this enormous tragedy was the improvement of the countryside for foxhunting. Villages, commons and smallholdings gave way, in 1,539 places, to parkland or more usually to grazing land – large, well-fenced fields of permanent grass ideal for both hounds and horses. The profitable stock to the grazier was not the docile milchcow but the turbulent beef bullock, who had to be kept in (especially when vexed by the gadfly) by solid obstacles. In the Shires these took the form of oxers of ditch, hedge and rail. The hedges grew into huge ragged bullfinches, often on top of a bank raised by the excavation of the ditch; they were later cut and laid.

The period of these changes also saw the beginning of organized pheasant shooting. This meant preserving and rearing imported birds. As early as 1780 Beckford was aware that the gamekeeper was becoming a major enemy of the Master of Foxhounds in some areas.[105]

9 Britain
The Golden Age
1800–1850

Melton and the Quorn

Mr Hugo Meynell sold Quorndon Hall and fifty couple of hounds to the 2nd Earl of Sefton, who brought his own fifty couple and his huntsman Stephen Goodall from Oxfordshire. Lord Sefton was almost as heavy as his huntsman, with 'cod's head and shoulders',[1] but he crossed the country magnificently on £1,000 thorough-bred hunters, and 'brought the second-horse system into fashion'.[2] Everything became more expensive and more flamboyant, and continued so under the 3rd Lord Foley: but farmers were as welcome as ever.[3]

Mr Thomas Assheton Smith, though very young, was invited to be master in 1806; he began hunting hounds himself, the first master of a Shires pack to do so. He bought in 1810 Mr John Chaworth Musters's South Notts pack – small, lively hounds in great contrast to the 'calves' of the Pytchley and Cottesmore. Though a good hound breeder, he was best remembered as a man across country. 'No man that ever came into Leicestershire could beat Mr Smith.'[4] 'Throw your heart over,' he said, 'and your horse will follow.' He had an enormous number of falls and bounced up undamaged. Where he failed was as a huntsman, drawing too fast (often over a fox) and getting away too quickly without most of his pack, and then waiting too long at a check.

He was followed after eleven seasons by Mr George Osbaldeston, a Yorkshireman who had hunted all his life, a champion shot, billiards player and turfite: and like

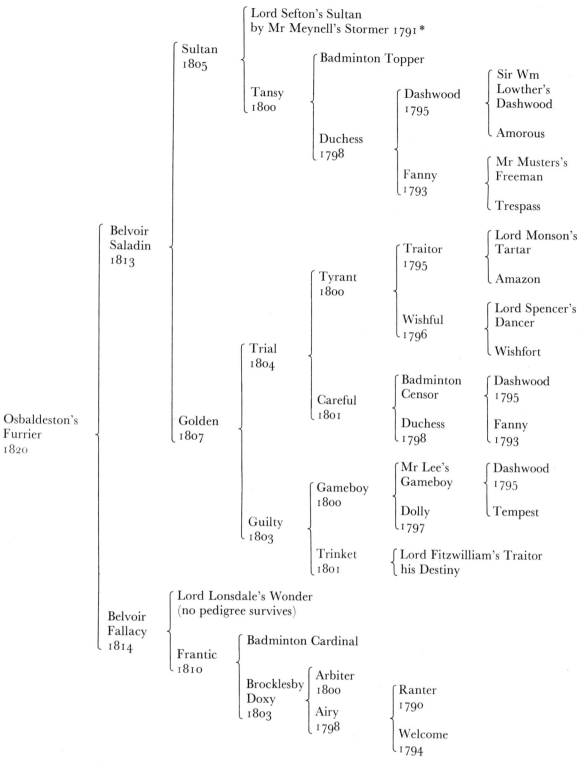

Osbaldeston's
Furrier
1820

Belvoir
Saladin
1813

Sultan
1805

Lord Sefton's Sultan
by Mr Meynell's Stormer 1791 *

Tansy
1800

Badminton Topper

Duchess
1798

Dashwood
1795

Sir Wm
Lowther's
Dashwood

Amorous

Fanny
1793

Mr Musters's
Freeman

Trespass

Golden
1807

Trial
1804

Tyrant
1800

Traitor
1795

Lord Monson's
Tartar

Amazon

Wishful
1796

Lord Spencer's
Dancer

Wishfort

Careful
1801

Badminton
Censor

Dashwood
1795

Duchess
1798

Fanny
1793

Guilty
1803

Gameboy
1800

Mr Lee's
Gameboy

Dashwood
1795

Dolly
1797

Tempest

Trinket
1801

Lord Fitzwilliam's Traitor
his Destiny

Belvoir
Fallacy
1814

Frantic
1810

Lord Lonsdale's Wonder
(no pedigree survives)

Badminton Cardinal

Brocklesby
Doxy
1803

Arbiter
1800

Airy
1798

Ranter
1790

Welcome
1794

** Mr Meynell's more famous Guzman used to be believed sire of Sultan;
Lord Bathurst revealed the mistake.*

his predecessors a polished man in society.[5] His hounds – 'de facto in the HIGHEST
REPUTE IN THE HUNTING WORLD'[6] – were principally Lord Monson's old Burton sort
and Lord Vernon's Sudbury. He was jumped on by Sir James Musgrave, an incor-
rigible thruster,[7] and retreated to the provinces; he came back in 1823 disinclined
to jump timber: 'I hate that d——d carpentry.'[8] His hounds were better than ever,
thanks mostly to Furrier (1820), a black-and-white hound drafted from Belvoir
because he was not quite straight. He got them a little mute,[9] but with great nose,

drive and steadiness under pressure from a crowd.[10] Mr Osbaldeston hunted six days a week before Christmas and effectively twelve after: he took out a fresh pack in the afternoon and drew fresh coverts: an unheard-of-proceeding.[11] This was made possible by many more foxes, because many more coverts, than in Hugo Meynell's time.[12]

Melton in this period was brilliant but bachelor, cultured, not drunken, church-going:[13] but 'While they sat at table, it was the constant habit of a few wretched, squalid prostitutes to come and tap at their windows, when those who were not too sleepy were seen to sneak out of the room.'[14]

Lord Southampton had a short mastership, Sir Harry Goodricke what promised to be a very long one. He was enormously popular, though self-willed and eccentric;[15] he died in 1833 of a chill caught otter hunting in Ireland. A bad period began: Sir Harry's heir, Mr Francis Holyoake, was rapidly followed by Mr Rowland Errington and Lord Suffield, the latter so damaged in fortune by the turf that the only tradesman who offered him credit was the pastrycook;[16] Mr Thomas Hodgson, who had liked the Holderness and disliked the Quorn; and Mr Greene of Rolleston, the fifth master of the fourth pack in six years.

In 1847 Sir Richard Sutton brought his Cottesmore pack (of Mr Assheton Smith's breeding) and the even better Fife hounds;[17] he was very rich, very experienced and the best horn blower in England.[18] He recovered the north-western Donington country, but gave the southern (Billesdon or Harborough) side to his son Dick. Initially he took a subscription, then chose to pay all expenses because his subscribers were interfering. He died during the 1855–6 season; Mr Assheton Smith wept openly when he heard the news, which was unlike him.[19] Sir Richard had spent a third of a million pounds on his foxhunting.

The Shires

Mr John Warde brought his large hounds to Northamptonshire about 1797,[20] joined them to the 2nd Earl Spencer's pack, and called the result the Pytchley hounds. The hunt was very popular but 'There was something like an affected disregard of appearances'.[21] He reunited the country, which 'knocked up for a time the old Pytchley meetings';[22] but the Pytchley Club was as merry as ever: 'all very well,' said Mr Warde, 'but the reckoning.'[23] He sold nearly all his pack to Lord Althorp in 1808, who became in effect (but not name) joint master with Sir Charles Knightley. They used Mr Warde's hounds to teach their young entry, but bred a completely new pack, much smaller and faster. Sir Charles was the greatest of all horsemen in the hunting field, with the best of all horses.

Sir Bellingham Graham had a brief mastership (disastrous) and Mr John Musters another (triumphant) and then Squire Osbaldeston arrived from the Quorn. His

MR HOLYOAKE, MR OSBALDESTON, SIR HARRY GOODRICKE, 1827
This was the last season of the Squire's second mastership of the Quorn, after which he took his hounds to the Pytchley for seven years. They were based on the Old Burton sort he had bought from Lord Monson, together with the best of Lord Vernon's Sudbury pack; he bred them with tremendous chase but also plenty of hunt, which made them uniquely steady to pressure from a hard-riding field. Many people thought them the best of their time, and they sold for a record-breaking price. The Squire rides Assheton. Mr Francis Holyoake (riding Crossbow) lived with Sir Harry (riding Doctor Russell) at Melton during the season. When Sir Harry's own very popular Quorn mastership was ended by his premature death, Mr Holyoake was found to be his heir. He kept the hounds at Thrussington for a short time, and returned with them in 1841. He later gave up hunting, according to Sir John Eardley-Wilmot, owing to the onset of an intense and morose brand of religion. Painting by John Ferneley Snr. By courtesy of Arthur Ackermann & Son.

DICK BURTON AND THE
TEDWORTH HOUNDS
Dick Burton whipped in to Mr Osbaldeston, succeeding Tom Sebright, during the latter's second mastership of the Quorn, then stayed in Leicestershire to hunt Lord Southampton's hounds. He went briefly to Mr Moreton (Lord Ducie, V.W.H.) as huntsman, and then lived for many years with Mr Thomas Assheton Smith at Tedworth. His last position was with Lord Henry Bentinck and the Burton; Lord Henry, who was hard to please, had a tremendous regard for him. He was a genius at getting a pack steady, especially to hare, and at teaching young hounds to draw. These Tedworth hounds were based on a draft from Sir Richard Sutton's Burton pack, which were of Mr Smith's own breeding; they were big hounds which he made still bigger by using Mr Horlock's stallions of John Warde's sort. He later brought down the size, principally by buying 60 couple of sharp small hounds from the Duke of Grafton. 'For a draft of young hounds,' said Mr Horlock in 1851, 'I think I should select the pack of the wonderful Squire of Tedworth.' Painting by William Barraud.

pack was now overbred for speed, and apt to flash over the line, but he showed great sport.

The much-loved, ludicrously spendthrift Mr George Payne had two masterships, interrupted by Lord Chesterfield, even more lavish, who went to bed too late after drinking too much.[24] 'Craven' or 'Gentleman' or even 'Another' Tom Smith, a poor man, was quite unable to collect his subscriptions after such munificence. Mr George Payne, returning, engaged Charles Payne as huntsman; by going on until 1865 the latter provided an element of continuity which was otherwise sadly lacking.

In 1799 Sir William Lowther bought back the family pack which the Noels had owned since 1732. For a time Sir Gilbert Heathcote had these hounds (Dick Christian sometimes hunting them) but Lowther, who loved hunting and had £200,000 a year to spend on it, took Cottesmore House and the country in 1806. From 1807 he was 1st Earl of Lonsdale of the second creation.[25] From about 1830 the hounds were managed by his son, Colonel Henry, who was a Member of Parliament for fifty-five years and never made a speech. Until this time they kept their character – big, rather slow, surprisingly prone to riot;[26] rabies nearly destroyed them, and the new pack was smaller and faster.

Tom Newman bred a small, sharp pack for the 4th Duke of Rutland. His successor Shaw 'bred the hounds a deal higher than Mr Newman – quite a high man'.[27] Tom Goosey whipped in to both, and was huntsman from 1817 to 1841; his wife was at the disposal of gentlemen visiting Belvoir.[28] The Belvoir was as fashionable as the Quorn in this period, attracting Beau Brummel and the Duke of Wellington. The most regular follower was 'Short Odds' Richards, a Croxton bookmaker, who carried an umbrella instead of a whip, and constantly nibbled pieces of stale bread, for which he had a passion.[29]

The 5th Duke retired in 1829 and appointed the 2nd Lord Forester field master. The hunt became grander than ever: Queen Victoria came out once and Prince Albert several times. Lord Forester worked extremely hard in both field and kennel; his pack was often described and deeply admired.[30]

In 1837 William Goodall, grandson of Stephen, came from the Bicester to whip in to Tom Goosey. In 1841, when Goosey went to Sir Richard Sutton, Goodall became huntsman: one of the half-dozen greatest in history, loved and admired in his own time[31] and revered ever since. 'Fox-hunting historians in the 2000th century will have rare stories to tell of him.'[32] His relationship with Lord Forester was close and happy; it was based on mutual respect and on shared ideas about hunting and hound breeding. This emerges from their voluminous correspondence, much of which survives, and on Goodall's hunting diaries.[33]

Lincolnshire and Huntingdonshire

Mr George Osbaldeston bought Lord Monson's Burton hounds in 1809; they were the basis of his great pack, and of major importance to hound breeding for the rest of the century. This was Osbaldeston's first mastership of foxhounds, although he was experienced with harriers; he was lucky in getting the younger Tom Sebright as whipper-in.

The Squire's temperament was better suited by Leicestershire; Mr Assheton Smith's by Lincolnshire; he came from the Quorn in 1814 and bred a pack as big as John Warde's. He sold part of it to Sir Richard Sutton when he went home to Tedworth; Sir Richard brought the size down with Osbaldeston and Brocklesby blood,[34] because he was 'too fond of the ride & the ride only, to have any taste for a hunting thing'.[35]

In 1842 Lord Henry Bentinck began his twenty-two-year mastership. He was son of the 4th Duke of Portland and brother of the formidable Lord George. He assembled a pack from Lord Ducie (V.W.H.), Mr Wyndham (New Forest), Mr Horlock (John Warde's sort bred to Cottesmore) and Mr G. S. Foljambe; he got a few hounds from Brocklesby and Sir Richard Sutton.[36] With these ingredients he bred the best working pack in England, full of drive, very self-reliant, enormously influential.

In the first half of the 19th century, north Lincolnshire was transformed. The wolds had been empty and useless. Now they were cleared and ploughed, miles of gorse grubbed up, tons of chalk put down. The most important crop was turnips, grown in fields of up to 600 acres, full of hares; there was a lot of wheat and some sheep pasture. At the same time the fens were drained. The expense and profit were both enormous; the result was a large and rich farming community, well-mounted and hunting in scarlet, which gave the Brocklesby a special and delightful character.[37]

Mr Charles Pelham was succeeded by his son (1st Lord Yarborough), grandson (1st Earl) and greatgrandson. Their huntsmen were the Smiths, following in similar

TOM GOOSEY AND THE BELVOIR HOUNDS

Goosey turned the Duke of Rutland's hounds to both Newman and Shaw; he hunted them from 1817 until he went to Sir Richard Sutton in 1842. The report that Mrs Goosey was available to entertain gentlemen visiting Belvoir is George Osbaldeston's; he is not a reliable source for this sort of story, but it would certainly appear that she entertained him at least. Goosey was a good hound breeder, maintaining the very high standard of his predecessors, but it is probable that from 1829 the decisions were taken by Lord Forester. It is interesting to see so much white in the pack (compare Sir Harry Goodricke's Quorn bitch, illustrated on p. 90) in relation both to the uniform tan of the 1880s and to the usual assumption today that a lot of white reveals Welsh-cross blood. Painting by John Ferneley Snr.

[94]

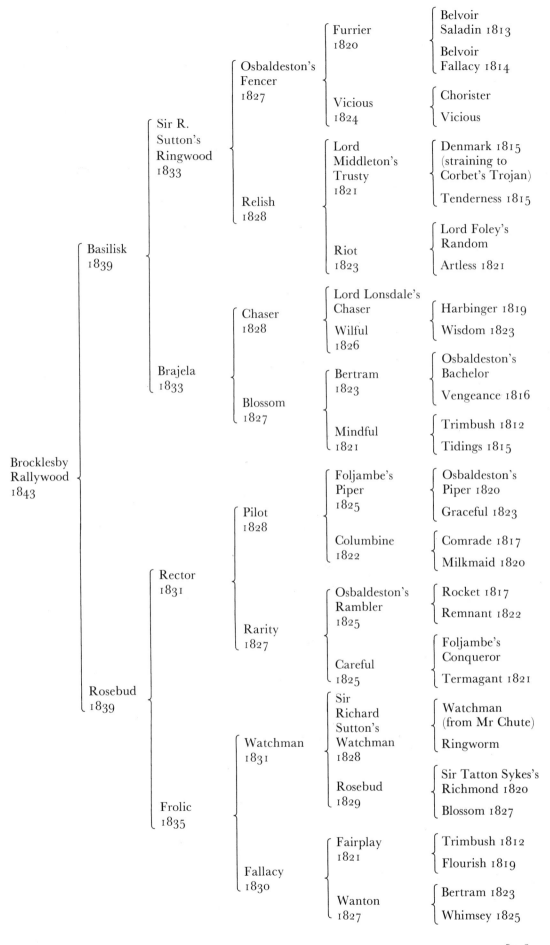

Simplified pedigree showing Belvoir Weathergauge's hits to Brocklesby Rallywood:

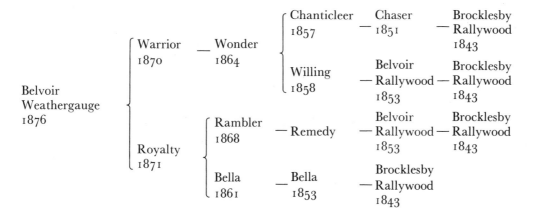

progression. The most important strain in the kennel was that of Ranter (1790), inbred to Charlton Ringwood (1741). Mr G. S. Foljambe said of Brocklesby about 1835: 'the hounds certainly are a mean looking pack, too weedy to please the eye, you never saw such narrow animals, but the mode of their hunting & running, & their style of killing, the head they carry, the pace they go, set aside all my prejudices.'[38]

After Ranter's day this was due most of all to Rallywood (1843). Will Goodall said he was '*the lowest* dog I ever saw in my life',[39] and was delighted to have him as a stallion at Belvoir in 1850. He was prepotent to a remarkable degree; having filled the Brocklesby kennel he filled the Belvoir. Belvoir Weathergauge (1876), a stallion of comparable importance, had no few than four hits to Rallywood (being inbred $5 \times 5 \times 5 \times 4$), two through Belvoir Rallywood (1853), entered the year of his sire's death. In 1926 every hound at Belvoir and Brocklesby descended from Rallywood.[40]

The southern half of the Brocklesby country was hunted sometimes by the Pelhams and sometimes by other packs. In 1823 Mr George Pelham, brother of the 1st Earl of Yarborough, started the South Wold. It then had a large number of masters, some distinguished, some of whom showed good sport in a country without coverts.[41]

Neither Lord Fitzwilliam's hounds nor his huntsmen were admired in the first twenty years of the century.[42] Then Tom Sebright came from George Osbaldeston; he built up a far better pack at once, and stayed for forty years. Will Goodall said they were 'a capital pack of hounds, and hunted beautifully'.[43] There were very large fields, which included very large numbers of parsons.

Nottinghamshire

Mr John Musters, the younger, married Mary Anne Chaworth, heiress of Annesley, whom Lord Byron also loved. The latter's disappointment is said to have caused the mad and melancholy turn which his poetic genius sometimes took. Mr John Chaworth Musters was master of his father's country discontinuously from 1804 to 1845.

Lord Henry Bentinck ranked him as a huntsman with Will Goodall and Mr G. S. Foljambe.[44] He was a fine horseman, though careful. He inspired the most adoring affection from his hounds, although he never fed them and seldom even saw them in kennel.[45]

The one dissentient voice in the chorus of contemporary praise of Mr Musters is George Osbaldeston's. To this other 'Squire', Musters was a handsome man and a great favourite with the ladies, but 'as a sportsman and a Master of Hounds he was less successful'. He used often to pretend that a fox was marked to ground when hounds had lost him; once he did this over a rabbit hole the mouth of which, as a yokel on foot pointed out, was full of cobwebs.[46]

The 6th Earl of Scarborough hunted the Rufford country until he inherited in 1807; he then moved to Sandbeck. His hounds were those of his father (4th Earl) and descended from Lord Thanet's and Lord Monson's. In 1822 he handed over his country and sold his hounds to Mr George Savile Foljambe of Osberton, master of the Grove until 1845. Mr Foljambe set about perfecting the pack, looking for 'zeal, keenness, and vermin anxiety, to pursue the wild animal'.[47] Lord Henry Bentinck said he was 'by far the best breeder of hounds and had the keenest eye for a hound's work'; he was also one of the three best huntsmen in England.[48]

The Rufford was hunted by the Rev. John Lumley until he succeeded as 7th Earl of Scarborough in 1832; by the 6th Viscount Galway; and from 1841 by Captain Percy Williams. He bred a marvellous pack, and came to be considered the best judge of a hound in England after Mr Foljambe himself. He was also 'as brilliant a rider over a country as ever cheered a hound', perfecting his seat by hacking to covert without his stirrups.[49] He had a great deal of trouble with pheasants; they 'have brought in their train envy, hatred, and malice, have dispossessed the fox, and demoralised the country'.[50]

West Midlands

Derbyshire and South Staffordshire were hunted at the beginning of the century by Lord Vernon of Sudbury. His hunt wore orange coats, except a tanner from Nuneaton, a tiny man on a tiny mare, who wore a long green coat and was called 'the Parakeet'. Lord Vernon's eyesight failed, and his hounds were managed by the Rev. George Talbot of Brereton. He was killed in the hunting field in 1812. The hounds were widely dispersed among several short-lived packs; some were bought by Mr Osbaldeston. The latter arrived about 1815; he united the countries which Lord Vernon and Sir Richard Puleston (raiding from Shropshire) had hunted, and in effect founded the Atherstone. Lord Anson (later 1st Earl of Lichfield) made the hunt celebrated; Sir John Gerrard made it ridiculous; Mr Applethwaite, accepting a subscription, made it respectable.[51] But his field made too much noise because his huntsman did not make enough.[52]

Mr Hugo Meynell's grandson, Hugo Charles, took over the Hoar Cross country (north and west) in 1816; his pack was of his grandfather's blood and his huntsman, Tom Leedham, had been his grandfather's coachman. He took a subscription. In 1819 he inherited the Ingram estates, adding to his name and his fortune; he returned the subscription he had just been paid, and was master, at his own expense, until 1868. He bred on an enormous scale because he could call on unlimited walks.

The countries adjacent changed their boundaries and names so often that a detailed analysis is scarcely possible and certainly purposeless. Woore, North Staffordshire, South Staffordshire, Enville, Shifnal, Worcestershire, and various shapes of Shropshire countries came and went. By 1850 there emerged from the welter distinct Albrighton, North Staffordshire and Worcestershire countries, their delineation attended by repeated boundary disputes.

Overleaf

TOM SEBRIGHT, 1850
This is the younger Tom, with the Milton hounds. His father had been huntsman to Mr Gilbert and his successors in the New Forest, where young Tom was entered and blooded. He became first whipper-in and kennel-huntsman to Mr Osbaldeston, and came with the latter on his dismal visit to the Hambledon; it was perhaps this experience which sent him to Milton and Lord Fitzwilliam's hounds in 1821. He succeeded Will Dean and Tom Clerk, neither of whom were able, by contemporary accounts, to control the hounds in the field or improve them in the kennel. Sebright's forty years brought about a gradual but immense improvement, and by 1850 Milton had a pack of first-class excellence and breeding importance. Huntsman and whipper-in are wearing the spare stirrup-leather traditional to the servants of this hunt; this practice was often remarked on but never explained. Painting by George Sebright. By courtesy of Arthur Ackermann & Son.

Warwickshire was taken over by Lord Middleton from Mr John Corbet in 1811; he bought the pack, and his stallions transmitted old Trojan's blood. Lord Middleton affected grandeur; his régime brought a black cloud of gloom[53] in spite of all the money he spent. It was dissipated at last by Mr Robert Barnard (later 17th Lord Willoughby de Broke).

Lord Middleton and his successors made no attempt to hunt North Warwickshire; it was hunted intermittently by the Atherstone and Hoar Cross. In 1834 Mr Robert Vyner was invited to start a new hunt; he bred a pack (to Belvoir) that could 'drive a fox to death, working his line all the way'.[54] His country was being transformed by the growth of Leamington; the crowds drove away Mr Vyner's successors; but he had acquired the experience which appears in *Notitia Venatica*, one of the best of all hunting treatises.

Shropshire's most spectacular master was John Mytton of Halston: remembered for his insane daring and his ludicrous exploits, best forgotten as a Master of Hounds. He liked two bagmen a day, but he was usually too drunk to hunt the second. For some years Sir Bellingham Graham and Sir Richard Puleston shared Shropshire; by 1850 there was a single Shropshire Hunt: but drab. It 'always stood high as a hunting country, when Corbet, Hill, Graham, Puleston, and Mytton were its scarlet kings; but its enthusiasm has been somewhat on the wane'.[55]

Trencher-fed hounds hunted the Wheatland country after Mr Baker's death in 1818; they descended from the Aldenham pack which came from Squire Forester of Willey. They were small, pale, harefooted hounds,[56] given substance by a blood-hound cross. After several removes this was highly effective. In 1845 Mr John Baker

Jack Mytton's father died when he was two; his mother spoiled him. He kept a pack of harriers as a child, was expelled from Westminster and Harrow, and knocked out his private tutor. As an officer in the 7th Hussars he gambled so heavily that he had to resign his commission. He was only 5′ 9″ but very powerful. Though he never learned to box he was always in fights because he was always fighting drunk. Seven bottles of wine a day was his ration until he graduated to seven bottles of brandy. His intake of filberts was partly responsible for this Homeric thirst: he got the nuts in cartloads from Shrewsbury. He never wore underclothes or gloves, or carried a handkerchief or a watch. He enjoyed jokes and disguises, his wit being crudely practical because he was deaf. Once he dressed as a highwayman and robbed his own butler. Once, in hunting clothes, he rode his bear into the dining room; he used a spur incautiously and the bear bit him in the leg. He was accustomed to fight not only men but also large dogs, using his teeth. He was Master of Hounds from 1817 to 1821, with two packs for his two countries. The remoter (Shifnal) kennels were forty miles from Halston; he used to hack there, and to coverts far beyond, hunt all day, and hack back for dinner. He hunted six days a week, but in spite of his fine horsemanship and truly insane daring he was not successful. His hounds were a scratch lot, and he was too impatient to be a breeder. After spending all his money he fled to Calais, where he attempted to cure an attack of hiccups by setting fire to his nightshirt. He died, bloated, paralysed and mad, in the King's Bench Prison, to be moralized over by 'Nimrod' but regretted by all the humble within many miles of Halston.

re-established his brother's hunt and got these hounds; they were an immense success in Shropshire and later in North Warwickshire.[57]

The Cheshire hounds were very large and the best were red tan.[58] They derived from Sir Peter Warburton's pack and from Bluecap. Their master from 1810 was the Rev. George Heron, 'a truly scientific sportsman',[59] and a brilliant hound breeder. Sir Harry Mainwaring followed him: vastly popular locally, unknown nationally because nobody visited Cheshire. The hounds remained completely distinctive.

Oxfordshire and Gloucestershire

Sir Thomas Mostyn brought a 'perfect little Welsh colony' to Bicester; it was all very friendly and convivial.[60] His hounds became remarkable for muteness, blamed on a Cottesmore bitch called Lady, but this was all anybody could find to criticize about them. He sold to Mr Thomas Drake in 1829, who bred in cry without breeding anything out.[61]

The 5th Earl of Berkeley hunted his enormous chain of countries until 1807. His eldest but illegitimate son Colonel Berkeley inherited the castle but not the pack, which formed the Old Berkeley Hunt at Gerrards Cross. To his home country the colonel added the Cotswolds, hunted from kennels at Cheltenham and Buckland. He built up a new pack, and got Harry Ayres as huntsman, 'Wot a little bit of a chap'.[62] The colonel sometimes hunted hounds himself at Cheltenham, and was once tipped half-a-crown by an Irishman.[63] The new pack was superb – small, not always straight, with great hunt and great drive.[64]

The colonel became Lord Segrave and then Earl Fitzhardinge. He tried to establish his legitimacy in the House of Lords, but succeeded only in creating a family feud of extraordinary bitterness. His (legitimate) brother Grantley consequently accused him of lechery, rapacity, theft and preferring amateur theatricals to hunting;[65] but he was one of the most original and influential hound breeders of his time and a very popular Master of Hounds.

Mr Henry Moreton took the Old Berkshire in 1830, decided it was too large, and overcoming opposition established the western side as a separate Vale of the White Horse hunt. He had kennels at Cricklade, then at Cirencester. He was a man of great kindness and generosity,[66] and a great houndman. He became Earl of Ducie in 1840.

One of the most unpleasant disputes in hunting history followed his resignation in 1842, between his successor Lord Gifford and Mr Thomas Morland, master of the Old Berks. A threat of thrashing by the former led to a warrant for arrest from the latter, all arising from a disputed covert.[67]

South Oxfordshire was part of Lord Berkeley's empire, then of the Old Berks. The Old Berks was still too large after the V.W.H. was formed; so was Sir John Cope's Bramshill, which had expanded into Oxfordshire. A new hunt was started by Lord Parker (later Earl of Macclesfield) in 1845. Its precarious infant life was saved by Mr John Shaw Phillips, who bought the hounds three years later.[68]

The 6th Duke of Beaufort succeeded in 1803. He inherited a good but imperfect pack. He engaged Philip Payne as huntsman from Cheshire: 'To appearance a duller bit of clay was never moulded by Nature', but he was patient, observant and scientific as a huntsman and above all as a hound breeder.[69] He bred a pack to give him 'palpitation of the heart in the first ten minutes';[70] the best pack in England after Belvoir.[71] The colours were badger-pie and hare-pie. The maker of the pack was Justice (1813). He was by New Forest Justice out of Sir Thomas Mostyn's

Britain: 1800–1850

Hopeful; the sire was by New Forest (Mr Gilbert's) Jasper by Lord Egremont's Justice, and was a perfect type of that celebrated sort; the dam combined the blood of Hugo Meynell, John Corbet and Lord Lonsdale. The Beaufort Justice was, perhaps, even more highly esteemed and more frequently mentioned than he deserved; Surtees suggests that his name was easily remembered and quoted by ignorant persons pretending to knowledge.[72]

The Badminton hounds still hunted the distinct Heythrop country from mid September until Christmas: every member of the household had to ride a hunter to Heythrop, including footmen and maidservants; the French cook hated it.[73] In 1843, just before his death, the 6th Duke handed over the Heythrop country to Lord Redesdale and his associates. The hunt nearly died when Mr T. A. Parker was killed in a riding accident and Lord Clonbrook ran out of money; Lord Redesdale saved it, and more particularly his huntsman Jem Hills, bred 'by an earthstopper out of a huntsman's daughter',[74] who had whipped-in to his brother Tom in Surrey at the age of ten. He was huntsman for thirty years and fourteen masters.

Berkshire and Hampshire

Until 1824 the Old Berks had very good masters, for a long time each, and after that very good ones for a short time each. Lord Kintore, one of the best, went home to Aberdeenshire, and Mr Moreton started the V.W.H. At one stage the hunt was only saved by Mr Harvey Combe's enormous fortune, and by amalgamation with the O.B.H. Mr Morland survived his unseemly battles with Lord Gifford, and Mr James Morrell a ghost with a carving knife, which plagued his Tubney kennel. A curious shibboleth declared that hunt and country were the Old Berks, but the hounds were the Old Berkshire.[75]

Mr John Warde followed Mr Charles Dundas (Lord Amesbury) in Lord Craven's country; he defined his territory as 'a simple triangle, bounded by London, Oxford, and Bath',[76] which magnificently ignored the Old Berks. His hounds were as good as ever, and the same as ever, though he twice bred new packs from a breeding nucleus. He sold most of them in 1826 to Mr K. W. Horlock. Mr Tom ('Another') Smith followed the latter for a few years, already celebrated both as huntsman and writer. Mr Frederick Villebois inherited his brother's H.H. pack and brought it to the Craven country: but it was not happy there; nor was his huntsman Ben Foot, who chased a fox by 'muttering after him all day long, and *worriting* him to death at last'.[77]

South Berkshire was hunted by the Rev. Ellis St John until his death in 1816. It was taken over by Sir John Cope, who as a Temple solicitor inherited from his brother and said: 'Hang the law; now for foxhunting.'[78] He hunted the country until 1850. The Duke of Wellington hunted with him sometimes: affable, but an awkward horseman and wearing the wrong clothes.[79] Sir John's country grew bigger and bigger, until it was too big. Part of it became the South Berks in 1843.

The H.H. hounds were bought in 1804 by Mr John Truman Villebois, co-heir of a brewing fortune. He bred an exceedingly fine pack, and trained very decorous servants: 'an oath, or a coarse expression of any sort, was never heard to escape them'.[80] But there was grave indecorum when, in 1817, the H.H. Bachelors' Ball was held at the Swan, Alresford: the waltz was introduced to Hampshire. Older people were greatly shocked that gentlemen's arms were permitted to encircle the waists of English virgins, and the Press resounded with their dismay.[81] Lord

FOXHOUND AND BITCH, 1792
George Stubbs, more than any other painter, gave animals character and individuality; he was also accurate, never, like his predecessors and contemporaries, falsifying conformation in the interests of fashion. We may take it that these hounds looked like this. But whose were they? Stubbs was expensive: this couple did not belong to a backwoods squire, but to a rich man, and they must have been the stars of his kennel. They look short-coupled, short-legged, burly-bodied; most pictures of the time show a very leggy hound to modern eyes. These also carry a lot of flesh; it has been suggested that they are a patriarch and matriarch of the kennel, retired from the field but still busy.

LORD HENRY BENTINCK'S FOXHOUNDS WITH A TERRIER
These are members of one of the most influential packs in the whole history of the foxhound, the constituents of which are listed on p. 94. They were reckoned the best working hounds in England – fast, not massively boned, full of drive, very stout, notably sorty because line-bred. The secret was breeding to work and ruthless selection – 'I breed a great many hounds,' said Lord Henry, 'and I hang a great many.' Concentration of blood produced prepotency, which made the stallions immensely influential: for example Contest (1848), full of Furrier blood, much used at Badminton and also sire of Lord Fitzhardinge's celebrated Cromwell. The terrier is a Jack Russell, one of the breed founded by the Rev. John Russell and descended from a little white bitch he bought from a milkman when he was up at Oxford. Painting by William Barraud. From the collection of Mr and Mrs Paul Mellon.

[102]

Palmerston hunted with Mr Villebois for the sake of his liver.[82] The Hursley side was first a private and then a subscription pack in loaned country.

The Hambledon was agog at the arrival of Mr George Osbaldeston and his pack in 1821. They were a terrible failure, both men and hounds all at sea in a cold-scenting, flinty country. They killed seven foxes in three months.[83] The only long mastership in the period was Mr John King's, who came from Devon and returned there in the end.

Mr John Warde brought his 'jackasses' to the New Forest; he found it very strange, especially when a hat addressed him from a bog, and there was a horse under the man under the hat.[84] Mr Sam Nicoll created a very quick and killing pack,[85] and Mr William Wyndham another, less quick but equally killing, of John Warde's blood: 'Better hounds need not be; and better sportsmen or a more pleasant gentlemanlike set of men I never met in any place.'[86]

Mr Thomas Assheton Smith came back to his father's Tedworth estate from Lincolnshire in 1826. His father utterly opposed his starting to hunt, as the cold-scenting country would damage his huge reputation; he was won over by local opinion. In 1827 he bought a draft of his own sort from Sir Richard Sutton. In 1828 he inherited. He built magnificent new kennels and stables, held up as a model to be studied,[87] and went to enormous expense cutting rides through the vast woods of the country. He was gradually converted back to small hounds from large ones, and in 1842 bought the Duke of Grafton's pack. With them came the great George Carter. 'Oh dear,' said Carter of his master, 'dear me, and he were an odd man, a very odd man were Mr Smith; why, he were unlike anyone else, and didn't care what he did or what he said.'[88] In 1858 Mr Smith died, on his Welsh estates, aged eighty-one. His widow gave the hounds to a committee.

Wiltshire, Dorset, Somerset

THE HURWORTH, 1846
The Wilkinson family of Neasham Abbey had the modern Hurworth country from about 1800. Part was absorbed by Lord Darlington's giant Raby, but enough was left to occupy the Wilkinson brothers, of whom Thomas (mounted) was the second. For many years Mr Frank Coates was amateur huntsman of this pack, a position later occupied by Mr Thomas Parrington, master of the Sinnington and father of hound shows. Will Danby (on foot) started his hunting life with the Duke of Leeds; he went to the York and Ainsty for a few troubled hours, spent many years with Mr Thomas Hodgson (Holderness), returned as huntsman to York, retired, grew bored with retirement, and came as huntsman to Neasham. The Wilkinsons' hounds were outstanding and their fields large. Their country was very good, but the scent was said to have been ruined by 'the tiles' – drainage which dried out the ground. Painting by John Ferneley Snr. From the collection of Mr and Mrs Paul Mellon. Photo by courtesy of Arthur Ackermann & Son.

The Wyndhams of Dinton resumed the hunting of Wiltshire, which had ceased with the departure of the Wardour hounds. Later Mr Wyndham's son-in-law Mr William Codrington came from the Old Berks. His methods were eccentric[89] but his skill was immense.[90] His huntsman was the brilliant Jem Treadwell. Mr William Wyndham left the New Forest in 1838 and resumed the South Wiltshire hunt at Dinton; his brother Frank followed him in 1848.

In North Wiltshire Mr Horlock of Ashwick House hunted the fox after Christmas. His son K.W. had a scratch pack as an undergraduate, then began to hunt at home in 1822 when he was twenty. Very little of the country had ever seen a foxhound; there were no foxes but many pheasants. In 1827 he bought most of Mr John Warde's pack, 'hounds which, in power, symmetry, and performance, have never been surpassed'.[91] All went well until the 7th Duke of Beaufort needed more country, owing to his father having given up the Heythrop. He resumed North Wiltshire; he was clearly within his rights, but Mr Horlock's bitterness shows repeatedly through the books which, as 'Scrutator', he began turning out in large numbers.[92]

Neighbours and close friends of Beckford, at Littleton, near Blandford, were the Farquharson family, rich London merchants originally from Scotland. J. J. Farquharson went to Eton and Christchurch; in 1805 he came of age and into a large fortune, and determined to use it immediately to hunt foxes.

He bought Mr Wyndham's hounds and Mr Sturt's; he built kennels at Eastbury, and began hunting six days a week, at his own expense, with ninety couple. Within

a few years he absorbed or fell heir to the whole of Dorset. He was very popular; there were soon plenty of foxes.[93] His country was much too large, and at various times he lent parts of it to Mr Thomas Grove (his brother-in-law, son of Beckford's successor) and Mr Portman; Mr Hall hunted the Blackmore Vale for two seasons with Mr Codrington's hounds and his huntsman Jem Treadwell; Mr Farquharson resumed the country, bought the hounds and engaged the huntsman.

In the 1830s Mr Drax (né John Sawbridge), Mr Portman and, later, Mr Wingfield Digby of Sherborne Castle, all wanted to hunt; Mr Farquharson would cede no territory and lent it with reluctance. In 1857 some of the Blackmore Vale coverts were closed to him; he resigned in great bitterness and his hounds were auctioned. His hunt broke up into four hunts.

In Somerset the Tudways' was the best-known (perhaps the only) private pack early in the century. In the West there was also (according to legend) a trencher-fed pack managed by a retired butler called Reid. The latter was succeeded by Captain G. F. Luttrell of Dunster in 1824; he got a very good pack principally from his friend Mr G. S. Foljambe.

Devon and Cornwall

'Devonshire is certainly the worst hunting country I ever was in; yet, strange to say, there are more hounds kept in it than in any other three counties in England.' One man hunted with seventy-two Devon packs.[94] They were practically all harriers.

In South Devon, Mr George Templer of Stover, singer and poet,[95] had a large pack for wild foxes, and the small 'let-em-alones' for bagmen. 'The Bold Dragoon' was hunted thirty-six times, and picked up by his brush unharmed at the end of each.[96] The big hounds became the Rev. Harry Farr Yeatman's Blackmore Vale harriers; the little ones went all over Devon. The Lamerton and Dartmoor countries were thoroughly hunted too, but there were very few foxes.

Mr Newton Fellowes (later 4th Earl of Portsmouth) of Eggesford had fine hounds with a fine cry, and a huntsman with a nose of the most brilliant red.[97] He started the Chulmleigh Club, at which three packs hunted turn about, which was much imitated. A protégé of his, of Mr Templer and of the Rev. John Froude of Knowlstone was the Rev. John Russell of South Molton, Iddesleigh and Swymbridge. He had very unsuccessful otterhounds, then very successful foxhounds, and dominated hunting in North Devon for a long time. His celebrated breed of fox terriers all descended from a little white bitch he bought from a milkman at Oxford.[98]

There were several packs in Cornwall, individually owned for very long periods; by 1850 four or five were entered solely to fox.

Yorkshire

The 3rd Earl of Darlington was by 1810 hunting the enormous Raby country, from South Durham to the middle of the West Riding, from a string of outlying kennels and with a string of local hunt clubs. He was a brilliant organizer, tireless, painstaking in kennel and dashing in the field. He both hunted and fed his hounds. His daughters hunted with him, in scarlet habits; they were 'too well-bred for foxhunting' to mind the smell of the broth which invaded the drawing room from the kennel.[99] He became a marquess in 1827 and 1st Duke of Cleveland in 1833. His grip slackened; he got involved in politics and racing;[100] by 1840 his pack was useless and valueless.[101]

In 1832 he made over his southern, Bedale, side to his son-in-law Mr Mark Milbank; the latter had fine hounds, fine country, plenty of money, a thriving hunt club and a foxhunting wife. He was fortunate; so were his neighbours.

The Duke of Leeds gave up his Hornby Castle hounds, under pressure from Lord Darlington; they went to a new York and Ainsty in 1816 in the care of a boy called Will Danby. New kennels had been built near York racecourse, with flimsy couches, which collapsed under the hounds. Will Danby fled to Mr Thomas Hodgson at the Holderness, returning years later as huntsman.[102] Lord Hawke had a very long mastership of the Badsworth; he was notable for his passion for blowing his horn, and for trying to start a Masters of Foxhounds Association. The 2nd and 3rd Earls of Harewood followed Mr James Lane Fox at the Bramham Moor; they bought Mr William Wyndham's New Forest pack of John Warde's blood, and engaged Charles Treadwell, son of Jem, said to be the best huntsman in Yorkshire history.

The Sykes family of Sledmere hunted most of the East Riding for much of the first half of the century. Sir Tatton Sykes withdrew to the Holderness side when Lord Middleton brought his (Corbet) hounds from Warwickshire; resumed the whole; but allowed an independent Holderness to be established in 1839. Mr Thomas Hodgson was its impecunious but brilliant master. Mr Richard Hill of Thornton-le-Dale followed the 'Gentlemen Farmers' in the Pickering country for nearly fifty years. The Sinnington and Bilsdale were unchanged by the course of outside events; the Farndale was started in 1835 with country from each. There was also an Eskdale (one of three in different parts of the North) which had foxhounds but no foxes. The Hurworth was hunted by the Wilkinson brothers – Tommy, Lozzy (Lozalure) and Matty – who had a very good pack, very big fields, and a country 'very good indeed for the provincials'.[103] The old Cleveland was absorbed by Mr Lambton at the same time as Tommy Page retired from the Roxby. The Roxby and Cleveland was formed as a trencher-fed subscription pack: the first year's subscription was £57 15s 6d.[104] John Andrew, the master, was sent to prison for a year for refusing to pay a smuggling fine; Mr Ralph Lambton sent him a draft the moment he got out.

The North

Mr Ralph Lambton 'treasured up for Durham County use every waif and stray that fell from the lips of his St. Hugo'.[105] His country became very large and his pack very good – 'Whoever has seen Mr Osbaldeston's hounds, *in their best days*, can form a very correct idea of what Mr Lambton's are.'[106] He lived at the kennels and, like Lord Darlington, practically in them. He sold his hounds to Lord Suffield at the Quorn in 1838; they were not used to Leicestershire manners and did better for Mr Robertson of Ladykirk (North Northumberland). In 1844 the Durham County Hunt was re-established, after various improvisations.

Several small countries were combined in 1818 by Sir Matthew White Ridley and his Blagdon or Northumberland hounds. To his north was Mr Baillie's Mellerstain country. Between there were at various times the Doxford or Belfort, Ladykirk or Galewood, Coquetdale, Alnwick, Tosson and other packs, all private. On Sir Matthew's fringes were the Prudhoe, and, after Mr Lambton gave up, the Slaley, Hamsterley (Mr Surtees's) and Castleside. In the 1854–5 season the area settled into its modern shape: Braes of Derwent, Tynedale, Border, Morpeth, with the Haydon and North Tyne beyond.

Neither Colonel Cook in 1826 nor 'Gelert' in 1849 had heard of any Cumberland foxhounds, but Mr Peel and Mr Crozier were famous locally. John Peel hunted from Caldbeck and Ruthwaite from 1799 until his death in 1854 with twelve couple, part trencher-fed, and a coat of local 'skiddaw grey'.[107] He stayed in the lowlands and hunted on horseback. Round Penrith, General Columb (or Colomb) of Arma-

MR RALPH LAMBTON AND HIS
HOUNDS
It appears that Mr Henry Lambton assembled a pack in 1793, which in 1795 was taken over by his brother and called the Durham County. According to 'The Druid' the first hounds were a 'Talbot pack' from Lord Vernon; it is possible that a draft went from the Rev. George Talbot, who latterly managed Lord Vernon's hounds: more likely that the pack came from Lord Talbot of Ingestre, who gave up his Staffordshire hunt in 1793. Mr Lambton's were very good indeed, and compared to Mr Osbaldeston's by 'Nimrod'. They were hunted by James Shelley until he died in 1809;

thwaite Castle had a pack called the Inglewood, which absorbed a farmers' pack at Keswick about 1825. Mr J. C. Salkeld of Holm Hill followed the general. John Peel's hounds sometimes joined the Blencathra pack of Mr Crozier of Threlkeld, who was succeeded by his son from 1836 to 1903. They embarked on 'the regular fell season', foxhunting, after Christmas, leaving their horses at home.[108] The Melbreak was ancient; the Coniston and Eskdale both started about 1825.

Throughout the period hound trails – races after a drag – grew more and more popular, attracting large prizes; the sport reached a peak in the 1840s, but then declined.[109]

South-east Midlands and East Anglia

The Duke of Grafton's hunt did not go well in the first third of the century: Tom Rose's hounds were wild and his son Ned's slack.[110] George Carter from the Oakley made an immense improvement. The 3rd Earl of Southampton took the country in 1842, lending half (the Whaddon Chase) to Mr William Selby Lowndes. Lord Southampton 'failed in innumerable huntsmen' until he got George Beers.[111]

Lord Tavistock resigned the Oakley hounds in 1829. Mr Grantley Berkeley brought a pack, mostly of his brother's sort, both inheriting and, because of the violence and arrogance of his character, exacerbating an intensely hostile situation.[112] The Duke of Bedford resumed the country, then Mr Hogg and Mr Arkwright, who had hunted jackal together in South Africa.

The Old Berkeley Hunt inherited the 5th Earl's hounds, tawny livery, and huntsman Tom Oldaker. The first master, the Rev. William Capel, was taken to court by his brother the Earl of Essex for trespass. This was the least of the hunt's troubles: the greatest was its swarm of Cockney followers. It was saved by Mr Harvey Combe's money and then by the 2nd Earl of Lonsdale, who hunted bagmen so that he should finish in time to get back to the actresses whom he entertained in Carlton House Terrace.

The Marchioness of Salisbury's Hatfield hunt was followed by the Hertfordshire Hunt of Sir Thomas Segrave, Mr F. P. Delmé Radcliffe (most intolerant of hunting writers) and Mr Brand, who became Lord Dacre. He had nearly thirty years in which to breed a marvellous pack. The Puckeridge had good times (Mr Samson Hanbury and Mr Nicholas Parry) and bad (Mr John Dalyell from Forfar). The Thurlow was sometimes independent and always devoid of foxes. The Cambridgeshire and Suffolk had very long masterships and very few visitors. Essex had good masters in a good country, East Essex superb ones (especially Mr Charles Newman) in a dreadful country.[113] Lord Petre in South Essex 'Maintained a pack of foxhounds in an unvarying style of excellence'.[114] Norfolk hunting had been very successful; in this period it was a great failure.

Sussex, Surrey, Kent

The 4th Duke of Richmond gave his pack to the Prince of Wales in 1813 as the new Buckhounds: 'what a pity they should have come to what they did!'[115] The 5th Duke had taken a bullet in the chest in the Peninsula, and had to go from hunting to racing. Lord Egremont therefore started hunting again. His heir Colonel George Wyndham (later Lord Leconfield) managed his hounds, bringing them south to Chichester and Findon. He withdrew from Findon in favour of Mr Napper. Colonel (later General Sir) Henry Wyndham had a separate pack at Leconfield. In 1837

thereafter the master hunted them, using a boxwood horn, until he was sixty-nine: but after a bad fall in 1829 he handed over increasingly to his kennel-huntsman John Winter. Mr Lambton 'used to cheer his hounds with, "Hi haro! Forrard! Hi haro!" a Norman hunting cry, not known since in England, but which is still [1870] heard in France when representatives of the old nobility in Bretagne are hunting boar or wolf, or leading a charge with bayonets, as at Inkerman.' Painting by James Ward. Collection of the Duke of Northumberland. By courtesy of Spink & Son.

Colonel George united the Goodwood and Leconfield countries. The Crawley and Horsham was formed by the turning of harriers into foxhounds and the absorption of Mr Napper's Findon country. East Sussex had a pack so unpopular that master and staff rode about in false beards. A military hunt was started at Ringmer barracks in 1820; after demolition and then bankruptcy the Southdown was established in 1843.

The Surrey has a history obscure as to date and detail,[116] but honourable as to sport and reputation.[117] Tom Hills was a great huntsman, brother of one still greater, and father of a clutch of hunt servants. The Surrey Union had a more precarious life.

The West Kent continued, almost totally unreported. Sir Henry Oxenden hunted East Kent from 1814 until he retired to Pau. Mr Frederick Drake Brockman really made the country between 1832 and 1870. The Tickham started as a farmers' subscription pack in the 1820s; Lord Sondes took it over in 1832, taking out seventy couple and coming home with forty.[118]

Wales

North Wales was patchily hunted by Sir Richard Puleston, Colonel Griffith Vaughan of Rug, Lord Mostyn and Mr Jones of Ynysfor. In Merioneth, Mr Vaughan of Penmaen had a 200-year-old family pack, tiny but effective, part Welsh, part English, part old blue-mottled harrier.[119] Sir Martyn Lloyd of Bronwydd had a pack crossed between Welsh hounds and old harriers, entered solely to fox. The Pryse family continued to hunt fox and otter in their enormous Gogerddan country with rough-coated Welsh hounds. A new Tivyside was started in 1815 by Captain Lewis of Llysnewydd, a very friendly and festive hunt; his successor Captain Howell of Blaendyffryn took his hounds forty miles up the coast for joint meets with the Gogerddan and Penmaen.

[110]

The South Pembrokeshire, Cresselly, or Castlemartin was hunted discontinuously by the Allens of Cresselly; some of the best half-bred horses in Britain were produced in their country.[120] Carmarthenshire had Mr Walter Powell's Maesgwynne and Mr W. J. Buckley's Penllergaer; the latter bought the former's pack and established the Carmarthenshire. Glamorganshire had many private packs, none hunting the fox. In Monmouthshire, Mr John Addams Williams's Llangibby was known as a first-rate pack far away in the south of England.[121] The Chepstow hounds were entered to fox, and became the 'True Blues', in 1820.

Welsh hounds were a great mixture. To the old rough-coated sort had long been added Old Southern blue-mottled harriers. Another ingredient was a pack of black-and-tan St Huberts of Margam Abbey, given about 1800 by Sir Thomas Mansel to the Gelli and used a great deal as an outcross. Another outcross arrived in the 1820s; when the Devon and Somerset staghounds were given up, the Rev. John Russell kept three lemon-pie bitches which he sent to Penllergaer. 'Thirty years afterwards I picked out their descendants in his kennell.'[122] Much whiteness descends from these hounds.

Scotland

The 4th Duke of Buccleuch kept hounds at Dalkeith. The 5th re-established a hunt not there but in part of Mr Baillie's Mellerstain country, with new kennels at St Boswell's. Willie Williamson joined him from Sir David Baird in East Lothian. In the 1830s 'the pack ranks third or fourth amongst the crack packs of the kingdom'.[123] Mr Baillie's Berwickshire side was taken over in 1833 by Lord Elcho, who became a very good huntsman of a very good pack.[124] His country became enormous and his hunt as fashionable as the duke's. For part of his very long mastership he withdrew entirely to Northumberland; Berwickshire became, temporarily, an independent hunt.

East Lothian was for a time joined to Berwickshire; when Mr William Ramsay Ramsay of Barnton withdrew for Lord Elcho he re-established the Linlithgow and Stirlingshire. He was one of the first Masters of Hounds to have switch-tailed hunt horses, and one of the last to hunt every Christmas day.[125]

Lord Kelburne (later Earl of Glasgow) took over Lanarkshire and Renfrewshire in 1820. He was so fond of his hounds that he forbade the use of whipcord entirely; they got very wild. He was in all respects very eccentric; he was also very well loved.

The Fife hounds were re-established in 1800. Things went well for a short time and badly for a long time. The Forfar side had to be given up (but it was never a great success as an independent hunt). Tom Crane, once the Duke of Wellington's huntsman, faced hopeless odds. John Walker from Lord Kintore, though pathologically nervous and excitable,[126] brought about an immense improvement.

The Turriff country in northern Aberdeenshire had been anciently hunted. Lord Kintore came from Berkshire to revive it. It went merrily until 1847, but when he retired it died. Another country now long unhunted was the Strathearn, Perthshire, thriving throughout this period, dying unaccountably and permanently.

Deer, Hare, Otter, Badger

The chase of the wild red deer was restricted to Devon and Somerset in 1800. Even there it repeatedly died, to be reborn only for short and ill-supported periods.

But carted-deer hunting was very popular, owing to its convenience and economy. The Royal Buckhounds were most popular of all. 'Great red deer as big as donkeys' were kept in paddocks at Swinley, Ascot. Lord Cornwallis was master and Wetherall huntsman. There were ten yeoman prickers, all with French horns and scarlet and gold coats. One of these was Tommy Coleman, later eminent as the father of modern steeplechasing; he described 'many a hard mile and a long day'.

The first yeoman pricker was Charles Davis, son of the huntsman of George III's harriers, brother of the sporting artist R. B. Davis, and himself previously second horseman to the Equerry in Waiting. In 1822 Davis became huntsman, and the great period of the revived Buckhounds began. The fields were extremely democratic and ill-behaved.[127]

The Buckhounds shared the London suburbs with a number of other hunts.[128] After Lord Berkeley stopped bringing his foxhounds to Cranford, Middlesex acquired more staghunts, notably those of Grantley Berkeley, Hubert de Burgh, John Elmore and Josh Anderson.

A hunt with much better country was Lord Derby's; the 12th Earl kept a pack of staghounds near Croydon from about 1800, usually enlarging his stag on Epsom Downs.

The Vale of Aylesbury was hunted by the Rothschilds from 1839. They showed magnificent sport, entirely at their own expense, for many years. Gentlemen sickened by the crudity of the Buckhounds' fields, business and professional men whose time was precious, took a train and had hair-raising runs over the stiff Vale country. They very much liked not being asked to contribute any money.

Fallow deer were hunted pretty regularly, by harrier packs, wherever they had become naturalized. One pack of hounds in this period was entered specially to roe deer: that of Mr Pleydell of Whatcombe, near Blandford in Dorset. Roe were extremely common and the pack, until about 1830, apparently effective.

The Royal Harriers had ceased in James II's reign, were restarted in 1730, and became celebrated when they were kennelled at Brighton in Prinny's time. They had excellent runs on the seaside turf, the hares, as in other unenclosed downland countries, usually running 'endways'. The fields were democratic, but often included the Prince of Wales in the active days of his youth. Prince Albert was more of a sportsman than his solemn reputation suggests. He had 'the most perfect beagles that could be procured in England' in 1841,[129] and harriers from the Isle of Wight in 1845.

[112]

THE STAG ENLARGED
Carted staghunting became popular in the early 19th century, although despised as false by some and condemned as cruel by others. The latter were ill-informed. The soft-hearted 'Harry Hieover', who fought a continuous battle in print on behalf of animals, called tame deer 'the most fortunate of beasts', comparing their pampered life and tranquil death with those of wild red deer. According to Lord William Lennox they were never hunted before they were three; they were fed 'good corn, beans, and clover. The paddocks should be dry and well-sheltered from the weather . . . In a grass country, deer may be hunted once a fortnight; but in a flinty country, it will be as well to save their legs, by turning them out only once a month.' Sometimes ribbons were tied to the antlers; more usually they looked like this one: 'The horns of the stag should be sawed off before the hunting season commences, as it prevents mischief to men and hounds.' Painting by Henry Alken Snr. By courtesy of Arthur Ackermann & Son.

At a less exalted level, there was as much harehunting as ever, all over Britain, with the greatest variety of countries and of hounds.

In the Welsh hills, and in the Lake District, the 'Mountain packs frequently hunt everything, from a foumart to a fox, from a hare to an outlying deer. . . .' 'In these counties every little farmer is a sportsman, knows every hound by sight and voice, understands the meaning of every note, knows the habits of hare or fox familiarly, and hunts with all his soul.'[130]

This was a far cry from the old slow harehunting, with blue-mottled Southern hounds, derided by 'Nimrod' and his friends. They called the harriers 'jelly dogs' – 'currant jelly', in Jorrocks's more exact words – because red-currant jelly was thought (correctly) to go with jugged hare. The Mole used a similar insult to the rabbits, in *The Wind in the Willows*, when he shouted 'Onion sauce'.

Beagles in the modern sense (not simply small hounds, but harehounds hunted on foot) were unknown to Delmé Radcliffe in 1838; he said the only foot hunting was with the Old Southern hound and in the fells.[131] He was quite wrong. Before 1800, 'A dozen packs of beagles not exceeding fifteen inches in height were generally hunted on foot.'[132]

Some hares were still killed for the pot by greyhounds, but match coursing in this period almost entirely replaced the old sport. It grew rapidly on the northern moors, among farmers and especially 'colliers'. It was buoyant in the south at a grander level. Surrey had meetings at Epsom and Leatherhead, Berkshire and Hampshire the Ashdown Park, Letcombe and 'High Clere' meetings, and Wiltshire the Amesbury and other clubs.

Otter hunting, in 1826, 'is at present but little followed. Of all field amusements otter-hunting is perhaps the least interesting . . . Those who have never witnessed otter-hunting, may form a tolerable notion of the business by imagining to the mind a superior duck-hunt.'[133]

In parts of Wales the old otterhound was by no means extinct: 'Nimrod's' grandson described in 1869 the 'pure-bred otter-hounds' of the Hon. Geoffrey Hill of Hawkestone, which hunted on the Teivi (Tivy) and were of ancient, unadulterated blood.[134] The otter was also vigorously hunted by rough-coated Welsh foxhounds.

Meanwhile Mr Henry Peyton (son of Sir Henry, a famous foxhunter) started a new pack of otterhounds near Bicester, hunting mostly on the Cherwell. He started at dawn and used spears, in the manner unpleasantly described by Somerville.

WATERLOO COURSING MEETING, 1840
Organized match coursing began with the foundation by Lord Orford of the Swaffham Coursing Society in 1776; one of the greatest devotees of the young sport was Sir Charles Bunbury, for a short unhappy time brother-in-law of the 3rd Duke of Richmond, and for a long and happy time 'Perpetual President' of the Jockey Club and benign dictator of Newmarket racing. The Waterloo Cup became the championship; greyhounds of this class were bred as carefully as racehorses and readied by professional trainers: one, Newby, is on his knee by the brace of greyhounds held by the Slipper, Mr William Warner. The greyhound farthest away, by the horse, is called O Yes, O Yes, O Yes; another is called Top; otherwise their names might be those of foxhounds. Distinguished noblemen and gentlemen are present, but few have names remembered in foxhunting (Lord Sefton, riding the horse with the lowered head, is an exception); to a remarkable degree it was a quite separate set of sportsmen. Painting by Richard Ansdell. By courtesy of Roy Miles Fine Paintings.

They once had a twenty-five-mile run. This success inspired imitation, and by 1842 there were five other recognized packs of otterhounds.[135]

But the real revival outside Wales depended on the disuse of the odious spear; it was abandoned in Devon in the 1830s, and very gradually elsewhere. Otter hunting thus became a more attractive sport, and grew moderately throughout the second half of the century.

Badger hunting was local. A few areas teemed with badgers. Mostly they were fought by terriers, underground, in the old way; but foxhounds were also used. Mr Lumley Savile's 'Dukery' hounds were rough-coated, and he used them for fox and badger. The Pytchley coverts in the first quarter of the century were full of badgers; the most successful killer, though not a good foxhound, was an Oakley hound called Outlaw. By 1850 the Pytchley badgers had almost disappeared. Thomas Assheton Smith had a great badgerhound in the foxhound Denmark, taught his work by Jack Shirley.

Hounds

The most important thing that happened in foxhound breeding in the first half of the 19th century was, perhaps, not change but absence of change, the continuity from the late 18th century of the great kennels. Brocklesby, Belvoir, Badminton all became more rather than less influential, as 'it is the custom', in 1820, 'to send bitches to the fashionable stallions of the day'.[136] There was also continuity, in blood and in influence, from packs which changed hands but retained their character.

Colonel Cook remarked in 1820 that 'Half the hounds in the Kingdom are of the blood of the later Mr. Meynell's "Guzman", and Lord Yarborough's "Ranter"'.[137] To Robert Vyner twenty years later all the best hounds in the country were descended from the blood of Brocklesby, Milton, Belvoir, Burton (by way of Osbaldeston), Badminton and Pytchley.[138] To 'Nimrod' the following year (1842) the most influential individual stallions were, in his order, Osbaldeston's Furrier, Pytchley Abelard, Beaufort Justice, New Forest Justice, Warde's Senator, Meynell's Guzman, Musters's Collier, Corbet's Trojan and Brocklesby Ranter.[139]

The intention, in using this outside blood, was of course to breed out bad characteristics, of conformation and temperament, and breed in good ones. 'The Masters of Fox-hounds and huntsmen of England, in continual communication with each other, have devoted their attention, for more than a century [since 1770], and have in that time got rid of the "crooked legs", the "dewlaps" of old English and Continental hounds, in some instances sacrificing scent and hunting qualities to speed, but always combining in a high degree hunting and racing qualities.'[140] As bow legs and neckcloths were bred out, so were the old colours. In 1842, 'What is known as "a blue mottled hound" is not to be found among fox-hounds of the present day, that variety of colour being peculiar to harriers and beagles.'[141]

Lazy and drunken feeders were a problem solved only by close personal supervision. Walks were not at all easy to arrange in countries where the master was not also a great landlord. But it was understood that confinement was very bad for young hounds, and that a kennel could breed only as many whelps as it could find walks for. The importance of condition was well understood: the afternoon fox found out the unfit hound.[142] Veterinary science made advances, but they were gradual, and often not only neglected but rejected: Robert Vyner always bled his puppies before cubhunting, although science was already telling him that this was folly. Cubhunting was perfectly modern in method and intention, although occasionally done in the evening (by the Brocklesby and Grafton as well as by Tom Smith).[143] Ears were invariably rounded, largely because of the gorse, much of it new, on which so many hunts relied for so much of their holding covert. Some ears were rounded far too close, leaving the inner ear unprotected, as this was thought smart.[144]

Horses and Horsemanship

'Give me 'em lengthy and short-legged for Leicestershire,' said Dick Christian. 'I wouldn't have 'em no bigger than 15·3 . . . Thorough-bred if you can get them, but none of your high show horses. Thorough-bred horses make the best hunters. I never heard of a great thing yet but it was done by a thorough-bred horse.'[145]

But the proportion of thoroughbreds, even in the Shires, remained very small: in 1842 'not more than a twentieth part of English hunters are at this time of quite pure blood'.[146]

All recorded opinion of the period acknowledged that, in grass countries, the speed of modern hounds called for a hunter 'at least three-quarters bred, if not seven-eighths';[147] but there was a school of thought, perhaps a majority, which actually preferred a cocktail to a pure-bred. 'Nimrod' ascribes this to prejudice, small feet and fat men.[148] But to John Lawrence twelve years earlier the seven-eighths bred was quite fast enough, had more power and toughness, and was not so much on the leg.[149]

The Lincolnshire farmers, generally the richest in the country after the agricultural revolution of these years, bred an enormous number of good hunters until they were again depressed; their sons half made them with the Burton, Brocklesby and South Wold, and then took them to Horncastle Fair: 'a legion of Hard-Riding Dicks are ever at work'.[150] The Shropshire farmers had excellent halfbred mares, mostly small; the foals were often substantial, but always had dainty heads.

The Irish imported a few English thoroughbreds, and with them covered their very various mares. Many had more optimism than sense: 'provided they get a good sire, they put the veriest jade on earth to him.'[151] But at best: 'In some of the rich grazing counties, as Meath and Roscommon, a large, long blood-horse is reared, of considerable value. He seldom has the elegance of the English horse; he is larger-headed, more leggy, ragged-hipped, angular, yet with greater power in the quarters, much depth behind the knees, stout and hardy, full of fire and courage, and an excellent leaper. It is not, however, the leaping of the English horse, striding as it were over a low fence, and stretched at his full length over a higher one; it is the proper *jump* of the deer, beautiful to look at, difficult to sit, and, both in height and extent, unequalled by the English horse.'[152]

The folly of some of the Irish was common in England too: 'Farmers are sadly careless what their mares go to.'[153] The exceptions were farmers who themselves hunted;[154] this goes far to explain the pre-eminence of Yorkshire, Lincolnshire and Shropshire.

Some heavyweight hunters were tried for by crossing thoroughbreds with Suffolk Punches. It was known to work: Lord Jersey (5th Earl) 'found one of his best hunters in the produce of a Suffolk Punch mare and an Arab sire'. But 'The more common result of such *mésalliances* is a monster, composed of two different kinds of horses badly joined in the middle.'[155] Certain breeds of moderate-sized harness mares, though trotters, were a feasible cross with a thoroughbred because they already had a large infusion of blood: notably Cleveland Bays and Norfolk Trotters.

Mares were seldom hunted, there being in the 1820s and 1830s, a new 'prejudice against riding mares in the hunting field'.[156] But Sir Tatton Sykes's Anna Maria, foaled in 1805, was hunted in Yorkshire until she was eighteen; she then had her first foal.[157]

Quite apart from their breeding, the condition of hunters was subjected to new demands. This was hardly realized before 1800; horses were knocked up and even killed by overstrain when they were unfit. There was, indeed, a ghoulish credit attached to riding so hard that your horse died under you. 'Nimrod', above all others, championed the luckless hunter. His central point, made again and again, was that horses had to go racing pace and must be trained up to it.[158] 'It would be useless to expect horses to live with hounds in such a country as Leicestershire, unless they were in condition to enable them to contend for a plate.'[159] The sustained campaign which he launched in 1824 was widely publicized and widely influential. By 1846 Leicestershire horses were trained much like racehorses, so that 'Horses being what used to be called knocked-up is now a matter of rare occurrence'.[160]

Condition influenced coat and the need for clipping. 'Nimrod' in 1824 was perfectly familiar with clipping, which was apparently introduced about 1815 by officers who had seen French and Spanish mules clipped with sheep-shears.[161] He tried it for the first time on a new horse which had already been allowed to grow a heavy coat. Normally, he said, it was simply a substitute for proper grooming and condition.[162] As might be expected, there was wide disagreement about this. 'Harry Hieover' held 'a clipped horse a beastly sight'.[163] John Lawrence suggests, amazingly, that it had been an 18th-century custom abandoned in the 19th – he refers to the 'old and worthily forgotten practice of CLIPPING or BURNING the coats'.[164] But Delmé Radcliffe[165] and Surtees were entirely in favour of clipping; the latter preferred shaving: 'we wonder it is not more generally adopted.'[166] Singeing was another method, much more usual later in the century with gas. Clipping was more widespread in provincial countries with heavier-coated horses of coarser breeding: the thoroughbred was thought not to need it. This is really very odd. Today every thoroughbred steeplechaser is clipped, as well as every horse in the hunting field which does not live out all winter. Partial clipping was an invention of the late 19th century.

Eighteenth-century tails were docked extremely short. This was cruel to a horse put out in the summer, but it was practically universal. Surtees said much later that, with fast hounds and fashionable hunting, 'whitening-brush tails were succeeded by long switches'.[167] But the change was gradual and resisted. In 1824 'Nimrod' said a switch tail looked terrible except on a Galloway.[168] Turner's illustrations of 1825 show very short tails; Alken's of 1835 and 1837 show tails about eighteen inches long. But by this time undocked tails were becoming fashionable. George Osbaldeston always docked, but before he left the Shires for the last time (1834) he was shouting to his thrusters: 'Gallop on, long-tails, you'll soon come back.'[169] Ears were no longer cropped.

Veterinary science probably killed as many horses in the hunting field as their riders did. They were weakened by purging and physic before hunting; they were further, often fatally, weakened by bleeding after it. Even the wise Tom Smith recommended that two or three quarts of blood should be taken from a distressed horse.[170] 'Harry Hieover' ten years later admitted the occasional necessity of bleeding, but greatly preferred giving a quart of beer with two glasses of gin in it.[171] In one respect, the hunter of the time was fortunate. 'In fashionable countries, on the days that the hounds are out, every public-house with a stable prepares gruel, and gets ready for the custom of returning sportsmen.'[172] Before the coming of the railways there were coaching and posting houses everywhere; tired hunters were given an hour, and often a night, with gruel, hay, water and deep straw bedding.

In horsemanship, the English seat, saddle and riding length had for a long time been quite different from anything known on the Continent. Abroad, legs were straight, the ball of the foot was on the stirrup iron, and in the high-pique or demi-pique saddle 'the rider was securely packed with the help of a sheepskin'. 'The ordinary saddle in use in England either for road-riding or hunting affords the rider no support beyond the stirrups. It is a purely English, and probably Yorkshire invention, the outcome of the taste for riding across country in pursuit of hare, stag, or fox.'[173] The legs were slightly bent and the foot was home in the stirrup.

In the late 18th century, as hounds and fields began to race, a new style of horsemanship became widespread, based, inappropriately, on that of flat-racing jockeys. John Adams, riding master, taught his pupils to shorten their leathers, stand up in the stirrups, and 'thrust your rump out farther behind'. The bottom (*sic*) was not to touch the saddle.[174] This was not generally approved for very long. Foxhunters were instead abjured: 'Sit down in your saddle; don't stand up and stick out your hind-quarters as if they did not belong to you.'[175]

The great influence on jumping style came from the first generation of professional steeplechase jockeys – Becher, Dan Seffert, Jem Mason, Tom Oliver. They began to lean back over the cantle as the horse approached the jump, keeping well down in the saddle. There is evidence, surprising but undoubted, that this back-leaning style was a revelation to hunting men.[176] Specifically to the example of steeplechasing was ascribed, in 1846, the general excellence of horsemanship: 'certainly since hunting was first followed, there never was a period that could produce such a number of fine riders in the field as the present'.[177]

Nearly all 18th-century horses were ridden with a simple snaffle: they were not thoroughbreds, they were not asked for an all-out gallop, there were few fences, and undrained ground rode deep. After the 'Leicestershire style' became popular the curb was necessary. A few hunting stables forbade it, including Pytchley and Sudbury,[178] but by 1800 it was almost universal in the Shires.[179] 'Nimrod'[180] and Whyte-Melville were enthusiastic about the Pelham, which some people disliked and others found bizarre; Whyte-Melville disliked nosebands.[181] 'Scrutator' acknowledged that he was exceptional in preferring a simple snaffle for any but a ewe-necked horse; he was unique (and improperly dressed) in never wearing spurs.[182]

There was violent disagreement about the martingale, some holding (as some do now) that a horse with its head tied down cannot save itself if it slips or knuckles over on landing; 'Harry Hieover' agreed with 'Nimrod' that a head-tossing horse which needed a martingale jumped better with it than without it.[183] Henry Alken thought a horse that needed one should not be used as a hunter.[184] 'Scrutator' said that many more horses carried them than needed them. Girths were usually too tight, as they were made of slippery wool; breastplates were probably not used enough.[185]

The best stables were well-found to the point of luxury, although many were badly ventilated. The best flooring was said to be of Dutch clinkers, set level, with a grating and drain. Cobbles were out of fashion; wood floors were the most usual. It was recognized as early as 1829 that looseboxes were better than stalls;[186] but they were still most exceptional.

The covert hack became a normal part of every leading man's stud soon after the beginning of the century: at about the same time as the second horse became usual. The latter was deplored by Cook and derided by Surtees,[187] except in the case of heavy, hard-riding men in flying countries. But the former, with a meet more than five miles away, was considered essential until country lanes improved enough for wheels. The perfect covert hack was almost thoroughbred, just under fifteen hands, with a smooth canter.[188]

An immense number of men – visitors, Londoners, soldiers and foxhunters whose studs were broken down – relied on hirelings. Tilbury, of Dove House, Pinner, was by far the greatest jobmaster, widely praised and trusted; he hired out good horses in good condition. There were innumerable other sources, in all hunting countries, like Trollope's Mr Stubbings of Stanton Corner in the Ufford and Rufford United country, 'a little man and rode races' (typically), and had a great deal of difficulty collecting his money.[189] He and his like had a greater problem, according to 'Harry Hieover': 'Half the persons availing themselves of the use of hired animals, seem to consider that their being hired does away with all calls of interest or humanity in the parties using them.'[190]

Clothes

Clothes continued substantially unaltered through the first decade of the 19th century. George Brummel, who hunted a few times from Belvoir, is generally credited with the enormous changes of the next few years. A sleek, streamlined look was found appropriate to fast hounds and fast horses. Even in such conservative backwaters as the Heavyside Hunt, 'the flowing bed-gown like coats' were abandoned by younger men.[191] Brummel's influence dictated that the new coat was a very tight, double-breasted swallowtail. About 1820 lapels narrowed and acquired notches: they were no longer intended to fold inwards to protect chest and throat. Meanwhile collars grew immensely high, and were worn over high starched cravats often of cheerful colours.

As coats tightened, so did breeches; skin-tight doeskin (most uncomfortable in heavy rain) became fashionable. The Prince of Wales tried white kidskin; it was not strong enough to contain the royal person, and modesty forbade repetition of this experiment. Doeskin, for all its toughness, lost favour rather quickly in the Shires: 'it looks slow'.[192] White corduroy replaced it, equally tight.

At the same time beaver hats replaced caps; they started quite low-crowned, but ascended rapidly during the 1820s. A few hunt servants wore them, but most wore caps or billycocks.

By 1830 consummation was achieved: 'the hunting-dress, in fashionable countries, had reached the lowest depths of vulgarity and inconvenience'.[193] The return to sanity started with breeches, which from about 1830 were cut much looser above the knee. This permitted a return to leather.[194] Sir Richard Sutton was the last prominent foxhunter to wear corduroy; his breeches 'were of a dingy blue colour, and very baggy'. The tight dresscoat gave way soon afterwards to a more comfortable single-breasted coat, cut square at the bottom, which could be done up over the throat in bad weather. There were usually five buttons, sometimes six.

Then desire for the practical and comfortable went too far: about 1840 the field abandoned its tall hats and reverted to caps, which had become the distinguishing badge of masters and their servants.[195] It became impossible to tell field and hunt staff apart. Lord Gifford, when master of the H.H. (1847), gave his hunt staff white browbands to their bridles; and some masters revived the practice of Thomas

Assheton Smith and wore tall toppers.[196] Cravats remained the proper neckwear, but they got lower; a real sportsman, said Surtees, could be recognized by his small cravat as well as by never wearing whiskers.[197]

Various sorts of boots came and went. Wellingtons with trousers over them, and a leather strap under the boot sole, were always possible if not in the highest *ton*. Jackboots worn over trousers were briefly in fashion, following Prince Albert; Delmé Radcliffe deplored this 'French postillion' mode.[198] Ironically, the Napoleon boot became and remained supreme over Wellington or Prussian, apparently rendered acceptable by the Duke of Beaufort. He wore 'napoleons' with loose-cut doeskins. The hunting boot has hardly changed since. Of colour: 'it is not absolutely necessary that port wine and black-currant jelly should be the chief ingredients of proper blacking, or that the boot-top liquid should actually be composed of champaign (*sic*) and apricot-jam'.[199] Pink tops, in fact, gave way to mahogany, the darker the better.[200] But until the railways brought more visitors to the remoter countries, there were fierce local snobberies about the colour of boot tops, by which strangers were made to feel unloved.[201]

The colour of coat for foxhunting had settled generally to scarlet long before the end of the 18th century, owing, perhaps, to the rural association between hunting and Toryism. Badminton was the only famous exception after the orange of Lord Vernon's and the sky blue of Lady Salisbury's disappeared. Red was known sometimes as red, usually as scarlet, and very occasionally as pink. (Cook, in 1826, is one of the first to refer to pink; he does so once or twice as a change from scarlet; this is true of 'Nimrod' into the 1840s, Surtees into the 1860s, Sidney into the 1870s. Scarlet remained the normal word into the last quarter of the century. The origin of 'pink' is obscure enough; its elevation into shibboleth is baffling. There was no leading tailor of the name – to dispose of a frequent explanation – in London or any hunting centre.) Contrasting collars were ancient (Tarporley and Pytchley Clubs) and always worn by invitation only. Most hunt coats were distinguished only by the button. Parsons were not allowed to wear scarlet; for many years they compromised on purple. Other men wore harehunting brown or green. But by about 1850 black was the only alternative to scarlet except unashamed ratcatcher, with which coloured tops were not allowed.

Hunts of any pretension had evening as well as daytime uniforms. They were much admired. Harriett Wilson said: 'The evening hunting dress is red, lined with white, and the buttons, and whole style of it, are very becoming. I could not help remarking that these gentlemen never looked half so handsome, anywhere in the world, as when, glowing with health, they took their seats at dinner in the dress and costume of the Melton hunt.'[202] When the Handley Cross Hunt was reformed, the uniforms, day and evening, were among the first items on the new committee's agenda.[203]

Parties; Races; Jargon

Hunt club dinners – gentlemen only, in hunt evening dress – became fairly usual in the last quarter of the 18th century, almost universal in the first quarter of the 19th. Where several gentlemen were leading bachelor lives, far from home, the dinners were often weekly; among local residents they might be monthly, three-monthly or annual.

Hunt balls of a recognizable kind began about 1800; the Stratford Hunt Club's, in Warwickshire in John Corbet's time, were perhaps the first. The idea went all over the country within a few years. The balls had various purposes (which did not yet include a profit for the hunt funds). Wives, excluded from the hunting field 'by their nature', were sometimes disposed to stop their husbands from hunting; the hunt ball was devised to change their minds.[204] Covert owners who liked pheasant shooting were often unreliable fox preservers: but their daughters wanted to go to the ball. On this ground Colonel Cook was 'a great advocate for a ball and supper. I have known it the means of saving many a fox from being trapped.'[205] Some of the most lavish and expensive balls were attempts by unpopular masters to earn the love of their countries; such were Lord Middleton's in Warwickshire from 1813.

The entertainments offered farmers by the hunt were the races. These affairs were informal and (usually) amateur; they find no place in the *Racing Calendar*. It is not clear when they started – perhaps about 1810 – or where. There were Members' and Farmers' races, and usually a Farmers' Cup presented by the hunt. The farmers and their wives were also regaled, in marquees and from the steps of carriages, with stout, port, brandy and gin and water. Colonel Cook makes clear the immense value of the goodwill thus earned.[206] Much the fullest record of such races concerns the various hunts of Hampshire, owing to the chance of the county's having a diligent sporting historian. 'Aesop' lists copious results for the 1820s and 1830s; all races were on the flat, nearly all two miles, some dashes and some in heats. Farmers' and Members' races were almost always included.

Early steeplechasing also grew out of foxhunting, but in a different way. The first jumping races were mostly matches (two horses only) between agreed points, go as you please. Typically, challenges were made after dinner between gentlemen who had 'ridden jealous' during the day. Between 1790 and 1830 there were quite a few of these races, mostly in Leicestershire; latterly there were sometimes considerable fields of horses, for which some very large sums were given. Bets were substantial. The most celebrated amateur rider (of many) was George Osbaldeston; the outstanding professional (of very few) was Dick Christian. Racing of this kind almost died out in the early 1830s, because organized steeplechasing started – St Albans 1830, Cheltenham 1834, the Vale of Aylesbury 1835, Aintree 1836.

The new sort of hunting called for a new language. 'In former days we rode *after* hounds, now [1829] we ride *to* them – we then *leaped*, now we *jump*. We formerly *leaped hedge, ditch, and gate*, now we jump *fences and timber*.' 'Fencer', for a good jumper, was an acceptable new word. 'Entire horse', also new, was tautologous and a cockneyism; 'huntress' savoured 'too strongly of Cheapside'.[207]

Most of the shibboleths (once known as the Terms of Art of Venery) were inherited from former centuries – pad, mask, brush, kennel, stern, couple. To say 'hound' instead of 'dog', except when specifying gender, was not new in use but new in required use. There was a curious development in spelling – the final 't' in 'covert', which is almost wholly illogical. All 18th-century and most early 19th-century writers throw their hounds into cover. Tom Smith did so. Delmé Radcliffe, in 1839, mocked this as a dreadful solecism.[208] Today he would be quite right: but 'cover' was a perfectly acceptable spelling at least until 1870.[209]

The 18th century called its fox Reynard. In about 1816, when George Osbaldeston was in the Atherstone country, a local gardener talked about 'Charley'. The Charles James Fox joke was new to Osbaldeston;[210] had it been current he, of all people, must have heard it. Possibly through him it caught on. When in 1834 Lord Kintore wrote from Aberdeen to 'Nimrod' in France, he used it as familiar jargon.[211] 'Nimrod' himself called a hunted fox 'pug'. 'Scrutator' has 'Charles James', 'Mr. Wily' or 'Wiley' (following Tom Smith), and, whimsically, 'Mr. Reynolds'.[212]

Masters, Servants, Subscribers and Laws

In 1800 there were several sorts of hunts, differing in origin, scale, and the relationship between masters and field.

There were the great family packs, maintained by territorial magnates at their
own expense. Some of these were born long before this period and survived long
after it – Belvoir, Badminton, Brocklesby, Milton. Some died, their countries being
hunted thereafter under a different dispensation – Sudbury, Craven, Goodwood,
Burton, Lord Scarborough's. Some were born which survived – Lord Fitzhardinge's
new-model Berkeley, Buccleuch, Wynnstay. Some were born to flower, in these
particular and traditional terms, only in the lifetime of a single man – Mellerstain,
Raby, Lord Elcho's, Cottesmore, Mr Farquharson's, Tedworth. Some changed
control without changing character – Bramham Moor, Middleton, Grafton.

Differing in degree, but that enormously, were the private packs of squires,
equally independent of subscription. Their owners were able to afford them because
they kept them small and unpretentious. Few hunted the fox only. Few survived
in the same ownership beyond 1850, except in Wales, the south west, and the fells.

At the other organizational extreme, there were packs got up as local co-operatives,
for sport or vermin killing or both. These were typical of Yorkshire and Wales, and
the hounds were typically trencher-fed. Sometimes an individual was found to farm
or manage the hounds; in such cases they were often kennelled, without the character
of the hunt being much changed.

Between 1800 and 1850 these poles came together, for reasons of pure finance.
By 1850 the cost of a middling provincial establishment – fifty-five couple, eighteen
hunt horses – was in the region of £2,500 p.a. A crack five day country would
double these figures.[213] In the first years of the century it was recognized that only
very rich men could stand this, year after year, unaided.[214] The answer was a
subscription.

Clearly subscriptions changed the character of hunts, if not of day-to-day hunting.
The master's authority might be absolute in the field, but it was severely qualified
elsewhere. Subscriptions had one great advantage (beyond the undoubted fact that,
by 1850, they made nearly all foxhunting possible) and two great disadvantages.

'A subscription pack', said Surtees, 'makes every man put his shoulder to the wheel, not only to keep down expenses but to promote sport, each subscriber feeling his own credit identified with the credit of the establishment.'[215] But putting shoulders to wheels shaded into unwarrantable interference, as Sir Richard Sutton found in Leicestershire; large subscribers felt able to say which coverts should be drawn, and even which servants dismissed. This was particularly galling if the subscriptions were unpaid – the other great disadvantage of the system.

Subscription hunts sometimes appointed a committee from among their number, in preference to individual outsiders. This was commonly disastrous: 'There is so much hesitation, so much stopping, so much debating, so much chopping and changing, that the indecision of the Master communicates itself to the field.'[216]

The only two well-known masters who hunted their own hounds in the 18th century were Mr (later Sir) Richard Puleston and Lord Darlington. The first in the Shires was Thomas Assheton Smith, in Lincolnshire George Osbaldeston, in Nottinghamshire John Chaworth Musters, in the far north Ralph Lambton, in Scotland Lord Kelburn. The number substantially increased, but it was never a majority or near it.

For many masters, hunting the hounds was the point of having them: it also solved the acute problem of finding a reliable professional. This was extremely difficult.[217] Some were cruel, some incompetent; a few of the best were drunken. The general level seems to have risen a great deal by 1850, but this brought a new problem with it: 'Nine tenths of all men who keep hounds allow their huntsman to be their master.'[218]

Huntsmen were adequately but not munificently paid. They lived well but few saved money. Early in the century the custom began, and rapidly spread, of capping after a kill; this, with a big field after a good run, was a substantial bonus for the huntsman. The fox was often treed by the huntsman, ostensibly for the good of the hounds; the real purpose was to let the stragglers come up so as to increase the cap.

The 19th century inherited perfectly clear ideas about the inviolability of a hunting country, and many boundaries had been firmly drawn for years. In a few places the precise position of the line was disputed. An example was the Holwell Mouth covert in Leicestershire: 'they're a bit jealous of each other, and they're never done drawing it. It's really in the Duke's Hunt, but I've seen the Quorn draw it for years and years.'[219] Colonel Cook recommended a new master to be sure that he and his neighbours, in writing, agreed in close detail where their limits lay.

Greater confusion arose when a hunt ceased to exist, either permanently like the Slaley, or temporarily like the North Warwickshire. Coverts lent (as by Quorn to Donington) could be resumed on demand, but coverts ceded (as by Craven to Tedworth) could not. Trouble then arose if a club or committee, succeeding the master, wanted the coverts back, claiming that he had acted *ultra vires*; this claim would be strenuously resisted by the recipient hunt, who were entitled to regard the ceded coverts as their own. Sometimes, however, the club was right in regarding itself as the custodian of the country, as against the master of the moment, owing to a specific delegation in the past; this was the case in the Albrighton country. The law was simple, but the realities were often complex; widely different beliefs were firmly held and feelings ran very high.

The greatest anguish was when a man made a foxhunting country, over years, by assiduous attention to coverts and their owners: and then found that the whole was claimed back by its legal but neglectful parent. The most vocal sufferer was 'Scrutator'.

'Nimrod' and his Successors

The first quarter of the 19th century saw antiquarians, travellers, diarists, encyclopedists and writers on horses and horsemanship. It hardly saw the one hunting book, John Hawkes's little pamphlet *The Meynellian Science*, which had a circulation so limited that no other writer saw it. The second quarter of the century saw Beckford's precedent several times followed: Cook, Tom Smith, Delmé Radcliffe and Vyner were all Masters of Hounds who wrote about their art. There was one hunting history, 'Venator's' of the Warwickshire, one hunting biography, 'Nimrod's' of Jack Mytton, and one hunting novel, the same author's *The Life of a Sportsman*.

The great invention of the period was hunting journalism.

The Sporting Magazine was started before 1790 by Mr Cooke. John Lawrence began contributing material about the horse in 1792. Cooke failed and a Mr Wheble took over for a few years. He introduced racing articles, which resulted in a modest growth. Then Mr Pittman bought the magazine. He asked Lawrence to find a hunting writer; Lawrence tried and failed (though he himself hunted and sometimes wrote about hunting). Pittman himself found Charles James Apperley: 'a greater than Beckford is here'.[220]

Apperley was born in 1778, son of the tutor to the heir of Sir Watkin Williams Wynn of Wynnstay. He was spoiled; he hunted in a scarlet coat at the age of eleven. He served briefly in the militia (Sir Watkin's Fencibles), then tried a life of trade and detested it. He married and set up house at Bilton Hall, Rugby. He hunted with John Corbet in Warwickshire, John Warde in Northamptonshire and Hugo Meynell in Leicestershire. He made ends meet, barely, by horse coping. After moving about the Midlands for twenty years he came to London (without his wife) to earn some money, and there met Pittman. In 1822, reluctant but desperate, he began writing as 'Nimrod' for *The Sporting Magazine*.

He visited various hunts, with some financial help from Pittman, and reported on them. In 1824–5 he contributed his challenging and influential articles about the condition of hunters. He was more and more widely read. Within two years he had doubled the circulation of the magazine, which became dependent on his reports. By 1825 he was touring with five or more hunters and a covert hack. By this time Pittman was paying for everything: 'Nimrod' took £9,000 in six years from the magazine. His visits struck terror, his judgments were read with awe. He was tall and good-looking, a fine horseman, with an impressive address. His prestige was such that he was used by clubs to report on prospective masters and by prospective masters to report on hunts. He was deeply concerned about appearances, and judged everything by Leicestershire. One prospective master on whom he had been asked to report had mounted a boy whipper-in on a mule with a crupper to the saddle. 'Nimrod' could stomach the mule but he was deeply shocked by the crupper.[221]

There are many contemporary mentions of his wonderful tours (as well as his own, published in book form in 1835); the cruellest and funniest is Pomponius Ego's visit to Mr Jorrocks. '*There's* a man with a cocoa-nut full of knowledge for you!' said Jorrocks before he came. 'He hiccups Greek, dreams o' Julius Caesar, the twelve apostles, and all them ancient Romans, talks Latin by the yard and like a native too.'[222] In the event, Ego turned out to suffer from supreme conceit (fair), and funked a fence (not fair).[223]

Pittman died in 1829, increasingly dubious about 'Nimrod's' expenses; his successors terminated the arrangement. 'Nimrod' lived economically in Hampshire for

TREEING THE FOX
It was put about by huntsmen (who had, it is true, good historical precedent) that it was good for hounds to be made to wait for their quarry. It was also good for the huntsman, who took a cap round after a kill and wanted time for all the stragglers to get up and contribute. The practice was much disliked: but in one case at least it was essential to a huntsman's performance. 'Harry Hieover' recalls a huntsman who, living with a poor Master of Hounds, always took a cap; he was a bold rider and hunted the hounds admirably. His success took him to a new master, a rich peer, who disapproved of capping, but who made up the huntsman's salary so generously that he was better off than before. But he neither rode so boldly nor hunted so effectively. 'I wish,' he said, 'to show your lordship and the gentlemen sport, and try all I can, but for the life of me I cannot ride or kill a fox as I did when I used to feel the money after a kill.' Painting by Henry Alken Snr. By courtesy of Arthur Ackermann & Son.

one more season (hating cold scent, flints and absence of Leicestershire swells) and then took refuge more economically still in Calais. He travelled a little, but his home was there until he died in 1843, during a visit to London.

Most of his work was written in exile. In 1832 John Gibson Lockhart commissioned *The Chace* (whimsically adopting Somerville's spelling), a brilliant long article on matters quite new to the sedate pages of the *Quarterly Review*; it was followed by *The Turf* and *The Road* (he was a distinguished whip), and the three were published as a book in 1837. In 1834 the warm-hearted Lord Kintore asked him to Scotland, which resulted in the *Northern Tour* (1835). That year he also wrote his half-admiring, half priggishly deploring *Memoirs of the Late John Mytton Esq.* In 1838 he was tricked, as he said, into contributing to a second-rate compilation called *Sporting*; and suffered from bad translation, ill-checked, with his book for the followers of the new sport of thoroughbred racing in France, *Nemrod, ou l'amateur de courses*.

R. S. Surtees had visited him in Calais in 1832, and later commissioned for his *New Sporting Magazine* the series of articles collected as *My Horses*. The same magazine serialized in 1841 the dreadful but fascinating novel *The Life of a Sportsman*, published as a book the following year. *The Horse and the Hound, Hunting Reminiscences* and the two-volume *Nimrod Abroad* followed (1842–3), and he embarked on his own *Life and Times* in *Fraser's Magazine*. This series was abruptly and insultingly terminated, which greatly upset him. His resulting mood probably explains his quarrel with Surtees. He died later in the year, aged sixty-five.

Robert Smith Surtees was born in Northumberland in 1803, the son, grandson and greatgrandson of Masters of Hounds. As a boy, Surtees lived near and hunted with Ralph Lambton, who used Hamsterley Hall, the Surtees property in County Durham, as his base for hunting that side of his country. The family consequently gave up their hounds, and their country was absorbed into Lambton's. The social informality and hunting good manners of the Durham hunt influenced Surtees's attitude all his life: he thought Leicestershire ridiculously overpraised by 'Nimrod', and mocked, with real dislike, the side and show of its fields.

He was trained to the law, but in 1829 replaced 'Nimrod' as hunting correspondent of *The Sporting Magazine*. '"Nimrod",' he said, 'originated a new style of literature which might not inappropriately be called the "sporting personal".'[224] As 'Nim South' Surtees carried on the new style, in close imitation but far more economically. In 1831 he tried to buy a share of *The Sporting Magazine* from Pittman's successors; failing, he started *The New Sporting Magazine* with the sporting-print publisher Robert Ackermann. 'Nimrod' asked for a job, but 'Nim South' was in the saddle. Besides hunting reports, he wrote a large number of other articles, including a series about 'Nimrod' and some stories about an uncouth wholesale grocer, hunting mad, called John Jorrocks.

In 1826 he resigned from his editorship, after a disagreement with Ackermann; two years later he inherited Hamsterley. He restarted the family pack, hunting hounds himself, and began writing novels.

As the inventor of hunting journalism, 'Nimrod' had a number of other followers: 'Nim North' (a Mr Sitwell), his provincial poor relation; the Irishman Pierce Egan, better known as the first boxing writer (*Boxiana*), but whose little newspaper *Book of Sports* often reported hunting and racing; 'Actaeon', thought to be Robert Vyner; and at the end of the period 'Scrutator' and 'The Druid'.

'Scrutator' purported to hide the identity of K. W. Horlock of Ashwick, Wiltshire, owner and huntsman of his own pack and for a time master of the Craven. In 1852 he wrote his *Letters on the Management of Hounds* for *Bell's Life*. Most of his books were written in the 1860s. 'The Druid' was Henry Hall Dixon. He was the son of a Carlisle cotton manufacturer. He went to Rugby in Dr Arnold's time and to Cambridge. Like Surtees he was a lawyer; unlike him he practised law. He began to supplement his income writing for the *Doncaster Gazette* in 1847, and became its editor. He came to London in 1850; he worked for *Bell's Life* and contributed to the *Sporting Life* and *Sporting Magazine*. 'It was known that never in his life had he been on the back of a hunter or followed hounds across country on horseback.'[225] But he gossiped interminably with hunt servants; in taking down Dick Christian's 'lectures', allegedly verbatim, in the gig in Leicestershire, he invented another sort of hunting literature.

At the end of the period one other sort of book was invented: the hunting guide. Two were published almost simultaneously, in competition. In 1849 Pittman and Ackermann jointly published the *Fox-Hunter's Guide* by 'Cecil', which was revised and reissued the following year, and in 1850 appeared *Fores's Guide to the Foxhounds and Staghounds of England*, written by 'Gelert'. 'Cecil' was Cornelius Tongue, who wrote a large number of books over the following twenty years – guides, histories, treatises – and in 1866 edited the first volume of the *Foxhound Kennel Stud Book*. 'Gelert' is identified (confidently but surprisingly) as the Rev. Edward W. L. Davies, the Rev. John Russell's curate and whipper-in at Swymbridge and later his biographer.

'HOLD HARD, THERE!'
The shout is to the engine-driver; hounds, with their kill, are not anxious to be moved. Railways were greeted with unanimous horror by hunting men, but this was enormously qualified, as early as 1850, by their extreme convenience – for horses and sometimes hounds as well as men – and by the way they swelled the subscriptions. Foxes learned at once, and hounds almost at once, to avoid trains. Whistles sometimes brought hounds' heads up. Fumes sometimes destroyed scent. Railway cuttings were a hazard: the fine if unorthodox hounds of the Old Surrey, hunted by Tom Hills, lost seven couple of bitches in 1852 when they fell 100 feet on to the Brighton line. But the worst hazard, by universal consent, was the navvies who built the railways. Print by J. H. Engleheart after Henry Alken Snr.

Countryside, Society and Opinion

The main changes to the physical countryside were drainage, reclamation and clearing, hedging and fencing, the growth of arable; canals and railways; and the depopulation of the land.

Drainage started on a large scale in the East Anglian fens and spread rapidly through all parts of England and southern Scotland. On hunting it cut both ways: it was blamed for the ruin of scent, but it improved the ground for riding.

Clearing removed both woodland and scrub, which in some countries was a good thing. A lot of gorse was also grubbed up to increase the productive area, such as the whole of the Lyneham Heath covert in the Heythrop country. Much gorse was also planted – the total in Leicestershire being at least doubled – although many people preferred to unkennel a fox in a wood, as it got away better and ran straighter.[226]

The enormous enclosures of the 18th century were subdivided: in many countries an average of fifty or seventy-five acres became an average of five or ten. This was more exciting for horsemen, but discouraging for people who liked watching the hounds. Hounds checked more often from the fox turning up a ditch, but it was easier for them to cast themselves, or for their huntsman to cast them, than in the middle of a 100-acre prairie.

Arable grew at the expense of pasture during the Napoleonic wars. It continued to grow as long as the corn laws made the harvest profitable; they were repealed in 1846. Much land was also put to the plough which had previously been waste.

Canals were an almost unmitigated nuisance – unjumpable, unfordable, with few bridges. They did bring great benefits directly to country people and indirectly to some hunts. Railways were at first bitterly opposed by most landlords and all hunting men. Both modified their views. Disraeli's Lord Marney fought against a local railway in the 1840s, until he had negotiated an enormous payment from the company;[227] this was quite typical. Delmé Radcliffe was aghast at 'this thrice-accursed revolution of railroads'.[228] The northern part of Ralph Lambton's country, gridironed with tracks, was becoming difficult to hunt even before his retirement. Smoke and fumes were bad; the killing of hounds was worse; the navvies building new railways were considered worst of all. But more and more people used 'the two best cover hacks in the world, the Great Northern and Euston stations'.[229] Railways gave hunting a broader base and brought many more subscriptions: but fields swollen with ignorant townsmen did more damage.

Enclosures of common land continued; there was also widespread eviction of country tenants. In 1845 'This town of Marney was a metropolis of agricultural labour, for the proprietors of the neighbourhood having for the last half-century acted on the system of destroying the cottages on their estates, in order to become exempted from the maintenance of the population, the expelled people had flocked to Marney.'[230] As a result of enclosures, evictions and the price of bread, the Return of Paupers of England and Wales at Lady day 1842 was 'In-door 221,687, Out-door 1,207,402, Total 1,429,089'.

This was blamed, with justice, on the landowning interest; and the fury against landowners was habitually linked to foxhunting. Who made the iniquitous laws? '"We!" answer the much-*consuming* Aristocracy; "We!" as they ride in, moist with the sweat of Melton Mowbray.'[231]

An equally emotive subject was the gamelaws. People contrasted (how could they not?) the tremendous slaughter of pheasant *battues* with the transportation of a poacher who snared a single rabbit.

To these indignations was added the moral disapproval of the Evangelical movement – the Clapham Sect, the prophetess Hannah More (*Thoughts on the Manners of the Great*). The Evangelicals did not disapprove of shooting, but they 'thought hunting a wicked indulgence'. As George Eliot said, 'Evangelicanism has cast a certain suspicion as of plague-infection over the few amusements which survived in the provinces.'[232]

Pheasant shooting was an enemy of foxhunting in a more direct sense. Gin traps set for poachers caught both foxes and hounds. (Poachers' own pheasant snares did so too.) More damaging still was the attitude of almost all gamekeepers, and many of their masters, to foxes. This began to be a problem at the very beginning of the century, especially in Hampshire. In 1829, 'For some time there has been a war between the Pheasant and the Fox . . . the former has generally been victorious.'[233] A few pheasant preservers closed their coverts to hounds and had all foxes trapped; but this so outraged local opinion that it was exceptional. Many more owners turned a blind eye to their keepers' vulpicide. Keepers were, according to 'Scrutator', ignorant and superstitious almost to a man; they never allowed themselves to learn that a fox and a pheasant can share the same covert, although this was often and conclusively demonstrated.[234] When shooting rights were let to absentee tenants the problem became much worse. Shooting rents, and keepers' tips, depended on foxes being trapped.[235]

Farmers, throughout the period, probably killed far more foxes than gamekeepers did, mostly by destroying litters of cubs. No one who has seen a fox-visited henrun can find it easy to blame them. Compensation of some kind was usually forthcoming from the old sort of master with a private pack, but in the early days of subscription hunting it was most exceptional. As damage also increased, hunts lost more friends and more foxes. The solution was a proper poultry and damage fund, provided by subscription; this was highly unusual before 1850; as a result there was throughout the period a serious dearth of foxes in many countries.

DIGGING OUT
Spade and terrier were used if hounds needed blood; if subscribers wanted blood; or if the country were overfoxed. In the first half of the 19th century very few were, principally because coverts were neither cared for nor preserved. Terriers had run with many packs, or been carried on horseback in a basket: but 'Nimrod' notes that this became quite exceptional. There were no foxes to spare, especially as so many were poached and imports and bagmen were so expensive and unsatisfactory. The leathers round the shoulders of these hunt servants suggest Lord Fitzwilliam's; his country was well foxed. Print by I. Clark after Henry Alken Snr. By courtesy of Sterling and Francine Clark Art Institute.

The Trade in Foxes

The dearth of foxes had several results. Countries were given up because there was nothing to hunt; spade and terrier were far less used; some countries became extremely large; and captured foxes became big business.

In underfoxed countries, foxes were bought either to be hunted from a sack, or to be turned down and hunted as wild game.

Bag foxes were pretty consistently deplored. Their stronger scent made them too easy to hunt (like an aniseed drag) which turned a pack idle. Unlike carted deer they never ran straight because, in strange country, they had no home earths to make a point to. But they were sometimes needed for blooding the young entry, and they were sometimes needed for any sport to be shown at all. And 'there is often on the borders of a fox-hunting country some scratch pack of curs, miscalled harriers, which often turn down a bag fox on their high days and holidays, sometimes secretly, but generally openly, in defiance of every law and rule by which real sportsmen should be guided'.[236]

But the number of bag foxes hunted was far smaller than the number of transplanted wild ones. The most important sources were France, Germany, Holland, Scotland, Wales – and England. They were imported from abroad by a number of dealers, and sold at Leadenhall Market, from the beginning of the century. They were quite expensive – ten shillings each, rising to fifteen. French foxes were considered worst, owing to their diet of moles, and they were thought to undermine the native breed by crossing.[237]

Reputable dealers sold to reputable masters foxes which were guaranteed to be foreign. It was well known that many were English, stolen from the coverts of one hunt to be sold to another. Poachers, and many gamekeepers, were engaged in this trade throughout the period; they could get ten shillings a head for young cubs. Apart from the alertness of well-disposed farmers, only two answers were found. One was energetic cubhunting, which dispersed litters and made cubs harder to find;[238] the other was good thick gorse covert, which no poacher could get into.[239]

Both legitimate foreign and illicit English importations had one further serious disadvantage. Having been kept in close and dirty quarters by the dealers, they almost all contracted mange.

10 Britain
Victorian and Edwardian
1850-1914

Shires and East Midlands

Sir Richard Sutton retired from the Quorn in 1856. Lord Stamford's mastership was thoroughly satisfactory except for his banishment of 'Skittles'. Caroline Walters had begun her career setting up the skittles in the alley of a Liverpool tavern. She rose to be Lord Fitzwilliam's protégée, and rode to hounds beautifully dressed and mounted. This enraged Lady Stamford, who had risen even further from similar origins. In 1860, 'They sentenced thee in judgement firm, To be a banished maid.'[1]

Mr Clowes had bad weather and no subscriptions. The 3rd Marquess of Hastings had no common sense and less and less money. Mr John Chaworth Musters preferred Nottinghamshire. Mr Coupland (1870–84) was said to be the best master the Quorn ever had.[2] He entered its most influential hound since Furrier – Alfred (1872), by Mr Garth's Painter out of Craven Affable. He engaged the best huntsman in history: Tom Firr, who had been dismissed for incompetence by Lord Eglinton, and crisply instructed by Captain Percy Williams: 'Stay at home with your hounds, and wear a white neckcloth. Keep your temper, and stick to the line.'[3]

In 1893 the country took the brave step of inviting the 5th Earl of Lonsdale to be master. He was passionately keen, tireless, dictatorial and almost rich enough to sustain his extravagance. The farmers loved him, the field obeyed him like 'trained wolves, going on only at the word of command'.[4] He gave Tom Firr room to work.

Captain Frank Forester and Tom Bishopp bred Mr Coupland's pack to Belvoir; the result was said to be the best Quorn pack since Osbaldeston's. If sport never quite recovered the glories of 'the best season on record' (1883–4)[5] it was very, very good.

Lord Stamford did not resume Mr Dick Sutton's Billesdon or South Quorn country. It was taken by Mr William Ward Tailby. He 'hated anyone to be in front of him',[6] took as many falls as Assheton Smith but hurt himself more,[7] believed in showing his field a gallop, and made 'Skittles' welcome. His 'brilliant lady pack'[8] was as fast as the Pytchley's.

When Sir Bache Cunard succeeded Mr Tailby, Mr Coupland wanted his country back. The dispute ended old friendships. Quorn men came out in ratcatcher to insult Sir Bache; he and his followers pretended to think they were pad grooms, and cursed them out of the way. Mr C. W. B. Fernie took the country in 1888; he was told he might live five years if he wintered abroad, but wintered in Leicestershire for thirty-three. He and Charles Isaac, then Arthur Thatcher, followed the steeple-

Right above
THE EARL OF MACCLESFIELD AND HIS HOUNDS, 1875
Lord Parker started the South Oxfordshire as an independent hunt in 1845; the country was provided by the shrinking needs of the Bicester and Old Berks. After two years Mr J. S. Phillips took over, saving the hunt from premature death. Lord Macclesfield, as Lord Parker had become, returned from 1857 to 1884; he was sole master and owner of the pack from 1860. 'Brooksby' called him 'one of the best authorities in England on the points of the foxhound,' and he bred a beautiful pack which he hunted himself. It was a compact, two-day country, happy in loyal and sporting farmers. The Prince of Wales (King Edward VII) saw his first fox killed by these hounds. Painting by the Hon. Henry Graves. By courtesy of Fores Ltd.

Right below
A FOXHUNTING CONSTELLATION
On horseback: the 9th Duke of Beaufort, Mr George Charles Wentworth Fitzwilliam, Sir Gilbert Greenall, first outside Master of the Belvoir since Lord Forester, the 4th Earl of Yarborough, the 5th Earl of Lonsdale, Mr Henry Chaplin (later 1st Viscount Chaplin), the 8th Earl of Harrington. Standing: Ben Capell, Belvoir huntsman from 1896 to 1912, and the 7th Duke of Rutland.

chasing tradition of Mr Tailby and Jack Goddard: Thatcher was considered the best ever,[9] but what he did was cast forward at a gallop and change foxes.[10]

The Pytchley had far too many masters but the same brilliant pack, and for many years Charles Payne hunting it. The 5th Earl Spencer might have been master for thirty-three years, but he kept going away to be a Cabinet minister; he also had a weak chest, to protect which he wore a long red beard. During one of his absences, Colonel John Anstruther Thomson was inveigled from Fife by George Whyte Melville;[11] he was 'A rum one to follow, a bad one to beat', and accustomed to big fields by his mastership of the Atherstone. On 2 February 1866 they had the legendary Waterloo run, three hours and forty-five minutes and hounds whipped-off in the dark. The $17\frac{1}{2}$ couple, hunted by the master, included one Beaufort hound, Ferryman by Beaufort Finder: thanks to him the pack hunted through several successive flocks of sheep. '"Hurrah for the Duke of Beaufort!" said I.'[12] One of the poems written about the hunt was by Tom Firr, the second whip.

Lord Spencer returned in 1874, bringing 'white-collar' Will Goodall, son of Will of the Belvoir, comparable to his 'Incomparable' father.[13] The Woodland Pytchley was hived off, to a qualified extent, at this period. It was also the time of the Empress of Austria's immensely popular visits. Mr W. M. Wroughton was party to a most interesting experiment: he borrowed two Welsh-cross bitches from Colonel Frederick Lort-Phillips of the Pembrokeshire. Dimple, by Llangibby Danger out of Taunton Vale Verity, 'was there from find to finish, she leads from first to last'.[14] Her merit was widely noticed,[15] but for some reason the idea was not followed up.

In 1906 Lord Annaly engaged Frank Freeman, taught how to hunt hounds by Mr Henry Chaplin[16] and by 1912 'the best huntsman in the world'.[17]

In 1855 Will Goodall 'saw Lord Lonsdale's hounds on my road home. I never saw such a miserable sight'.[18] By 1870 Sir John Trollope had restored their excellence, breeding the old Cottesmore sort mostly to Belvoir. From 1880 to 1900 Mr William Baird was master of a pack which had become one of the best and a country which was now quite the best.[19] According to Lord Lonsdale, Arthur Thatcher then ruined the pack:[20] in curing it, Lord Lonsdale went far to ruining himself.

ARTHUR THATCHER AND
MR FERNIE'S HOUNDS, 1908
Thatcher was Charles Isaac's second
whip; he went to the Essex Union as
huntsman in 1898 and the Cottesmore
in 1900. He was there subjected to
ferocious criticism by Lord Lonsdale
who, becoming master in 1907,
immediately replaced him with Sam
Gillson, son of George Gillson who had
been a great Cottesmore huntsman for
Mr William Baird. Thatcher came
back to Mr Fernie. He was not as good
a hound man as Charles Isaac (Mr
Higginson said he drafted better
hounds than he kept): but he was
spectacularly brilliant in the field.
Mr T. F. Dale was one of many
experienced hunting men who said he
was the best ever. But good judges
thought differently. Lord Lonsdale
said he was a disaster. Mr A. H.
Higginson said he was a brilliant
bluffer, casting his hounds forward
at a gallop at the briefest check and
so always changing to a fresh fox.
Guy Paget said that he kept his hounds
moving so fast, and changed foxes so
adroitly, that few people realized they
were not foxhunting at all. Mr Charles
McNeill said he was blessed with
fields so ignorant that his bluff was
seldom exposed. These hounds, from
the left, are Ferryman, Trimbush,
Daystar, Fireman, Trueman and
Somerset. Painting by H. F. Lucas
Lucas. By courtesy of the Athol
Gallery.

The 5th Duke of Rutland took over his hounds from his cousin Lord Forester in 1857. Will Goodall, still young, died after a fall in 1859, leaving a pack that ran a little mute owing to Furrier blood. James Cooper bred back cry before he took to the bottle, and then Frank Gillard arrived and bred Weathergauge (1876), the most influential stallion of the second half of the century, 'not to be beaten',[21] the 'acknowledged bedrock of all modern day excellence'.[22] The pack by 1880 was so sorty that it was difficult even for Gillard to draw hounds by name.[23]

Other masters joined with or acted for the 7th and 8th Dukes, but the breeding policy and the reputation of the pack were unaltered.

A pack of comparable influence but wholly different type was Lord Henry Bentinck's at the Burton, which Mr Henry Chaplin bought in 1862 and took charge of in 1865. He was Lord Henry's devoted pupil and disciple[24] and the recipient of the letter published as *Goodall's Practise*. Though heavy and short-sighted, he was the best amateur huntsman and one of the best horsemen of his day.[25] His country was too much for one pack, even going out six days; in 1871 he divided it, keeping the southern side as the Blankney.

At Brocklesby, tradition was broken when Nimrod Long succeeded Will Smith in 1864, and in 1875 Mr J. Maunsell Richardson was acting master for Victoria, Lady Yarborough (widow of the 3rd Earl, whom he later married). But there were no changes in either kennel or country:[26] nor under the 4th Earl and his great huntsman Will Dale. When they used outside blood, such as Weathergauge and his sons, they were always breeding back to Brocklesby.

The South Wold offshoot was 'bandied from hand to hand every few years', and had 'many a struggle for bare existence',[27] until the forty years of Mr E. Preston Rawnsley; he started as an invalid and ended as one of the very great Masters of Hounds.

Mr George and his son Mr George C. W. Fitzwilliam followed the 5th Earl from 1857. Their country deteriorated in the agricultural depression;[28] their pack retained all the Milton savagery and its rough coats and hackles: they were 'George Carter's shaving brushes'.[29]

In 1860, at the age of twenty-two, Mr John Chaworth Musters of Annesley revived the South Notts hunt which his greatgrandfather had started and his grandfather made famous. Frank Gillard, his kennel huntsman, called him 'the finest of sportsmen and the truest of friends'.[30] Mr Chaworth Musters confirmed this judgment: his own account of the great Harlequin run of 16 February 1872 ends with a tribute to his second horseman.[31] The hunt was so popular with the 'teeming manufacturing population' that Mr Lancelot Rolleston had to draw coverts near factories surreptitiously and from distant meets.[32] The 8th Earl of Harrington bought the hounds in 1882; he and Fred Earp hunted six days a week with three packs.

'The Rufford and the Grove are very far from first class, but picturesque, romantic, and rare for cub-hunting.'[33] Captain Percy Williams made an enormous reputation at the Rufford in these rather special circumstances. Most of his hounds went to Lord Fitzwilliam's new Wentworth country in 1861. His successor bred hounds of the same type and from the same sources. The 6th Viscount Galway came back to the Grove in 1858; he was a disciple of Mr G. S. Foljambe and used his blood. The 7th followed him for thirty-one years, his pack closely similar, and closely related, to Mr Henry Chaplin's. His greatest problem was fish manure, which enraptured even the steadiest hound.[34]

The 6th Earl Fitzwilliam lived in Yorkshire, not at Milton, and bravely started the Wentworth in an industrialized corner of the Grove country. The 7th took over the Grove as well when Lord Galway retired in 1907.

West Midlands

The Atherstone had a series of distinguished masters and some very interesting hounds: especially Colonel Anstruther Thomson's twenty-five couple of yellow-and-white Welsh cross, 'sharp as terriers in their work . . . in kennel they bit like vipers'.[35] Mr William Oakley (1871–91) was an extremely fine hound breeder, and so popular that when his resignation was rumoured 1,000 tenant farmers signed a petition begging him to stay. His son-in-law Mr W. F. Inge and Mr Gerald Hardy kept the pack exactly as they found it. It was an exceptionally happy hunt; Siegfried Sassoon records the hospitality and friendliness he met during Mr Norman Loder's brief mastership just before the first war.[36]

When Mr Meynell Ingram died during the 1868–9 season, aged eighty-six, he had done for his country almost what his grandfather had done for Leicestershire. His son died after a fall two years later. The hounds were given to the country, became a subscription pack, and were called the Meynell. Tom Leedham the younger was succeeded by his nephew Charles, of whose success as huntsman Tom was desperately jealous.[37] The atmosphere was like Lincolnshire – no visitors because there was nowhere to stay.[38] Mr Gerald Hardy came home from the Atherstone in 1903, and the next year entered Whynot (or Why Not) by Belvoir Vagabond, bred by Mr Reginald Corbet in South Cheshire (Mr Corbet hunted only bitches). He was said to be the best sire in England between 1900 and 1914,[39] and created the

'modernized Meynells',[40] which Mr Charles McNeill said was the best pack in England.[41]

South Staffordshire was created out of Meynell and Atherstone territory in 1865. The new hunt had very few and very good masters. The Woore was renamed the North Staffordshire and had the same good fortune. So did the Albrighton: except that there were no walks[42] and the country was too big. It was divided in 1908, which should have been done thirty years earlier.[43]

In Warwickshire the 18th Lord Willoughby de Broke followed the greatly-loved Mr Charles North and the liked but incompetent Mr Lucy in 1870. He had to create a new pack, which he did with Ravager, by Lord Coventry's Rambler out of a Brocklesby bitch called Skylark. Warwickshire then had one of the best packs, best huntsmen and most unspoiled countries in Britain.[44] North Warwickshire was from 1855 lucky in its masters and its hounds, and also in Leamington: the Spa was the making of the hunt, and the hunt was the making of the Spa.[45]

Worcestershire went from very happy times in the 1850s and 1860s[46] to very unhappy ones of wire, pheasant preserving, vulpicide and poison.[47] The Croome was re-established in 1873 by the 9th Earl of Coventry, who brought his private pack from the North Cotswold. He entered Rambler that year, a marvellous hound largely of Mr G. S. Foljambe's and partly of Lord Fitzhardinge's blood. The pack became very good indeed, and the field were under control: 'The followers crouched before his beck, His iron heel was on their neck.'[48]

The Ledbury had 'joyous and spacious days' with very fast hounds and fields of farmers.[49] Shropshire was absorbed by the Wheatland for a time and divided for a time. In 1880 it was reunited; it 'keeps up a pack of hounds for its own amusement'.[50] But for many years the farmers were too poor to be amused. The United had a Welsh-cross pack that 'came up the valley like a peal of Lancashire bellringers'.[51] The Ludlow had few masters, the right number of coverts, and a vast number of stout foxes. Herefordshire divided, quite wrongly;[52] South Hereford had another effective Welsh-cross pack. Cheshire was festive but underfoxed owing to pheasant shooting.[53]

Oxfordshire and Gloucestershire

The Bicester had a sequence, only occasionally and briefly interrupted, of six masters in 122 years. It also had the same pack, added to but not changed by Mr Charles (later Lord) North. Lord Parker returned to South Oxfordshire, as Lord Macclesfield, for nearly thirty years. He was lucky in his farmers, and they in him. Mr Albert Brassey of Heythrop House was master of the Heythrop from 1873 to 1918. He bought Lord Redesdale's pack of Jem Hills's breeding: distinctive and very fast indeed: they even kept clear of Oxford undergraduates being run away with.

The V.W.H. had no such luck. Lord Gifford was still arrogant and ill-judging,[54] Mr W. F. Croome was not popular enough to get his puppies walked, Captain Wilson's huntsmen and whips all kept getting drunk in Cirencester,[55] Sir William Throckmorton was unable to extract money from his subscribers, Lord Shannon had to dismiss a very good huntsman for impertinence, and George Whyte Melville was killed hacking slowly from covert to covert. All previous unpleasantness paled before that which followed the arrival of Mr C. A. R. Hoare. His lavishness to the farmers bought their loyalty, but his private life scandalized the country: rumours which he denied turned out to be true: he was ostracized and coverts were closed to him: the country was divided in 1886.[56] All was well in the end because the 7th Earl Bathurst and Mr T. Butt Miller of the Cricklade side got on very amiably.

THE V.W.H. AT BLUNSDON HILL, 1885
This was the most dreadful season in the history of this or any other hunt. During the previous season the name of the master, Mr Hoare, was linked to private scandal, for which it was the wrong era, and on 12 January 1884 the Committee asked him to resign. He denied the rumours. He was allowed to stay. Many landowners were incensed, some threatening to warn him off their coverts. The farmers, whose goodwill he had bought with money and hospitality, stumped town and country on his behalf with banners, as though in a Dickensian election or modern protest march. It then emerged that the scandalous rumours were true. Lord Bathurst (6th Earl) refused Mr Hoare the use of the Cirencester kennels. There was a general meeting of the hunt on 25 April 1885; the landowners present refused to let the master draw their coverts; most refused to speak to him. He hunted the country for one more miserable season. His fields were limited to farmers and a few personal friends; many of his coverts were closed to him. He vacated the kennels in February 1886, leaving not so much as a broom behind. The hounds descended from Mr Morrell's fine Old Berkshire pack, bought from Mr Duffield by Captain Matthew Wharton Wilson in 1863. Painting by Thomas Blinks. By courtesy of Fores Ltd.

The 8th Duke of Beaufort succeeded in 1853. His son began hunting hounds in 1868. The Greatwood run in his third season (22 February 1871) was said to be the greatest of the century because of the variety of country they crossed.[57] The hounds retained their character – 'extraordinary dash and enormous stride'[58] – and some still had the badger-pie colour from old Justice. The duke still bore almost the entire cost, but the agricultural depression compelled him first to lend Mr Horlock's old country to Captain Spicer, and then, like the Duke of Rutland, to accept a subscription. It was about this time that Lady Meux, incensed because her coverts were drawn just before she wanted to shoot, arrived at a meet on an elephant and turned it into a terrified stampede.[59] When the 9th Duke succeeded, the hounds were better than ever before; identical to Belvoir but a little bigger;[60] their music 'was better than the Boston Symphony Orchestra, by far!'[61]

Admiral Sir Maurice Berkeley succeeded his brother in 1857; he shortly afterwards became Lord Fitzhardinge. He was nearly seventy, which is probably why he gave up the Cotswold country. Harry Ayres was huntsman for another nine years, completing forty. The hounds were slightly unusual: they had been, and continued to be, bred entirely to work without regard for appearance;[62] indifference to Peterborough made them increasingly distinctive; they would have been more used as an outcross but for the risk of an unfashionable pale colour. They were nearly as savage as Milton.[63] Nothing changed under the 2nd and 3rd Lords Fitzhardinge except the introduction, which was fully in line with the kennel's philosophy, of Welsh-cross blood from Itton.

Mr C. F. Cregoe Colmore divided the Cotswolds – an unpopular move – in 1868. There was one good pack under several masters in the south, and several good packs under several good masters in the north.

Britain: 1850–1914

Berkshire, Hampshire, Wiltshire, Dorset, Somerset

Mr James Morrell's years at the Old Berks were 'clouded with vexation, undeserved and bitter enough to make many a less staunch sportsman throw up the cards'.[64] The Duffield brothers and Lord Craven had a much happier time. The Craven itself suffered wire 'twined through the tops of thorns'[65] and disputes between master and committees; it emerged into sanity and got a fine and influential pack. Mr Thomas Colleton Garth took Sir John Cope's reduced country in 1852. Charles Kingsley reported fine runs and fine big hounds;[66] the latter in 1880 were the tallest in England. Mr Garth took no subscription, did everything 'extremely well',[67] and was master for fifty years. At the South Berks everything was '*superb*' under Mr John Hargreaves,[68] and continued so under Mr 'Doggy' Dubourg, who hunted hounds four days a week without ever attempting a jump.[60] At the Vine, Lord Portsmouth was followed by Mr Marsh (whose real name was Walker). He had such a bad first season that he resorted to a desperate expedient. On 30 January 1859, a Sunday, he had a fox dug up. The next day he caused his whipper-in to cut off one of its hind legs. The maimed fox was put in a bag and turned down in front of the pack; it was naturally killed within 200 yards. 'Marsh' was summonsed by the Society for the Prevention of Cruelty to Animals (not yet Royal) and appeared before the Kingsclere bench. He was acquitted because the fox was not held a domestic animal, which alone enjoyed the protection of statute. Local enthusiasm then created and maintained a 'capital pack'.[70]

Things went well at the H.H. under Mr Henry Deacon, who got Lord Portsmouth's young draft every year, better under Mr George Evans, who bred a Puckeridge draft to Belvoir. The Hursley was quiet and untroubled by either strangers or pheasants; Mr Tregonwell was so good-tempered that he showed no annoyance when his horn was stuffed with buttered toast during a hunt breakfast at Winchester Barracks.[71] The Hambledon became large (expanding into Sussex) and comparatively flamboyant and fashionable. It got a marvellous pack of Cottesmore blood. The best pack the New Forest had was Sir Reginald Graham's: Blankney bitches from Mr Chaplin; Mr (later Sir) George Meyrick took them over. At the Tedworth, George Carter continued for a long time, in full control of the kennel. The hounds had to be steady to hare, and themselves hare-footed because of the flints; they were still the Assheton Smith sort, but bred down.

Wiltshire hunts formed and reformed themselves in various outlines; they settled down into Lord Radnor's (modern Wilton), reunited South and West Wilts (1881) and Captain Spicer's (modern Avon Vale).

Mr Farquharson's heirs in Dorset bickered for a time about their coverts; in 1858 boundaries were agreed between Lord Portman, Mr Wingfield Digby (Blackmore Vale) and Mr Radclyffe (South Dorset and Cattistock). The 2nd Lord Portman bred one of the best packs in the South of England, and eventually had enough foxes to hunt. Mr Radclyffe withdrew from the Cattistock, which became Lord Poltimore's; the 7th Earl of Guildford was killed there while hunting hounds; the Rev. Edgar Astley Milne arrived for thirty-one years in 1900, probably the toughest parson in the Church: 'if he sat on a tack he'd bend it'.[72] He bred a fine big pack, mostly Belvoir by way of Lord Rothschild's. The Blackmore Vale was the 'Queen of the West', with good scent and handsome country;[73] Mr Merthyr Guest permitted only grey hunt horses, to match his beard, and having bought the Brocklesby doghounds refused to let other breeders use them.

Colonel G. E. Luttrell added Mendip to his West Somerset country in 1859; he

[134]

withdrew in 1865 owing to 'entire absence of support in any shape'.[74] Mendip was unhunted for twenty years, which was 'scarcely credible',[75] and hardly hunted except by harriers until 1914.

Devon and Cornwall

In one part of the Rev. John Russell's country (at its largest extent) Mr Nicholas Snow hunted a pack called the Stars of the West for twenty years; it became the Exmoor in 1889. Rabbit trapping made foxes very scarce early in the 20th century. The country to the south – the heart of Mr Russell's – became a separate Dulverton under Mr Froude Bellew in 1875. The old Tiverton remained sporting but unpretentious until the 1890s, when it went into scarlet and attracted much larger fields. Sir Ian Heathcote-Amory was, like his father Sir John, an extremely fine hound breeder. Lord Portsmouth (5th Earl) succeeded his father – better known as Mr Newton Fellowes – at Eggesford in 1858; he brought from the Vine the pack he got from Mr Henry Villebois, and made it one of the most celebrated in Britain – his hounds went to, and his stallions were used by, kennels in Northumberland and Scotland. The Mid and South Devon were old, the East Devon and Silverton new; they were all short of foxes, and suffered, probably in consequence, from brief masterships. Dartmoor was more fortunate in both regards; Mr William Coryton bred a beautiful pack described as a small version of Belvoir. The western end of Mr Russell's country broke away in his time (and to his rage); in 1859 it was taken by Mr Mark Rolle of Stevenstone. Frank Gillard was his huntsman until he went to Belvoir. The Arscotts' old Tetcott was re-established as an independent hunt by Mr Calmady, whose whole pack descended from one bitch given him by Lord Willoughby de Broke. Mr Scott Browne and Mr George Brendon divided the country in 1896. The twin Leamon brothers (one hunting hounds, the other turning them) took the reunited Lamerton in 1853; they did everything in kennel but nothing in the field, letting their hounds hunt entirely unaided.[76]

East Cornwall was Mr William Coryton's, then Mr Connock Marshall's. North Cornwall was created in 1874 by the amalgamation of two countries. The Williams family began their connection with the Four Burrow in 1854. Mr John Williams's Whipcord (1905), by Berkeley Vanguard, was an immensely valuable stallion, and crucial to the development of Colonel Curre's crossbred pack. In 1910 Mr Aubrey Wallis brought his pack of 'pure original black and tan, the same as the Scarteen':[77] the only Kerry beagles in England. They were better in Cornwall than at the Woodland Pytchley. The Western country was taken over by the Bolitho family from 1864 to 1939; Mr T. R. Bolitho, with or without other Bolithos, was master until 1925. Not counting joints, the Western has had five masterships between 1820 and today, a blessed condition possible only in great family packs or those of the remotest countries.

Yorkshire and the North

The 2nd Duke of Cleveland re-created a foxhunting country round Raby. He died in 1861. Mr Christopher Cradock was highly successful with a pack of Lord Henry Bentinck's sort, until it all got too expensive;[78] Lord Zetland was better able to bear the cost. The Bedale got a new pack at Captain Percy Williams's sale in 1861; hounds and country were so good that the hunt deserved to be fashionable;[79] but the fields, like Lord Zetland's, were all farmers. Mr Simon Scrope of Danby briefly revived the Wensleydale in 1906 with a Welsh-cross pack; but the more familiar sport of the area was the hound trail, like Cumberland's but with less heavy betting. Neasham and the Hurworth hounds were inherited by Mr James Cookson from the Wilkinsons. He improved a fine pack; he merited large fields but was delighted with very small ones.

The Cleveland hounds were at last kennelled in 1870, between the railway and the ironworks at Kirkleatham – healthy but noisy and dirty.[80] Mr W. H. A. Wharton moved the pack to Skelton Castle. The Bilsdale were kennelled in 1888. Their whipper-in for sixty years was Bobby Dawson; he once found a vixen in a trap: 'I was'na half as sorry when me 'ard mother deed.'[81] The Sinnington was much more social owing to the presence in its midst of the Duncombe family (Lords Feversham, Earls from 1868); but the pack was still trencher-fed, 'an anomaly, or at all events a curiosity, to be found scarcely anywhere else in this year of 1883'.[82] It was kennelled in 1891. The Farndale was still trencher-fed in 1914. The Goathland hunted two days a week with twenty couple for a total outlay, in 1913–14, of £50. The Eskdale was revived in 1867, but there were no foxes and no subscriptions. The Staintondale were inexplicably hunted on foot until 1880, kennelled in 1910, trencher-fed again in 1913. All the hounds had to be home-bred because draft hounds fell off the cliffs. The Pickering country was taken over by Mr Harcourt Johnstone (later 1st Lord Derwent) and his son in 1862; it then had private packs known by their masters' names.

The Bramham Moor went back from the Lascelles to the Lane Fox family in 1848; Mr George Lane Fox was master until 1896. Charles Treadwell was a very good huntsman, Stephen Goodall a very bad one,[83] Tom Smith, son of Brocklesby Will, a very good one. The pack was magnificent – John Warde's blood bred to Lord Henry Bentinck's – and the master the best judge in England after Captain Percy Williams.[84] At the York and Ainsty, Sir Charles Slingsby was a first-rate breeder and huntsman. He, the kennel huntsman, and four others were drowned when their horses overturned the Newby ferry crossing the Ure after their hounds. The farmers were very keen, but lost their money; the fields were very small, except near York, where they were far too big. The 8th and 9th Lords Middleton followed Sir Tatton Sykes in the East Riding, taking over his pack and moving it to Birdsall. Once forty couple were taken out cubhunting at 5.30 on an August morning. In a large, dry wood two miles from the nearest water there was a crash of music from the whole pack such as had never been heard before; they killed an otter.[85]

The Holderness had two very long masterships after Mr Hodgson, to which was ascribed the excellence of the pack.[86] The Badsworth had a pack of the same blood, but a country in sharp contrast: as early as 1880 it was thought brave of them to try to hunt at all.[87] It was even braver of Lord Fitzwilliam, but his efforts at Wentworth were very popular. 'Two colliers bought a horse and hunting kit between them, and in turn worked them three days a week.'[88]

Durham was divided in 1872, although the northern side was getting as bad as Wentworth; the miners sometimes spoiled a hunt by being drunk, but when a fox was dug out late at night they were always there helping.[89] The Braes of Derwent was started in 1854 in the old Prudhoe country; Mr William Cowen and his brother Colonel John were masters until 1895, with an unusual but most effective blood-hound–foxhound first-cross pack. Mr Lewis Priestman was then master for fifty years: though brilliantly successful he was not obsessed with hunting; he saw *Floradora* thirty-five times in London. The Haydon in this period was remarkable for repeated changes of name. The Tynedale had on 21 February 1868 a run celebrated

not by the usual poem but by a two-act play, *A Run with the Tynedale Hounds. A Romantic Drama*. The Morpeth was the 'Belvoir of the North' owing to its hounds, its country and the expensive dressiness of its fields.[90]

Lord Elcho's country went through various divisions, which settled down as the Alnwick (later Percy), Callaly (later Coquetdale, later still West Percy) and Glendale (later North Northumberland). The Border remained the Robsons', the North Tyne the Dodds'. The Border seldom went out with more than eight couple, and seldom had a tally of fewer than fifty brace.[91]

The Cumberland reached so low an ebb in 1870 that 'The Druid' thought it was dead.[92] It revived and in 1890 was divided. Some of the true fell packs were amalgamated; they continued typically to have both masters and huntsmen with almost incredible lengths of service.

The old sport of hound trailing became much bigger business; the first major trail was at the Grassmere Sports, the 'Derby of the Dales', in 1852. About fifteen couple ran in each race; training was crucial, and each family's secrets of work and diet were closely guarded. Heavy betting led to fraud, which led to the Hound Trailing Association in 1906.[93]

South-east Midlands, East Anglia, the South East

The Duke of Grafton's was Lord Southampton's until 1861. It became the Grafton. Frank Beers succeeded his father, and by 1888 had 'the most fox-killing lot that ever drove a line'.[94] Mr Charles McNeill bred almost entirely to Belvoir; but also, and quite separately, used Welsh-cross blood from the Curres. Mr Selby Lowndes was allowed back to the Whaddon Chase by the 6th Duke of Grafton. The Oakley went very well indeed, especially under Mr Robert Arkwright and his grandson Esme; but 'The steam plough has been driving its villainous grooves through the soil.'[95] The Old Berkeley had too few foxes, too many Cockney followers and better masters than it deserved; its existence was precarious and discontinuous. Hertfordshire remained rural and sporting; a great deal of money was spent in kennel and country, but none on ostentation. Mr George Smith Bosanquet began hunting a loaned section in 1908; he was the first builder of hunt jumps in wire fencing on an extensive scale.

The Puckeridge pack had been carefully bred by experts for over 100 years when Mr Edward Barclay bought it in 1896. He re-created it as the purest Belvoir outside Belvoir itself. The Suffolk had keen farmers and ruthless gamekeepers. The Newmarket and Thurlow was restarted in 1884; it had a lot of masters and very little hound breeding. The Cambridgeshire was considered very valuable, as Cambridge

[137]

undergraduates learned hunting instead of the steeplechasing which Oxford men got with the Heythrop and Bicester.

Essex had every advantage – scent, country, masters, huntsmen, hounds – except that its foxes were all stolen and sold in London. East Essex had fewer advantages but more foxes. The Essex and Suffolk had a very good pack and very small fields. West Norfolk hunting had failed, but under Mr Henry Villebois it succeeded: the reason was the friendliness and good sense of covert owners, who understood that foxes preferred rabbits to their pheasants.[96] About 1909 there were five crowned heads at a meet.[97]

In Sussex, the 2nd Lord Leconfield and from 1901 the 3rd maintained a princely establishment at Petworth. In 1883 Lord Leconfield withdrew from the south to make room for a new Goodwood hunt; but it only lasted twelve years. The Chidding-fold Harriers were entered only to fox (having killed a lot of foxes) in 1860. They were never bothered by Cockneys. The Crawley and Horsham had a lot of Londoners; but they had a lot of absentee shooting tenants too. The new Southdown was almost too successful, attracting large fields which overrode the pack. The East Sussex was started in 1853; it was well-run and well-supported in spite of hopfields, mud, mange and shooting tenants. An Eastbourne hunt existed between 1891 and 1916.

The Old Surrey would have been all right, in spite of building, but for shooting.[98] The Burstow Park harriers became foxhounds in 1866. These two amalgamated in 1915 to get an adequate country. Half the Surrey Union was lost to suburbia by 1876 and there were no walks. Jack Molyneux said the kennels were full of rats and the country empty of foxes.[99]

When Mr Ralph Nevill was master of the West Kent, his Tunbridge Wells country paid a separate subscription for its one day a week. This became an independent hunt, the West Kent Woodland, under Mr Nevill's nephew Lord George. It became the Eridge in 1887. The young Siegfried Sassoon found it very slow.[100] Although some of the Tickham's country was very good, most of it was bad: orchard, market garden and pheasant covert. The owners of the last shot at home and hunted elsewhere.[101] In East Kent, Mr Brockman's long and heroic mastership ended in 1870. He was perhaps tired: foxes and subscriptions were few. The 7th Earl of Guildford pulled things round the moment he attained his majority, by dint of enthusiasm and money, but when he and they went to Dorset the hunt was in a bad way again. Mr Henry Selby Lowndes worked a new miracle in 1900.

Wales

Sir Watkin Williams-Wynn (6th baronet) assembled the first serious pack at Wynnstay in 1842 and took charge of it in 1843. Under John Walker the pack became very good very soon, and under Charles Payne even better. He even learned Welsh. Sir Watkin's nephew and heir was manager from 1883 and master, as 7th baronet, from 1885 to 1944. The Flint and Denbigh was re-established as an independent hunt, at first with names of great length and strangeness. The efforts of the Ynysfor were supplemented by professional foxcatchers, of whom the most famous were women. The Plâs Machynlleth was hunted as a separate country by the Gogerddan in the 1880s, but had first harriers and then its own foxhounds in 1908. Mr David (later Lord) Davies of Llandinam established a pack of great interest in 1905: pure Welsh hounds, unknown so far north except for the Ynysfor. The Teme Valley replaced harriers with foxhounds in 1892. The Radnorshire and West Hereford replaced a private pack in 1868, hunting Welsh–English first-cross hounds.

Colonel Edward Pryse had the Gogerddan Fox and Otter Hounds at Peithyll from 1859 to 1889; his hounds were rough-coated and often white. He also had a pack of harriers. He was followed by his two greatnephews. A separate hunt was started in the southern side called the Aberayron and then the Neuadd Fawr; the latter (Mr and later Mrs Hughes's) had one of the purest and most influential of all Welsh packs. The Llangam March was started in 1909 to keep foxes down with a pack like Mr Hughes's but from Glamorgan; it became the Irfon and Towy. The Rhandirmwyn (now Towy and Clothi) was established with a Neuadd Fawr draft. The fox-killing Brecon harriers were entered only to fox in 1906.

Pembrokeshire was divided in 1866, reunited by Colonel Frederick Lort Phillips in 1888, but divided again five years later; Mr Seymour Allen revived his grand-father's hunt. His English hounds were in great contrast to Colonel Lort Phillips's brilliant crossbreds. Half Carmarthenshire was full of coalmines, the other half of rabbit traps. Glamorganshire had more than a dozen private harrier packs, of which the Cowbridge became foxhounds. Mr Theodore Mansel Talbot of Margam Abbey founded the Glamorgan in 1873, planting coverts and turning down foxes. After his death the hunt lived on. The Llanharan fox-, hare- and otterhounds became the Llangeinor foxhounds in 1885. The Gelligaer was re-established in 1885.

The Monmouthshire hounds were English because Welsh hounds killed the small mountain sheep. They became largely Welsh, but remained steady. The Llangibby was taken by Mr John Lawrence of Crick, who created the then best crossbred pack. He usually lined a Welsh bitch with a Berkeley stallion, and greatly influenced Colonel Curre. The Chepstow was re-established as an independent hunt in 1884. The pack was first-cross by Heythrop sires. In 1896 Colonel (later Sir) Edward Curre bought it and took it home to Itton. He set about creating a strain which bred true, combining Welsh blood (especially Glôg Nimrod's) with the most active and athletic kind of English. After twenty years he regarded his task as only half completed.

Lord Tredegar started a hunt known by his name in 1870; his pack was crossbred and much like the Llangibby.

Wales had, about 1890, an interesting tally of packs: forty-two hare, fifteen fox and hare, fourteen fox only, four hare and otter, three fox, hare and otter, two 'fox &c.', two otter only, one fox and otter, and six beagles. Of the harriers, two packs were described as 'Welsh' and one as 'Red Harriers'.[102]

Scotland

The 5th Duke of Buccleuch hunted a country of great but varying size. The 6th Duke's was sometimes even larger, but reduced by the formation of the Jed Forest in 1885, a delightful little hunt, amateur but not amateurish.[103] Partly also in the Duke's country was Mr Scott Plummer's, later the Lauderdale, formed in 1889. The Eskdaill (*sic*) was formed in country round Dalkeith which the dukes had once hunted.

Berwickshire was intermittently separate from North Northumberland, and when Sir James Miller died in 1906 nobody could be found rich enough to hunt the combined countries and the separation became permanent.

The Dumfriesshire was started in 1848 by Joe Graham, who had been Mr Salkeld's Cumberland huntsman and was given some of his hounds. In 1850 Lord Drumlanrig bought them and engaged him. It was sheep country, wired but good-scenting.

The East Lothian and Linlithgow and Stirlingshire joined in 1869 to form the

fashionable but short-lived Lothians Hunt. There were not many foxes and the ground was covered in quicklime, but Edinburgh people came out by train in large numbers. Ladies always went home early because their squires deserted them.[104]

Sir David Carrick Buchanan of Drumpellier was master of the Lanarkshire and Renfrewshire for nearly half a century, but Lanarkshire was virtually unhuntable. They expanded into Ayrshire until Lord Eglinton started his hunt in 1861. A day with his hounds in their first decade is one of Trollope's best hunting passages.[105] Lord Eglinton was almost gratuitously cruel to his young huntsman Tom Firr: from which Firr said he greatly profited.[106]

Fife had no foxes, but with Forfar it was too big. The hunt was only really successful when Colonel Anstruther Thomson was there: but he also liked being master of the Atherstone and Pytchley. Both Forfar and West Fife had periods of independent life, but their foxhunting died of apathy.

Deer, Hare and Otter

Mr Fenwick Bissett, a giant with a giant personality,[107] revived the chase of the wild red deer on Exmoor in 1855. He made the first success of it since the 18th century. Deer became scarce, then flourished and spread; the Tiverton staghounds could be started in 1896 and the Quantock in 1902.

Red deer were removed from the New Forest, but there were plenty of feral fallow. The Buckhounds were started in 1854 and became a success from 1858.

A few packs still chased carted deer. The Royal Hunt became increasingly uncouth, and by 1897 'an object for which halting apology has to be made annually in discussing the money voted for them'.[108] They were disbanded in 1901. 'The Barons', in sharp contrast, 'are doing the thing in tip-top form.'[109] Mr Nevill of Chilland and Lord Wolverton at Iwerne Minster hunted carted deer with bloodhounds. Mr Nevill's also hunted badgers, bag foxes, a tame jackal, swans and thieves.[110]

There were sixty-two harrier packs in 1850, ninety in 1902; by then they were nearly all dwarf foxhounds, and really too fast for the quarry.[111] This prompted the establishment of packs of basset hounds, and was part of the reason for the growth of beagling. (Economy was the other part.)

Otter hunting had a great resurgence owing to the abandonment of the spear.

58TH REGIMENT BEAGLES AT COLCHESTER, ABOUT 1890
Over the centuries a few people had a few couple of beagles – often as small as ten inches – with which ladies and children hunted rabbits in parks. The first serious beagler was the Rev. Philip James Honywood, of Marks Hall, Essex, who went out in a tall hat and a short green coat and killed a great many hares. Captain John Anstruther Thomson got a draft of Mr Honywood's little hounds, which he sold in 1845 to Cheshire; this was the origin of the Royal Rock, the oldest extant pack. By 1870 there were eighteen packs, most bred up to twelve–fifteen inches. They were welcomed in foxhunting countries: beagles displace foxes from hedgerows into coverts where they belong, reducing the incidence of outliers which cause a change of fox. Examples were Mr Otho Paget's pack in the Quorn country, and these regimental hounds in the Essex and Suffolk country.

[140]

Hounds

The most important influences on hound breeding were Belvoir, Peterborough and 'Cecil'.

About 1880 300 bitches came annually to Belvoir to be lined by Weathergauge and his relations. Breeders were getting colour as well as conformation. Tan was not uniform at Belvoir itself before about 1875;[112] but by 1880 'Brooksby' remarked on the beautiful uniformity of colouring.[113] Belvoir tan became the fashionable colour for a foxhound, and a bad but widespread reason for breeding to the kennel. Belvoir's influence in the matter of bone was equally marked. In 1914, 'legs and feet in the foxhound have been brought to the highest state of perfection during the last quarter of a century'. There was far more bone below the knee than in the hounds of the 1870s, and 'The best models of today knuckle over very slightly.'[114] Even Mr Chaplin bred for much more bone than Mr Foljambe or Lord Henry Bentinck had liked. The only major exception was Lord Fitzhardinge.

In 1859 the Cleveland Agricultural Society 'boldly broke the egg by associating an entry of foxhounds with its pristine endeavours in the way of encouraging the breeds of cattle and sheep'.[115] The Society's secretary was Mr Tom Parrington, Lord Feversham's agent and later master of the Sinnington; the idea was his and he gave the first cup. Peterborough took over from various Yorkshire *venues* in 1877, by which time a number of smaller local shows had also started.

Hounds bred at Belvoir but entered elsewhere won a great many prizes at the shows, and home-bred hounds of Belvoir blood and stamp a good many of the rest: but Belvoir itself never entered. A number of other masters also stood out. Lord Bathurst voiced the opinion of a large minority when he concluded that Peterborough did more harm than good because breeders were aiming for a winner on the flags.[116]

Pedigrees had always been recognized as important, especially by men who knew thoroughbred horses, but they were not always easy to come by. There was an enormous gap in the breeder's equipment, filled at last by 'Cecil'. This was Mr Cornelius Tongue, who hunted in the Albrighton country and had been one of Sir Bellingham Graham's original subscribers there in 1823. His researches enabled him to trace pedigrees back to 1787. The labour was enormous, largely because to a hound's name are attached the year and kennel of its entry, not of its breeding.[117] In 1864, at his own risk and cost, he published the *Foxhound Kennel Stud Book*, of which he then brought out a second volume. As Mr Weatherby's comparable *General Stud Book* was bought by the Jockey Club, so the *F.K.S.B.* was bought by the M.F.H.A. 'Cecil' died in 1884; he was succeeded as editor by the Rev. Cecil Legard, and he in 1905 by Mr Harry Preston.

Britain: 1850–1914

Horses and Horsemanship

There were very few thoroughbred hunters outside Leicestershire. Until about 1880 there were a lot of good halfbreds, but all over Britain the agricultural depression stopped farmers hunting and therefore hunter breeding.[118] Although they fully recovered the halfbred hunter never really did.

A lot of bad horses had been bred even in the prosperous days: farmers chose bad stallions – weedy cast-off thoroughbreds toured by dealers, or cocktails which often produced monsters out of halfbred mares – because their services were cheap. Sometimes there were no good stallions available.[119]

This problem was clearly recognized, and a solution proposed: 'Let the Master and Managing Committee of the County Fox-hounds make it part of their business to see that the district is never without the command of a good, sound thorough-bred stallion . . . Let such a horse, if necessary, be even the property of the Hunt, to stand at the kennel stables.'[120] This did happen, on an extremely limited scale.

The first major attempt to improve hunter breeding was by way of shows. The Royal Agricultural Society had toyed with them, but its committee had no interest in well-bred horses and in 1860 'There has never been a thoroughly good entry of hunter stallions'. This was also true of the Yorkshire, Lancashire, Lincoln and Dublin Societies. The serious pioneer, as in hound shows, was the Cleveland Society. Its 1860 show at Middlesborough offered a £100 premium for the best thoroughbred stallion for non-racing as well as turf purposes; the winner was Lord Zetland's immortal Voltigeur, then thirteen. The Royal at long last copied this idea at its shows at Leeds (1861), Battersea (1862) and Worcester (1863).[121]

In 1885, at a time of clear crisis in hunter breeding, the Hunter Improvement Society was founded and held its first London show. In 1888 its fourth show provided eight fifty-guinea premiums and four more of twenty-five guineas. Premium stallions were each to serve twenty mares belonging to tenant farmers at a fee not exceeding £2 10s. The year before this the Duke of Portland, as Master of the Horse, told the Jockey Club that the money provided for the Queen's Plates at various racecourses could be put to better use, and in 1888 the Royal Commission on Horse Breeding, of which the duke was *ex officio* president, held the first Queen's Premium Stallion show at Nottingham. In 1889, at the Royal Agricultural Hall, Islington, the two movements combined: twenty-two premiums of £200 each were offered by the Royal Commission, and a further three by the Royal Agricultural Society. In 1911 the Board of Agriculture took over the Premium Stallion scheme from the Royal Commission; it gave fifty premiums, the value varying with the number of mares covered and foals sired.[122]

The major drawback to all this was the dearth of suitable mares. The light-legged cart mare was rare by the end of the century and virtually extinct in the next, as was the similar pack mare, because transport no longer required them.[123]

The covert hack was an invariable part of a good hunting stud in the Shires in the first half of the century, though not elsewhere; in 1860 there were still a great many covert hacks in Leicestershire, of which the best were thoroughbreds either too small for training or – like Mr Sawyer's Jack-a-Dandy – the victims of peculiar careers.[124] But in the next twenty years the covert hack became quite unusual, owing to the wheel or to economy.

The double bridle was almost universal in the first half of the 19th century. Many people continued to believe that even the best-mouthed horses went better in a curb,[125] but the simple snaffle regained its popularity so fast that by 1864 it was said to be used by the majority.[126] The Pelham, though popular in Ireland, was never much liked in England.[127]

In the early 19th century the hunting saddle invariably had half-inch pads in the flaps to support the knees. From about 1840 hunt servants began to use plain-flapped saddles, which were cheaper though more slippery; these grew in popularity, and Whyte Melville was one of many serious horsemen who actually preferred them.[128] They became almost universal in the Shires, but in countries less sensitive to fashion padded flaps were still usual. Elderly persons used quilted saddles.[129]

The woollen girth was commonest, but leather began to be used in two forms. Mr Froude Bellew said about 1880, 'I prefer and use the open stamped leather girths, a great improvement on non-ventilating woollen girths.' There was also a colonial pattern, introduced about 1870, of plaited rawhide, 'used and praised by hunting men' because it did not slip.[130]

There was a swing away from the extreme ideas of 'Nimrod' about keeping hunters in all summer. They were given their grass and their freedom, their tails being left long to deal with flies. The important part of 'Nimrod's' crusade did survive: hunters were brought in in good time, and worked and fed to get fit, before they were asked to gallop all day in November.

Clipping became almost invariable. Good clippers – English, French or American – were freely available by 1870. The practice of shaving was dead. Instead singeing became quite widespread, growing with the availability of gas. No one thought of trace or other partial clipping before about 1870; leaving the saddle mark was then introduced, but by many people much opposed on the grounds that there, more than anywhere, a horse sweated. Legs were always fully clipped to make life easier for grooms.

Stable design was gradually but entirely changed: new stables had looseboxes instead of stalls. All good stables had their own boilers: 'It is a great mistake to permit the grooms to be dependent on the cook for supplies of hot water.' Lighting of stables was by oil lamps instead of tallow-dip or horn lantern.[131]

Stable management, feeding and routine veterinary attention all immensely improved. The writings and teachings of Captain Horace Hayes acquired an almost biblical authority, to the benefit of tens of thousands of horses.

Hunting Clothes

'*Correct costume* is essential in the hunting-field,' said Lord Henry Bentinck.[132] Serious persons, said Whyte Melville at about the same time, will 'order coats from Poole, boots from Bartley, and horses from Mason to display the same wherever they think they are most likely to be admired'.[133] The scarlet coat did not much change in cut after it had re-acquired a practical shape: but it was subjected to new hazards of grease and top dressing. *Eau écarlate* – principally pure nitric acid – was the specific for taking out stains; it cost a guinea a bottle.

The proportion of scarlet coats in the field diminished with distance from the Shires. In some hunts there were none except for master and staff, and in very many others, in remoter places, a maximum of half a dozen. Parsons always and farmers usually wore black coats. The few farmers who vaingloriously wore scarlet because they subscribed £10 a year were mocked by Trollope and by their neighbours.[134]

Velvet caps had been used to distinguish hunt staff, then spread to the field for the reasons of comfort and safety. In 1868, says 'Scrutator', 'they are adopted by every sporting man who would be thought a sportsman'.[135] 'Scrutator' was a

'COME HUP! I SAY – YOU UGLY BEAST!'
Mr Jorrocks is here uttering the phrase perhaps most often quoted of all his remarks, owing to its continual relevance. He would, in many people's view, be better to turn away from his horse: they follow the backs of heads more readily than faces, a lesson demonstrated daily behind the starting-stalls during the flat-racing season.

provincial. When Mr Sawyer went to Market Harborough his provincial's cap rendered him identifiable, at a great distance, in the largest field: it was not *mal vu*, but it was unique in a Pytchley field.[136] All the rest wore tall hats, which had gone from beaver to silk when Sir Robert Peel removed the duty on silk.

The high cravat gave way to the neckcloth (still so-called), normally of 'blue bird's eye', about 1850. The white stock became usual some twenty-five years later.

Top boots of the modern type almost universally replaced the Blucher or Wellington types, although fashion flirted with 'butcher-boots'. A good boot required a thin leg. Mr Sawyer's thick calves dismayed a fashionable London bootmaker: 'I could have made you, now, a particularly neat *provincial* boot; but with this pattern it's exceedingly difficult to attain the correct appearance for the flying countries.'[137]

Gloves went from buckskin to doeskin to calfskin, usual by 1870; worsted gloves were worn in wet weather to grip the reins better.

The experience of the cavalry in the Crimea universalized the flannel shirt, 'one of the greatest comforts of the hunting man. With the flannel shirt came another friend in cold weather – elastic woollen drawers.'[138]

One aspect of dress, seldom seen by subscribers but taken seriously by Masters of Hounds because it reflected on the hunt's local reputation, was that of the hunt staff when taking out hounds or horses in the summer. '*At exercise* the men are all to be dressed alike, either round hats and leggings, or high hats and boots.'[139]

Hunting Ladies

In 1850 the number of women who hunted was very small, and was limited, with few exceptions, to the immediate families of Masters of Hounds – to ladies brought up in the shadow of stable and kennel.

In the second half of the century growth was continual, rapid and widely deplored. It began in the Shires. Mr Sawyer, emerging from the provinces to Market Harborough, found ladies hunting in numbers that amazed him.[140] It spread quickly to other fashionable hunts, even those far from Leicestershire, such as the Duke of Beaufort's and Lord Eglinton's. In other areas it remained unusual – 'Aesop' makes a point of mentioning, as locally without precedent, that a handful of ladies rode to Mr James Dear's harriers near Winchester in the 1860s.[141] The 'hunting-horn' crutch and the tight skirt had made jumping feasible, but hunting without jumping, as with the Devon and Somerset Staghounds, had an early and obvious attraction to ladies.[142]

'Huntresses' (a word sometimes deplored, but used by Trollope)[143] were seen at once to fall into several categories.

Two groups rode really well and knew how to behave in the hunting field: the daughters of great houses and the professionals. Most spectacular of the former was the Empress of Austria; one of the bravest was Lady Harrington, who lost the sight of one eye while hunting with Mr Coupland, and got it back after a fall in a race.[144] There were many professionals, well known in Rotten Row and the Shires; they 'pursue and improve their business as horse-breakers in the hunting-field with extraordinary skill and nerve – a very useful class. These perfectly well know how to take care of themselves. Young ladies may derive many useful hints by noting, in silence, their performances.'[145] There were also teachers and exhibition riders, such as Lady Stamford who worked in a circus before her marriage.

A third group was equally competent but far less elegant. They 'acquire a really strong seat, ride hard to hounds, handle the reins with more or less skill, but present an appearance painful to contemplate. Amongst such may be counted the daughters of hard-riding hunter-breeding farmers, as well as ladies of fortune who never hear the jokes of their flatterers or see the caricatures that are handed round when they have left the room.' 'Not to put too fine a point on it, the majority of horsewomen ride abominably.'[146]

A fourth group followed the others in time and, beginning slowly, at last overwhelmed them in numbers: ladies who liked going hunting and to whom means and emancipation permitted it. With reservations Trollope welcomed them: 'Women who ride, as a rule, ride better than men', having been, by 1870, better taught; they had naturally better hands; they improved the atmosphere of the hunting field.[147] Old-fashioned and provincial persons like 'Scrutator' disapproved because hunting was unfeminine: but his real complaint was that gentlemen had to stop and help the ladies when they fell.[148]

This points to the central male objection: the creatures needed looking after. They needed pilots and jumped far too close to them; they needed gates opened; they talked too much. Kitty Trewson 'considers her presence at the covert-side one of the great attractions which give distinction to the Meadowmere Hounds'; she is pretty; she is quite brave; but she heads foxes and whips hounds, and she wants her girth tightened just as hounds burst out of covert for the run of the season.[149] Whyte Melville saw, with unaffected admiration, Victorian feminists becoming pre-eminent in shooting, deerstalking, tennis and hunting: but how they do press hounds![150] Lord Henry Bentinck's anonymous female collaborator commanded: 'Be careful never to presume on your sex by jumping out of your turn, or by elbowing your way through a crowded gateway . . . People out hunting – and, sad to say, women in particular – are often so selfish that they think only of getting to the front themselves, even at the expense of other people.'[151] But ladies continued to ride jealous and to override hounds: and they were far harder for a master to stop than men, especially if their husbands or fathers were big subscribers.[152]

There were other hazards for incautious ladies. 'A middle-aged woman of fortune can do anything she likes without exciting the anxious sympathies of lookers-on, whether she is ducked in a brook or rides home in a fly *tête-à-tête* with a horse-breaker.' But a young lady had to be extremely careful what she did and whom she talked to. It was impossible to go to a distant meet by train or chaise with a gentleman; it was impossible to come home in a coach unchaperoned, as Arabella Trefoil did with Lord Rufford to the shocked dismay of her relations.[153] There was a worse trap still: 'the young lady who has become of the horse horsey has made a fearful, almost a fatal mistake.'[154]

Women continued privileged exotics until sheer numbers changed masculine attitudes. Half the field cannot be a special case. This had happened in some countries by 1900, in many by 1914.

A very tight habit was at first considered indelicate, as revealing the contour of the hips concealed by bustle or crinoline: but it was much safer than a full one because it did not catch on pommel or stirrup in the event of a fall. More indelicate was the loss of the skirt; a lady who falls 'may cut a very ridiculous figure in her trousers without a skirt – an incident which really happened to the daughter of a distinguished master of hounds'.[155] Once again attitudes changed: the safety habit became invariable by the end of the century, its merit being that it came off if it got caught. Colours of habits varied; they were usually black, green or snuff-coloured.

In 1850 ladies sometimes hunted in beaver hats, but usually in low-crowned hats with plumes. The silk hat with a veil was invented, about 1865, in Leicestershire, allegedly by Skittles. A large false hairpiece was often part of the Diana's headdress; it sometimes fell off.

In most places a lady riding astride was unheard of before 1914. But the scandal had begun: Lord Annaly had to forbid it to the ladies of the Pytchley.

Manners, Parties, Races, Parsons and Boxes

The fulltime hunting men of the early 19th century – the 'Four Ms', the members of the Melton and Pytchley Clubs – disappeared towards its end. A Leicestershire first flight would by 1860 include 'a soldier, a statesman, a poet, a painter, or a Master in Chancery, whilst "maddening in the rear" through the gates come a posse of authors, actors, amateurs, artists, of every description'.[156]

A landowner new to the country had problems. 'For a new man, in the sense of the French term *nouveau riche*, to obtain admission into a county hunting club is almost as difficult as to be balloted into the most exclusive clubs of London, say White's or the Travellers'.' A frequent means of securing acceptance was to entertain master and field: 'When a rich migrant from town to country life, with all his way

THE HORSE SHOW AT ISLINGTON: TRYING THE HUNTERS

The Royal Agricultural Hall, Islington, saw in 1889 the second Queen's Premium Stallion Show, and the first in which the Royal Commission on Horse-Breeding combined with the Royal Agricultural Society and the Hunter Improvement Society, then four years old. The show was held in this hall except in 1918–19, when it was at Newmarket; it moved to Derby after World War II. Working hunters, as well as show horses and ponies in various categories, had their own classes; sometimes, but not always, the judges rode them as part of judging them. It remains a matter of dispute whether this is desirable, but it is hard to see why.

to make in the country, settles down in a mansion to which a famous fox-covert is annexed, where it has been usual from time immemorial to precede the drawing by a breakfast-meet . . . the arrangement of the entertainment becomes a matter of serious consideration . . . When the meet runs up to and over a hundred horsemen, no one but a millionaire should attempt hot dishes.' Joints requiring much carving were a mistake. As to drink: 'Six dozen of really good sherry at a hunt breakfast have been known to establish the reputation of a new resident, and £10 would probably represent the difference between a superior and a common article. The brandy should be old; the ale the cleanest tap that Burton or Stratford-on-Avon can produce.' There should be mulled claret and cherry brandy (Danish, not English) for gentlemen not wishing to leave their horses: for the others fifty countrymen should be engaged, at a shilling each, to hold two horses apiece.[157]

The trouble was that hunt breakfasts were too lavish. Finch Mason's socially aspiring Mr and Mrs Peter Piper, determined to lure the duke to their hunt breakfast, filled the parson so full that he was unable to take the service on Christmas day.[158] Into the 20th century many gentlemen (though few ladies) were more seriously injured when they fell from eating too much, and fell more frequently from drinking too much.[159] Mr Leonard Hatton of Kempsey, Worcestershire, gave such tremendous champagne breakfasts just before the war that hounds were almost always injured by drunken riders.[160]

Hunt Club dinners had long been normal. The Keepers' Dinner (at midday) was an exercise in public relations of fully equal importance in pheasant-shooting countries. The M.F.H. always presided; the songs and toasts were interminable.[161]

As the womenfolk of landowners were wooed at the hunt ball, so were farmers and their families at the hunt races. These continued to vary enormously, some being normal professional racing (often on the flat) organized by a hunt instead of by a municipality, an innkeeper or a regiment: and some being amateur cross-country scrambles of the old kind, at which the spectators were hardly considered. These were still being got up in the Shires in the 1850s, but many people disliked them. The races were apt not to fill; dubious 'gentlemen' were put up by some owners; and it was difficult to find a handicapper everyone trusted.[162] Between these extremes there were 'very inferior' hurdle races and steeplechases, like the Hambledon's in 1855 and 1856, which were in effect professional 'flapping' races, and such amateur hurdle races as the H.H. put on in the same period.[163]

In 1857 Dr Fothergill Rowlands proposed a great race in the Shires for genuine hunters ridden by genuine amateurs; the first (a failure) was at Market Harborough in 1859, the second (a success) at the same place the following year, and the third at Cheltenham. These events inspired the formation of the National Hunt Committee and the drawing up of its rules. They also inspired widespread imitation. There were during the 1860s plenty of races, held under various auspices, limited to hunters; these had to be certified by Masters of Hounds as having been fairly hunted. Masters were far too lenient. Horses only had to show themselves beside the first covert. In the 1870s the certification of hunters became 'something which bears a very close resemblance to an impudent swindle'.[164]

The racing put on by hunts and the racing of certified hunters came together, at an uncertain date, to produce the first point-to-points in the modern sense. The first members'-only hunt steeplechase was apparently the Oakley's in Mr Arkwright's time,[165] and the Worcestershire held a Red Coat Race, *eo nomine*, in 1883.[166] Many hunts followed almost at once and most by 1900. Members rode in scarlet and top hats. There were also farmers' races, very popular until 1914, equally amateur in theory and often in practice; farmers wore black coats and billycocks. Only strangers wore racing colours. Although the prizes were small, betting was sometimes heavy: much point-to-point racing was therefore extremely dishonest. Its function was nevertheless achieved – the farmers' families had a great day out and a great deal to drink, and the festival attracted far larger crowds than the puppy show.

There was little discussion about parsons in the hunting field before 1850, not because parsons did not hunt but because their hunting was taken for granted. Other professional men rode to hounds – lawyers, doctors, politicians, soldiers – and parsons were not deemed different. This changed dramatically. Bishops Philpotts of Exeter and Wilberforce of Oxford took a high moral line with their clergy on the subject, and then the whole Evangelical movement, low-church and censorious, raised its middle-class voice. Parsons in the 1840s could play whist, dance a quadrille, go to the theatre and ride to hounds: but twenty years later Trollope noted that even the most experienced foxhunting parsons were self-conscious and shamefaced about it. They no longer dared wear purple coats; they often, for decorum, wore black trousers over their hunting breeches.[167] 'There is a strong feeling', in 1868, 'against a clergyman who hunts.'[168] A few years later, 'their number and wholesome influence on the hunting-field is rapidly diminishing'.[169] There was pressure from bishops, newspapers, old ladies and – strongest of all – non-hunting clergy: 'We know how many of them deny themselves a harmless pleasure rather than offend "the weaker brethren".'[170]

Opinion relaxed in the tolerant Edwardian period: but the Rev. E. A. Milne was as rare a bird in the early 20th century as he would have been common in the early 19th.

If the church hunted less, royalty hunted more. Prince Albert had his own harriers and hunted a few times from Belvoir. The Prince of Wales (Edward VII) first went out with Lord Macclesfield's South Oxfordshire hounds; he saw his first fox killed in February 1860. He later hunted regularly with the Blankney, Pytchley and Belvoir. Queen Victoria did not really approve, but she much preferred hunting to the raffishness of the turf or the plutocratic exclusivity of pheasant shooting.

Hunting boxes were special to countries where people came to stay for the season. The first were in or near Melton: converted farmhouses or inns and, by 1850, a few built specially. There were some hunting boxes, though never many, in outstanding provincial countries like Warwickshire and the Duke of Beaufort's. The requirements of such houses were special. Ideally they were designed so that good service was possible with a small indoor staff. A big boot room downstairs stopped mud being carried all over the house; a big drying room was necessary; so was a big drink cupboard near the dining room in order that constant journeys did not have to be made to the cellar. 'To have full-sized hot baths for half a dozen persons is simply impossible' in 1870. The answer lay in cold or tepid baths, douches, hot-air baths, sitz baths, sheet baths taken in a pig-scalding tub, and packing baths, in which the foxhunter buried himself in hot-water bottles. Hot pipes were, at this early date, to run along all passages. 'Roberts's portable terra-cotta slow combustion stoves should be in the bedrooms of every hunting-box', as should 'Tobin's ventilating tubes'.

Breakfast was normally 'a hot cutlet, a couple of eggs, a plateful of cold meat, washed down with two cups of tea, a glass of curaçao, and a pint of ale'. Claret and water was a recommended breakfast beverage. The flask was to be filled, without fail, before setting out: a nip of neat brandy or whisky had replaced bleeding as the accepted treatment for a man knocked unconscious in the hunting field.

The requirement of a hunting dinner was that it could be kept hot without spoiling, or cooked quickly. Clear *potage* was considered more easily digestible than thick *purée*; dry sherry was drunk with it; alternatives were *pot au feu* or Aberdeen tinned soups. Fried sole was a favourite fish course because it could be cooked while the soup was being drunk; the game course, for the same reason, was snipe or plover rather than grouse or pheasant. One *entrée* was enough: cutlets or rissoles, cooked quickly, or stewed mutton, which could be kept hot; and 'There is nothing easier of digestion or more succulent than a steak of red deer venison broiled'.[171]

Masters, Servants, Subscribers and Laws

The *Rural Almanack* of 1874 listed fourteen packs of foxhounds in Britain maintained without subscription. There were a few others, known only locally, of which the compilers of the *Almanack* were unaware. The remaining 122 packs were maintained by subscription, this either coming from a club (sometimes exclusive) or 'open to any man willing to pay the fixed minimum contribution, and behave with common decency in the field'. Such payment did not of itself entitle the contributor to button or collar.[172]

Some subscription packs had the same management for a long time. The local standing of the hunt, and breeding continuity in the kennel, were then comparable to those of the great family packs. This was true even when the master's fortune was a new one. At the other extreme, a subscription pack like the South Wold was 'bandied from hand to hand every few years', to the detriment of its kennel and its relations with the country. Persons took on the mastership for the wrong reasons (usually snobbery), and resigned, on financial grounds, as they began to learn the job.[173]

More competent, but still bad for a country, were the 'professional' Masters of Hounds, itinerant like Osbaldeston and Sir Bellingham Graham but without their own packs, whom club or committee picked when no local candidate could be found. 'Does he do all that cursing and swearing for the £2,000?' asked Senator Gotobed of Captain Glomax, who tried to show sport more for the sake of his professional reputation than for the members of the 'Ufford and Rufford United'.[174] It was possible for a master of this kind to live on his guarantee, having paid all expenses, as late as 1914;[175] but such 'itinerant contractors for hunting' were naturally tight-fisted: they mounted their men deplorably, they skimped on feed and fuel, they referred all claims to the committee. This was always a mistake and often a disaster. The M.F.H., said Trollope, should be local if possible, but above all he should be rich. 'Grease to the wheels – plentiful grease to the wheels – is needed in all machinery; but I know of no machinery in which ever-running grease is so necessary as in the machinery of hunting.'[176]

Under these circumstances the proper scale of the establishment, and the consequent size of the outlay, was a matter of disagreement. 'Scrutator' thought expenses had got completely out of hand by 1860 in 'our huge overgrown fox-hunting establishments'. Twenty-five couple were taken out instead of sixteen to eighteen; eighty couple were kept in kennel instead of forty or fifty, ample for a three-day country.[177] But 'Scrutator' hunted economically as a squire with a private pack; in 1870 Trollope declared that it was proper even for a very rich man to take £500 for each day a week he undertook to hunt. Clearly no one could manage kennel, stable, staff and country, hunting three days a week, for as little as £1,500; the master

THE HUNT STABLES AT BADMINTON
The stables were rebuilt by the 8th Duke of Beaufort; the last row of boxes was finished in 1860. The horses in them benefited immensely by the experience and teaching of the previous forty years. Every one had a loose-box, which gave it freedom to walk about and lie down; every box was thoroughly ventilated. The mangers and hay-racks were oak; each had an iron bar so placed as to prevent crib-biting; the troughs were slate (an idea introduced by Mr Thomas Assheton Smith at Tedworth) for the same reason. The floors were exactly level, with no drainage; it was thought better to clean them out completely and fork in fresh straw than to risk the stink and contagion of drains. It was also considered better for a horse to stand on the flat than on a slope. This is, in both regards, a more disputable point of design.

Reference to Plan.
A. Part of stable. 13 loose boxes.
B. Part of stable. 6 stalls.
C. Drug room.
D. Little coach-house.
E. Coach wash-house.
F. Fire engine.
G. Open yard.
H. Horse wash-house.
J. Cleaning room.
K. Saddle room.
L. Stable. 9 loose boxes.
M. Groom's room.
N. Stable. 18 loose boxes.
O. Stable. 20 loose boxes.
P. Covered pathway.
R. Straw house.
S. Hay house.
T. Granary with floor over.
V. Covered shed for unloading hay and straw.
X. Water taps.

must have money to spend and he must spend it.[178] Even £1,500 was not easily raised. The usual minimum subscription in 1870 was £25; and visitors were not asked for anything until they had been out three or four times.[179] This was asking too little. In 1868 a man could hunt four days a week, with seven horses, for £840 a year; his subscription should be at least £70.[180] 'With harriers', about 1870, 'a collection called "a cap" is generally made before the hounds throw off, of from two shillings and sixpence to five shillings, from each non-subscriber.'[181] This was introduced to foxhunting on only a very limited scale before 1900.

Apart from its absolute inadequacy, the two dreadful disadvantages of subscription remained exactly the same. In 1868, as at earlier periods, subscribers 'always think themselves entitled to have a hand in the game, or, rather, a voice in the vote; they have a right to holloa whenever so disposed; to ride over hounds if in their way . . .'[182] Big subscribers had to be treated with a deference which was barely tolerable: the master has to wait half an hour for Lord Giltedge, and then watch his nephew, unreproved, jump on to a favourite hound.[183] Almost worse was the man in the Bicester country of whom Mr T. T. Drake said: 'He doesn't know the rudiments of hunting. He doesn't know how to subscribe.'[184] As many masters as ever gave up for non-payment of subscription, of the Quorn as well as of the North Durham.

In the field the master should be 'an urbane man, but not too urbane'.[185] Lord Spencer showed that it was possible to keep even a Pytchley Wednesday field under control without swearing, but soft masters allowed sport to be spoiled and damage to be done. Personal popularity was more important among the farmers even than among the field; when a master was disliked in the countryside walks became impossible, foxes were trapped, gates were locked and wire appeared where it had never been before.[186] But popularity could be bought at too high a price: over-lavish wooing of the farmers, like Mr Hoare's in the V.W.H. country, lost a master respect among the gentry. Mr Hoare's career also reminds us that Masters of Hounds were eminent public persons – said, by enduring if baseless legend, to take precedence in the county only after the Lord Lieutenant – in whom private immorality must not be detected.

If an outsider was a confession of local failure, a committee mastership was a greater one. 'Nothing for hunting purposes can be much worse.'[187] But not always. There were committees of experienced local sportsmen, one of whose members acted as master with the loyal support of the others, which were much better than an incompetent or dictatorial individual, or an outsider with a living to make.

'Scrutator' in 1865 counted thirty packs, of 130, hunted by amateurs.[188] The 100 professional huntsmen of the time were 'as a body, an intelligent, sober, thoughtful class'.[189] There were exceptions. Certain localities seem to have exerted an evil influence on successive generations of hunt servants, especially, for obscure reasons, the respectable town of Cirencester.[190] Huntsmen were moderately paid. Collections, sometimes munificent, were taken when they retired. They no longer capped at a kill, but they sometimes sold the brush, even though the dead fox was the property of the master. The pads were a perquisite of huntsman and whips: for this 'The second Earl of Lonsdale gave Hugo Meynell for his authority'.[191] Whippers-in were usually more serious students of hunting than earlier in the century; they hoped to be huntsmen and many were very well taught. Second horsemen were still a problem; some wanted to go hunting and many left gates undone.

Hunt staff were without question more considerately treated towards the end of the century. An example was the timing of meets in the spring. In early March, hounds had met at 9.30 instead of 10.30 or 11; in late March as early as 8 a.m.; in April 6.30 or even 6. But in 1900, March and April meets were noon or afternoon, the reason being that hunt staff were busy with young hounds and whelps.[192]

The Masters of Hounds who belonged to Boodle's Club continued to meet and to discuss, in a way at once casual but influential, the questions of disputed coverts which were brought to their attention. In 1856 it became clear that a somewhat more formal tribunal was desirable. Twenty-four members of Boodle's, all being present or past Masters of Foxhounds, agreed on the formation of a committee, which was chosen at a meeting on 19 July 1856. Lord Redesdale was elected Chairman of a committee of six. The Masters of Foxhounds Committee, or Foxhunting Committee of Boodle's, functioned with energy and goodwill. It was called upon many times, the most widely discussed dispute being that between Mr Coupland and Sir Bache Cunard in 1878. This regrettable affair reminded all concerned of the central weakness of the arrangement: it was only after much time and argument that Sir Bache consented to arbitration by Boodle's, and he was in no way bound to submit to it.

In 1880, for reasons now obscure, there was a quarrel between the management of Boodle's Club and its foxhunting members. 'The hunting men retired in a body, and Boodle's seems likely to lose all that made it distinguished.'[193] Foxhunting's government disappeared. The Duke of Beaufort therefore wrote a circular letter to all Masters of Foxhounds, inviting them to a meeting the object of which was to form a new body. This meeting took place at Tattersalls on 2 June 1881, and the Masters of Foxhounds Association was formed. Its role as arbiter was the same as the Boodle's committee's, but its standing was far higher because it represented a much larger number of masters and therefore of packs, clubs, and hunting people. Previously, a hunt had been 'recognized' if people had heard of it; the new organization made possible the new concept of an officially recognized hunt, which in turn made possible the rigid enforcement of foxhunting's unwritten laws. In 1886 the M.F.H.A. took over the *F.K.S.B.* from 'Cecil'; its writ thus ran, following the invaluable precedent of the Jockey Club, over hound pedigrees as well as hunt conduct. In 1891 the Association of Masters of Harriers and Beagles was formed in imitation. By this time the hunting men had rejoined Boodle's.

Foxhunting was subject not only to its own unwritten laws, but also to the written ones of the realm. The relevant laws related to trespass. A tradition had existed time out of mind that hounds could go wherever their quarry went, followed by anyone riding to them. The case of Essex *v.* Capel in 1809 had firmly disposed of this notion, but it crept back. In 1850 it was generally believed that hounds could be debarred from drawing a covert, but a hunt could not be forbidden to cross an estate once hounds were running. In 1878, however, the case of Paul and another *v.* Summerhayes was heard in the Queen's Bench Division; Lord Coleridge held that foxhunting did not give unrestricted right of trespass, and Mr Justice Mellor remarked, 'no one can suppose that ladies and gentlemen of position go down to Melton to kill vermin'. This did not change rural opinion in sporting areas; it did remind the world that foxhunting existed on sufferance.

Countryside, Society and Opinion

In 1859 'The Druid' looked back on the golden age of fifty years earlier: 'Never was a period more propitious for the chase . . . The country was not grid-ironed by railways, nor did steam-engines impregnate the air with noxious gas. There were not two or three men draining in every field. Hunting was then at its culminating point. Modern science has doubtless filled the pockets of the jobber and the speculator, but it has gone far to destroy the noblest pursuit which the Gods ever bestowed on mortals.' Railways were still being built, and all round Melton itself, in 1880:[194] 'Railways *in being* are hateful and sport-spoiling enough; but railways in progress are to a hunting country as the Colorado beetle to the potato.' While hounds and horses could get used to rails and engines, no country could be hunted while gangs of navvies, poachers to a man, beat every covert an hour before it was drawn.[195] Trollope concluded that all the damage railways had been expected to do they had done: but in the upshot hunting benefited: 'hunting has more than doubled, instead of being crippled by the railroads'.[196] Not only the jobber and the speculator profited. Oakham, Leamington, Leicester, Rugby, Northampton, Oxford, Swindon, Chelmsford, Basingstoke could all be reached conveniently by rail from London; an early start enabled a Londoner to make an 11 o'clock meet of the Pytchley, and there was time for a civilized breakfast before catching a train for a day's hunting with the O.B.H., Puckeridge, Whaddon Chase, or the Kent and Surrey packs. 'The multiplicity of railways and the existing plethora of money has so increased the number of sportsmen, that to keep a nag or two near some well-known station, is nearly as common as to die.'[197]

The railway journeys of the period arouse today a nostalgia as keen as 'The Druid's': 'The railway directors of the best hunting lines run specials, and put on *drop* carriages to express trains, for the accommodation of hunting men. A party of from half a dozen to a dozen can engage a saloon carriage, provided with a dressing-room and even cooking arrangements. The finishing stroke has been put to the luxuries of hunting by the addition of American sleeping-cars – dressing-rooms by day, bedrooms by night – so that you may breakfast going down, dine, or take tea, and sleep or play whist returning. The Midland and London and North-Western Companies have found it worth while to make direct extensions for the accommodation of hunting-men; and all over the kingdom the locomotive has become a hunting machine.'[198]

Horses often, hounds occasionally, were carried by train too. A hunt with a big country or one of awkward shape had always used outlying kennels to draw its remoter coverts, a week or two being spent there. It became convenient for some hunts (the Duke of Buccleuch's and the York and Ainsty regularly, others occasion-

THE QUORN, 1895
This was the second season of Lord Lonsdale's mastership, in which the turnout of the hunt staff and the quality of their horses were as superb as at any time even in the Quorn's resplendent history; and the field was disciplined with a rigour never before or since suffered in the Shires. The great merit of the master's tyranny was that Tom Firr was given room to work. The latter had been breeding the pack for twenty-three years at the date of this picture, building on Mr Coupland's great work and cherishing the blood of Alfred. He was also – even he – beguiled by the beauty of the notorious Rufford Galliard, a Peterborough winner, who began to fill the kennel with softness until his influence was identified and bred out. Hounds are here drawing Walton Thorns, one of several famous coverts drawn after a meet at Six Hills, six miles from Melton. 'The Thorns,' said 'Brooksby', 'are seldom untenanted, no matter how often appealed to.' Painting by Major G. D. Giles. By courtesy of Fores Ltd.

ally) to make brief excursions to faraway places, which the train alone made possible until the invention of the motor hound van. This was first used about 1900.

Cars were by the turn of the century beginning to be covert hacks. There was no harm in this, as the car went no farther than the meet. But people were beginning to try to follow the hunt in cars: to an M.F.H. as early as 1901 they were 'those inventions of the Evil One, motor cars'.[199]

Besides the steam plough, major agricultural novelties in many places were winter wheat, seed clover, reseeded grass reclaimed after the depression, and various sorts of fertilizer. By small fields, and when the ground was not very wet, wheat could be ridden over without much damage; but clover and new grass were badly damaged either by the breaking of the stem or by little puddles forming in the hoof prints. The result was an earlier end to the season; nearly everywhere in 1850 foxes were hunted to the end of April, but in 1900 most hunts closed the season early in the month. Only in wild or hill areas, where foxes had to be killed and no damage could be done, was late-April hunting still usual.[200] Fish manure, pig muck and chemicals all stained the ground and sometimes destroyed scent entirely; chemicals also destroyed hunting coats.

A lot of new coverts were planted between 1800 and 1850, but many more in the next sixty years. Some countries, and especially the very best, had far too many

[153]

small gorse coverts too close together; the very long runs of the past became impossible without repeated changes of fox. The new coverts, being impenetrable to poachers, were also full of rabbits, the effect of which was to make foxes less inclined to travel. This, with railway navvies, swarming foot people, and hard-riding 'captains', was blamed for making sport in the Shires far worse in 1888 than fifty years earlier.[201]

One other factor was blamed: the much greater numbers of sheep and cattle. These brought more stain, more people, more cur dogs; and in the 1850s they brought wire. 'Wire-fencing and the increase of sheep-feeding are the greatest obstacles to fox-hunting.'[202] Sheep could be contained by a dense hedge or a wall; at a heavy labour cost they could be folded in hurdles; but their increasing financial importance coincided with the availability of wire and the result was inevitable. Well-stretched wire on good posts also contained cattle as effectively as a cut-and-laid that took thirty years to grow, or rails that cost far more in materials and labour. Wire appeared in the Quorn country in Sir Richard Sutton's time and became a problem in Lord Stamford's (1856 *et seq.*). It was said to be a danger to life in the Atherstone country in 1862; Mr Tailby had to make efforts to remove it in south Leicestershire in 1863.

'The *curse* to hunting in the present day', said Lord Henry Bentinck, 'is *wire* – in very many cases put up without necessity or without regard to common sense.'[203] Wire was a godsend to undercapitalized tenant farmers; but its appearance in a country followed a pattern controlled by other things than agricultural method or available credit. Where many farmers hunted, however unpretentiously, there was no wire, as in Worcestershire in the 1860s.[204] Where a Master of Hounds had tremendous popularity and influence there was no wire, as in Warwickshire in the 18th Lord Willoughby de Broke's time or the Cattistock country in Mr Milne's. But where a master or his huntsman was unpopular with the farmers, wire appeared where it had never been and where it was hardly needed. It must be added that, where sheep were the principal industry, wire was inevitable even in a country as sporting as the United's in Shropshire.

Wire came (as it comes still) visible and invisible, predictable and unexpected. In the Shires it was 'set up broadly and ostentatiously with a line of posts'; in provincial countries it was 'twined through the tops of thorns', hard to see and very dangerous indeed.[205] There were several deaths.

Barbed wire first appeared in England in 1882.

There were thought to be three usual reasons for the use of wire, right up to 1914. First, small tenant farmers could genuinely afford no other sort of fencing. Secondly, socially resentful or personally vengeful farmers strung it up in a spirit of pure bloody-mindedness – a motive portrayed by Kipling.[206] Thirdly, large landowners, pretending to be friends of foxhunting in order to retain local popularity, used it or allowed it to be used so that they could save money to spend on their racehorses, their pheasant shoots or, worst, their hunting establishments in other countries.[207]

In the early years of wire, Masters of Hounds tried to persuade farmers to build fences or plant hedges. Some succeeded to a remarkable degree. But by 1900 money spoke louder than Masters of Hounds. Some masters, like Lord Dudley in Worcestershire, replaced wire with rails which remained in position only until their backs were turned. Mr Smith Bosanquet, in a heavily wired country just before the first war, was the first to use on a large scale the modern idea of a hunt jump. With all its irritations and disadvantages, of zigzagging and waiting in line, this idea made unridable countries ridable, and kept hunting alive in places where it must otherwise have died.

In many countries an enemy to hunting at least as terrible as wire was pheasant shooting. Coverts were closed to hounds, sometimes until Christmas and sometimes all season, in all but the best grass countries or on empty hill. In Kent, Sussex, Surrey, Hertfordshire and even in more deeply rural areas like Worcestershire, a substantial proportion of the coverts were lost to the hunt. The mortality of foxes in pheasant coverts was as dreadful as ever. It remained true that absentee shooting tenants caused the severest closing of coverts and the greatest destruction of foxes, but resident owners who did their hunting elsewhere were still an unforgivable part of the problem in the home counties.

The trouble did not arise on bare hill, moor or wold because there was no pheasant shooting; it did not arise where the covert owners hunted as well as shot; and it did not arise where, simply, there was goodwill between the two fraternities: this was the glory of Norfolk, although its pheasant shooting was among the best and most expensive in England.

The most curious phenomenon of the period is that of the wholly unsporting area. This was commonest in Scotland. The first half of the 19th century had seen vigorous and well-supported hunting in Forfar, Perthshire and Aberdeenshire; about the middle of the century the people of these areas simply lost interest. Later the same thing happened in the Lothians. In England the most startling example is East Somerset – rural, ridable, with the right amount of covert, and with a long and lively foxhunting tradition. Even in the most unpromising parts of Kent hunts could establish themselves and, after a fashion, thrive: but neither the farmers nor the gentry of the Mendips showed a flicker of interest for half a century. This was inexplicable to 'Scrutator' and 'Brooksby' and it is inexplicable still.

Heavy industry was already damaging some countries by 1850; by 1914 it had virtually destroyed North Durham and the Wentworth country and wholly destroyed Lanarkshire. The suburban expansion of London, Bristol and Birmingham made large inroads into Hertfordshire, Surrey, Gloucestershire and Warwickshire. But hunting on balance benefited greatly from the growth of towns and their wealth: if the South Notts and Warwickshire fields were sometimes unmanageably swollen, subscriptions were plumper too. Even the Quorn felt this in 1880: 'the sporting proclivities of the city of Leicester are increasing in proportion as its hosiery and elastic web manufactures grow in importance.'[208] Resort towns continued crucial to the finances of local hunts, as Leamington to the North Warwickshire and Cheltenham to the Cotswold.

There were two changes in social attitudes, pushing in opposite directions.

On the one hand, the commercial middle class, enfranchised by the Reform Bill and enriched by the industrial revolution, made a deliberate and successful attempt to identify itself with the old squire class. Merchants sent their sons to the new public schools, of which many were founded, in imitation of Eton and Winchester, in the 1840s. They went to live in the country. They became gentlemen. This process was virtually unique to Britain; there was nothing new about it except its enormous scale. Hundreds of thousands of new gentry were recruits to foxhunting.

But the class next below stayed in the towns and began to voice its resentful disapproval. This was also new only in scale, but the scale became tremendous. Trollope's resentful lawyer's wife hated gentlemen and hated foxes; she bracketed the two; she was envious and ignorant, but she spoke for a large part of the lower middle classes.[209]

11 Ireland
to 1914

Background

Medieval Ireland killed stag, wolf, boar, fox, hare and marten in great numbers, because pelts were an important export. They had wolfhounds, deerhounds and 'beagles'; they also set traps and dug pits. The English occupation introduced the hunting of parked deer in the 'civilized' area round Dublin. Wild deer were hunted in the West and South by trencher-fed packs of staghounds. Harehunting was also popular.[1]

During the 18th century the Anglo–Irish aristocracy built large Georgian houses with stables and kennels in exact imitation of their cousins in England. There is no computing the number of private packs all over Ireland about 1750. There would probably have been more foxhunting if there had been more foxes. The hounds were Old Southern harriers. It is conceivable that hounds of this sort came to Ireland from England or even from Gascony at a much earlier date, but more likely that the bulk of them came in the late 17th and throughout the 18th centuries. They were regarded in 19th-century Ireland as 'old Irish hounds', but this only dates their arrival before living memory.

Establishment of Foxhunting

At the end of the 18th century Ireland was still full of the private packs of the gentry. Some were quite grand: Mr W. B. Ponsonby's Bishop's Court Hunt in Kildare wore 'Blue coat and velvet cape lined with buff, broad striped blue and buff waistcoat, and yellow buckskins. A fox's pate was embossed on the coat buttons, which bore also the words: "B's C.H."'[2] More typical were the neighbouring hounds of Mr Thomas Conolly of Castleton; the Squire was 'a very eccentric, jolly soul', who never asked anyone to dinner after hunting but expected everybody to come.[3]

All over huntable Ireland packs like these gradually amalgamated, under some person of strong character, who thus created a viable foxhunting country. The pack became known as the County Hounds, and was supported, in every way except financially, by a Hunt Club.

The pioneer of this process was Mr (later Sir) John Power, who in 1797 was invited, with his brother Richard, to Kilkenny. Mr Power had hunted at Quorndon, and everything that he did was in respectful imitation. He was the first man in Ireland to breed a pack of pure English blood, to hunt it on the Meynellian system,

MR WATSON, CARLOW AND ISLAND, 1871
The Watson family of Ballydarton, County Carlow, had hounds for a very long time. They were said to have killed the last wolf in Ireland. Grandson of the owner of that pack was Mr John Watson, pupil and protégé of Sir John Power of the Kilkenny, in imitation of whom he imported English hounds in 1808, planted gorse, and began foxhunting. About 1822 his hounds became a subscription pack named for the town of Tullow and managed by Mr John Whelan of Rath. In 1826 Mr Watson resumed control, now hunting hounds himself. In 1845 Mr Robert Watson began hunting his father's hounds, becoming, by universal consent, the best amateur in Ireland. The hounds were kennelled at Ballydarton; they were all home-bred, mostly by Belvoir, Brocklesby and Milton stallions. In 1853 Mr William Bolton's Island pack and country were offered to Lord Milton (later 6th Earl Fitzwilliam): he accepted, and handed them on at once to his close friends the Watsons. The Tullow or Ballydarton became the Carlow and Island. Mr John Watson, still titular M.F.H. at the age of eighty-three, died in 1869. Mr Robert Watson became owner and master. He hunted hounds – for a total of fifty-six years – until 1901. He retired in 1904, aged ninety-three, selling the pack to the country. The 7th Earl Fitzwilliam resumed the Island country, adding it to his Coollattin, but the two were hunted separately from 1907. Painting by Alfred S. Bishop. By courtesy of Arthur Ackermann & Son.

to plant gorse, and to define his boundaries; his was also the first County Hunt Club in the modern sense. Sportsmen came from all over Ireland to ride to his hounds, and to take part in the elaborate productions of Mr Richard Power's Kilkenny Theatricals.

His first imitator was Colonel William Wrixon in County Cork. He had inherited his family's Ballygiblin hounds, which had absorbed the near-by Castlecor; in 1800 he started the Duhallow Hunt Club, held frequent hunt dinners, changed to scarlet, and put on races twice a year. The next was Sir Fenton Aylmer in County Kildare. After Squire Conolly died and his hounds were sold out of the country, Sir Fenton got a new pack from England, renegotiated with the covert owners and with the heirs of Castleton and Bishop's Court, and started a new hunt. He went from blue to scarlet in 1808, and founded a Kildare Hunt Club in 1812. The club had outlying cellars wherever Sir Fenton had outlying kennels.

In County Wexford, Colonel Pigott of Slevoy Castle had a well-known private pack; it remained wholly private, but he started the Wexford Hunt Club in 1810. In Queen's County (Leix) the countries of many private packs were amalgamated as the Emo about 1800; Sir Walter Burrowes of Lauragh succeeded the 3rd Earl of Portarlington, and in 1814 started a hunt club which met and dined regularly. His pack was English and mostly Belvoir. Next door in King's County there was a similar club soon afterwards.

Equally important aspects of Mr Power's mastership were imitated in Tipperary; Mr William Barton hunted with him until he inherited the Grove hounds at Fethard; he bred to English stallions, hunted in the English way and planted gorse. Another follower of Mr Power's hounds was Mr John Watson of Ballydarton, County Carlow; he imported hounds, planted gorse and tried to turn Ireland into Leicestershire. A County Pack was established in Louth with the amalgamation of two private packs, Mr Filgate's and Mr Brabazon Disney Shields's, in 1817. Several packs were joined to form the Union Hunt Club, south west of the Duhallow in County Cork.

A considerable part of hunting Ireland was thus functioning, within a quarter of a century, in a recognizable way, in indirect imitation of Quorndon.

In some places, however, completely private establishments continued to hunt; in others clubs were formed intending change, but met only expensive disaster; in others there were no changes at all.

Mr William Bolton of The Island, County Wexford, inherited a family pack and country; he then absorbed the countries of the Careys of Munfin and the Esmondes to the north; he hunted the whole large area until his death in 1853, at his own expense and consulting no one. Lord Lismore's private Ormond hounds became a subscription pack, known in 1830 as the Ormond and King's County; but this collapsed for reasons which are unrecorded but almost certainly financial. Thereafter for thirty-three years there was no county pack. The same thing may have happened in County Carlow, but with happier results: about 1822 Mr John Watson's Ballydarton became a subscription hunt called the Tullow: but in 1826 he took it back again. He hunted hounds; his son Robert, who later did so, was by universal consent the best amateur in Ireland.[4]

A more successful subscription effort was in Kildare. In 1814, to fill the gap left by Sir Fenton Aylmer, a meeting was held at Morrison's Tavern, Kildare, and the hunt was reorganized. Mr (later Sir) John Kennedy of Johnstown (son and grandson of pack owners; then only twenty-eight) became master until 1841. He planted gorse, hunted hounds and kept a voluminous hunting diary.[5] But the subscription never added up to anything more than a small covert and poultry fund; if Sir John had not been rich there would have been no more foxhunting in Kildare. He and his members had the very best horses in Ireland.[6]

Westmeath had many private packs, with one of which Mr John Fetherstonhaugh hunted round Killucan and Grangemouth from about 1800. His hounds were all drowned in a lake; they kept swimming towards their own cry echoing from one bank and then the other. There were attempts to amalgamate other packs. In 1835 Mr Sam Reynell got together a pack; he tried to persuade covert owners to preserve foxes, but with no success. He took his hounds away in 1841.

The Union Hunt Club's troubles were more of their own making. They started with two packs, one pure Irish and one mixed Irish and English: both were failures. At the suggestion of the younger members an English pack was imported. Hunted by an Irishman it was a failure. An English huntsman was sent for; pack and huntsman still failed. In ten years the Union had four Masters of Hounds, four huntsmen and three packs, none of which showed any sport at all. The club faced bankruptcy; the hounds were offered for sale but found no takers.

In 1837 an Irish master, Mr Roche, got a pack of small Irish hounds (presumably black-and-tans) and an Irish staff; once they got the hounds steady to hare they had tremendous sport in an almost purely bank country. In 1840 the 4th Earl of Shannon of Castlemartyr reversed this policy, getting drafts of the very best English blood, and to hunt them Tom Smith, son of Will the elder of Brocklesby, who had been whipping-in to Mr John Watson in Carlow. This English establishment was as successful as the Irish.

In some areas entirely 18th-century arrangements continued until nearly the middle of the 19th century.

County Waterford had about six private packs hunting more or less defined areas until the 1840s, including the Ballynatray, Blackwater Vale, Salter Bridge, Tinvane and Ballylegget. The Sullivans, who owned the last, were a merry family who once drew for and hunted a fox at midnight after an intemperate dinner. In the country between Cork and Kinsale, many generations of the Knolles, Knowles or Knowlles family[7] kept hounds. In 1830 the Mr Knolles of the time formed the South Union Hunt Club, which was hardly more than a gesture towards the 19th century: he continued to hunt hare and fox with 'old Irish hounds'. In far south-western County Cork, Mr John Beamish of Cashelmore hunted his private pack from 1787 to 1820, and was succeeded by his son, also John. Their pack was all home-bred, 'grizzled hounds', with Kerry beagles used for an outcross. Still farther away, the West Carbery country was hunted from 1760 by Colonel John Becher of Hollybank, Skibbereen, and from 1824 by Mr T. Somerville of Drishane. He was one of the landowners of whom his granddaughter wrote: 'How many Anglo–Irish great-great-grandfathers have not raised these monuments to their English forbears – and then, recognising their obligations to their Irish mothers' ancestry, have filled them, gloriously, with horses and hounds, and butts of claret, and hungry poor relations unto the fourth and fifth generations?'[8]

A more celebrated example of such a family were the Eyres of Eyre Court, County Galway. Colonel Giles Eyre inherited his uncle's pack in 1791. His hounds were large and savage, having both a mastiff and a bloodhound cross: they ate their huntsman Nick Carolan one night when he went, drunk, into the kennel without his kennel coat. Colonel Eyre was entirely a sportsman and almost illiterate. He is assumed to be the original of Godfrey O'Malley of Castle O'Malley, who hunted the fox only with a completely private pack, was spendthrift, improvident and totally unreliable, and was much loved in the countryside.[9]

This was one of the few owners of private packs who had a considerable reputation outside his own country, which was the Killucan and Grangemouth part of Westmeath. The family's hounds came to a strange and tragic end (see *opposite*). Westmeath was not yet a foxhunting country, and did not become one until the second half of the century. Not much is known of Canon Kearney, but he represents an important element in early Irish hunting history: the sporting Anglo-Irish parson, with a well-endowed living in the gift of a relative, and with a Protestant flock sometimes numbering no more than a family or two. Some such parsons were very rich and several had their own packs.

Herbert Fether is one who is all for a
  start,
And Toby, of that ilk, is wild for a
  dart ;
But the Canon "goes off" at the very
  first note—
Our honoured and reverend pastor from
  Moate.

HERBERT FETHERSTONHAUGH.

CANON KEARNEY.

Further west, Mr Persse of Persse Lodge (rebuilt as Moyode Castle) dressed his staff in orange plush and established himself as 'the Irish Meynell', a title more properly bestowed on Mr Power of the Kilkenny. In 1803 Mr Persse divided his pack and country, giving half – all his big hounds – to his nephew Mr Robert Parsons Persse of Castleboy. The Castleboy hounds had many joint meets with Colonel Eyre's, after which the dinners were amazingly strenuous. The combined hunts once burned down the hotel where they were dining; either this event, or the number of hard-riding redheads, is supposed to be the origin of 'Blazers'.

Famine and Land League

There were parts of Ireland where the people, even when not hungry, acted towards hunting with an apparently motiveless savagery. This first struck Tipperary. The 3rd Marquess of Waterford in 1840 bought from Captain Jacob of Mobernane the hounds which had been the Bartons'. Schooled for years at Melton, Lord Waterford began to show fine sport in a country which was steadily improving towards his Meltonian ideal. Then, in 1843, he 'was compelled to relinquish the country he was hunting, in the county of Tipperary, on account of the numerous demoniacal

attempts, not only to poison his lordship's hounds twice, but even to destroy by incendiarism the stables occupied by the horses of the hunt'.[10]

This violence was local. Five years later came famine. On people the potato blight caused starvation and mass emigration; on some hunting, but only some, it caused the end of all financial support because landowners paid their local expenses out of local rents. The Kildare was almost given up. Hunting stopped in Queen's County and at the Union Hunt Club in County Cork.

In other countries there were no ill effects or few. Meath was a country of very large grazing farms and no one starved. There the old Mountainstown and Gibbstown packs had amalgamated as the Clongill about 1813, and with the Michaelstown formed the Meath in 1832. This hunt was still without distinction until Mr Sam Reynell came from Westmeath in 1851. Though not a great huntsman or hound man,[11] he was of the utmost importance to the hunt because he made its country, especially on the Dublin side. He 'found Meath without a gorse-covert, and drew between thirty and forty "sure finds" in it before he died'.[12] He was motivated, it was said, by jealousy of Burton Persse of the Galway.[13]

Louth was largely unaffected too, and for the same reasons; so was Wexford.

In Waterford things went better than ever before. The 3rd Marquess, driven from Tipperary, established Lord Waterford's Hounds at Curraghmore, and over the next four years greatly expanded his country. On 29 March 1859 he was hunting for the first time after coming back from the Grand National at Aintree. He jumped a little fence on to a road, fell on his head and was killed. He was a bad judge of a horse and the horse he was riding was a bad one.[14] Mr Briscoe of Tinvane, whose pack he had bought, was luckily an extremely diplomatic successor.

All went well in Carbery, too, although Mr Thomas Beamish inherited the pack at the worst possible moment in 1848. He never sweated, even when very hot. One of his followers reported: 'His head and face alone seem affected – they reek doubly, and when he has taken off his hat, a smoke like that from a small furnace has

MR REYNELL LEAVING WESTMEATH Westmeath was hunted by a number of small private packs in the 18th century. Following the nearby examples of Louth and Kildare, various attempts were made to amalgamate the heirs of these, but with no success. In 1835 Mr Samuel A. Reynell attempted to start serious foxhunting. His grandfather had had a pack at Killyman, inherited by his father Richard who died in 1834. They probably hunted hares. Foxes were extremely scarce, and Mr Sam Reynell's first concern, having imported English hounds, was to get covert-owners to preserve something for them to hunt. His failure to do this was the main reason for his departure in 1841. Ten years later he went to the Meath, formed by amalgamation in 1832, where, during a twenty-year mastership, he made a foxhunting country. The Westmeath was started *eo nomine* by Sir Richard Levinge of Knockdrin in 1854; it then had far too many masters, staying each for far too short a time, until 1913, which suggests a continuing shortage of foxes and of finance. Painting by James Walsham Baldock, 1841. By courtesy of the Leger Galleries.

issued from his head, and his face streaming, but all else as dry as possible.'[15]

Another hunt which thrived, more surprisingly, was the Galway. In 1840 a County Galway Hunt was formed; Mr John Denis of Bermingham, near Tuam, had a small private pack hunting in Mayo and Roscommon which he joined to the Moyode and maintained with a subscription. 'Black Jack' Denis – Trollope's 'Black Daly' – was a man of no fortune and obscure background; he farmed a tiny acreage and coped horses; he was a bachelor and 'his hounds were his children'. He was a very great horseman and a fine hound breeder and huntsman; 'he never carried a horn; but he spoke to his hounds in a loud, indistinct chirruping voice, which all County Galway believed to be understood by every hound in the pack'.[16]

Kilkenny had bad times, but not because of famine. Mr H. W. Meredyth of Morlands had his foxes poisoned and his hounds burned; and he was the victim of 'unpleasant incidents' from his members as well as the peasantry. 'On more than one occasion the Kilkenny Hunt, and with it the Old Club, was perilously near extinction, and probably has had more hairbreadth escapes than most packs.'[17]

Limerick was hunted by private packs until 1829; when Mr Croker of Ballynagard gave up, the gentlemen of the county formed a club for foxhunting. Mr George Fosberry of Curraghbridge, 'Red George', was master until his death in 1845. A committee, which included his son, then ran the country with well-remembered incompetence. Another member was Mr Edward Green of Greenmount, whose sole mastership from 1853 to 1861 was considered one of the least successful in history: when he retired there was 'but a scant subscription, a wretched pack of hounds . . . the country in very bad order, as regards coverts, and hardly a fox to be found'.[18]

There was general recovery from the famine, where it had struck. In many countries hunting was gayer than ever before: 'Many go out now to have a gallop across the country, many to "show off" in faultless costume, others to escort some fair friend, and carry on a flirtation . . . but few to enjoy the working of the hounds.'[19]

This was the atmosphere in which the Land League, led and financed from America, suddenly began to try to destroy the fabric of Anglo–Irish society in the countryside. Foxhunting was the most obvious of all its targets.

Kildare had had the mastership of Lord Naas, 'no less distinguished for his daring horsemanship, than his tact in managing a country, and his skill in hunting a pack of hounds';[20] the immensely popular Baron de Robeck; and Sir Edward Kennedy (2nd baronet) whose tact got rid of most rabbit traps and much wire; but Mr W. Forbes of Callender, a Scottish 'foreigner', was given a bad time. In Queen's County, Mr Hamilton Stubber had first the Land League, then rabies in the kennel, then lack of subscriptions; the hunt died until 1902. The Ormond and King's County was also stopped from hunting, but only for three years. In Wexford Captain Walker had his hounds poisoned several times; the hunt went into a slough from which it did not really recover until 1912. The 5th Marquess of Waterford suffered at Curraghmore all that the 3rd had suffered in Tipperary; after three seasons of struggle by other masters the country was unhunted for sixteen years. In Tipperary itself the Land Leaguers went shouting round the coverts to stop them being drawn, and then poisoned the hounds. The hunt was saved in 1887 by Mr Dick Burke, who had gone to America and come back a millionaire: a most able and energetic man who continued to make money owing to his knowledge of old silver and furniture.[21] In Limerick, Mr John Gubbins of Bruree called on all the reserves of an extremely strong character to withstand the Land League until 1886; he then resigned with great abruptness after an attempt to bully him.[22] He dismantled his very large hunting establishment and went to England; his thoroughbred stud stayed in Ireland to breed two Derby winners.

Mr John Tonson Rye had to stop hunting his ancestral country in County Cork. After two seasons Colonel Mangles started hunting it again with the 10th Hussars regimental harriers. From then until 1898 a succession of cavalry regiments stationed locally took over the pack, each giving its name to the hunt for a season or two. Captain Forester of the 3rd Hussars here underwent the apprenticeship which equipped him for the Quorn.

In 1853 Mr Burton R. P. Persse of Moyode, son of R.P., united the Galway and East Galway countries, adding the county hounds to his private pack. He hunted this huge territory most successfully until the Land League spread down from Mayo. The hunt was boycotted; Mr Persse and his hounds exhausted themselves trying to find a covert that the mob had not crashed through; he carried a pistol in the pocket of his hunting coat; it was universally believed in 1881 that it was 'impossible that hunting should go on in County Galway'.[23] It did go on, just; Mr Persse died not by the bullet he expected but after a fall in 1885.

A few hunts were as unaffected by the Land League as by the famine. After the brilliant Captain Jock Trotter, the Meath very nearly collapsed in 1888: but only through lack of subscriptions. It was saved by Lord Fingall and made glorious by Mr John Watson, a great horseman and a very great hound breeder.[24] His followers went as well as he did. 'You ought to see the ladies go!' said an American visitor in 1902. 'My Lord! how they do go!'[25] Mr William de Salis Filgate was master of the Louth from 1860 and 1916. His father, though latterly blind, continued to hunt on a sensible old horse and with a groom in attendance. The younger Filgate's son-in-law, Captain R. A. B. Henry, was his joint huntsman; he changed his name to Filgate and was master for fifty-one years.

One hunt in the south east had similar fortune. Mr Bolton's Island country was offered in 1856 to Lord Fitzwilliam, who had an enormous estate in County Wicklow.

THE WARD HUNT
The Ward or Wards was formed in 1830, as the local Dublin hunt, by Mr Gerard of The Bay; it was the amalgamation of the Dubber and Hollywood packs, and was named for a tavern where hounds often met. Mr Gerard's principal game was bag-foxes. In 1836 Mr Peter Alley of New Park changed to carted deer, of which a great many had been, and still were, hunted in contemporary England, especially near London. Mr Alley hunted first fallow and then red deer. The pack became the Ward Union in 1854, still under Mr Alley, when it amalgamated with the Garrison hounds. Painting by William Osborne.

Lord Fitzwilliam handed it on at once to Mr John Watson. The Tullow became the Carlow and Island. Mr Watson died in 1869, still titular M.F.H. at the age of eighty-three. His son Robert became owner and master; he hunted hounds until 1901, for a total of fifty-one years.

As in the 1850s, there were hunts whose problems were not the fault of the Land League. The Westmeath had nineteen different masterships between 1854 and 1913, most of only a season or two, and several being committees. The most surprising régime was that of Mr Harry Worcester Smith, who arrived in 1912 from America with a retinue of hounds, horses, vehicles and black grooms. He was concerned to prove what he had claimed in 1904, that American hounds could hunt a British fox in Britain better than English. A professional hunted the club's hounds, Mr Smith his own on bye days; they were not at all successful, but this was blamed on the months they had spent in quarantine. Mr Smith himself said they were wonderful.[26] The Kilkenny had further hairbreadth escapes from extinction. Sir Hercules Langrishe of Knocktopher revived the hunt's greatness. He was so popular that he could have sent 100 puppies out to walk. His skill on the horn was such that he could blow 'gone away' on his gun barrel.[27] Mr Isaac Bell, half American but brought up to English hunting, brought in 1908 the hounds he had been hunting in Galway. At this point Mr Nicholas Lambert of Dysertmore had turned his New Ross Harriers into the East Kilkenny foxhounds, and he had one remarkable crossbred hound of Colonel Curre's breeding. Mr Bell was told about it by Commander Forbes (the writer 'Maintop'); he went himself to Itton, and got Colonel Curre's Fiddler, a lemon-and-white hound of only twenty-two inches. From this beginning developed one of the most influential breeding experiments of the 20th century.[28]

Three other hunts demand mention:

A new Lord Milton (later 7th Earl Fitzwilliam) began to bring the Wentworth pack to Coollattin for cubhunting. In 1897, when he married, he came to live at Carnew Castle. He built a kennel and began hunting the east side of County Wicklow. This became the Coollattin in 1902.

In 1891 Mr Aylmer Somerville of Drishane started a new West Carbery. His whippers-in were his sister Edith and her friend Violet Martin, the 'Martin Ross' of the literary collaboration. Miss Martin adored hunting in spite of physical frailty and short sight; she was crippled by a hunting accident. In 1903 Miss Somerville succeeded her brother, becoming Ireland's first woman M.F.H. The atmosphere and country of the hunt are consequently better described than any other.

Between the Tipperary and Limerick countries lies the Scarteen.

Mr John Ryan of Ballyvistin had a pack of distinctive hounds of disputed origin. By one account, Spanish fishermen came to the south-west coast of Kerry in the 17th century, bringing their own black-and-tan hounds which became acclimatized in large numbers all over Kerry. The Ryan family, having moved to Scarteen, heard about them and acquired a few couple from which their pack was bred.[29] By another and more credible account, Mr John Ryan himself imported hounds from Gascony in 1735, which he may have crossed with English Talbots; from these all Kerry beagles descend.[30] Mr Thaddeus Ryan inherited the hounds at his father's death in 1789; it appears that he moved to Scarteen with the black-and-tans in 1798.

Not all Kerry beagles were black-and-tan. As might be expected with hounds of Gascon origin, there were blue-mottled and black-and-white hounds at Waterville, and at Scarteen in the early 19th century some white, some red, some buff.[31] These variations survived in Maryland and Kentucky, where Kerry beagles were so immensely influential, but at Scarteen breeding and drafting turned a predominant into an invariable colour. The hounds were sensationally fast, casting themselves forward with a fox-killing drive all their own; they were sadly prone to riot.

County Clare to the south of Galway, County Mayo to the north, Roscommon to the east, had a great deal of hunting, under conditions verging on the impossible. It was to this part of Ireland that Anthony Trollope was sent, at the age of eighteen, as an official of the Postal Service. He was introduced to foxhunting, three days a week on government horses; it changed his life. One result was to give fiction its best hunting, and hunting its best fiction, after Tolstoy, Surtees and Miss Somerville. He describes, especially, what is otherwise undescribed: the long-established but precarious foxhunting of Clare and Mayo.[32] By the time he died it had all died too, at the hands of the vulpicides and Land Leaguers.[33]

Stag and Hare

Wild deer were hunted all over Ireland while there were any to hunt. In the 18th century the Anglo–Irish gentry evicted their tenants and established deer parks. In the 19th several packs were formed to hunt carted deer.

Near Dublin there were two packs, the Dubber and the Hollywood, amalgamated as the Wards in 1830. Lord Howth also had staghounds in 1840, which became the Garrison Staghounds of the Dublin soldiers. This pack amalgamated with the Wards in 1854 because of the Crimean War. The result was the Ward Union, the most successful and celebrated hunting establishment in Ireland.

Deerhunting grew considerably in the 1870s: the Limerick in 1872; the Roscommon in 1873, because no other kind of hunting there was possible; the Lissagon in 1874 because the Cavan hares were all poached; the County Down in 1881.

The history of Irish harriers is as unwritable as that of American hill-top fox-hunting, and for the same reasons. There is no computing the number of packs – private, subscription and trencher-fed – which have hunted all over Ireland in the last 200 years, nor has any list, at any moment, the smallest chance of being comprehensive.

Some of the private packs had reputations far wider than local. Some of the clubs

THE IRISH WOLFHOUND
This is Captain Graham's Scot, 'by a Kilfane dog out of a Red bitch of Capt. Graham's Strain'. The breed is compared by early writers with the Scottish deerhound, and by some considered virtually identical. In remote history this is probably right, and the Scottish deerhound probably derived from Ireland. The breeds thereafter grew apart. The Irish, like other wolfhounds, was required to hunt by the nose (although it was normally assisted in this phase of the chase by a much smaller scenting hound, the beagle, equivalent to the English brachet) and then by sight: the wolf was kept out of covert once it broke, if possible, and then coursed, the method of early 19th-century Russia described by Tolstoy (see p. 243). There were still plenty of wolf-hounds, so presumably some wolves to hunt, in the mid 17th century (Dorothy Osborne was embarrassed by the prodigious size of one she had sent to her in Bedfordshire); but the last wolf was killed early in the 18th century, allegedly by the hounds of Mr Watson of Ballydarton, County Carlow. The breed became rare, special, expensive, and functionless.

owned packs. But the most ancient and celebrated never did. This was the Downe. A few of the many private Ulster packs used to forgather at the house of a squire, there to hunt for a week. The house was seldom big enough, and 'Dick, Tom, or Harry was always put up in *outquarters*, and had to stumble across the farmyard at midnight to find them . . . Therefore it was desirable to form a regular Hunt Club.'

Fitzpatrick listed, as at 1 November 1877, forty-eight packs of harriers; this was the tip of an iceberg the rest of which, to Fitzpatrick in the fashionable East, was invisible; the Sunday harriers, trencher-fed, not advertising their meets but simply assembling after Mass. Mr Ikey Bell describes with high admiration a pack of this kind in Kerry in about 1905 – 21½ couple, astonishingly level in condition, the M.H. the postman and his whippers-in local tradesmen, many of the hounds Kerry beagles but some crossbred to foxhounds, the sport first-class.[34]

Hounds

The enormous old Irish wolfhound continued to exist: there were plenty in the 17th century, but very few by the end of the 18th. Whatever the old Irish deerhound was, it seems to have been replaced by English lemon-pies brought over from Elizabeth's reign onwards, and then by blue-mottled Old Southern hounds. The beagle of Irish antiquity was any small hound.

In the south west there were two distinct breeds: the Kerry beagle (sufficiently described) and an old white kind which carried the black-and-tan's good and bad attributes to extravagant lengths. They were savage, riotous and completely self-reliant, 'hunting with bloodthirsty intentness and entirely after their own devices'. Quite humble families in County Cork had kept small packs of these hounds for a very long time.[35] Their origin is utterly obscure.

Mr Conolly had Belvoir hounds at Castleton in the 1760s, and both Sir Fenton Aylmer and Sir John Power had English packs about 1800. The use of English blood became widespread towards the middle of the century, though very seldom kept pure. By the 1870s every leading kennel had had English drafts and bred to English stallions. The resulting packs did not, however, much resemble English.

The first hound show in Ireland was added to the Clonmel Horse Show largely by Mr Assheton Biddulph: he intended an Irish Peterborough. But although Irish M.F.H.s went to Peterborough they did not want a real Peterborough in Ireland, and in 1900 Clonmel was still the only hound show, and the hounds shown there were still a pretty rough lot.[36]

Walks were difficult to arrange in some countries, owing to agricultural extremes: either the farmers were enormous graziers or tiny smallholders.

Puppy shows were started in King's County; by 1900 most Irish hunts held them.

Horses

Irish horse breeders about 1800 had several great advantages and one huge disadvantage, all of which lasted.

They had wonderful, bone-making grazing, since much of Ireland is old turf laid on limestone. They had open winters, which made feeding cheaper. They had excellent foundation stock: 'Till within a few years [in 1878] there was literally *no* cart-horse blood in Ireland':[37] and there was very little thereafter until the first war. The Irish disadvantage was poverty, which meant that young stock was ill-fed and worked too soon.

The use of top-class English thoroughbred stallions for hunter breeding began about 1800, with the arrival of Meynellian foxhunting in Kilkenny.

The Irish were considered marvellous at making and breaking their hunters. 'Whatever we may think of her natives,' said George Whyte Melville, 'the most discreet and sagacious of our hunters come now from the Emerald Isle.'[38] Foals learned to bank by running with their dams over stiff country; at two they were schooled with a long rein very patiently and gently. Lucky ones were put out to grass until they were backed at four; the poorer breeders had their colts ploughing at three – even those by the very best thoroughbreds – because they could not afford them in idleness. This, as much as heredity, made them small, and shortened their useful life to eight or nine years instead of an English hunter's fifteen or more.[39]

When they were backed they were apt to be treated rough. By the account of 'Nimrod', who hunted one season in Ireland: 'If an Irishman has got a clever young horse, which he means to make a hunter, he puts a fellow more than half drunk on his back, with a pair of sharp spurs and a *cutting whip* (Anglicé, a hand-whip), and he gallops him at all sorts of fences, regardless whether he goes into them or over them – though with the help of the instruments just mentioned, and a good "Horough! by Jasus, the devil a balk you're going to make now!" the latter is generally accomplished.'[40]

Shows to encourage breeders with prizes and premiums were suggested in the 17th century, but the first of any importance was in Waterford in the 3rd Marquess's time. Its purpose was thwarted by dishonest judging: 'the worst horses succeeded to the best places'.[41] Lord Howth was the prime mover in the Dublin Horse Show in 1865. In the late 1880s the Hunter Improvement Society brought the Royal Dublin into the Premium Stallion scheme. The intention was to subsidize the use of thoroughbred stallions capable of siring fifteen-stone hunters; in the event this was, in Dublin, a ludicrous failure, the winners being eye-filling weeds, often unsound, fit only for light weights and minimum distances.[42]

Clubs and Country

The organization of Irish hunting evolved like that of England, but more slowly and on a more penurious scale. All early packs were entirely private, except those which were formed *ad hoc* of trencher-fed hounds. The early clubs either met with their private hounds to hunt together, or supported the owner of a pack; in the latter case their support was not financial, but provided the master with loyalty and the members with parties. Even in those establishments known as the County Hounds – Kilkenny, Kildare, Wexford, Louth – the packs were the master's property.

Subscriptions for the maintenance of hounds, as against wine cellars, started in Kildare in 1814: but the sums subscribed hardly covered poultry claims. Ormond and Tullow followed a few years later, but only temporarily. The first celebrated pack maintained principally by subscription was Mr John Denis's Galway in 1840. The idea spread slowly.

The reforms of the last years of the century made much of the countryside far more prosperous. This created the possibility of adequate hunt subscriptions: but the potential was seldom realized. Even the Meath and the Kilkenny very nearly collapsed from lack of financial support, and many lesser hunts did go under, for greater or lesser periods.

While all costs were lower than in England – horses, feed, wages, covert-rents – they were not low enough for hunts to be carried on, except by very rich individuals,

GALWAY, ABOUT 1810
'Charles O'Malley' has a wild impromptu pounding-match with the English Captain Hammersley, both inspired to mad daring by romantic rivalry. The Captain rides a Leicestershire thoroughbred, Charles his Irish halfbred. The former has refused at a typical Galway obstacle; the latter banks it. Another hazard is a five-foot wall of crumbling stone on the crest of a difficult hill, and another a twenty-foot sunk fence (a gigantic haha) with bricked walls; Charles O'Malley, maddened by jealousy, jumps it; Captain Hammersley goes in, killing his mare. It is suggested that 'Godfrey O'Malley's Castle O'Malley' hounds are a picture of Colonel Giles Eyre's.

THE MEATH, 1907
This was the penultimate season of Mr John Watson, one of the greatest Masters of Hounds in Irish history. His father Robert and grandfather John were masters of their own hounds (which became the Carlow and Island); his Uncle George started the first pack of foxhounds in Australia (see p. 246). He learned his hunting from his father, often acting as deputy or field master. He came to the Meath in 1891, hunting hounds five days a week and going out with the Louth or Ward Union on the sixth. He was a man of immense physical toughness and courage, openly contemptuous of weakness. He had become a great polo player when serving with the 7th Hussars in India, and captained the first British team to go to America (he auctioned their ponies to pay expenses). The Meath pack was destroyed by rabies, and he replaced it with a draft from his father's kennel (rich in Milton blood from Coollattin) and drafts from Brocklesby and the

on any but a pinchpenny scale. A result in many countries was a turn-round of masters far too rapid to be healthy. Another result was the cap, general in Ireland but still most unusual in England in 1900. English visitors would have helped. Near Dublin they did. Elsewhere, however, there were almost no comfortable hotels in hunting countries, and the only available boxes were mansions so huge they needed armies of servants and tons of expensive coal. To compound all these problems, the finances of many Irish hunts were run, according to an Irishman, with the utmost incompetence.[43]

What made hunting possible in most of the remoter parts was amateurism. The master owned the hounds and hunted them. His brothers and sons whipped-in. Wages were paid only to kennelman and groom. Such hunts, clearly, could not run to stables of thoroughbreds or kennels of Peterborough or even Clonmel hounds. What they could do was survive bad times far more resiliently than the fashionable establishments, which were broken up in the 1880s and reduced to cadre strength in 1914.

The Irish field was rather different from the English. Nowhere were there many hunting farmers; in some countries there were none. There was a much greater reliance on soldiers wherever there were any within reach: this was good for finance but dangerous for hounds. The difference most noted by many writers was the number of ladies: far more in Ireland and a remarkable number, to English eyes, all over the country in 1900.[44]

Ireland was nearly all grass (though much of the grass was bog). There were few big woods. There was very little corn. Potatoes were planted in the spring and dug in the autumn, and they were in small patches. There was little frost: loss of more than a day or two was rare (for this reason there were no good skaters in Ireland).

There were no timber fences, no cut-and-laid and very few bullfinches. The obstacles were banks and walls. The banks were in some areas stone-faced, in some stone-flagged on top. Many were double, with a deep dyke amounting to a carriageway between – a bohreen. In some places enormous stone-faced banks divided minute enclosures. It was a matter of amazement that the Irish, at some unrecorded time and before a change in the national character, should have undertaken so prodigious a labour.

Cheshire; on this basis he bred what 'Maintop' called the best pack ever seen in Ireland. He was also considered, as his father was, the best living amateur huntsman. His country continued to appal English visitors, for reasons even better than those here visible: the strangest hazards were ditches so deep that they swallowed horse and man, leaving only the latter's head visible. Meath ladies were said to go better than any others anywhere. Print by G. D. Giles. By courtesy of Fores Ltd.

They were not tempted to repeat it when wire became available. It was worse in some parts of Ireland than in much of England because it was still needed all winter; the open weather meant that the stock stayed out. It was, however, less insidious, as there were no thorn hedges to hide it in. All farmers were tempted; many could not afford to resist; the very worst offenders were the Scottish estate managers of absentee Anglo–Irish landlords.[45]

Sometimes the wire was put up with regret: sometimes, clearly, with glee. In the 1880s this was apt to be undifferentiated bitterness against the squires and their sport, but later it was usually personal. The same is true of poison, which remained a menace in several places to hounds as well as to foxes.[46]

12 America
Colonial Times to Civil War

Arrival of the Colonists

Some tribes of the North American Indians were farmers and some fishermen, but most were primarily hunters. In Virginia, 'The men bestowe their times in fishing, warrs, and such manlike exercises.'[1] Job Hartop saw the Indians of Mexico hunting deer in 1568,[2] and John Davis those of the Canadian coast hunting seal and bear in 1585.[3] Inland in the north, moose were followed over great distances on snowshoes.

The white man transformed Indian hunting techniques. In the early 17th century in Massachusetts, Thomas Morton, 'haveing more craft than honestie', set up the scandalous settlement of Merry Mount, near Plymouth, as the headquarters of unseemly revelry. 'Now to maintaine this riotous prodigallitie and profuse excess, Morton, thinking himselfe lawless, and hearing what gaine the French & fisher-men made by trading of peeces, powder, & shotte to the Indeans, he, as the head of this consortship, begane the practise of the same in these parts.' By 1650 the Indians were making their own bullets and shot.[4]

White men also introduced the hound to Indian forest hunting. De Soto took hounds as well as horses to Florida in 1539. Both the French and the English brought scenting hounds to the northern forests; Hawkeye was perfectly familiar with hound work and with tufting a deer out of covert. He would then, however, shoot it, in the French and New England fashion.[5]

Jamestown was founded in 1607. The settlers included, from the very first, sporting gentry who brought their lifestyle with them from the English countryside. About 1650 the Parliamentary victory in the Civil War sent more cavaliers across the Atlantic – racing and hunting men.

The earliest importation of hounds of which there is firm record is that by the cavalier Colonel Robert Brooke. He arrived in Prince George's County, Maryland, on 30 June 1650 with his wife, ten children, twenty-eight servants and a pack of hounds from England. He kennelled the hounds at de la Brooke. He died in 1655 and his family moved to Montgomery County. All his eight sons, and all their sons, kept hounds descended from his. All hunted the fox – mounted by day, on foot by night – and the blood survived in the Brooke family packs and in most of the well-known strains of American foxhounds.

In the tidewater region of Virginia, 'Every House keeps three or four mungril dogs to destroy Vermin, such as Wolves, foxes, rackoons, Opossums, etc.'[6] In the areas still heavily forested, 'vermine hunting' for the same four beasts was 'perform'd a Foot, with small dogs in the Night, by the Light of the Moon and Stars'.[7] In 1691 Mr Michael Dixon of Northampton County had a pack of dogs to destroy 'foxes, wolves and other varmint'; his dogs attacked people passing his house with the result that, by order of the County Court, the road was moved.[8]

In other parts of the colony sport, as sport, began to flourish. Hounds from Colonel Brooke's kennel, and probably from others in Maryland, came into Virginia from the 1660s. The country was beginning to be cleared on a large scale for tobacco, the staple of Virginia's economy. Horses increased rapidly – the colony was exporting them by 1668. The result by perhaps 1690 was recognizable hunting on a fair scale, wolf being the favoured quarry until its virtual extinction.

Early in the 18th century Virginia became, rather suddenly, very rich indeed. Fine houses, carriages, racehorses and foxhunting were the most obvious signs of wealth. Middle and Northern Neck were the principal hunting countries. The fox became the principal game.

In 1736 a traveller met a Master of Hounds who had eleven couple out and a group of friends on horseback. They all came back to dinner and got very drunk.[9] Three years later, on the uplands, 'Some hunt the foxes with hounds as you do in England'.[10]

In 1742 Dr Thomas Walker imported six or eight couple of hounds from England, built kennels, bred a pack and formed the Castle Hill Hounds of Albemarle County. In 1749 Dr Walker crossed the Alleghenies into Kentucky, taking his hounds and hunting for food on the way.

Lord Fairfax, Colonel Washington and their Friends

Thomas 6th Lord Fairfax inherited from his mother an estate in Virginia between the Potomac and Rappahannock rivers. He visited it in 1746. He stayed with his cousin William Fairfax, who had built a house called Belvoir in 1731 and whose daughter Anne married Lawrence Washington of Mount Vernon. William Fairfax had a pack of hounds and his whole family hunted.

After a year or two Lord Fairfax went home. He wrote from Yorkshire announcing the arrival of $1\frac{1}{2}$ couple of English hounds for 'mending the breed' at Belvoir.[11] The next year he came to live with his cousin. He began to hunt energetically. A frequent visitor and pupil was his connection by marriage the sixteen-year-old George Washington, Lawrence's halfbrother.

In 1752 George inherited Mount Vernon. He continued to hunt regularly, with Lord Fairfax and at Belvoir. In 1767 he assembled a pack of his own. 'The pack was very numerous and select – the colonel visiting and inspecting his kennel morning and evening, after the same manner as he did his stables. It was his pride, and a proof of his skill in hunting, to have his pack so critically drafted as to speed and bottom, that in running, if one leading dog should lose the scent, another was at hand immediately to recover it; and thus, when in full cry, to use a sporting phrase, you might cover the pack with a blanket.

'During the season, Mount Vernon (the general's residence) had many sporting guests from the neighbourhood, from Maryland, and elsewhere. Their visits were not of days but weeks, and they were entertained in the good old style of Virginia's ancient hospitality. Washington, always superbly mounted, in true sporting costume of blue coat, scarlet waistcoat, leather breeches, top-boots, velvet cap, and whip with long thong – took the field at day-dawn with his huntsman, Will Lee, his friends, and neighbours.'[12] With Washington sometimes hunted Martha, in a scarlet habit; Thomas Jefferson, 'as eager after a fox as Washington himself';[13] and the McCarty

America : Colonial Times to Civil War

and Chichester families. Captain Daniel McCarty of Cedar Grove, near Mount Vernon, kept a pack of hounds started soon after Fairfax's; Washington often hunted with him. In 1766 Captain McCarty's daughter married Richard Chichester, who also owned hounds. The Chichesters took over Lord Fairfax's country.

The Mount Vernon pack was given up in 1775, but re-established after the war. The largest draft was from Mr Chichester's Fairfax County Hounds, which had been the next best pack to Washington's own.[14] There was also a draft of French stag-hounds, a gift from Lafayette, which arrived in August 1885;[15] some hounds from Philadelphia; and some from England.[16]

The fields which followed Washington's and the other packs were local gentry or guests, and sometimes their ladies. A notable feature of Virginia hunting in the generation before the Revolution was the large number of sporting parsons, who were also among its keenest turfites. They went at these pursuits energetically: 'The race must end in a dinner, and the dinner must end under the table. The day's hunt must be followed by a night's debauch.'[17]

In the first half of the 18th century most of the horses were inconveniently small owing to their Chickasaw blood, and short of stamina for the same reason. In 1730 the first thoroughbred stallion arrived – Bulle Rock, by the Darley Arabian. A few more thoroughbreds arrived in the 1740s, and several extremely important sires between 1750 and 1765. They got enormous numbers of carriage, saddle and hunting horses out of halfbred mares. The result, by about 1770, was a population of three-quarter-bred and seven-eighths-bred hunters entirely comparable to those of the English Shires.

Colonial Maryland, Pennsylvania, New York

Maryland squires owned packs which, like Lord Fairfax and Sir Roger de Coverley, they brought out to amuse their neighbours. But there were few establishments as grand or as well organized as Mount Vernon or the Chichesters'. 'The planter's porch was always crowded with yelping foxhounds.'[18]

Pennsylvania had active foxhunting in the 1740s and 1750s. Some was quite different from Virginia's or Maryland's because its followers were townsmen.

The best-known Philadelphia pack was managed by Mr Butler, who was supported by a subscription from twenty-seven gentlemen. Just before Christmas 1765, thirty horsemen had breakfast at 5 a.m., met at Darby, and killed three foxes by 11. Four days later they had '30 dogs, 35 gentlemen, but no foxes'.[19]

On 13 December 1766 this loose association was formed into a hunt club, America's first, which later became known as the Gloucester Fox-Hunting Club. Its first president was Captain Samuel Morris. The 'President of the Day' was to act as Master of Hounds, leading the field until a fox was found; riders could go as they pleased while hounds were running, but at a check came under the President's orders; the first man up was to get the brush, sit on the President's right at dinner, and give a dollar to the huntsman.[20] The first meet was on 1 January 1767. In 1774 a uniform was adopted: brown coat with white buttons, buff waistcoat and breeches, black cap.

In New Jersey the spreading red fox became a scourge, and a bounty was offered in 1713. This undoubtedly led to vulpicide by smoke, trap, poison and gun, but also to vigorous foxhunting. There were many private packs in the colony before the Revolution, of which the best remembered was Mr Heard's: he was 'a dignified and venerable personage in a scarlet coat, black jockey-cap, broad leather belt, and a hunting-horn'.[21]

There were many small packs round Oyster Bay and in Westchester County, but New York had two large ones: those of James deLancey and Lewis Morris, both of Westchester.

In 1767 deLancey went to England, visiting relations in Yorkshire and Leicestershire. In the latter place, while hunting, he persuaded Mr John Evers to come back to America with him to manage his hounds. They brought 'several *hunters* and a number of *fox-hounds* fresh from the renowned *kennels* and *studs* of their friends, *Hugo Meynell, Esq.*, and *Col. Thos. Thornton* . . . this importation was combined with the old *Morris* and *deLancey* pack [itself apparently by now combined], and weekly hunted the coverts of *Westchester* and *Long Island*.'[22] The establishment was known as the Riding Hunt or Evers'.

A few small packs of dubious type and organization hunted on Manhattan Island; they were probably kennelled; they hunted on Long Island also. The Brooklyn Hunt advertising a meet on 14 November 1781 was apparently not a regular hunt but a scratch pack got together for a day in Brooklyn. Charles Loosley the advertiser (who wanted to buy bag foxes) was proprietor of the King's Head Tavern; his hunt, like much contemporary racing, was designed to create a festive and thirsty crowd.

Hounds

New England, New York, Pennsylvania, Delaware and the Eastern Shore of Maryland all got, overwhelmingly, the Old Southern hound: tall, long-eared, deep-voiced, slow, with a splendid nose and little drive. This breed suited perfectly the unsporting

GENERAL WASHINGTON WITH HIS HUNTSMAN AND HOUNDS
Washington began hunting when he was sixteen. He inherited Mount Vernon on his half-brother's death in 1752 and married in 1759: both events had the effect of increasing the time he spent hunting. In 1767 he formed his own pack. From then until 1774, as his diary constantly shows, hunting occupied a great deal of his spare time. His kennel was 100 yards from the family vault – 'a rude structure, but affording comfortable quarters for the hounds, with a large enclosure paled in, having in the midst of it a spring of running water'. He went out three days a week, breakfasting by candle-light, leaving the house at cockcrow, and often unkennelling his fox before sunrise. He was an accomplished and daring horseman, and he rode up to his hounds in a way hardly yet attempted in England. His favourite hunter was Blueskin, 'a fine but fiery animal, and of great endurance in a long run'. Will or Billy Lee usually rode Chinkling, a short-legged powerful horse and a brilliant jumper. 'Will had but one order, which was to keep with the hounds; and mounted on Chinkling, a French horn at his back, throwing himself almost at length on the animal, with his spur in his flank, this fearless horseman would rush at full speed through brake and tangled wood, in a style at which modern huntsmen would stand aghast.' Painting by John Ward Dunsmore, 1924.

needs of the north east and the sporting of the south. In the north, the Old Southern hound flushed game out of covert to be shot; deer, turkey and fox were all killed thus with a conscious absence of enjoyment. In the south, the same hounds hunted very well the hare-like grey fox: the slowness of both hound and quarry was a merit in country often very difficult to cross.

In the best kennels breeding was selective and drafting ruthless; the Mount Vernon hounds were level and they carried a grand head. This was evidently quite exceptional. In other kennels, and among thousands of trencher-fed hounds, breeding was utterly casual, as was that of even the best thoroughbred horses.

Everywhere hounds were crossed, deliberately or haphazardly, with other breeds and with pointers, greyhounds, and various crossbred guard dogs and herd dogs. It is doubtful if any pure-bred Talbots or English staghounds survived the Revolution. The only pure-bred English foxhounds to survive were probably Mr Evers's at Hempstead. But it is clear that the Old Southern survived in pure form in parts of Pennsylvania, Eastern Maryland and Delaware (to be the ancestor of the Penn-Marydel) and of New England. The Virginia mountain hound – uniquely light-framed, uniquely self-reliant, often and uniquely red in colour – also survived in pure form in places where its owners had contact with the owners of no other type.

The Grey and the Red Fox

The sporting colonists of Virginia and Maryland found an unfamiliar fox in their woods, jackal-like in its habits, hunting by scent like a pointer, having, of itself, less scent than the foxes of England, being less fast and less stout a runner, going in rings, taking refuge in trees, and grey in colour.[23]

When the red fox began to appear in sporting districts, it was generally believed that it had been imported from England for sport. 'A gentleman of fortune in New England, who had a great inclination for hunting, brought over a great number of foxes from Europe.'[24] In fact a red fox was native to Canada and the northern states. It was well known to the Indians and trappers, and was hunted for its pelt. Its reputation for devious cunning was the same as its European cousin's – the Huron Magua was known as *le Reynard Subtil* to the Mohicans.[25]

The red fox spread southward during the 17th century; unlike the forest-loving grey it throve in partly cleared land, and it found easy pickings near farms and villages. It multiplied enormously. This process was artificially accelerated. In 1730 'eight prosperous tobacco planters' of Talbot County, Maryland, imported English foxes 'in order to secure the same sport that many of them had enjoyed in England'.[26]

In the hard winter of 1779–80 Chesapeake Bay was frozen, and it is supposed that red foxes crossed the ice to Baltimore. They spread rapidly thence through Maryland and Virginia, transforming the demands made on hounds and huntsmen and – as much as the Revolution itself – starting a new era in American foxhunting.

Virginia, Revolution to Civil War

'Hunting, or coursing, *proper*,' said the Englishman 'Frank Forester' in 1848, 'does not exist on this Continent.'[27] This had been heavily qualified sixteen years earlier by a native writer: 'There are, however, Foxhunters in almost every state; but their number is so small, and excursions comparatively so few, to those of the Southern states, that it may properly be called a *Southern sport*.'[28] The fact was that in almost every county in Virginia, Maryland, the central regions of North and South

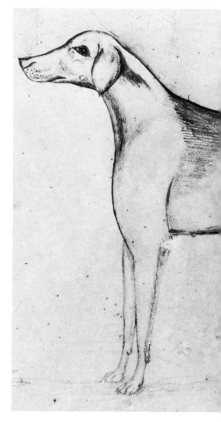

Carolina and the extreme south east of Pennsylvania, there were two or more private packs of foxhounds and numberless farmers with one or two couple.

The best pack of foxhounds in Virginia was given up when its owner became president. The next best was at Messrs William H. and George M. Chichester's Fairfax County kennel. There were two other packs in the county; the three often combined. On 1 and 2 January 1830, for example, they all met at Ravensworth – twenty-one horsemen, twenty-one couple; they killed four red foxes, all after fine runs. The sport was 'wanting nothing but a uniform dress to give it all the splendour of an English fox hunt'.[29]

In Fauquier and Loudoun Counties there were large numbers of trencher-fed hounds which met to hunt. The one well-known pack was that of General William 'Billy' Payne ('Captain Pepper' because of his rages) of Clifton, near Warrenton. In Rappahannock County several gentlemen 'each keep from ten to fifteen well-bred hounds'.[30] John Tayloe III of Mount Airy inherited hounds from his father as well as Virginia's most important thoroughbred stud.

Mr Hancock Lee, a foxhunting man, hotel owner and connection of the Chichesters, started the Hunt of the White Sulphur Springs to entertain his customers; Colonel Charles Green started a Rappahannock Valley pack; a pack was established at Upperville which became Colonel Dulany's. By 1845 there may have been a dozen packs in Fauquier County alone. Mr Percival started one in the Southside which became the Petersburg Hunt Club.

By this point hounds in all parts of Virginia were changing. The red fox had arrived, and was not to be killed above ground by the old Virginia hound. English and Irish hounds were therefore imported, mostly by way of Maryland, and used as outcrosses. There was great complaint about this: in 1834, 'the constant search for *fast dogs*, has left us with but few dogs of *good tongue or cold nose*'.[31]

Drive without loss of nose or tongue was provided by blood which was quite free of English foxhound and quite unknown in England: the Kerry beagle. Fellhounds were perhaps also imported.

The Virginia horse continued to improve. Dozens of thoroughbred stallions were imported after the Revolution; there were consequently a lot of good hunters. There were fine horsemen too. 'Some of our riders would be in the first flight, even at Melton.'[32]

Maryland

Chesapeake Bay divides Maryland as sharply in hunting history as in other matters.

The Eastern Shore was dense forest when settled, and remained heavily wooded. Consequently the grey fox much outnumbered the red even after the latter's dramatic southward and westward expansion. The land was owned by farmers quite prosperous enough to own a few hounds and horses, and quite sporting enough to use them, but without the great wealth or Anglophil sophistication of Baltimore, Washington or Northern Virginia. The result was that the Old Southern hound, right for the country in the 17th century, was still right for it in the 19th, and kept its purity as nowhere else. Eastern Shore hounds were owned in small parcels rather than packs, and organization remained minimal and relaxed. Under these circumstances hunting was hardly recorded.

Hounds of identical character had arrived in Prince George's County, on the other side of the bay, in 1650. Mr Roger Brooke Taney, later Chief Justice of the Supreme Court, inherited a pack of hounds in Calvert County descended from the colonel's.

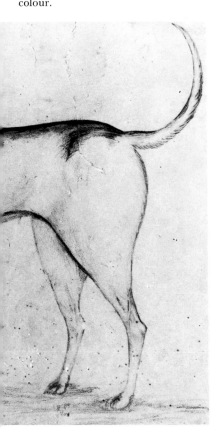

MR OGLE'S SOPHY
The old Virginia and Maryland hounds, both black-and-tan and blue-tick, were incapable of killing a red fox above ground, like their English ancestors the Talbot and Old Southern. When the red fox came south, breeders got hounds from Ireland. The most celebrated of many were Mountain and Muse, which went from Mr Bolton Jackson of Baltimore to Colonel Sterett Ridgely, and from him to Mr Benjamin Ogle of Belair, Maryland. Sophy was the best of their numerous offspring. She was ancestress of the Henrys and some of the Julys (the latter following the former into Georgia): thence of the Birdsongs and so the Triggs. Although it is not quite proved that Mountain and Muse were Kerry beagles, it is morally certain. No other kind of Irish hound of the time (except pure-bred English importations, of which there were few) had the amazing drive of these hounds; Sophy's forelegs belong to no relation of any English foxhound; black-and-tan was already a frequent but by no means an invariable Kerry beagle colour.

His father, about 1795, would unite his pack with that of a visiting neighbour; they would hunt for a week, with a party of eight or ten. Life was exactly like that of Mount Vernon thirty years earlier: they breakfasted by candlelight, 'most commonly on spareribs (or bacon) and hominy, – drank pretty freely of eggnog, and then mounted and were in the cover, where they expected to find a fox, before sunrise'.[33] But Colonel Maynadier of Ann Arundel had a pack near Annapolis early in the 19th century which already showed far more drive and self-reliance than the pure-bred Eastern Shore hound: they once ran eighty miles in a straight line, nobody near them at all; a farmer kept them for two weeks until the colonel found them.[34]

Early in the century, Baltimore and Washington had small private packs which joined together *ad hoc* for a day's hunting. But there was a new departure in these places.

In 1825 the anonymous owner of a pack offered it, by a letter in the Press, to anyone who would keep and hunt it near Baltimore. The offer was taken up by Mr John Stuart Skinner and Mr Robert Oliver. They formed the Baltimore Hunt Club.[35] They still drew before sunrise. They had joint meets with other packs such as the Bridge or Potomac hounds, and often went into Virginia. The hounds were probably an uneven mixture of blue-tick, Virginian and Kerry beagle. English hounds were also tried – $1\frac{1}{2}$ couple from the Quorn given to Commodore Richard Stockton by Sir Harry Goodricke. But their noses were not good enough for the cold-scenting country, they ran mute, and they were far too fast for pack and field; they went to Virginia to hunt deer.[36]

Near Washington at this point there were at least six private packs. By 1828, additionally to these, a Washington Hunt existed, its president being Sir Charles Vaughan, British Ambassador since 1825. It was no larger than the others, which it regularly joined. Sir Charles provided English hounds. The subscribers included the whole of the British Embassy staff, with numbers of congressmen and diplomats.

The pack grew from 'seven couple of topping red fox dogs'[37] in 1828 to forty or fifty in 1834. The huntsman Mason Clark 'rides manfully to his hounds'. The elegance and eminence of the members, the efficient organization, the fine hunt horses, and the size and quality of the pack made the Washington Hunt by 1834 'the best appointed hunting establishment in the Union'.[38] Bagmen were occasionally hunted when some diplomatic occasion made a run desirable. Cockneys (*sic*) sometimes turned out in distressing numbers, spoiling sport by their ignorant indiscipline.[39]

Baltimore and Washington started a rapid formalization of Maryland hunts, on lines specifically imitated from England, and urged by J. S. Skinner in the *American Farmer* and, from 1829, the *A.T.R.*

'The most remarkable and distinct family of hounds, recollected in Maryland, sprang from two that were brought some twenty years odd since from Ireland, by Bolton Jackson, Esq.'[40] Mr Jackson of Baltimore was allegedly given the hounds by the Duke of Leeds, whose wife was a Marylander. They arrived about 1814. They were called Mountain and Muse. They were astonishing for speed, bottom and 'ardour' – they cast themselves forward at a check, which had hardly ever before been seen in America. Mountain was on the point of being destroyed for killing dogs; his life was saved and he was given, with Muse, to Benjamin Ogle Jr of Belair.

Mr Ogle bred a whole pack from them, keeping the blood pure. The very best whelp was Sophy. She was lined by Traveller, her own but not litter brother, and whelped Captain. Captain came, by way of two other owners, to Dr Thomas Y. Henry of Virginia.

RULES

OF THE

OUCESTER HUNTING CLUB.

TALLY HO!

ARTICLE I.

'he association shall be called, **THE GLOUCESTER
X HUNTING CLUB.**

ARTICLE II.

'here shall be annually chosen by ballot, on the first
ursday of January by a majority of the members pre-
t, due notice having been given to each member by the
retary, at least three days before said election, a Prent, Vice President, Treasurer, Secretary, and four

**RULES OF THE GLOUCESTER
FOXHUNTING CLUB**
An informal association of citizens of
Philadelphia was given formal organization in 1766: this was America's
first Hunt Club. It owed its formation
to what was then rare but became
common: the fact that business and
professional men, living in a city,
wanted to hunt. The farmers of nearby
Chester and Delaware Counties had
no need of clubs until much later.

Other Irish hounds were still coming into Maryland. General Hood imported
some about 1835; their descendants included Tickler and, through him, Colonel
Nimrod Gosnell's July. Nimrod Gosnell, of Baltimore and then Howard County,
was a successful farmer, a hard rider of good horses, and a hound breeder of immense
historical importance.

Maryland hunting had other attributes that deserve mention. One was a greater
number of ladies in the field than elsewhere in America, and a far greater number
than in England; they rode to hounds in scarlet habits.[41] A second was the length
of the runs. Colonel Maynadier's eighty miles was unique, but thirty miles was not
uncommon in 1800 owing to the slow but tireless way the hounds hunted. By 1830
it was normal to kill a grey fox in thirty-five minutes to an hour, a red in one to two
hours. It had been 'a very rare thing to kill a red fox on the ground'; it became
frequent.[42] As in England, degenerate foxes were blamed, but better hounds were
probably the main reason. A third special feature were the blackjack thickets: scrub
oak, four to six foot high, very dense, a favourite covert for foxes. In 1837 two visiting
Englishmen, full of Meltonian hubris and used to bullfinches, were humiliated by
the disintegration of all their clothes.[43]

Maryland, like Virginia, had slave labour and plenty of trees. The result was
massive and excellent fencing; the traditional type was the snake fence, in which
heavy rails were laid in a shallow zigzag so as to overlap at each end.

Pennsylvania and New Jersey

The Gloucester Fox Hunting Club was restarted by Captain Samuel Morris and
his friends immediately after the Revolution. It had great sport (with a brilliant
but eccentric huntsman)[44] but it relied all too much on one man. After Captain
Morris died this was Captain Charles Ross. He died in 1818 and with him the club.

Hounds kept in twos and threes were as numerous in south-eastern Pennsylvania
as in Maryland and Virginia. Meets were advertised with the words: 'Those gentlemen having dogs, are invited to bring them.'[45] In Chester County hunting continued
'from the force of habit': but it was said to have come downhill from the better days
before the Revolution. Hounds had degenerated, 'not being restricted to close
communion'; even rich farmers were unable to afford good horses; and some opinion
was becoming more openly hostile. When a bag fox was turned down at Kennett,
Chester County, in 1796, the only man up at the death was riding a plough horse. It
was all 'but a very faint shadow of the old English pastime'.[46] All the same it continued.

The hunting of trencher-fed packs did not draw attention to itself. William Cobbett, visiting from England in 1817–18, saw no hunting at all in the English sense –
only shooting over dogs – except by one pack of hounds, 'those kept by old John
Brown in Buck's County, Pennsylvania, who was the only *hunting Quaker* that I ever
heard of'.[47]

Another private pack was kept by Mr Charles Pennell, from immediately after
the Revolution. With it he hunted in Chester and Delaware Counties. It was
inherited by Mr Mark Pennell. The best hound was 'blue and white'. They scorned
to hunt a bag fox; they had no need to.

Meets of trencher-fed hounds were often at taverns, one of which was the Rose
Tree Inn at Media, Delaware County. In 1852 Messrs J. Howard Lewis and Mr
George E. Darlington combined their 'white-speckled' and 'blue-speckled' hounds,
were joined by other friends, and in 1859 formed a club. They kennelled the pack at

the Rose Tree. There was no regular master or huntsman. None was needed. 'The sport was truly hunting, and not steeplechasing with hounds across country.'[48]

Western Pennsylvania hunting was more influenced by Canada than by the east. A number of farmers' trencher-fed packs are presumed; a number belonging to ironfounders are recorded. One of these very rich industrialists, Peter Marmie, had twenty couple of hounds which he hunted in orthodox English fashion. Once, enraged by their failure on a bad-scenting day, he had the whole pack thrown alive into his Alliance Furnace.[49]

New Jersey hunting was exactly like eastern Pennsylvanian. The many trencher-fed packs were mostly along the Hackensack and Passaic rivers.

The only regular pack recorded is that of John Frame of Hackensack, who had ten couple of English foxhounds about 1820. His hunt was popular with farmers while foxes were a nuisance; but after damage became more annoying than foxes they grew truculent, and Mr Frame took his pack to Long Island.

In the southern part of the state there was a sharp difference between east and west. Throughout eastern New Jersey in 1823 foxes 'are yet hunted in the laudable old-fashioned style, on horseback'. This style had once flourished in the west too, but it was given up before 1820. Foxes were shot over dogs; near Salem they were shot on the beaches of Delaware Bay.[50]

New York and New England

Mr John Evers kept his English hounds kennelled at Hempstead, Long Island, throughout the Revolutionary War, with English horses and hunt staff. On 23 April 1783, St George's day, a group of gentlemen met and formed the St George's Hunt Club, agreeing to subscribe to maintain the hounds and keeping Mr Evers as master. Eleven horsemen turned out at the first meet; they had 'a nine-mile run and a six-bottle dinner'.[51] The membership became resplendent, including General Washington, Alexander Hamilton and General Charles Lee.

One of the members of the St George's Hunt Club was Mr Nathaniel Prime; his sons Edward and Rufus bought '10 couple of fine hounds' from Mr Biglow of Boston in 1812. Their Belvidere Hunt met at Cato's (now Third Avenue at 52nd Street) until building made hunting there impossible. They moved to kennels at the Higbee Farm, at Foster Meadows, Long Island. Their pack was there joined by Mr Frame's from Hackensack. The other Manhattan hunts either closed down or moved to Long Island or Westchester by 1821. Bag foxes were still hunted in the Bronx for some years after this.

Then hunting died in and about New York. It was revived in 1856, when Mr T. C. Carpendale, son of an English parson, acquired a pack and called it the Brooklyn Hunt. His founder members included the great trotting-horse man Hiram Woodruff, Henry Herbert ('Frank Forester') and William Porter of the new *Spirit of the Times*. 'For the first time for many years the majestic hills in the neighbourhood of Brooklyn will respond to the notes of the merry horn and hound.'[52] But the hunt was disbanded in 1861 when war was imminent.

With only two known exceptions, there was no recognizable foxhunting in New England.

To an extent this was a matter of physical conditions. The game was in hardwood forests with dense undergrowth. The Puritans killed foxes at night, using codfish heads as bait. Their successors shot over one or two Old Southern hounds. But the main reason was a matter of political and social tradition. 'There have been two

Place and artist are unknown; date is doubtful. The beautiful plantation house is a rich man's home and these very large deerhounds are his own. Deer were hunted as well as grey foxes by the 'Silver Greys' at Raleigh, North Carolina; there were many more of them in South Carolina, the 'middle country' of which, between mountains and coastal swamp, was extensively cleared at about this time for crops and cattle. The deer hunting season started as soon as the harvest was in. The hounds were mostly black-and-tans of clear Talbot type (tall, fast, unlumbered pack bloodhounds of the English north country, not the delicate grotesques of modern dog-shows). Carolina tradition allowed hounds, once running, to be followed on to any man's land: at a trial for trespass on the South Eastern Circuit of South Carolina about 1845 a witness, himself a rich landowner, maintained as ' "hunter's law" his right to follow his hounds wherever they led him, *regardless of damage to fences or growing crops*'. Georgia, Alabama, Mississippi and Louisiana all had rich planters and many private packs of deerhounds; in all the wonderful-nosed hounds were used for runaway slaves as well as grey fox and deer; they were known as 'nigger-dogs', and were an important ingredient in the Georgia Birdsongs and thus in the Kentucky Triggs. Painting attributed to Rufus Porter.

great distributing centres of the English race on this continent, Massachusetts and Virginia,' said James Russell Lowell. 'New England abolished caste; in Virginia they still talk of "quality folks".'[53] In 1794 Connecticut was compared to Europe by the President of Yale: the former was practically paradise, while in the latter,

Hounds and horses riot on the store,
By HEAVEN created for the helpless poor![54]

The two exceptions were both in the Boston area, and at the same time. Mr Biglow had a kennel of foxhounds five miles from the city for an uncertain period; his hounds must have been good, since a draft of them in 1812 satisfied the Primes in New York, who knew the St George's pack. And in 1814 Colonel Samuel Jacques founded the Charleston Hunt Club, with ten to fifteen couple of working hounds which he owned until 1830. He was succeeded by Mr John Tapley of Spring Hill, Charleston. Mr Biglow's hounds no longer existed; Mr Tapley's did not survive him.

The Carolinas and the Deep South

In the 'middle country' of the Carolinas, between the mountains and the coastal swamps, there were large numbers of hounds. 'In the old planting days many kept large packs' – often twenty couple and more, far larger than most private Virginia and Maryland packs. Hunting grew steadily from the Revolution, and rapidly from 1830 to 1850 when a great deal of forest was cleared for maize, cotton and cattle grazing. 'In the middle country, where the ground, comparatively open, is more favourable to equestrian exercise, the sport is followed with great spirit by the Hamptons, Taylors, Singletons, Mannings and other familiar names.'

Most Carolina hounds were the old black-and-tans. They were effective enough: at Greenville, between 1 October and 1 November 1832 one man and his pack killed thirteen full-grown foxes. A few years later the Carolina hound began to be influenced by a new sort. Mr Percival of Petersburg, Virginia, bred by his Rattler out of an English bitch a hound called Byron, which was acquired by Mr Thomas Goode Tucker, who had hunted, with his father, since 1814. In 1837 the Tuckers moved from Virginia to Gaston, North Carolina, and Byron was the patriarch of a new strain which Mr Tucker bred and hunted for forty years.

Hunting was as enthusiastically followed near the coast as in the middle country, but under great physical difficulties. Colonel Elliott's huntsman, a black slave, was told to dismount to follow hounds across a nasty piece of country; he said, 'If he be water, I swim 'um, if he be bog, I bog 'um – if he be brier, I kratch tru 'um – but who de debble, but otter, no so alligator, go tru all tree one time!'[55]

South Carolina had from about 1830 the best and most fashionable thoroughbred racing in the Union. The famous hunting families were all horsebreeders; Richard Tattersall exported a steady stream of good stallions to the Hamptons and Singletons and their friends, which meant excellent thoroughbred and halfbred hunters. Even the one Colonel Elliott rode in the swamps was a great-great-grandson of Gimcrack.

Like South Carolina, Georgia was notable for big estates and rich men. Many private packs were kept. The sport was deerhunting and some hounds were Talbots. In 1827 the Camden Hunting Club was formed; its members rode out in scarlet, but what they did was shoot driven deer.

The state's best-known sportsman was Colonel George L. F. Birdsong of Thomaston, Upson County. 'He was a man of delicate sensibilities, and of aristocratic dignity . . . a writer of prose and poetry of more than local repute.'[56] Once, while hunting, he stumbled on the camp of a stranger. This was Dr Thomas Y. Henry on his way, on foot, from Virginia to Florida, hunting all the way with his Irish–Virginia hounds descended from Mountain and Muse. Colonel Birdsong stayed and hunted with him for three weeks. When Dr Henry reached Quincy, Florida, he found that his hounds were eaten by alligators when they ran deer into a swamp. Consequently he sent them to Colonel Birdsong.

Alabama had vigorous hunting of greys by the 1830s. Church Hill, Mississippi, was the centre of a sporting region. In Louisiana, enthusiasm for hunting is shown by the gigantic price of $100 each paid for ten couple of hounds from Kentucky.

Kentucky, Tennessee, the Middle West

The western foothills of the Southern Appalachians and the grass plains beyond began to be settled at about the time of the Revolution. The settlers brought hounds and some of them brought horses. They found the grey fox and chased it with enthusiasm.

In 1852 a Kentuckian wrote: 'Fox-hunting in the Middle and Southern States, is quite as much a subject of enthusiasm, as it has been in England; although it is neither so expensive nor so technical with us.'[57]

The red fox was first seen in Kentucky in 1856, to the chagrin of hunting men. As it multiplied they had to provide themselves with a new kind of hound. To meet this need, Mr General George Washington Maupin (so baptized), whose father had brought black-and-tans from Virginia, acquired in 1857 a small draft from Britain, said to be from the Duke of Buccleuch. 'Uncle Wash' Maupin was 'Kentucky's most famous and successful hunter': a man of enormous physical strength and a bruising horseman.[58] He and Mr John W. Walker bred a pack of this imported blood, crossed with their Virginia hounds which had already been crossed with a mysterious black-and-tan stallion called Tennessee Lead. The new strain, originally the Maupin-Walker, was remarkable for self-reliance, cold nose, refusal to pack and fondness for clever skirting.

These qualities made it ideal for the new sport of hill topping or high-ground foxhunting, which became popular in Kentucky and Tennessee soon before 1850. It was done at night and by ear. Competition entered the sport at once, to the point that all over the South and Middle West a hunt of this kind was habitually known as a fox race.

WOLF HUNT ON THE ICE, 1831
Wolves as well as red foxes were coursed with greyhounds kept by the garrison at Fort Dearborn, Chicago; a chase like this was first class cavalry training. Wolves were also hunted, by an account contemporary with this picture, in a fashion familiar to the Russia of the time. Four couple of staghounds and a leash of greyhounds were taken out in December. The hounds drew 'the little woods on the east side of the Chicago river, and started in it one of those midnight prowlers. He was trailed up handsomely by the hounds, the woods echoing and re-echoing with their loud, deep notes.' The greyhounds were slipped when the wolf at last broke covert, and got him on the ice of the frozen river, often with the help of a bullet.

In the extreme east of Ohio, at Zanesville, Mr Usual Headley and his sons Ealam and Nealem kept the Headley Inn; from 1802 they kept a pack of hounds for the amusement of their guests, hunting all available game.

Indiana and Michigan had dogs, guns and traps. Foxes, like wolves and bears, were trapped for their pelts.

Near Chicago the red fox was abundant and stout. It was hunted with deerhounds and coursed with greyhounds from early in the 19th century. Greyhounds were well suited by the treeless country.

Far to the south west, the U.S. Army brought hunting to Oklahoma. The Fort Gibson Hunt Club, 1835, was probably America's first military hunt. According to its rules, the kennel was to contain 'bear, wolf, deer and fox dogs'.[59] The first president was Major R. B. Mason of the Dragoons.

Canada

Canadian forms, methods, hounds, hunt staff and followers were English, and the fox was red.

Early settlers in Quebec Province (the minority who were English) acquired hounds very soon; they hunted with them in as orthodox a way as they could manage in dense forest and with months of iron frost. Their numbers were swelled by loyalists who came north after the Revolution.

The Montreal Hounds (the oldest extant organized pack in North America) were 'said to owe their origin to a sporting English butcher, who brought a few couples with him from the mother country. A club was afterwards formed.'[60] The butcher's name was Outhet; he was hired and his hounds bought by Mr John Forsyth, who also got Mr Matthew Bell's Three Rivers hounds. The Montreal Hunt Club first met in 1829, hunting wild foxes.[61] The subscribers were all English and mostly officers. They had a swampy and thickly-wooded country, but this was not the greatest of their problems: '"Jean Baptiste", harped on by Monsieur Papineau,

[179]

occasionally turned out with pitchforks, and even with guns, to stop *les sacres chasseurs du roi*, as they termed the lads in scarlet.' The huntsman was once surrounded by a furious French family armed with guns and pitchforks. He pulled out his horn to warn the field, 'when, to his astonishment, down on their marrowbones dropped his formidable foes, crying out most heartily, "*O mon Dieu, ne tirez pas.*" '[62]

Upper Canada hunting is earlier recorded. Mr William Jarvis owned a pack, of unknown origin, which in January 1801 hunted a fox on to the ice where the mounted field were displaced by skaters.

In 1805 Mr James Durand imported English hounds, the first in Ontario; he hunted a large country near Long Point, Lake Erie. Red fox was their principal chase, but probably not the only one. Mr Charles Durand inherited his father's hounds and lent them to the officers at York, Toronto; this was the foundation, about 1840, of the Toronto Hunt. The pack was enlarged by more English drafts during the 1840s; like Ontario racing, it depended almost wholly on the army.

When the Crimean War took the soldiers away, the Toronto Hunt suffered even more severely than the Montreal.

HUNTING HORNS
The natural cow-horn was very little used in England by the late 17th century. Most huntsmen carried either the French horn or, like the Duke of Buckingham, the little shrill, straight metal horn of the modern type. There were a few boxwood horns (a kind known to Chaucer) and other varieties. In the late 18th century Peter Beckford recommended the short metal horn especially for use in wooded countries, because its shrill twang, though not beautiful, cut through the covert. In spite of this advantage, and in spite of very big woods, most Americans remained loyal to the natural horn.

13 America
Civil War to 1914

Virginia

After the Civil War stables were empty and packs dispersed. Even in 1873: 'At present fox hunting and fox hunters alike have gone to decay in the south, and but few first-rate packs have survived the calamities of the war.'[1]

The result was the growth in Virginia of informal and especially of moonlight hunting, which required no organization, no expense, no kennels, no servants. The pack owner of 1860 became the hill topper of 1865, even in Fairfax and Fauquier Counties, and even among the First Families.

Recovery began soon but it was slow. Colonel Richard Hunter Dulany of Wellbourne, Fauquier County, formed a pack about 1870 and hunted a large country round Upperville. A number of Englishmen arrived at Warrenton, of whom Captain William Assheton bred an interesting English-cross pack;[2] this was taken over by Mr James K. Maddux and became the Warrenton. Another Englishman, Mr Archibald Bevan, started the Blue Ridge in the Shenandoah Valley in 1888: their country was 'the Ireland of America'.[3] In Loudoun County small packs and trencher-fed hounds were all that hunted until 1894; then the packs of Mr Arthur Mason Chichester, Mr William Heflin and Mr William C. Eustis were joined to form the Loudoun County. They bought the Dulanys' Piedmont hounds, but after this pack killed twenty-nine sheep in one day they got a new lot from the Bywaters family. Mr Robert Frank Bywaters had had a pack in Culpeper County before the war; his son Burrell Frank and grandson Hugh were commercial breeders.

This new pack was too small to hunt the Loudoun County's country properly, so Mr A. H. Higginson was invited to bring his English hounds from Massachusetts. They were remarkable for their steadiness. The next season (1908) Mr Harry Worcester Smith brought his Grafton hounds, which were not nearly as successful. Apathy invaded the country, bringing wire.[4]

Mr Smith had come from the Piedmont. He was followed there by Mr John R. Townsend, master of the Orange County, a hunt with a curious history. The Orange County was not that of Virginia, but of New York. A hunt had been started at Goshen in 1900, principally financed by Mr E. H. Harriman, a railway tycoon. They hunted a drag; they wanted to hunt foxes; consequently they came to Virginia where they were asked to share the Warrenton country. Most members came south in seemly fashion, but Mr Harriman fitted up a private train for his hounds, scarlet-coated staff, thoroughbred horses, family and friends. It had a grand piano and

'Fox-racers' and 'hill-toppers' had cows and could make horns; they did so with skill and pride, and at no expense. They inherited a technique of hunting and changed it with the greatest reluctance. Much more important, every natural horn has a distinctive note: if a man can recognize his hounds at a great distance by ear, so can his hounds recognize him. Most important of all – as General Roger D. Williams said, an orthodox Master of Hounds as well as a field triallist – men loved the mellow booming of their cow-horns, and would never forego its evocative magic.

gold-plated taps in the bathroom, which amazed even the richest rural Virginians.

The other Orange County men took increasingly to hunting with Mr William Skinker's private pack of Madison County red ringnecks at The Plains. They were so good that in 1904 the New Yorkers bought the pack, and in 1905 they bought the kennels too.

A confusing situation then arose. Mr Dulany had asked Mr Harry Smith to hunt the Piedmont country; he also asked Mr Townsend; he also did so himself. The immediate result was the departure in dudgeon of Mr Smith from Virginia, and then the formation, at his instance, of the M.F.H.A. of America in order that such scandalous things should not occur again.[5]

Meanwhile Mr Joseph B. Thomas had been assembling a private pack since 1910, mostly of the Bywaters' blood. In 1911 he built superb kennels at Huntlands in the Piedmont Valley and engaged Charles Carver as huntsman. He made the whole establishment available to Mr Daniel Sands. The latter was master of the combined Piedmont and Middleburg countries, but his kennels and hounds were Mr Thomas's property and his huntsman was Mr Thomas's employee. This situation was pregnant with trouble, which exploded into a dispute of extreme bitterness in 1915.

Mr Harriman's flamboyant personal invasion left a spirit of display and exclusivity in the Orange County's part of Virginia. Day visitors were not allowed; they had to spend the night before hunting with a landowner in the country (hence 'Toothbrush Hunt'). Because of these rules there was once a serious doubt about whether the Prince of Wales could be permitted to come out with the Orange County.[6]

Hunting in the Southside began its organized revival about twenty years after the end of the war.

Near Lynchburg, several private packs joined to form the Oak Ridge in 1887. Near Richmond, the Deep Run was either formed as the result of a visit by Colonel Fred Skinner, or he visited it soon after its formation; the date is variously given.[7] A Charlottesville Hunt, previously small and private (and supported by the University of Virginia) became organized in 1894 and then became the Albemarle County. The Keswick was started in 1896; under too amiable a master there was more damage than finance.[8] An Orange County hunt was started in 1902, but it had to change its name to the Tomahawk because of the New York gentlemen in Fauquier County.

Dr Thomas Walker had had hounds at Castle Hill, Albemarle County, in 1742. In 1905 his descendant Mrs Gertrude Rives Potts refounded the hunt, justly considering herself hereditary master. She first got the goodwill of seventy-two farmers (it was the warmest goodwill, and so remained), which assured her an adequate country. Impressed by Mr Higginson's pack, she got English hounds, which amazed the region. At a combined hunt at Barboursville one Christmas, with a huge scratch pack mostly of American hounds, Mrs Potts's three couple were all up when the fox went to ground, with only two couple of all the rest.[9]

Another English pack was established as the Blue Run, Orange County, by Mr William du Pont and some friends. The du Pont family also brought a private pack to Montpelier Station in 1912; the master was Mr William du Pont Jr.

The Petersburg area had an ebullient revival of foxhunting: there were six packs within fifteen miles of the Riverside in 1908. They all died.

Maryland and Delaware

Just after the Civil War Anthony Trollope wrote: 'A pack of fox-hounds was for a time established in Maryland, which, of all the United States, is perhaps more than

other like to England in its mode of life. But it has been found impracticable to establish the sport in other lands, even among men who are thoroughly English in their
ways and thoughts.'[10] Although Trollope's information was scarcely complete, it is
true that in Maryland as in Virginia there were no regular foxhunting establishments
at the time when he wrote. But there was a great deal of foxhunting. The farmers
of the Eastern Shore continued to assemble their trencher-fed packs of pure-bred Old
Southern hounds, and hunt the grey and sometimes the red fox sonorously through
the woods. This skilful, unhurried, inexpensive and deeply rural sport did not in
essence change between the American Revolution and the first war.

At this period farmers and citizens of Baltimore were joining up their hounds for
meets at Elkridge Landing, south west of the city. On 6 March 1878 they established
themselves as the Elkridge (often Elk Ridge) Fox Hunting Club.

In 1880 General George S. Brown and his son came back from Europe, both
widely experienced in English hunting. The general became president of the hunt
and his son master. Mr Alex Brown undertook his duties as he had learned in
England – he looked after the farmers and did all he could to encourage them to
hunt.

Mr Brown got Maryland hounds and crossed them with imported English. This
was the foundation of one of the great crossbred packs, widely imitated and widely
admired.[11]

By 1890 there was clearly room for another Baltimore pack. The Stewart family
had come to Philadelphia from Ireland about 1760, then become leading citizens
of Baltimore. Redmond C. Stewart, following family tradition, had hounds at the
age of ten. His hunting tutor was John Bowen, a white-bearded resident of Green
Spring Valley who had a little pack of red hounds descended from the Brookes and
from Mountain and Muse. At the age of eighteen, in 1892, Mr Stewart established
the Green Spring Valley. He started with Maryland hounds, but became convinced that the Elkridge were right.[12]

Of several other evanescent hunts in the area, the Patapsco was the best and best-
known; it was engulfed in buildings in 1913.

The Elkridge roamed far north into Harford County; in 1906 the Green Spring
Valley took its place there. In 1912 Mr Frank Bonsal, Mr Stewart's nephew and
whipper-in, was given twelve couple to start an independent Harford Hunt. It was
an immediate and sustained success.

Following the successful examples of Annapolis and Baltimore, Washington again saw formal hunting, on a modest scale, in the early 1880s. Mr Haskins, an eminent grocer, kept a small pack in a kennel behind his store. Riding to his hounds on his wagon horse, he revived hunting in Washington, but to the wounding of his business. The Dumblane Hunt Club was a formal successor, but a failure. Mr Samuel S. Howland picked up its pieces and started the Chevy Chase in 1892; Mr Clarence Moore then showed such good sport that he made hunting near Washington more popular than golf. But support dwindled. It recovered enough to justify a visit to England in 1912; Mr Moore got more hounds; he and they went down with the *Titanic*.

Annapolis had a Naval Riding Club until about 1889, then an Ann Arundel Hunt Club from 1904. Because it depended on naval officers it was a casualty of the first war.

Delaware hunting was almost entirely of the Eastern Shore type, with the same sort of farmers using the same sort of hounds. One of the few organizations was the South-Side Fox Hunting Club of Wilmington, which hunted into Cecil County, Maryland. There was also a Delaware Fox Hunting Club in the 1880s. There were thousands of hounds, hundreds of two- and three-couple lots, but into the 20th century very few private packs much larger than this. One was that of Mr James C. McCoomb at Claymount, to which Abner Garnell came as huntsman from Delaware County, Pennsylvania, when the Uplands Hunt came to an end.

Northern Maryland carries better scent than most of Virginia, and the country needs power to get across. This does not really explain the use of pure-bred English packs round Washington, but it does account for the development of the Baltimore crossbred packs. Mr Redmond Stewart's was essentially a cross of Belvoir and July, the latter having been developed specifically for the red fox. English stallions lined American bitches, which argues unusually large American hounds.

Pennsylvania and New Jersey

Until 1873 the Rose Tree Fox Hunting Club was no more formal than any of its forgotten contemporaries. In that year, however, it was put on a regular basis. Mr George W. Hill became president and acting master (there had never been such an officer before) and the club took a subscription. Hounds bred by individual members had been all that were ever entered with the pack, but now drafts were bought from Virginia and Maryland.

The country was almost entirely fenced with very stiff post and rail. In 1876 two visiting Englishmen, Masters of Hounds, 'absolutely refused to ride with the Rose Tree, frankly confessing their fear of riding over such a country at the pace set'.[13] It was still normal for the Rose Tree to join with one or more of the many other hunts in Delaware County: on 5 March 1877, 100 'hunters' and 133 hounds turned out for a joint meet of the Rose Tree and Germantown clubs.[14]

In 1878 Wells Rogers was engaged as professional huntsman, another departure; he served until 1905. A convinced admirer of the American hound, his method was typical of American huntsmen; he brought the hounds to the meet in couples, and took home as many as he could find at the end, but while they were hunting he left them completely alone.[15]

West Chester is a few miles west of Media, in an area equally thronged with sporting and hound-owning farmers. About 1871 some of these formed themselves

MR TRUEHART'S HOUNDS, ABOUT 1810
Mr Bartholomew Truehart (1770–1834) had a private pack in Powhatan County, Virginia, where there was probably at least one other and perhaps several. Mr Truehart's huntsman (a slave, like most others) has a curious long bugle. The hounds are large, slow line-hunters, the old Virginia hounds which were ideal for the hare-like grey fox but virtually incapable, through lack of pace and drive, of killing a red above ground. They look underfed, which was normal and deliberate: huntsmen believed into the 20th century that hounds had to be hungry in order to want to hunt. Mr Truehart's hat is 'coon- or fox-skin, a trophy of the chase. The fence is the characteristic snake, product of unlimited timber and labour. Paintings by an unknown artist.

MEADOW BROOK HOUND
The Meadow Brook country was hunted, successively, by: Mr Griswold's Irish harriers; Mr Joe Donahue's Hackensack hounds; Mr Purdy's, also Irish; Mr Griswold's again; Mr Ralph Ellis's American hounds; Mr Foxhall Keene's fellhounds from Colonel Salkeld's private pack in Cumberland, hunted on Long Island by Bob Cotesworth; Mr H. I. Baker's Arkansas pack; Mr Paul Rainey's, another private pack, which he later took, in dudgeon, to hunt lion in Africa; Mr J. E. Davis's Virginia hounds, hunted by Thomas Allison from 1911, who also brought hounds of his own; and some others. None of these packs were really successful except with drags. In 1913 Mr Harry I. Nicholas turned failure into real foxhunting success. He bought many of Mr Harry Worcester Smith's Grafton hounds; when English hounds started coming to America as refugees in 1915, Mr Nicholas secured some bitches and lined them with carefully chosen dogs of the Grafton sort. He thus bred a pack which combined the nose, cry and self reliance of the sires with the stamina, steadiness, levelness and pack discipline of the dams; by line-breeding to the cross he created a type (of which this is Revel) which bred true. Painting by C. Muss-Arnolt, *c.* 1920.

ROSE TREE HOUNDS, ABOUT 1880
Chil, Trailer, Hunter and Tuck. In the 1874–5 season a few English hounds were imported and tried by the Rose Tree, but it was found that 'the English hound could not compete with the American in our hunting fields, either in nose, voice, or endurance'. Thereafter hounds of the type shown were exclusively used, bred and hunted from 1878 by Wells 'Doc' Rogers. This group shows the influence of Virginia and Maryland blood in the kennel (the black-and-tan) but also the dominance of the old Pennsylvania sort, visible in the high-crowned heads and long ears as well as in colouring. These dog-hounds have plenty of bone but they do not carry it to the ground; they look somewhat hare-footed. Their collars remind us that Wells Rogers, typically, always brought his hounds out in couples. He never attempted to hunt them once they were in covert: hence he could allow them monosyllabic names which no English kennel would ever have used. Print by Armstrong after Alexander Pope Jnr.

into a loose organization. Three years later Buffalo Bill came out with them; by his own modest account he was terrified by the stiff timber until he stopped at a tavern and had some drinks; then he rode very bravely, was up at the death and was given the brush.[16] In 1879 the members adopted formal organization, electing a committee and master, choosing a uniform and committing themselves to subscriptions.

Immediately north of the Rose Tree's country in Delaware County, Mr Thomas Mather, a Quaker, had a private pack from about 1870. His neighbours joined him, some informally subscribing, and there was a clubhouse. On 13 December 1883 a regular club was organized; in 1886 it became the Radnor Hunt.

The following year Mr Charles E. Mather (no relation) became master, his grandfather having had a private pack at Coatesville, thirty miles west, early in the century. He continued to hunt the club's Pennsylvania hounds, but with increasing dislike; he found them undisciplined, jealous, given to babbling and riot, and incapable of breeding true because of ill-judged outcrossing.[17] He accordingly imported, for himself and at his own cost, a draft of thirty-one couple, young and old, from Belvoir, with which came Frank Gillard Jr, who had been whipping-in to his father. The club meanwhile assembled a new American pack. Frank Gillard hunted both in the Radnor country for five years; sometimes they went out together.

Pressure from members grew in favour of the American hounds, on grounds of nose, cry and patriotism, until deadlock was reached in 1901. Mr Mather refused to hunt only an American pack and resigned his Radnor mastership.

Mr (later Colonel) John R. Valentine found a nice compromise between these extreme views: he bred a really fine crossbred pack, lining active light-framed bitches from hilly countries like the Fife and Blackmore Vale with American dogs of similar conformation.

Mr Mather had already been hunting a new Brandywine country and continued to do so with his own pack. He called his hounds not English but West Chester. 'I feel positively convinced that my home bred hounds are faster and have better noses and voices than their imported progenitors. Also I think they have become more self-reliant, because of the necessity of giving them a wider range when drawing our large woods.'[18]

The Lima Fox Hunting Club was formed in 1885 by the amalgamation of small packs. In 1908 it was going very well indeed, with local support and consequent lack of wire. Within a few years 'waning hunting interest' and growing wire killed it.[19] This was a common fate: there had been in 1895, within fifteen miles of the Radnor, 'no less than twelve packs of hounds, and of all of them the Radnor and the Rose Tree are the only ones not entirely supported by farmers'.[20] The farmers' sons seem to have been different.

Farther west, the old Whitelands had died, revived, died, and revived in 1896 as the Chester Valley. It went as well as any hunt in America, owing to local support which owed nothing to big cities. Its country and membership were absorbed into a new Whitelands in 1913.

Between the Rose Tree and the Lima there were individuals hunting, but room for a hunt. The Uplands was founded in 1900, its pack mostly Mr Edward Crozer's Maryland hounds. In 1910 the Uplands was given up. Mr Samuel D. Riddle of Glen Riddle (who later bought Man O' War) formed a pack to hunt the country. He found that there were 5,000 hounds within thirty miles of his kennel; he therefore bred a uniform black-and-tan pack so that his hounds would not be blamed for depredations committed by others.[21]

America: Civil War to 1914

At Valley Forge, the Taylor had absorbed the Washington, but in 1910 a new Valley Forge absorbed the Taylor. This was taken over by the great tennis player Mr William C. Clothier, who called it the Pickering. He added the Glen Moore in 1914, which became the Eagle Farms in 1918.

Mr W. Plunket Stewart, while whipping-in to his brother at Baltimore, wanted to hunt his own pack. But there was nowhere near home that he could do it. He found at last a country next to the Brandywine and in 1914 started cubbing with a pack mostly of English hounds.

In Lancaster and York Counties, the miscalled Pennsylvania Dutch were not the farmers to welcome orthodox foxhunting. Nor did they. Mr Richard P. McGrann tried very hard with his Killashandra hounds in 1907, but in 1913 the farmers stopped him, more gently than Irish peasants but just as effectively.

At the other end of the state, a Pittsburgh hunt was born and died. It was born again as the Harkaway, but died when its master moved away. Hunts supported by businessmen in cities were still as frail in 1909 as they were when the Gloucester was given up ninety years earlier.

At Hackensack, New Jersey, Mr Joseph Donahue was master of an ill-assorted pack of blue-mottled foxhounds, harriers and beagles. He was joined about 1867 by Colonel F. G. Skinner. Fred Skinner was the son of John Stewart, the Baltimore publisher who, in his three periodicals, made foxhunting a subject for journalism a very few years after *The Sporting Magazine* was doing the same in England. J. S. Skinner was a friend of Lafayette; Fred was brought up partly by Lafayette in France, and hunted there and in England as a boy. After the Civil War he was field-sports editor of *Turf, Field and Farm*. He and Joe Donahue made the Hackensack a popular and respected hunt, in spite of rough pack and country.

A few miles west of Hackensack, the Montclair Equestrian Club was started in 1876 by Miss Florence Wilmer, daughter of English residents. More than half her club were young ladies. Within two years, influenced by Joe Donahue and Fred Skinner, the club became the Montclair Hunt. In 1880 the Montclair became the Essex County. In 1890 the pack was bought by the industrialist Mr Charles Pfizer, an outstanding horseman. He built new kennels on his own land at Bernardsville, and hunted a country farther west in Morris and Somerset Counties.

Far to the south east, there had been active hunting in Monmouth County early in the 19th century, but little recorded between 1830 and 1890.

In 1890 Mr Peter Fenelon Collier, an Irish resident, imported a draft of hounds and a stud of hunters from Meath and began draghunting near Eatontown. He had hunted for several years each season with the Meath, and Mr John Watson (M.F.H. 1891–1908) was a close friend. In 1893 James Blute, the huntsman, went to Ireland to get fifteen couple of staghounds and some tame deer from the Ward Union, and more horses. The Monmouth County began hunting carted stags, which enraged the S.P.C.A., who did not realize that the deer joined in the fun and were never hurt.

The Watchung Hunt Club was established at Plainfield in 1902 by Mr Middleton O'Malley Knott, an Irish veterinary surgeon. His first pack was one couple of beagles and a single American hound called Chief, sold for $5 because he was gun-shy. His opening meet was on Christmas day 1902; his pack hunted a cat. He got a larger pack for the next season, equally bobbery and equally wild. In 1906 Mr Charles D. Freeman, lately master of the Richmond County, paid a visit and liked what he saw. He put up money for a new pack. Mr Knott's father in Ireland found them a draft of Mr Aubrey Wallis's Millstreet pack, Kerry beagles from County Cork; these hunted enthusiastically a drag laid with a piece of dead fox.[22]

THE GENESSEE VALLEY HOUNDS Mr (later Major) W. Austin Wadsworth formed the basis of his pack in 1880 with a draft from the Meath, Captain Jock Trotter's very fast hounds. In 1884 he got a draft from Lord Fitzhardinge, the distinctive Berkeley hounds, often pale-coloured, seldom perfectly straight, famous for pace and drive; and in 1887 one from Sir Bache Cunard, descended from Mr Tailby's brilliant bitches. He also got hounds from the Duke of Beaufort, tremendously fast and powerful and uniquely steady; the Holderness, then a very fine pack of almost pure Belvoir blood created by Mr James Hall and Mr Arthur Wilson; and Lord Tredegar. The last had formed his pack in 1870; his hounds were Welsh cross based on the Penllergaer. These constituents should have produced a pack of tremendous drive and substance: and they did.

THE QUEEN'S COUNTY, 1878
This was the hunt's first season. Mr Griswold had procured a pack; Messrs William E. Peet, A. Belmont Purdy and Robert Center had found a country, bought a farm at Meadow Brook, built stables and kennels, collected hunt horses, and negotiated with the farmers. The first meet was on 3 or 4 October 1877. They hunted a drag. On 10 October they dropped a red fox. Fields grew rapidly and included many ladies; the farmers were friendly. The second season was disappointing; Mr Griswold took his hounds away. They were replaced by 'Mr Purdy's Hounds' – some Irish, some from the Duke of Beaufort – which in 1881 became the Meadow Brook.

New York

In 1875 Colonel Fred Skinner came from Hackensack to Long Island intending to start a hunt. He got support from the young men who had learned their hunting at Hackensack. In 1877 they formed the Queen's County. Mr Frank Gray Griswold went to Ireland and bought a pack. He had hunted in England and at Pau as a boy; he decided that the Pau precedent of bagman and drags was better for Long Island than that of the English.[23]

America: Civil War to 1914

Mr Griswold went away with his hounds in 1879. 'Mr Purdy's Hounds', Irish and English, became the Meadow Brook in 1881. Mr Griswold, returning, shared the country. Meanwhile at Far Rockaway, then a place of high fashion, a pack of black-and-tan Virginia hounds began to hunt bag foxes.

Rockaway, Meadow Brook and Queen's County earned, at this point, some resentful comment: 'They object to smiling, speak in loud tones, and tap their boots loudly with their English whips. They wear silk hats, pink coats of which they are intensely enamoured, hunting breeches that are somewhat severe on their legs, and boots. Often they are accompanied by fresh-faced English grooms clad somewhat like themselves, but looking vastly more at ease. The huntsmen (*sic*) usually wear the single glass, and exhibit a tendency to ignore and gaze over the heads of other people who do not hunt the fox.'[24]

But 'Brooksby' was full of admiration for Mr Griswold's hounds and his 'quiet and masterly' handling of them, and awed by the size of the timber and the speed at which it was jumped.[25] Thereafter there were repeated attempts to hunt naturalized wild foxes with all sorts of hounds; but only draghunting was really successful. The first pack that turned out right for the country was Mr Harry L. Nicholas's, crossbred out of English bitches.

There were several other Long Island packs of short life and two of longer: the Bayside, which became the Smithtown, and the Suffolk.

'The early hunts of the Staten Island Club ended so ingloriously that the organization was dissolved after the second meeting, and the chase abandoned in disgust.' Twenty-five dollars were spent on a bag fox, which escaped from the ship which brought it from New York. Forty dollars were spent on a second fox, but the members, who wore scarlet, uncoupled all their hounds without giving it any law and it was killed after a run of twenty feet.[26]

In 1876 the hunt had recovered from these traumatic beginnings, and with seven couple of local hounds and $4\frac{1}{2}$ from Hackensack was chasing bagmen satisfactorily. The club became the Richmond County. Repeated vicissitudes turned gradually into success: but the hunt was developed to death.

Mr Griswold had visited Westchester County with his hounds and aroused local enthusiasm. An ill-managed hunt resulted in 1885, followed by a well-managed one in 1888. After twenty-five years building destroyed not so much the country as interest in hunting.

Dutchess County had hunting, remote from its Dutch and trotting-horse traditions, in 1889. German hares were imported ten years later and were hunted by a private pack. The Millbrook was started in 1907 with the Watchung's Kerry beagles and O'Malley Knott. Mr Oakleigh Thorne was persuaded to overcome his reluctance, and taught to jump; he became a great Master of Hounds. He tried English foxhounds with an English huntsman after the German hares: but replaced them with English harriers and an English hare huntsman in 1913. This was one of the very few authentic harrier packs in American hunting history, and it was immensely successful. Wire spread, but according to O'Malley Knott this was a blessing in disguise. Farmers left blind clumps of scrub each side of their post-and-rail, but going and visibility were perfect each side of a 'Club Panel'.[27] There were foxes too: Mr Higginson brought his Middlesex hounds to hunt them.

Two hundred miles west of Saratoga, the Genesee river runs north into Lake Ontario. In 1790 the Wadsworth family settled in the valley, coming from County Durham by way of Durham, Connecticut. At about the same time the Fitzhughs, a family with hunting traditions, came up from the south. For the next three-

GENESSEE VALLEY, 1892

Mr W. Austin Wadsworth and his pack, seen at the meet and drawing a covert. By this date, probably, every working hound was home bred of imported English blood (and a little Welsh). The pack was Mr Wadsworth's own and he paid all expenses. The field were his guests. A hunt club had been formed in 1881, but like the Quorndon and Pytchley clubs of an earlier period in England it was a social organization among followers of the hounds. It did put on horse shows and, from 1887, point-to-point races. Scarlet was only worn in the evening. Older men came out in the uniform of blue with buff facings, younger men in 'mufti' (then often so called). There were plenty of wild foxes, and plenty were killed although the master never used a spade. There was no need for drags, but the 'crowd' wanted them; Mr Wadsworth reluctantly and occasionally permitted them, and then created the Livingstone County Draghounds specifically, he said, to give horse-dealers and jockeys a steeplechase and keep them out of his hunting field. The country was stiff and sporting, full of solid timber up to five feet high.

quarters of a century foxes were hunted by hill-topping farmers and by guns over dogs.

In 1876 a local group started the Livingston County Hunt, the hounds being trencher-fed and brought to the meet in couples by their several owners. Mr (later Major) W. Austin Wadsworth was master, and Mr C. C. Fitzhugh amateur huntsman. Mr Fitzhugh found the hounds totally uncontrollable. He died in 1878.

Mr Wadsworth decided to get a proper pack under proper control. From 1880 he began importing very good English hounds. By 1900 he had what Mr Higginson roundly called the best pack in America.[28] It was wholly private; the field were his guests; the country was sporting and the foxes plentiful.

In spite of all precautions, Major Wadsworth had the usual trouble with ill-disciplined thrusters, which in turn caused him trouble with the farmers. He therefore drew up a celebrated set of rules, widely printed and read – a marvellous document which manages to be stern without hectoring, and to be witty without loss of seriousness. Essentially the rules were: farmers must be shown consideration, as the hunt depends on their hospitality and goodwill; the M.F.H. is absolute master – he must not be spoken to or interfered with, though may at any time be offered a flask; horsemen must keep well clear of hounds and never head a fox. Printed in the English *Field*,[29] the Genesee Valley 'Bible' earned the warm approval of English hunting men, warmly expressed by 'Brooksby'.[30] A central part of his hunting philosophy was also far more characteristic of any part of England than of the Orange County or Meadow Brook: 'I would rather see a farmer's boy on a mule at a meet than the most elaborate creation of a London tailor.'[31] It was inevitable that, when the Masters of Foxhounds Association of America was formed in 1907, Major Wadsworth should be the first president.

New England

Throughout the 19th century, and into the 20th, wild foxes were killed all over New England by a gun used over one or two hounds. The 'fox dogs' were of clear Old Southern type, but outcrossed in various directions.[32]

In Maine in 1870: 'I'm going into fox-hunting . . . I've got hounds and a famous *fox-bait*; also snow-shoes, and everything necessary for a jolly burst at it.' The hounds were three, the bait horseflesh; the most needful equipment was gun and rifle.[33]

About 1875 a group of sporting young Bostonians came together in an informal club to play tennis and baseball. Many of the members wore spectacles, including the four Prince brothers; in 1876 the club was therefore called the Myopia. In 1881 it became the Myopia Fox Hound Club, getting hounds and secondhand pink coats from Montreal.[34] Both astonished local farmers, but were welcomed by the Press.[35]

Soon afterwards Mr E. F. Bowditch of Framingham, Millwood, started a private pack with Myopia hounds; so did his neighbour Mr Robert F. Perkins at Owl's Nest.

South west of Boston, several members of the Dedham Polo Club started the Norfolk Hunt in 1895, hunting a drag with English hounds. 'It is English, you

know, but lacks the fox, the peasantry, and some other English essentials.'[36] Mr Henry G. Vaughan was master from 1902 to 1937; he was first secretary of the M.F.H.A. and later its president; he led one of the most loyal and friendly hunts in America.

In 1903 Mr Harry Worcester Smith of Grafton, Worcester County, Massachusetts, assembled an American pack from various sources. He began hunting round the Grafton Country Club. He also rejuvenated the Brunswick Fur Club, which had first (in 1889) turned hill-top foxhunting into a field trial at Albany Hills, Maine.[37] He made, in print, extravagant claims for the sort of hound he preferred.[38]

Meanwhile Mr Alexander Henry Higginson had absorbed, from books, a devotion to English foxhunting. A rich and infinitely indulgent father gave him, successively, beagles, harriers and foxhounds from Mr Fernie. He established a private Middlesex pack at South Lincoln. Just before he began hunting he ate a bad oyster on a train, and in bed read Mr Smith's pronouncements. He replied intemperately. A heated correspondence followed. Mr John E. Townsend suggested a match in the Piedmont Valley, for which he offered a cup.

The story of the great hound match of 1905 has been told many times.[39] They hunted on alternate days for two weeks, starting 1 November. Neither pack killed fairly. The Grafton were adjudged winners, but 'Mr Higginson's hounds furnished such excellent sport that many clubs thereafter adopted the English hound'.[40] Mr Higginson himself was asked to hunt various Virginia countries and later the Millbrook. Mr Smith, who had been hunting in Virginia, was now squeezed out of it. He was, perhaps, hardly treated: but he had made himself a good deal disliked, especially by trying to sell Grafton hunt buttons during the match to raise money.[41]

Mr Higginson got more Fernie hounds, and Ned Cotesworth succeeded his brother Bob as kennel huntsman. The whole establishment was extremely influential.

ORANGE COUNTY AND MIDDLESEX HOUNDS, 1908
These two sorts are as different as they could be, and represent the extremes of American pack foxhounds. The Orange County hounds (*below*) had been bought by the club from Mr William Skinker, who continued to hunt them. He had inherited from his mother's family in Madison County a pack of red ring-necks (red hounds with white necks), crossed to Bywaters. They hunted as an orthodox pack, and very well, but in conformation and blood they were far more like Walkers than like the Middlesex. Mr Higginson's club dated from 1900, this pack from 1904; he then went to England and, advised by Mr George C. W. Fitzwilliam, bought a draft largely of Belvoir blood from Mr Fernie. He got another draft from the same kennel the following year. They were hunted by the English Bob Cotesworth, who came from Mr Foxhall Keene on Long Island. Bob retired in 1907. His brother Ned replaced him, too old to cross country but wonderful in the kennel. Ned brought back fifty couple more from England the season of this photograph – the whole Fernie draft and the Brocklesby young draft.

Western Massachusetts, Connecticut, Rhode Island and New Hampshire all flirted with foxhunting. One part of Vermont became married to it. Mr J. Watson Webb of Shelburne, far north on Lake Champlain, got beagles in 1902, harriers in 1903, and English foxhounds in 1904, with which in 1910 he began hunting wild foxes instead of a drag.

Carolina and the Deep South

Some Carolina families became rich again after the war, but most remained informal hill toppers like their poorest white and black neighbours. Mr Thomas G. Tucker's pack at Gaston was the only one known outside the state.[42]

Mr Thomas Hitchcock began spending his winters at Aiken, South Carolina, and in 1891 he brought the Meadow Brook hounds there. Their English noses were unable to follow the scent of the grey fox in hot, sandy conditions. In 1894 he invited Mr James M. Avent of Hickory Valley, Tennessee, to bring his hounds. They were an immense success and Mr Hitchcock bought half the pack. He became a leading exponent of the American hound and his hunt was one of the most popular in the country.

There was a great deal of hunting and hound breeding in Georgia, but almost none organized into clubs. Colonel Birdsong was still breeding the hounds named for him, of which the most celebrated was Hodo, a dog of phenomenal speed and drive.[43] These hounds owed most to the Henrys, but much to their 'Redbone' or 'Nigger-hound' ancestry. The other leading breeder was Colonel Miles Harris; he had the original July from Nimrod Gosnell. Many other hounds of similar type came from Maryland; their descendants were all called Julys in honour of the first.

Kentucky and Tennessee

'From 1845 to 1860,' said Colonel Haiden Trigg, 'I owned a pack of those long-eared, rat-tail, deep-toned, black-and-tan Virginia foxhounds. In those happy byegone days I could on a moonlight night ride to the covert-side, throw my leg over the pommel of my saddle and listen for hours to the most magnificent music made by the ever-to-be-remembered dogs.'[44] The red fox came. Colonel Trigg began buying a few hounds from Colonel Birdsong and from 'Wash' Maupin and the Walkers, and from all these bred the 'Trigg red fox dog'. The Walker brothers, heirs of John W., were at the same time breeding hounds of different character to meet the same challenge: but they usually hunted by night in thickly wooded country and their strain was developed accordingly.

In sharp contrast to the conditions faced by the Walkers, the blue-grass country round Lexington was open grazing, with no wire because thoroughbred horses were raised there; it was fine galloping and fine scenting country. Colonel (later General) Roger D. Williams was the fourth generation of a family of hound-owning Kentuckians, and in 1880 he started an orthodox hunt. He called it the Iroquois after Mr Pierre Lorillard's great horse, the first American-bred to win the English Derby. He had great difficulty organizing a hunt on English or East Coast lines, because of the immensely strong local tradition of informal 'fox chases'. He was himself an heir of this tradition and was a hill topper and field-trial man as well as a rider to a pack. Besides being master of the Iroquois he was a director of the National Fox Hunters' Association, Keeper of its *Foxhound Stud Book* and official judge of the

MR A. H. HIGGINSON

Mr Higginson's father was the leading lawyer in Boston and one of its foremost citizens. Like many New Englanders he was entirely unsporting. But he was in generous sympathy with his son's sporting obsessions, and financed them with immense and unfailing generosity. This permitted the successive packs the young Higginson owned, culminating in the Middlesex Foxhounds, the most influential of all English packs in America owing to its extensive travels. These were themselves the result of the length and severity of Massachusetts winters. Mr Higginson edited the early volumes of the American F.K.S.B.; he was president of the M.F.H.A. of America until he moved finally to England; he was there master of the Cattistock, joining and then succeeding the Rev. E. A. Milne. He was the most prolific of all hunting writers, producing history, biography, journalism, fiction, reminiscence and treatise. He was also a great collector of sporting books, like his rival (and, alas, personal enemy) the equally influential Mr Harry Worcester Smith.

Brunswick Hunt Club and the National Association Field Trials. His major ambition was to bring the exact methods of English breeders to American hounds.[45]

Tennessee's tradition was the same as Kentucky's; the scale was smaller because the state was poorer. Organized hunting was tried, but not for long.

Middle and Far West

Ohio filled with foxhounds as it filled with people from 1800 onwards. Individuals and small associations in vast numbers chased foxes by night and day, blowing cow horns and hunting by ear. There were also a number of private packs, hunted scarcely more formally, such as the Killbuck Hounds of Wooster and Colonel A. B. Whitlock's Shaggies. When the great Annie Oakley starred in *Miss Rosa*, the stage was filled in one scene with hounds, horses and scarlet coats; the hounds were Whitlocks.

There was also a tradition of horsemanship, associated most particularly with Troop A of the First Ohio Cavalry at Cleveland. Its members in the late 1890s began learning about hounds from local farmers, tried beagles and draghunting, and in 1908 formed the Chagrin Valley under Mr Windsor T. White. Ned Cotesworth came from Mr Higginson in 1911, and after various experiments they settled for an English pack of Belvoir blood.

A number of hunts came and went in the Chicago area. The most successful were the Onwentsia at Lake Forest and the Midlothian near by; both wanted to hunt foxes but neither dared because of the wire.

Detroit had a hunt club in the 1890s and a new Grosse Pointe in 1911; luckier than the Chicagoans, they found a huntable country and chased foxes.

California made strenuous and repeated attempts at hunting, defeated by apathy, wire or fog. Oregon's Portland Hunt Club had a slightly longer life, but only slightly.

U.S. Army

The earliest recorded military hunt was the Fort Gibson Hunt Club in Oklahoma Territory, started in 1835. The largest was General George A. Custer's. He took hounds with him to Michigan, and thence to Fort Riley, Kansas and into Texas. His pack grew larger and larger, consisting of foxhounds, deerhounds and setters, with which he hunted everything that ran until his ill-planned last battle in 1876.

The Sixth Cavalry had a Fort Meyer Hunt Club from 1895, and the First and Second the better-known Fort Riley Hunt Club a year later; this latter became the Cavalry School Hunt, with a recognized training value. In 1908 coyotes were hunted by 'trail hounds' and jack rabbits coursed by 'sight hounds'.

The Eleventh Cavalry Hunt was started at Fort Oglethorpe, Georgia, in 1909, with a pack of American hounds to which they added English hounds and some Kerry beagles. Hunting was obligatory, becoming part of the training programme: but it was extremely odd both to the officers and to the local farmers, whose own hunting was in a widely different tradition. All the officers went out every Friday. When the regiment was posted to Texas the hounds were left with a farmer who starved most of them to death. The hunt restarted in Texas in 1911 with five couple of English hounds from Mr A. H. Higginson, and with Bob Cotesworth. As foxes were scarce they used a fox drag – not aniseed, but 'drainage' from a captured fox.

MR JOHN W. WALKER
The Walker family, like the Maupin, came into Kentucky from Virginia with old black-and-tan Virginia hounds. Both sorts were said to descend from Colonel Brooke's importations of 1650. The Walkers settled in a densely wooded part of Garrard County where they hunted the grey fox, using horses but not attempting to stay with their hounds. In 1852 a black-and-tan doghound was stolen in the Cumberland Mountains by Tom Harris; he was named Tennessee Lead, and went to John Walker, who used him with great success as a breeding outcross. This suggests that he was at least partly Kerry beagle. In 1856 the red fox arrived. Mr Walker immediately crossed his hounds with an English draft acquired by 'Wash' Maupin, and with the Maryland hounds, almost certainly of Kerry beagle blood, of Mr Ben Robinson. He and later his sons thus created the Walkers, remarkable for self reliance, cold noses, refusal to pack, and a fondness for skirting. These qualities made them the pre-eminent hounds for hill-top foxhunting and later for field trials. They were also a most valuable outcross in orthodox packs, especially those of Mr Harry Worcester Smith, Mr Burrell Frank Bywaters, Mr J. B. Thomas, and the Warrenton and Orange County.

The officers became extremely keen on the style of hunting Bob Cotesworth taught them, and on his English hounds; many of them got scarlet coats.[46]

Canada

The Montreal Hunt recovered from difficulties and short masterships in the 1860s. It became again popular and prosperous. The Toronto was reunited after a schism in 1864, but remained precarious. It languished without large military garrisons. The London was started between Toronto and Detroit in 1885; the Toronto went to draghunting because of wire, but the London because its members were busy. The Ottawa, started in 1873, went very well when there was a keen master, and did not go at all if there was not.

A number of other hunts were started, some in the Prairie Provinces: none was able to survive development, wire, apathy and war.

Hounds

Judged by English standards, or those of English hound men in America, there were several oddities about American hound breeding. Although breeders regarded themselves as scientific, only a small minority paid much attention to conformation and very few indeed were influenced by pedigree. They bred wholly to working qualities. Having bred, they misdescribed. Mr George Garrett in 1919 refused to register as a July a single hound whose pedigree was submitted to him: he concluded that there were no July hounds, properly so called, left in Kentucky or Georgia. Single-syllable names were frequent. The old school of Southern foxhunters habitually, like the rural Irish, talked about dogs. Although American hounds were normally taken out and brought home in couples, 'nine' was more usual than '$4\frac{1}{2}$ couple'.

There were vast differences of opinion among breeders, owners, Master of Hounds and judges about what constituted merit and about what an American hound ought to look like. In the early years of 'bench shows', it was impossible to predict what stamp of hound would win.

Volume I of the *Foxhound Stud Book* was published in 1898 by the National Fox Hunters' Association, edited by General Williams. This was a register of field-trial hounds and the beginning of a serious attempt to establish standards: but the only reliable pedigrees were English. The M.F.H.A.'s *American Foxhound Kennel Stud Book*, edited by A. H. Higginson, was exclusively English until Volume 5 in 1931: this was not prejudice, but purely because of the appalling difficulties of establishing pedigrees for all but a few American hounds. There were very large numbers of stud books of field-trial hounds, kept especially by commercial breeders from about 1900: but they were as unreliable as the old Virginia pedigrees of horses which combined romance with fraudulent advertising. 'The American stud books show an utter disregard for accuracy, thereby destroying the value of stud books.'[47]

Hill topping had a huge growth from about 1850 and trials from about 1900; both numerically overwhelmed orthodox foxhunting. But this grew rapidly too; there were seventy-six recognized hunts by 1906, modelled more or less faithfully on England, and this number later doubled. Imitation of England was qualified by circumstances, especially in the kennel. Even in the most orthodox established hunts, puppy walking and puppy shows were almost unknown in America.

Clubs, Members and Servants

There were two completely different kinds of foxhunting, conducted by different kinds of people. Informal 'night running' and 'fox races' were not by any means only a poor man's sport, like the hound trails of Northern England – very rich men and important hound breeders in Georgia, Kentucky, Missouri and Arkansas went out in the old way from choice as well as from habit and for reasons of climate. But to a lamentable extent organized hunting *was* only a rich man's sport. Major Wadsworth might prefer to see a farmer's son on a mule, if he behaved himself and enjoyed his hunting, to an outsider in London-made scarlet: but clubs like the Orange County acted like French aristocrats before the Revolution.

The trouble was the confusion of club with field. English hunt clubs were often extremely exclusive; tradesmen and farmers neither came to the dinners nor wore the button. But these humbler people were always welcomed in the hunting field. The ridiculous thing is that in being snobbish some Americans – and this is an American comment of 1909 – thought they were being English.[48]

In another sense the American hunt club was quite unlike anything in Britain. In most of the north, men rich enough to hunt lived in cities. They therefore subscribed heavy sums to create rural or suburban headquarters for sporting activities, the country clubs to which there is no British equivalent because there is no need of one. Many American hunt clubs grew out of, joined, or even gave birth to country clubs. The members' horses were stabled at the club; they slept in club bedrooms and drank at club bars; the hunt was a club function.

A HUNT-BREAKFAST ANECDOTE, 1897
The young lady in the habit, telling her vainglorious story, is not placed geographically: but she is almost certainly a New Yorker about to go out with the Meadow Brook (*Harpers*, where the drawing appeared, was keenly and sometimes critically aware of Long Island hunting, owing to the social *réclame* it enjoyed in New York society). Although the girl is making a fool of herself, it is likely that later in the day she went very well indeed, on her thoroughbred, over the stiff timber of the country, to Mr Griswold's hounds. The latter, as restless as 20 years earlier, had come back to Long Island in 1893, replacing Mr Thomas Hitchcock, and amalgamated the Meadow Brook and Queen's County.

Since American hunting men were neither squires nor farmers, their time was not their own. They could not squander the hours of daylight drawing covert after covert. Hence the 'businessman's drag'. Draghunting also recommended itself because of lack of scent, shortage of foxes, and wire. English hounds could own a line of aniseed on hot dry ground when a fox, if there was a fox, defeated them. The drag could bypass hostile farmers and steer the field to jumpable places. This was often the crucial factor. In 1909, 'on account of the advent of wire, there will in a few years be no riding to foxhounds in America (as witnessed by the discontinuance of several hunts in the last few years)'.[49]

A large number of hunt servants in this period were English. There was an element of snobbery in this – an English huntsman conferred distinction like an English butler. It was also necessary, as no American had the experience of hunting English hounds in the positive English manner, lifting and casting. Most American huntsmen, coming from hill topping, left their hounds completely alone. By 1914 these schools had learned a good deal from each other. English huntsmen recognized the virtue of American hounds for the country, and Americans like Charles Carver were capable of hunting hounds with the control and forward impetus of the English Shires.

Organization and Authority

Steeplechasing, both amateur and professional, grew rapidly in the last years of the 19th century. Just as at the end of the Civil War Messrs August Belmont Sr and Leonard Jerome imitated England in forming the Jockey Club to control flat racing, so in January 1895 a new generation formed the National Steeplechase Association, in imitation of Britain's National Hunt Committee, to control professional steeplechasing, while a National Hunt Association controlled amateur hunt racing.

These two bodies amalgamated in 1897, under bizarre circumstances. Mr Sam Howland bought an estate called Belwood in the Genesee Valley, near Major Wadsworth's country but in a section which the pack did not draw. He successfully urged the formation of an enlarged National Steeplechase and Hunt Association; hunts were to register with it, thus becoming recognized, in order that their hunt racing should also be recognized. Mr Howland hoped that hunts would also register the precise extent of their countries. His idea was that Major Wadsworth would declare a border which would enable a new Belwood country to be delineated. But Major Wadsworth refused to register; he refused to recognize any limit to the country he hunted. Mr Howland did not start hunting; he did exercise his pack on roads well away from any coverts drawn by Major Wadsworth. In a spirit of mischief or of loyalty, certain members (allegedly) of the Genesee Valley laid a drag across a road Mr Howland used, and took it over several important farms. The Belwood hounds followed the drag and did a lot of damage. The ranks closed behind Major Wadsworth; poor Mr Howland had to sell his house and take his hounds away again.[50]

The N.S.H.A. was now, however, in existence. It recognized hunts strictly for racing purposes, but its recognition was the only recognition. It was not concerned with disputes between hunts or the conduct of hunting: it neither sought nor was given any status as a tribunal.

Meanwhile Virginia was filling up with recognized hunts, and Mr Harry Worcester Smith rightly saw the need for a body like the British M.F.H.A. He tried to turn the N.S.H.A. into such a body by filing a map of his Piedmont country. Mr John R. Townsend did not acknowledge the lines as Mr Smith drew them. Adjudication was needed, but the N.S.H.A. refused to provide it. Mr Smith went away, extremely angry with both Mr Townsend and the N.S.H.A. In October 1906 he wrote to a number of Masters of Hounds (probably all those registered with the N.S.H.A.) urging the formation of a M.F.H.A. of America and enclosing the rules of the British association. A meeting was arranged on 14 February 1907 at the Waldorf-Astoria, New York, to which six M.F.H.s came. The M.F.H.A. was formed. Major Wadsworth was inevitably, if ironically, elected president.

Opinion

American attitudes to foxhunting varied enormously: growing from richly emotional attitudes to England, trespass, social distinctions, carpetbagging, value for money and killing.

The peasants of French Canada had inherited violent Anglophobia, as well as a folk memory of the *ancien régime* trampling their crops. The New England farmers were heirs of a tradition of nonconformity, social as well as religious; their dislike of squires, red coats, and trespass was as deep-seated as the French. They were, however, better educated and much more amenable to reason. Both these groups were puritan in ethic, if not in theology, with the result that neither was in any real sense sporting.

In eastern Pennsylvania, Maryland, Virginia, the whole South, Kentucky, Tennessee and the southern Middle West, the farmers inherited the Virginian rather than the Massachusetts tradition: in so far as their roots were English they were a different sort of English. They were sportsmen: they chased foxes with their hounds. They had a different attitude to trespass and to things English. Orthodox hunting might be a strange exotic, but it had a chance, given tact, of being warmly welcomed. There was, however, in Virginia the complication that flamboyantly expensive hunting was Yankee: Mr Harriman's private railroad car was as inflammatory in the Piedmont Valley as the Montreal's scarlet in Quebec Province.

Educated opinion – in the rare cases where it made any response at all – was divided on lines familiar to earlier civilizations. At one extreme, Washington Irving reacted exactly as Voltaire had reacted a century before: 'The fondness for rural life among the higher classes of the English has had a great and salutary effect upon the national character. I do not know a finer race of men than the English gentlemen. Instead of the softness and effeminacy which characterises the men of rank of most countries, they exhibit a union of elegance and strength, of robustness of frame and freshness of complexion, which I am inclined to attribute to their living so much in the open air, pursuing so largely the invigorating sports of the field.'[51] At the other extreme, Harriet Beecher Stowe followed the Sophists and Sir Thomas More; dining with Earl Russell she heard foxhunting discussed, and was appalled 'that in the height of English civilization this vestige of the savage state should remain'. When she put this view the company laughed.[52]

Fundamental to a large part of the American attitude to hunting, at all economic and social levels, was its *pointlessness*. 'Is it worth the while of all those men to expend all that energy for such a result? Upon the whole, Mr Morton, I should say that it is one of the most incomprehensible things that I have ever seen in the course of a rather long and varied life.'[53]

14 Britain
1914 and After

First World War

In the 1914–18 war hunting suffered from lack of people, feed, horses and money, and from strong hostile pressures.

A high proportion of masters and hunt servants were away in uniform. Hunts were kept going by women, old men, committees and unexpected candidates. Prodigies of menial work in kennel and stable were done by the families of masters. Earth stopping become impossible and coverts got in a bad state.

Subscriptions dropped to almost nothing, but shortage of feed was more serious than shortage of labour or money, especially when German submarines became active. The Food Commission wanted the wholesale destruction of hounds and it was joined by a shrill popular outcry in the cities.[1] A great many hounds were put down and very few bred. It took ten years for most kennels to recover: the registered hound population of Great Britain was 7,212 couple in 1913, only 5,584 as late as 1921.[2]

Between the Wars

In some ways this was a glorious period in the Shires, but there was much which was widely deplored. Quorn, Cottesmore and Belvoir were lucky in long master-ships, and it was a great age of huntsmen: Arthur Wilson and George Barker at the Quorn, Arthur Thatcher and Bert Peaker at the Fernie, George Leaf, James Welsh and Major Hilton-Green at the Cottesmore and Frank Freeman at the Pytchley. Frank Freeman was generally regarded as the very best in history after, or with, Tom Firr. Stanley Barker followed him; in 1938 his voice and horn were recorded in action by Ludwig Koch.[3] George Tongue at Belvoir was by some considered a master breeder, but by others bitterly criticized for diluting the old Belvoir sort.[4]

To all this professional competence was added more royal glamour than ever. All the royal dukes hunted in the Shires. Her Royal Highness Princess Elizabeth was at the covertside on Frank Freeman's last day; at 4 p.m. on 4 April 1931 she viewed away the last fox he hunted. There was no breath of that strident urban dismay which greeted Princess Anne's day or two in Yorkshire in 1972. There was one unfortunate result of this royal participation. The Shires had always attracted a certain number of social climbers, at best ignorant and at worst full of the arrogance of their new money. What was particularly unfortunate was that farmers were very

Britain: 1914 and After

short of money after prices fell about 1925; though many came out with certain remote provincial packs like the South Dorset and the Ledbury, extremely few could afford it in the Shires; those who did were apt to be obtrusively despised by people who, like the imitation F.F.V.s of the Orange County, thought snobbery was socially correct.[5]

The eastern counties had the enormous merit that they were hard to get to and comfortless when reached. The superb though very different hounds of their packs were followed by local people. There was probably no major hunt in Britain which changed so little in atmosphere, kennel or country as the Brocklesby: or, until the eccentricities of Sir Julian Cahn, the Burton. The Milton hounds were as distinctive as ever: they were uniquely fierce in the chase and savage at the death, and retained their strong coats and bristling hackles.[6]

Nottinghamshire and south Yorkshire were as completely different as ever both from the Shires and from Lincolnshire. The dukeries were still huge estates with huge woods, while in the South Notts, Barlow and most of all the Wentworth countries industry was advancing at a rate which even the slump seemed hardly to slow down.

The countries west of the Shires enjoyed a good many long masterships. The countryside, on the whole, changed less than in the south but more than in the east. There was a slight tendency to subdivision, and a marked tendency, violently resisted, to Welsh-cross blood.

The Badminton hounds had earlier been described as indistinguishable from Belvoir; in 1930 they were called 'as like Brocklesby in work and looks as two peas'.[7] This was the old Badminton sort, but two new strains were being introduced: those of Sir Ian Amory's Tiverton Actor and Mr Isaac Bell's South and West Wilts Godfrey, both used for nose, speed, activity and above all cry. For a few years the three strains were visibly distinct, but by 1938 were merged into a single homogeneous sort. The colour, once uniform tan, was now extremely varied, and included pale, badger-pie and some blue.[8]

The Heythrop relived the 19th century when Mr Albert Brassey died after forty-five years in 1918, and his son had to give up the hounds in 1921: the hunt, used to being carried financially, was plunged into bottomless despair.

The Berkeley remained a family pack as distinctive and consistent as Badminton's, but of a quite different stamp: Berkeley was never influenced by Peterborough or the fashion of heavy shoulders and 'bedpost' forelegs; its active, killing hounds were of Lord Henry Bentinck's type and all strained to Cromwell (1855) of his breeding. This blood was immensely influential between the wars.[9]

Mr 'Ikey' Bell brought his long Irish experience and his audacious hound-breeding ideas to the South and West Wilts in 1925. His own most important hound was Godfrey (1928), by Kilkenny Gory and bred at the Carlow kennel: one of the most influential stallions of the century.

At the Cattistock, the Rev. E. A. Milne was joined in 1930 by Mr A. H. Higginson, who moved to Dorset from Massachusetts. Mr Higginson was dissatisfied with the big Belvoir hounds which Mr Milne had been breeding so lovingly for so long, finding them short of cry and nose; following the example of his friend and compatriot in Wiltshire he began introducing blood of a very different sort, first by Badminton stallions by Tiverton Actor, then by Curre Tuner (1927) and other white Itton crossbreds. Mr Milne was revolted by this policy.[10]

The swarm of hunts in the far south west were less affected by 20th-century change than any in Britain except those of Cumberland and parts of Wales.

BELVOIR POINT-TO-POINT, 1919
This is Barrowby Hill, an eminence quite uncharacteristic of the Shires. Most hunts held their own races by 1900; the atmosphere of the Southdown's just before the first war (typical enough) is nicely described by Siegfried Sassoon. In 1919 hunting was in some respects in a bad way – there were few hounds, coverts had deteriorated, stables and kennels were often dilapidated, wire had crept everywhere – but requisitioned horses were, like men, released from the service in a flood; there were more mounted followers and many more subscriptions in 1919 than in 1913. A notable result was a boom in hunt racing, which almost more than hunting itself appealed to men just out of uniform. It sometimes continued, alas, to be possible to have a racehorse leniently certified as a hunter, and to win a great deal of money in bets. Detail of painting by Sir Alfred Munnings. From the collection of Mr and Mrs Paul Mellon.

[202]

Yorkshire hunting changed very little in the smaller or remoter countries but there was a large change, for the worse, in the south of the West Riding. North Durham, like Wentworth, succumbed to industry; elsewhere in the far north there were very long masterships and some very good hounds. The fell packs throve and increased. The average height of fellhounds between the wars was $22\frac{1}{2}$ inches; they were shorter coupled, with ribs carried further back, than English hounds; they were usually back at the knee and harefooted.[11] In 1919 a Fell Hound Show was started at Applethwaite, which moved to Rydal two years later. This was viewed with alarm in case it led to a fell 'Peterborough type', bred to please the eye rather than to kill the fox.[12] Most fellhounds had some trail-hound blood, which gave them a good dash of greyhound quite close up in the pedigree; this was why Sir Alfred Goodson's fell-cross College Valley hounds needed a thoroughbred horse to stay anywhere near them.

The spirit of Welsh hunting is illustrated, perhaps quite unfairly, by a meet of the Brecon hounds at a public house about 1920. The master was in the front room drinking a beer called 'Royal Stand Back', the farmers were in the kitchen drinking 'Bouncer', and the labourers were in the barn drinking 'Swell Belly Vengeance'; all these beers were home-brewed; of the thirty farmers out on ponies, twenty fell off when the first fox was holloa'd.[13] In Captain Jack Evans's time (1922–35) the breeding was mostly of Brocklesby to Curre, and with a continuing debt to the great Glôg Nimrod.

Sir Edward Curre was followed at Itton by Lady Curre from 1930 to 1956. Their breeding, influential before 1914, became much more so after the war as more and more Masters of Hounds followed the brilliant example of Mr Isaac Bell. The extent of this movement is shown by the fact that the blood of Glôg Nimrod (1904), a pure-bred Welsh hound, was in 115 out of the total of 175 kennels by 1939, mostly by way of Curre stallions. Nimrod was one of the private pack of rough-coated lemon-and-white hounds established by Mr Thomas Williams near Pontypridd, Glamorganshire, and hunting fox, hare and otter in very rough country. Sir Edward's influence also increased as his hounds improved: he regarded his objectives as only half achieved in 1916 after twenty years, but fully realized in 1926 after thirty.[14] Not only were rough coats and faulty forelegs bred out, but also wildness, ill temper and spiritlessness at the end of a hard day.

Between the wars, only four packs in Wales were of pure English blood. An increasing number were crossbred, only the first cross normally being used. The most important Welsh parents of crossbreds came from Glôg, Neuadd Fawr, Llangibby, Ystrad and Gelligaer. Pure Welsh hounds improved greatly in conformation and levelness, as breeders (like their American contemporaries) brought more science to their matings. Although traditionalist English breeders recoiled from these unpedigreed savages, Welsh breeders like Sir George Bowen of the Tivyside and Captain Jack Evans of the Brecon knew their Welsh pedigrees, or at least blood lines, quite well enough to breed with full regard to pedigree as well as to conformation and work;[15] a point which was not appreciated by Lord Bathurst. The first Welsh Hound Show at Wrexham in July 1922 was a necessary, if slightly dangerous, step towards a standard; there were classes for Welsh, English, fell and crossbred hounds; twenty-six packs were represented; the Curre entry swept the board in the crossbred classes. The show later moved to Builth Wells.

Another breeding experiment of great interest was conducted by Sir John Buchanan-Jardine of Castle Milk, who took over the Dumfriesshire hounds in 1921. He was a learned student of the world's hounds and wrote an indispensable book

THE QUORN, 1973
Hounds are moving off from the opening meet at Kirby Gate. This was the fourteenth season of Mrs Ulrica Murray Smith's mastership (a lady who has recently shown herself to be a most diverting hunting writer, in the tradition of such M.F.H.s as Miss Edith Somerville and Miss Frances Pitt of the Wheatland), and the second of Captain Fred Barker, notable for the beauty of his wife and the eminence of his aunt Miss Effie Barker, like her father a most popular master of the South Berks. The Quorn hounds owe a lot to Sir Harold Nutting (master from 1930 to 1940) and George Barker (huntsman from 1929 to 1959) who made extensive if heterodox use of Mr Bell's South and West Wilts Godfrey.

about them. His approach in practice was highly original and included the re-discovery (miscalled the creation) of the Gascon hound, which he used both pure and as an outcross. His hounds were black-and-tan, exceptionally big, and had a marvellous cry; he demanded the same cry from his bitches and drafted them for light tongues.

Second World War

The second war was much harder than the first. Feed and money were even shorter, transport more difficult, able-bodied manpower rarer, opposition even more vociferous. The point has been made that hunting men joined up at once, while urban intellectuals and clerks divided their energies between calling for the destruction of all hounds and evading the indignity of uniform.[16]

In a dozen countries hunting stopped, usually for these reasons but sometimes because of military activity. A breeding nucleus was kept by some of these kennels; other packs were altogether dispersed or destroyed. All kennels were drastically reduced to save money and oatmeal. A few hounds went to America and a few to India and elsewhere, but a great many were destroyed.

Ladies were even more important to hunting than in 1914–18. Lady Curre's, Albrighton, North Staffs, Wheatland and Hurworth had long-serving women masters who continued in office; Cottesmore, Brocklesby, Blankney, South Wold,

THE DUKE OF BUCCLEUCH'S Hounds have just moved off from Micklem Burn, Selkirkshire, in the western side of the duke's country. Lord Dalkeith was deputy master of his father's hounds from 1920 until he succeeded to dukedom and mastership in 1935. George Sumners was huntsman from 1902 until he retired, aged 74, in 1946; he was the son and grandson of huntsmen, and had been second and then first whip here from 1892. The country has been substantially reduced from its earlier vastness by the creation of the Jed Forest and Lauderdale; it remains large enough to sustain four days.

Atherstone, North Warwickshire, V.W.H., Middleton and others were indebted to wives, widows and daughters. There were lady huntsmen (notably Miss Annette Usher) and very many whippers-in.

The effects of the war were a very small hound population, a great increase of arable, dilapidated buildings, airfields, and in some countries military barbed wire, slit trenches, unexploded bombs and the devastation left by tank training. For a long time transport became no easier, and money was still very short. But as fields came back so did labour, and earths could be stopped and puppies walked.

Deer, Hare, Otter

The staghound packs between the wars were the Devon and Somerset, Tiverton, Quantock, Lunesdale and Oxenholme; the New Forest Buckhounds also unharboured an occasional red deer although their usual game was fallow. These packs all relied primarily on unentered foxhounds drafted because oversized. The three West Country packs, and the Buckhounds, survived into the 1970s.

Baily listed eighty-five harrier packs in 1923–4, only twenty-seven in 1972–3 of which three are also recognized by the M.F.H.A., one (the Minehead) hunts fox only and some chase fox and hare. The country left unhunted by harriers has been taken over by beagles and basset hounds. Forty-nine recognized packs of beagles in 1923 have grown to eight-six, and the eleven active packs of basset hounds are confidently expected to increase. The popularity of beagling has grown steadily and enormously.

Sixteen otter hunts are recognized, of which two clubs have no packs and three are in abeyance.

Hounds

English foxhounds, even of impeccable pedigree, still varied greatly until the differences were almost everywhere smoothed out by the combined influence of Belvoir and Peterborough. The kennels which maintained a marked individuality in 1926 were, according to Lord Bathurst, Belvoir, Milton, Brocklesby, Blankney, Badminton, Warwickshire and above all Berkeley.[17] Elsewhere a Belvoir look was apt to be sought at any cost. Belvoir itself only bred from hounds with the highest working qualities, but lesser kennels and sillier men used Belvoir blood simply for forelegs, tan, and prizes on the flags.[18]

Conditions changed quickly, fashion slowly. The conditions in the 1920s included far more stain, especially from traffic, and foxes far more often headed. This meant that hounds had to turn sharply and recover the line on ground which they or the field had foiled; they not only needed better noses, but also the power to stop, turn, and accelerate with more adroitness and elasticity. Lord Bathurst, while accepting that the old Peterborough hound was inappropriate to these conditions, was principal spokesman of a large school of thought which believed that the necessary qualities could and must be achieved by selective breeding from existing stud-book material.[19] But the Welsh cross was another solution; it was used with most *réclame* by Mr Bell at the South and West Wilts, Sir Ian Amory at the Tiverton, Captain Esme Arkwright at the Oakley, Mr Higginson at the Cattistock, Mr George Evans at the H.H., and, of a younger generation, Sir Peter Farquhar at the Meynell and Portman and Major W. W. B. Scott at the North Cotswold. The influence of the blood has since become far wider.

The problem facing masters who wanted to breed on these lines was that they were usually custodians of a pack which they were bound to hand back to the country in acceptable condition: and this included registration of a stated number of hounds in the *F.K.S.B.* The issue of admission to the stud book occasioned some of the most violent disagreements.

The debate has not been much heard since 1945, partly because so many breeders have been converted, like the Duke of Beaufort, to a cautious use of Welsh-cross stallions, partly because the conditions which occasioned the change have all intensified. These include, relevantly, more plough, more cattle being out in winter, more fertilizers and tractor fumes, far more roads, especially motorways, and more afforestation. All these call for more hunt and the last for more cry.[20]

Horses and Horsemanship

Hunter breeding was said to be at rock bottom in the 1920s, mainly because very bad mares were sent to premium stallions.[21] The latter, however, markedly improved, as judges looked for weight-carrying hunter getters rather than showy sprinters. The War Office took over the financing of premiums, but the entirely private Hunter Improvement Society had to accept the burden in 1931 because the War Office had no money. The premiums were no longer 'King's'.

After the second war the scheme got going again gradually; by 1971 3,860 mares were served by the H.I.S.'s sixty-three premium stallions. The percentage of live foals had become far higher, rising from about fifty per cent before the war to better than sixty-three.[22]

Horsemanship between the wars showed a general tendency towards the 'balanced

THE CURRE, 1971
Lady Curre kept on the late Sir Edward's hounds from 1930 to 1956, preserving the 'new breed' of true-breeding white Welsh-cross hounds which over thirty-four years he had created. Mr J. O'M. Meade became master in 1956, joined two seasons later by his wife and in 1966 by Mr F. M. Broome; the latter's son David has latterly joined the mastership, though better known in the show-jumping ring. With hounds near Llansoy, here pictured, is George Headdon, huntsman since 1969. The hounds, of which there are twenty-five couple in kennel, are now owned by the Hunt Trust.

THE DUMFRIESSHIRE, 1972
This is the unmistakable black-and-tan pack created by Sir John Buchanan-Jardine between 1921 and 1950 with Gascon blood; it has been owned and hunted by his son, Major Sir Rupert, since 1950. The latter was joined in the mastership in 1970 by Mr David Culham. Their country is isolated owing to the sea on one side and moorland on two others; the woods here are typical of much of it. Sir Rupert is on the right; left is Ted Cockerell, whipper in since 1937 and kennel huntsman since 1953.

seat', a modified version of Caprilli's style. The full forward seat was not regarded as safe or suitable for hunting. Today it is. Young people coming into hunting in the years just before the second war were often far better taught than their parents, owing to the Pony Club. This movement has continued to grow, and the great majority of children now hunting have Pony Club instruction and pass Pony Club tests.

Hacking to meets more than a very few miles away became most exceptional with the availability of motor horseboxes and trailers; in 1930 a full-sized two-horse trailer cost £75.

Ladies; Clothes

In 1922 there were said to be twenty-five women hunting to every one in 1880; in many countries they were half the field, which, being thus swollen, made things difficult for hounds and impossible for huntsmen.[23] In the Belvoir field the astonished 'Sabretache' saw young females busy with their lipsticks while hounds were drawing, and then going very well indeed.[24] Since 1945 there have been more women than men in the fields of, probably, every hunt in Britain; in some countries the proportion is overwhelming, at least on weekdays.

The number of women masters has grown steadily throughout the century. Wars pressed women into service as amateur huntsmen and whippers-in (as well as grooms and feeders) and peace confirms their competence in these roles.

Sidesaddle was still regarded in 1930, by men, as 'the safer, the smarter, and the better seat'.[25] Women agreed that it was the safer and the smarter, but by 1932 about half were riding astride. The reasons for the change were that cross-saddle

[209]

riding was much cheaper and less trouble, and that even experienced horsewomen found it difficult to keep a horse straight at its fences without a leg each side of it. Ladies who rode sidesaddle always did so with a double bridle unless the horse had been schooled in Ireland, and usually with a martingale.[26] Ladies in breeches used to wear bowlers; most now wear caps.

Many gentleman would like to wear caps also, on grounds of safety and economy. But the rule is still that caps are for masters, hunt staff, and sometimes farmers.

The old hunt breakfast was hardly seen after the first war: catering for the inflated fields of the 1920s required a social climber with unusual determination and wealth. The lawn meet is the 20th century's economical equivalent. As early as 1931 it was noted that helpers with trays of drinks were mobbed by free-loading foot people, many locally notorious and some inimical to hunting;[27] this phenomenon is still to be observed.

Masters and Finance

The difficulties of masters were reckoned to have increased enormously in the 1920s, the principal problems being fields, money and changes in the countryside.

Larger fields encouraged masters, especially those who hunted their own hounds, to delegate the disciplining of the mounted followers to field masters. This was a new use of a phrase which had previously meant a master in the field, a deputy acting for the owner of the pack. Field masters have become almost invariable where fields are large. The numbers of people out have still been too great to control, and some hunts have consequently taken to excluding visitors on Saturdays and in the spring.

The shortage of money meant capping, which became usual in the 1930s. Field money also began to be taken – an Irish invention, introduced in Warwickshire in 1933 – from subscribers as well as strangers.

For masters, the problem was, and still is, the difference between the country's guarantee and the actual outlay. A committee asked to make up an annual deficit is inclined to want greater control over the hunt's management. This should under no circumstances – as a distinguished Master of Hounds insisted in 1973 – extend to interference in the running of the country or the choice of hunt servants.[28]

A happy development since the war has been the growth of hunt supporters' clubs. These have two mains functions – financial help, and public relations in the countryside; they enable foot and car followers – many extremely keen, many infinitely vexatious – to give practical backing to the hunt.

No one has ever doubted the immense benefit to a country and to its kennel of a long mastership: under all post-war circumstances it is surprising how many have been lucky. But many of the most celebrated subscription packs have had a terrible lot of changes since 1945. The ill effects of a kaleidoscope of masters are reduced by a long-serving huntsman; several fashionable packs have been lucky or wise in this regard, but the longest service has, predictably, been in places like the Cumberland fells, the far north, the Welsh Marches and Essex.

Politics

Between the wars there was sporadic opposition to hunting, expressing either the views of the Sophists and Humanists or resentment at privilege and display.

After the second war the League Against Cruel Sports and a part, but only a part, of the membership of the R.S.P.C.A., became far more weightily vocal. In February 1949 a private member's bill was introduced in the House of Commons which sought to make illegal the hunting of any deer, otter or badger and the coursing of hare and rabbit. It was defeated by 214 votes to 101, in a parliament with a large Labour majority. A measure to forbid foxhunting was withdrawn before coming to a vote. The effect of this political activity was to give immense impetus to the British Field Sports Society.

The debate continues. Journalists and persons connected with television are usually townsmen and often committed to a left-wing view of society, so that the mass media have by and large taken an anti view based on moral outrage. They have not yet suggested an alternative method of killing foxes which does not involve slow death by gangrene or suffocation, or the exposure of other animals to poison. The principal objects of disapproval have been staghunting and coursing, but plenty of extremists are violently against foxhunting. Activists among these have formed hunt sabotage groups, laying drags and otherwise trying to spoil sport. They have so far been an irritant but not much more. If they studied and could copy the methods of the Irish Land League of the 1880s they could destroy foxhunting over-night: but to do this they would need the wholesale support of the countryside. This they show no signs of getting.

THE BORDER, 1972
These hounds were owned by successive generations of the Robson and Dodd families; Messrs Jacob Robson, father and son, were masters until 1951 and Mr S. Dodd with them until 1949. Their pack was fellhound outcrossed to Tynedale and Cleveland; many were pale, as they still are, and all hare-footed. The Robsons only kept a dozen couple, which they took out three days a week. The younger Mr Jacob Robson gave them to the country in 1951, acting for a committee for another three years. In 1954 Mr Ian Hedley became master. Mr John Dixon whips in. Both are here shown, having caught their fox on the banks of the Fulhope Burn. The pack still numbers only eighteen couple of what the hunt calls 'hill hounds'. The hunt coat remains steel grey.

15 Ireland
1914 *and After*

First World War

Ireland, being still an integral part of Britain, was in the first war similarly short of men, money, horses, feed and transport. Men and money were in most countries shortest, and hunts were kept going by women very much as in England. Some countries – fewer than in England, but a much higher proportion – had private packs owned and largely financed by individuals; these suffered much less dislocation.

The most serious and enduring effect of the war was on horsebreeding. A lot of Clydesdale and Shire horses came to Ireland, where there had been extremely few before, and during the war the draught mares – not drayhorses but fast trotters with plenty of thoroughbred blood – were sent to them instead of to thoroughbreds. The result was a new race of cold-blooded mares of a much heavier and more phlegmatic sort, and very few indeed of the kind which had foaled the old Irish halfbred hunter.[1] This situation repaired itself, but it took a long time to do so.

The 'troubles' and the Civil War had a widely varied impact on the countryside, more so even than the Land League of forty years earlier but of shorter duration. In some places the Civil War stopped hunting; in others it was hardly noticed.

The Hunts in the 20th Century

In some countries, and some of the very best, all the old problems remained: lack of confidence, lack of support, quick turn-round of masters.

In Meath the problem was eased by a great huntsman, Will Fitzsimmons, and solved by the long mastership of Mrs Nancy Connell of Leixlip. In Kildare, continuity was only achieved by the defeatist expedient of a committee. Masters of the Tipperary turned over with Irish speed until the arrival of Mrs Sylvia Masters; she could blow her horn, at full gallop, with a cigarette in her mouth; she was the first woman to ride 100 point-to-point winners.[2] After 1932 the Duhallow had masterships of one or two seasons until after the second war. North Kilkenny – a revival of the old Castlecomer hunt – has survived appalling difficulties. East Galway failed to survive even greater ones – unappeased local hostility, making the country unhuntable. It has started again but its existence is precarious. Galway itself has always been intensely sporting, and intensely reluctant to subscribe. Mr Joseph Pickersgill was the first long-serving master since 1885 and the last until 1963.

With few exceptions, Ireland has enjoyed the incalculable benefits of long master-ships only when the master has owned the hounds, and especially when he has been rich enough to pay for them. The Louth is a private pack: consequently Captain R. A. B. Filgate was master from 1916 to 1967, followed by Mr W. R. Filgate, who hunted hounds from 1947 to 1972 with Mrs Filgate as second whipper-in. Major Dermot and Major Victor McCalmont have owned and hunted the Kilkenny since 1921. Mr Dermot Doyne managed the Coollattin for his cousin the 7th Earl Fitzwilliam from before the first war to the middle of the second. In Wexford, Major Lakin replaced the committee's pack with his own, and was thereby master from 1912 to 1937. Mr Dick Russell followed his father in Waterford, father and son spanning the years 1914 to 1957. Mr C. A. Love was master of the civilianized Muskerry from 1919 to 1959. The Carbery was given up by the Beamish family, owing to lack of support, in 1914; since when the O'Driscoll family of Bandon, all of whom are solicitors in their spare time, have owned, hunted and whipped-in. The new Bermingham and North Galway (1946) seems likely to enjoy the same good fortune as long as the Cusack-Smith family are about: but if they leave the lesson of Irish history is that the hunt has a thin chance.

Well over half of the whole island is unhunted by foxhounds. Three small patches of Ulster now are (by the Strabane, East Down and Dungannon) owing to a shift in the balance of nature: more foxes, fewer hares. In the whole of the west up from Galway hunting remains improbable: there is too much bog and too little money.

Deer and Hare

The Ward Union and County Down continue to hunt deer, the one in the Meath and the other in the East Down countries. The former's support traditionally comes more from Dublin than the countryside, the latter's more from the countryside than from Belfast.

There were thirty recognized harrier packs in 1972–3, two (Clonmel and Killeagh) admitting to hunting fox only, others to fox and hare. A high proportion are, as always, in country unhunted by foxhounds, which puts them in a very different position from that occupied by English harriers. The actual number of harrier packs, especially in the south west, remains anybody's guess. Mr Charles Lanier was told that there were at least forty 'Sunday harriers' in County Cork about 1925, all black-and-tans, almost all followed on horseback, almost all hunting the fox.[3] It appears that many more are now hunted on foot. Some of these packs advertise their meets in the *Cork Examiner*; more have their meets fixed when the members come out of church after Mass. One man has a bugle, used not to hunt hounds but only to collect them at the end of the day. The method of hunting the foot packs has much in common with American hill topping, each man listening for his own dog. When hounds hunt a fox they try to kill it; when they hunt a hare they are usually stopped because hares are scarce (hares are never shot in County Kerry). Besides fox races of the American sort there are trails of the Cumberland sort; at some meetings prizes are big and betting heavy. The mounted Sunday harriers very often run drags.

The Irish Masters of Beagles Association was formed in 1950, several packs already being well established. In 1972 there were thirty-five recognized packs, some trencher-fed and some private, but many kennelled and maintained by a normal subscription. In spring and autumn there are all-Ireland interhunt meets (normally including Ulster), for which one club or another is host; coats of all colours and headgear of all designs are seen.[4]

Changes and Absence of Change

The second war affected Ireland less than the first; although many things were short and many men away, neutrality was a good deal different from involvement in total war.

The great change after the war was caused by events in England: continued austerity and punitive taxation. A lot of rich hunting Englishmen came to Ireland as refugees from surtax; they and their wives had the effect of turning unpretentious hunts into grand social affairs, expensively mounted, elegantly dressed and entertaining lavishly. Americans also came in greater numbers than ever before, enhancing this effect. Many an Irish field was first abashed by, then emulous of, Pytchley and Orange County migrants.[5]

Englishmen had for a century been drawn to the grass, scent and wirelessness of Ireland. Immediately after the war these included several important Masters of Hounds: Lord Daresbury, Major Beaumont, Major Scott. The first is in Limerick still, the second was in Kildare until his death, the third went back to England and to the Portman after only two seasons, which was much regretted.

Love of sport and lack of money have always combined to give Ireland a strongly amateur personnel, which is now stronger than ever. Of thirty-two recognized packs of foxhounds in 1972–3, twenty-five were hunted by amateurs; thirty amateur whippers-in are listed in *Baily*, nearly half women.

The roving master and amateur huntsman became rare in England in the 20th century, though he had been frequent enough in the 19th; in Ireland there are several 20th-century examples – Sir Thomas Ainsworth, master successively of the Meath, Galway, Kildare and Tipperary; and Mr A. P. Pollok, who hunted hounds for the Galway, Waterford, Tipperary, Kildare, Westmeath and Limerick.

THE LIMERICK
The 2nd Lord Daresbury was joint master of the Belvoir from 1934 to 1947 (his father, as Sir Gilbert Greenall, had been master from 1896 to 1912). When he came to Limerick in 1947 he found the Welsh cross hounds which Mr John Alexander had brought from North Kilkenny in 1934, a pack which owed a great deal to Mr Isaac Bell and his blood. Lord Daresbury disliked it; he bred and breeds still a pack of Belvoir blood, his own property, and with eighty couple as numerous as Belvoir itself. The pack is now nearly all sired by homebred stallions. Hugh Robards (pictured) came from the Heythrop in 1970 and hunted hounds two days a week; in 1972 he began hunting all four days. In that season Lord Harrington joined Lord Daresbury, heir of an equally glorious and – in South Notts – almost equally distant hunting tradition.

16 America
1914 and After

First World War

The impact of the war on American hunting was, for a dozen obvious reasons, far gentler than on English sport. A number of hunts were nevertheless disbanded because they depended on groups of men who all went into khaki; these hunts were small clubs instead of traditional institutions, broadly based in the countryside, which could weather years of virtual abeyance.

In 1900, seventy-five per cent of all recognized packs were in Virginia, Maryland and Pennsylvania. For a decade after 1919 there was an enormous growth of foxhunting, mostly in new regions; by 1929 fifty-two new recognized hunts brought the American total to over 100, and there were hundreds of less formal new foxhunting organizations. The crash of 1929 killed a few, but in the second decade of peace far more were started than had died. In 1940 there were 130 recognized hunts, including those of Canada.

Virginia

Mr Daniel B. Sands was hunting the Piedmont and Middleburg countries as tenant of Mr Joseph B. Thomas and using his hounds and huntsman. Increasing friction developed between owner and master, and in 1915 Mr Thomas suggested that Mr Sands should go. Mr and Mrs Sands were bitter; they warned Mr Thomas off their own land; a number of landowners, their old friends, did likewise. But Mr Thomas had for years spent an immense amount of effort and money (especially on panelling) and had bought and bred an outstanding pack. Mr Thomas became master of the Piedmont; with Charles Carver hunting hounds better than any other American huntsman in history they showed brilliant sport. But Mr Thomas was an outsider and a Yankee, and Mr Sands lived locally and worked on local opinion while hunting the Middleburg country. Bitterness flared into open war a second time, and Mr Thomas took himself, his hounds and Charles Carver to another part of the state.

In 1921 Mr Sands returned to the Middleburg, where he was master until 1954. Bob Maddox was his huntsman until he died in 1948, followed by Charlie George, whipper-in since 1929. Mr Sands built up over this period a very good pack, from which he rigorously excluded any blood used by the detested Mr Thomas; he liked black-and-white hounds which he could see at a distance.[1] He was able to send his puppies out to walk like an English breeder, and combined the puppy show with the point-to-point; this event attracted an enormous crowd.[2]

Mr William Skinker of The Plains hunted the Orange County hounds until 1920. He was followed by Mr Fletcher Harper, master until 1952, who had hunted as a schoolboy with the Brandywine and Genesee Valley, and whipped-in to the Westchester. The pack was still of Mr Skinker's inheritance and management – red hounds, unusually sorty. Hunted by Ned Chadwell until 1924, and then by 'Dukes' Leach until 1967, they were better looking, better fed and better behaved than any other American pack; they were even brought to the meet uncoupled.[3]

Mrs Kennedy hunted with the Orange County when her husband was President. She was asked, 'What does your husband do?'[4]

Of the other existing Virginia packs: the Warrenton has had H. D. (Dick) Bywaters as huntsman since 1934, son of Hugh and like him a marvellous hound breeder. The Casanova died of poverty in 1925 but was born again in 1927. The Loudoun County died from lack of a huntsman, but was born again as the Loudoun. The Blue Ridge in Clarke County had and has a comparatively untroubled life.

When Mr Thomas left the Piedmont Valley he hunted for one season the part of Rappahannock County which was later Mr Larrabee's, then established a new base adjoining the Blue Ridge. Relieved of the expense of the Piedmont, he began breeding hounds on a much larger scale but exactly the same lines. Charlie Carver was able to put a great many puppies out to walk with the local farmers, then take them cubbing and teach them their business; he did this brilliantly, and his breeding and handling was, according to Mr Thomas, a major factor in the latter's success.[5]

In a typical year Mr Thomas had 118 days actual hunting over almost eleven months – July to December at Millbrook, December to March in North Carolina, March to May on Long Island. The influence of his breeding was enormous. The point that he himself made was that of the million and a half foxhounds in America in the 1920s, extremely few were in packs of more than seventeen couple, which made evenness impossible; at the same time he believed that the old Virginia hound was the best pack foxhound in the world, if properly handled, and was identical to the English foxhound of the late 18th century.[6]

Four years after Mr Thomas left Rappahannock County, Mr Sterling Larrabee started a private pack in the same country; it became the Old Dominion in 1931.

The Bywaters family had, in a different fashion, been doing what Mr Thomas did, breeding hounds, of something like a sort, for sale as well as for their own hunting.

ORANGE COUNTY HOUNDS
Hounds are breaking up a grey fox on Mr Howell Jackson's Oakendale Farm near Middleburg, Virginia. These hounds were taken over by Mr Fletcher Harper from Mr William Skinker in 1920; Mr Harper was master until 1952 (a mastership described in his own book); Ned Chadwell and 'Dukes' Leach were his huntsmen. Mr A. H. Higginson said that their feeding and handling were better than those of any other American kennel: their breeding was also an enormous success. Mr Skinker's sort was outcrossed principally to Mr J. B. Thomas's; a later outcross much used was the Foxcatcher, which were red Virginia hounds from Greene County also bred to Mr Thomas's from 1933. The Orange County pack had an influence comparable to Mr Thomas's – forty-eight different kennels had hounds or drafts directly from The Plains during Mr Harper's mastership, and twenty-seven more in the next fifteen years.

In 1926 Mr Hugh L. Bywaters joined with another breeder Mr Joseph D. Johnson of Sperryville to start the Rappahannock Hunt.

In the Southside, the Deep Run closed down because of building. Draghunting was started again in 1923, and foxhunting in a new country in 1928. The Keswick stopped with the first war and started again in 1927. The Albemarle County died, but before it did so the Farmington was started. Mr William du Pont moved his Foxcatcher Hounds from Montpelier Station to Maryland; the Montpelier was revived in 1927 by Mr du Pont's sister Marion. A number of other hunts were started; the Eagle Hill had a difficult country, but was defeated not by conditions but by apathy: 'The people preferred movies and Ford cars.'[7] On balance, new hunts outnumbered those which died.

Hill topping and trials continued to grow in popularity throughout the state. In 1970 every farmer, and many storekeepers and workmen, kept a hound or two, and always had, in 'the Valley'.[8] Many organized packs were largely bred from these hounds; the results were apt to be uneven, and looked to Edith Somerville in 1929 like 'well-shaved Irish setters'.[9]

Virginia horses became much more expensive as Northerners and Middle Westerners began hunting. Dress was pretty smart and usually scarlet; scarlet was, in fact, much more generally worn by members of some fields than in Britain, even those least experienced. Many hunts adopted the short shrill English metal horn, but the big and mellow old cow horns were still used.

Maryland and Delaware

The Elkridge had benefited from being near Baltimore, but in 1919 it was too near: development drove it farther out. The tradition of Mr Alex Brown was well maintained: the Elkridge Farmers' Day was an old-style point-to-point, with real farmers' races, mule steeplechases and other diversions, all as valuable as they were entertaining.[10]

Mr Frank Bonsal's Harford, farther north, kept its fine open grazing country almost wholly unspoiled. The English, American and crossbred pack had a bobbery look like the Elkridge's, but was equally effective and very well hunted by Mr Bonsal. He died after a hunting accident in 1924.

By 1934 the Elkridge had lost a great deal of its country to a new artificial lake dammed for Baltimore's hydroelectric power. This occasioned the merger of the Elkridge and Harford, mostly in the Harford's country.

Mr Redmond C. Stewart left the Green Spring Valley in 1914; his breeding policy remained unaltered (and so remains): very big coverts demand the cry and self-reliance of the American hound, rough country the power and stamina of the English.

Mr William du Pont brought his very good pack of red Virginia hounds to Elkton. He bought thirty-two couple from Mr J. B. Thomas in 1932, which nicked beautifully with the Foxcatcher. The hunt briefly amalgamated with the New Market in Frederick County.

The Howard County was started in 1930; following the best Maryland precedent, the right pack has been found to be an English–American cross.

In 1931 Mr Wilbur Ross Hubbard introduced formal hunting to the Eastern Shore, establishing Mr Hubbard's Kent County at Chestertown with hounds of the local type. To his south, the Corsica were a pack of identical type but less formal organization. An important private pack was Mr John B. Hannum's at Rising Sun;

he collected his hounds from farmer friends in Chester and Delaware Counties; in 1934 he was one of Mr Roy Jackson's co-founders of the Penn-Marydel organization.

In Delaware there was a great deal of foxhunting but no organized hunt. In 1920 a group in the north of the state formed a club under Mrs Victor duPont, and bought Mr Benjamin Funk's private Pennsylvania pack from Embreeville, Chester County. The hunt was called the Vicmead.

Pennsylvania and New Jersey

The Rose Tree kennel went in the 1920s from local to Virginia and Walker hounds, in order to get both drive and, by one account, pack discipline.[11] In the 1930s old and new were crossed. But by the time it found a new country far west in York County the hunt had gone back to Penn-Marydel.

The Radnor's famous crossbreds still struck some observers as wonderful: others as riotous babblers.[12] When Mr Roy Jackson became master in 1929 he wanted Pennsylvania hounds but he had to have crossbreds; he therefore, like Mr Charles Mather long before, had both. His private Kirkwood hounds, not the club's, were the member pack when he started the Penn-Marydel Fox Hounds Inc. in 1934. The purpose of this organization was to register, formulate standards and keep the breed pure. Shows started at Kirkwood in 1936, which within a few years had an immensely salutary effect on the breed.[13]

Mr Charles Mather bred what he called his 'West Chester' hounds of Belvoir blood for the Brandywine until he died in 1928. He was succeeded by his son Gilbert. Almost immediately the latter was out on a bad-scenting day; his hounds were joined by a farmer's beagle, which was the only one to speak to the line. Mr Mather fell out of love at once with his father's English hounds;[14] in 1930 he bought a draft from Mr J. B. Thomas and a few Walkers from Tennessee, and bred a new pack.

The Whitelands still had open country and plentiful foxes. In 1924 the Perkiomen Valley was started next door; in 1959 the two combined.

MR ROY JACKSON
Mr Jackson was a Pennsylvanian and a lover of Pennsylvania hounds. When he and Mr John Bowman followed Mr Charles Lanier at the Fairfield and Westchester, it was a Pennsylvania pack they brought, probably the first ever seen in New York or Connecticut. In 1924 they found a new country, just northward round Golden's Bridge, where they started hunting the same hounds in 1925. Mr Jackson went back to Pennsylvania in 1929, succeeding the unhappy Mr Horace B. Hare as master of the Radnor. He bought the farm of Mr Samuel Kirk, who had a good pack of local hounds; he bought the Vicmead hounds, which had come from Ben Funk of Embreeville, Chester County; he called his pack the Kirkwood. He hunted it three days a week; Will Leverton hunted the Radnor's crossbreds another three days. In January 1934 he enlisted three other like-minded hound-men and formed Penn-Marydel Fox Hounds Inc.; member packs included the Rose Tree, Westchester, Huntingdon Valley, Mr Hubbard's, Golden's Bridge. Extraordinarily, the Bryn Mawr show did not have a Penn-Marydel division until Mr Walter Jeffords successfully urged one in 1946.

ELIAS CHADWELL

The Chadwells are a Virginia hunting family of long standing and of a renown which shows no signs of diminishing. In 1927 the Millbrook (New York State) was reorganized in its modern country; Mr Oakleigh Thorne's daughter Margaret, Mrs Lawrence Smith, was master. The writer Gordon Grand, living in the country (which he so often described), was asked to find a huntsman. He consulted Mr Fletcher Harper, whose own Orange County huntsman had been until 1924 Ned Chadwell. Mr Harper recommended Ned's brother Elias. Elias brought hounds from Virginia (many bred by his own family) which were very successful; he outcrossed them to the hounds of small individual breeders, rather than to the bloodlines of established packs; yet he achieved both levelness and pack discipline. Though retired from active hunting he is still in charge of the kennel; his son Earl whipped in from 1935 and has hunted hounds since 1950. Ned Chadwell went from the Orange County to Mr Sterling Larrabee, who took over Mr J. B. Thomas's country in Rappahannock County, later the Old Dominion. His son William 'Buster' Chadwell has been the brilliantly successful huntsman of the Essex (New Jersey) since 1944; his son Rodney became his whipper-in in 1965.

Mr William C. (Bill) Clothier was master of the Pickering and the Eagle Farms until 1926. This became too much even for a man of his energy and wealth; he took thirty couple to a new kennel at Phoenixville for the Pickering, and made over the Eagle Farms to Mr Joseph Neff Ewing. Mr Clothier, hunting in a grey coat, was master of the Pickering until 1951. His hounds were in 1929 the best American that Miss Edith Somerville saw – black, white and tan, with long ears, very like Kerry beagles.[15]

Mr Plunket Stewart came back from the war in 1919 and began serious operations. He got many more English hounds, and in 1931 a specially valuable draft of bitches from the V.W.H. (Cricklade). On 6 February 1932 they had the great Lenape run, one of the best ever recorded. The bitches went from Saw Mill Wood to Lenape, a ten-mile point and fifty as they ran, the first forty minutes all on good grass with hardly a check; then the field climbed a flight of concrete steps to someone's summer bungalow, no one dismounting, and then interrupted two lovers in a car on the bank of the Brandywine. The lovers followed the hunt in their car. Hounds crossed the river four times, and hunted through the Lenape amusement park: they 'sniffed at a merry-go-round, led us under the scenic railway'. There were three up at the end, on other people's horses – Mr Stewart, the huntsman Charlie Smith and (luckily) Mr Stanley Reeve, most voluminous of hunting diarists.[16]

Mr Samuel D. Riddle gave up in 1917. His country and hounds were taken over by Mr Walter M. Jeffords. In 1927 Mr Jeffords moved his private kennel to Andrews Bridge in Lancaster County, in spite of the fate of the old Killashandra. Tact and good sense have persuaded the Amish farmers into friendliness, since neither field nor Penn-Marydel hounds do any damage.[17]

North of Philadelphia, the Huntingdon Valley started in 1914 and Mr Newbold Ely's in 1929. The latter did not survive its master's death. Both were influential Penn-Marydel packs.

Western Pennsylvania is a different world. Most of its hunting is young. Four of the six packs are draghounds. One of the exceptions is the Chestnut Ridge, re-established in 1932 in Fayette County. The other, better known, is the Rolling Rock.

About 1916 Mr Richard B. Mellon began to buy property in the Ligonier Valley; he started a shooting club, in order to entertain his friends without embarrassing them; in 1920 the club began hunting under Mr Richard K. Mellon. He tried American hounds, but replaced them with a Belvoir draft. He employed, uniquely, a salaried earth stopper and a mounted terrierman, and thus killed many more wild foxes above ground than most packs. The hunt has been described as the most English in America.[18] But its hounds are now American.

In New Jersey, the Essex had sustained success, thanks first to a new pack bred from Trigg dogs and Orange County bitches, and secondly to William 'Buster' Chadwell, son of Ned and nephew of Elias; one of his achievements has been to get his pack – of a kind prone to riot – steady to the country's teeming deer.

The Monmouth County turned into harriers; it turned back to foxes but still wore green.

New York

The Meadow Brook at last got the right crossbred pack for hunting foxes on Long Island;[19] but their situation was 'dire' in 1929[20] and bricks and mortar swallowed them. The Suffolk had the same sort of hounds and the same fate. The Smithtown survives, using English hounds for fox and drag, in spite of sandy soil and big coverts.

Long Island hunting continued to arouse a certain resentful envy among commuters, as well as farmers, who were not rich enough to afford it. J. P. Marquand describes the kind of country club which admits anyone, and holds membership drives, bitterly contemplating the club with a waiting list, and with stables for the members' hunters and polo ponies.[21]

The Goshen lived for a little after most of its establishment left for Virginia; died; lived again; and found no local support.

The same thing happened in Westchester. In 1915 a new hunt was started, straddling the state line, called the Fairfield and Westchester. Mr Lunsford Pitts Yandell brought an enormous pack of Walkers in 1924,[22] which never quite hunted as a pack. But a very good pack was bred from them.

Mr John Bowman and Mr Roy Jackson, with Ben Funk of Embreeville, started a hunt in 1925 which became the Golden's Bridge; their Penn-Marydel hounds were the only ones in New York state.

Mr Oakleigh Thorne shared his Millbrook country with Mr Eugene Reynal's excellent foot beagles. Mr Higginson came to hunt the fox for a time, then came Mr J. B. Thomas. In 1928 Elias Chadwell came as huntsman; his son Earl whipped-in from 1935; in 1950 they changed places.

The country, so often described by Gordon Grand, was still remote and very rural. Fields were small and included farmers. The panelling was so well managed that every enclosure could be jumped out of in every direction.[23]

Major Wadsworth retired in 1917. He invited Mr Higginson to take over the Genesee Valley hounds and country. But Mr Higginson was committed to the Millbrook. The hunt seemed to die. It, and its pack, were revived after two years. In 1933 Mr William J. Wadsworth, son of the Major, became master. He built up a completely different sort of pack with Welsh-cross hounds from Lady Curre.

New England

The Myopia kept its crossbreds and returned to foxhunting after the war. There was great continuity – too much, in one view[24] – but not many foxes. They turned entirely to draghunting.

Mr Bowditch's hunt was given up, but a new start was made in 1922, inspired by the Norfolk hounds. The Millwood hunted foxes as long as they could: but it was not long.

The Norfolk hunted drags at home but foxes on Cape Cod for two weeks at the end of the season. The Myopia also had an 'away country', in the far south of Massachusetts; this country was taken over by the highly successful Quansett (Mr Almy's) until it was swallowed by development in 1954.

Hunting near Boston, like hunting on Long Island, still arouses mixed feelings. The farmers, sturdily independent to the point of perversity, can be rendered amenable by dint of tact and damage funds: but middle-class persons, as portrayed by John Updike, deride the older, richer, horsy set, the 'big H' of Millbrook and Scituate. The sophisticated young wives nevertheless accept all invitations from this oafish hunting group.[25]

Rhode Island had draghunting for its summer visitors, then a more legitimate Jacob's Hill Hunt (1924) at Providence, and Bradbury (1950) in the west.

In Connecticut the Fairfield County was established in 1924 next to the Fairfield and Westchester, which it has outlived. A Penn-Marydel pack replaced one from

THE BLUE RIDGE, 1974
Hounds are moving off after meeting at Carter Hall, Clarke County. Mr William Bell Watkins followed Mr Edward B. Jacobs as master of these hounds from 1921 to 1925 and from 1931 to 1942. By 1928 foxes were being preserved, and reds still made very long points over good-scenting ground. In 1937 Mr Raymond Guest was given a loan in the southern part, which he hunted with a private pack called the Rock Hill, mostly from Mr Hugh Bywaters. Mr Alexander Mackay-Smith, America's most eminent recent hunting historian (to whom the author has elsewhere expressed his indebtedness), was master of the Blue Ridge for a total of seventeen seasons. Mrs George P. Greenhalgh Jnr has been master since 1965. The hounds were American, mostly from Mr Joseph B. Thomas, and bred by Mr Mackay-Smith to the Orange County; they are now half English and half crossbred.

Mr J. B. Thomas. The Westmoor Hunt at West Hartford hunted a drag not because there were no foxes, but because they were trapped or shot in the time-honoured local fashion. In 1929 Mr Haight's Litchfield County was started, hunting wild foxes at home until Christmas and near Aiken after it.

The Shelburne survived as the sole orthodox hunt (and very orthodox indeed) in northern New England until after the second war. The Green Mountain, also in Vermont, hunts a drag.

Carolina and the Deep South

Before 1914 there was virtually no organized foxhunting anywhere south of Virginia, with the exception of Mr Hitchcock's establishment at Aiken. This was no longer the result of poverty, but of taste and climate.

In 1914 Mr James 'Drums' Boyd started the Moore County, in the very empty Sand Hill section of North Carolina. Soil and climate meant no frost and also no scent.

Mr J. B. Thomas visited Mr Percy Rockefeller at Overhills, North Carolina, with sixty couple of hounds, for part of every winter from 1921 to 1930. This was a densely wooded country like the Aiken, with sixty-foot-wide rides cut in which the field often galloped for miles.

Two hunts were started in the 1920s, and two more since the second war. The most recent, the Triangle, has made the surprising choice of a pure English pack.

The trencher-fed hounds of farmers teemed, and teem still, throughout the state. To the shocked Edith Somerville they seemed entirely wild, running everything from rabbits to wildcats; she was awed by the amount of 'moonshine' drunk during the night by the foxhunters.

Miss Somerville also visited Mrs Thomas Hitchcock, queen of Aiken and master of its draghounds and beagles. By this time (1929) Mrs Hitchcock was usually in her buggy – one of many – but large fields followed her hounds on horseback at tremendous speed, including a lot of girls riding astride with the greatest elegance and dash. There were two boarding schools at Aiken – boys' and girls' – and forty or fifty of the pupils were regularly out, riding, said Miss Somerville, dangerously jealous.[26] There being no natural jumps in the forest, artificial ones were made – brush, eight feet wide, with a four-foot rail in the middle, always taken at a gallop.

A problem greater than any in the forest faced Mrs Hitchcock when Mr Harry Worcester Smith came to stay at her home 'Mon Repos' and refused to leave. In despair she had a house built for him. He declined to move to it. She burned his room down.[27] (This story, though denied, is believed true.)

The Camden has hunted foxes in Kershaw County since 1926, with American and crossbred hounds. The Woodside was started in 1961, adjoining the Aiken but hunting foxes. The American pack was joined after Christmas by Mr Sherman P. Haight Jr's Litchfield County hounds from Connecticut. The Greenville County was established in 1963 near Gowensville, foxhunting with American hounds.

Georgia probably had even more and better hounds than the Carolinas, but no organized foxhunting after the death of the Chatham until 1943. Since then four hunts have been established: growth startling in a state with an intense but very different foxhunting tradition.

Mr Bowman brought his Golden's Bridge to Florida in midwinter; his hunt staff wore white coats, jodhpurs and topees. The Two Rivers (1965) is remarkable in wearing scarlet, hunting foxes and having an English pack.

THE SCARTEEN, 1967
Mr T. F. 'Thady' Ryan with his family's celebrated black-and-tan Kerry beagles, here seen near Longford Bridge, County Limerick. Mr John Ryan entered then solely to fox only after the first war. He hunted them until 1929, when a bad fall in his own hunt races made him give up the mastership, though not the ownership. Outside masters reappeared, of whom Mr D. E. C. Price (1934–8) found it necessary at last to outcross to English foxhounds: but he did so with great care, using only black-and-tan stallions of appropriate conformation. Mr Thady Ryan became joint master in 1946, hunting hounds. He was joined by Mrs Dermot McCalmont in 1971.

Kentucky and Tennessee

The growth of hunting west of the southern Appalachians compares with that of the south: there was one orthodox hunt before the first war, which died when its master retired; that was restarted and two others started between the wars; six have been established since 1945.

The revival was the Iroquois. General Williams's huntsman Bonnie Stone was still in Lexington, and in 1926 he got ten couple of hounds together, for a young group.

In 1930 Mr Joseph B. Thomas brought his pack to Gallatin, Tennessee, and for two seasons his Grasslands Hunt was a lavish and successful venture, yellow-clad, locally welcomed. The large plans of the Gallatin gentlemen collapsed with the slump, and in 1932 Mr Thomas sold half his pack to a new hunt at Hillsboro, near Nashville.

Tennessee has, since the second war, acquired the Oak Grove at Germantown (1954), the Longreen at Rossville (1957), the Mells at Waco (1964), and the Cedar Knob at Cornersville (1972). The first two have American packs, the others cross-bred. All hunt foxes, all in scarlet except the youngest, which wears green.

Kentucky's orthodox hunting, aside from the Iroquois, is smaller and more recent: the Long Run near Louisville (1961) and the Licking River at Carlisle (1962); both hunt foxes.

THE CHAGRIN VALLEY
Mr Windsor T. White's establishment of this hunt is of first class historical importance, because its successful example is what really started the lusty growth of orthodox foxhunting in the Middle West. Already converted to English hounds, Mr White bought the Millbrook young hounds in 1924 when Mr Oakleigh Thorne gave up – these were descended from Mr Higginson's, and were mostly of Mr Fernie's blood. This policy has been continued, although the country is almost entirely wooded (except the parts lost to building) and might to some clubs seem to call for the cry and self reliance of American hounds. The Chagrin Valley has been consistently lucky in very long masterships: Mrs Gilbert Humphrey has been master since 1954 and Mr Robert Y. White since 1956.

Middle West and West

The Middle West has seen a still lustier growth of regular foxhunting. In 1914 there were only the Chagrin Valley near Cleveland; the Onwentsia and Midlothian (both draghunting because of wire) near Chicago; and the Grosse Pointe near Detroit. There are now twenty regular packs, of which seven are in Illinois, five in Ohio, and others in Indiana, Michigan, Minnesota and Missouri.

Mr Windsor T. White was converted by Ned Cotesworth to English hounds for the Chagrin Valley; he latterly believed in breeding them down to harrier size. The pack is still English. Two other hunts were started between the wars near Cleveland; one died, the other was reabsorbed by the Chagrin Valley. Near Cincinnati the Camargo (1925) has the stuff of survival because its country is mostly large estates. The Rocky Fork and Headley were started between the wars and joined in 1940.

Indiana had a single hunt between the wars and two more since 1967.

In Illinois, the Onwentsia and Midlothian were both killed by development, but there were new hunts between the wars and four since 1960. Illinois hunting could hardly be more buoyant; nearly all of it involves wild red foxes.

Michigan added the Bloomfield Open to the Grosse Pointe, and then joined the two as the Metamora. The pack is now mostly English; the hunt is thought by its members to be very English too, but was described by a recent English visitor – admiringly, not critically – as completely different.[28]

Two packs have been started west of Detroit. But it is strange that Michigan, with plenty of undeveloped country and plenty of red foxes, has no recent growth to compare with that of Illinois.

Minnesota has one draghunt, Missouri one foxhunt (the Bridlespur, 1927). Wisconsin had a pack but has it no longer.

A group of gentlemen started an informal hunt at Denver, Colorado, in 1907. The stables were by the eighth tee of the golf course. The hunt was recognized as the Arapahoe; a modest country was registered, a vast one actually hunted. Some of the stockmen tried hunting with Western saddles; they quickly got English ones. English hounds were also found best because steady to the teeming riot. Some foxes are hunted now as well as coyote.

Some way south of Denver, the El Paso County Hounds were started at Colorado Springs with a draft from the Arapahoe and a number of bobbery trencher-fed 'dogs'. At the El Paso's first meet, the pack was kept in couples, opposite to opposite, in a barn. The hounds fought each other and, when they were let out, attacked the field.[29] The Roaring Fork (1967) hunts fox and coyote.

Kansas has a hunt dating from 1927; Nebraska, Arizona and Texas have one each, all started since 1965.

Washington's hunting started between the wars, Oregon's died. California's died but has been reborn; two packs, both partly of English hounds, hunt fox, coyote and drags.

In Mexico, Mr Patrick Tritton embarked on the most adventurous pioneering of all. In 1965 he got hounds from the Meynell and various Irish packs; he hunted fox, hare, and different kinds of deer in several parts of Mexico. His country, potentially, was conterminous with the whole republic.

Meanwhile, fox and coyote are regarded as predators by the laws of some states, though not by conservationists, and the red-fox pelt is worth money. In the winter of 1972–3 more than 20,000 red foxes were shot from aircraft in South Dakota alone, earning the hunters about $500,000. The consequence is an explosion in the jack-rabbit population, which is extremely destructive.[30]

U.S. Army

At Fort Riley, Kansas, the Cavalry School's English pack (from Major Wadsworth) had gone from coyote to drag for better training. After the first war the pack became much more varied, through people's generosity and after the acquisition of the Coblenz pack.

The Coblenz hunt was the creation of General Henry T. Allen, commanding the U.S. Army garrison round Coblenz in 1920. He was given five couple by the endlessly generous Mr Joseph B. Thomas, got a draft from England, and secured individual hounds from various old French packs. The American forces left Germany in 1923 and the hounds went to Fort Riley.

The Infantry School and its hunt were at Fort Benning, near Columbus, Georgia. The first hounds, in 1923, belonged to the huntsman, Sergeant Thomas Tweed.

The important surviving military hunt was started at Fort Leavenworth, Kansas, in 1929; it lapsed, and restarted in 1962. The country is mostly a military reservation, together with some farmland. There are red fox and coyote, and drags are run; the pack is English.

Canada

The Montreal, having been driven away from the city, was driven farther in 1920 by wire and railroads. In 1940 it nearly disintegrated; in 1942 the pack was dispersed. Active hunting started again in 1947; in 1950 foxes were more plentiful than ever before, and could be hunted properly as the wire was well panelled.[31] The Lake of Two Mountains was started in 1947 and the Belle Rivière in 1967.

In Ontario, wire drove Mr George Beardmore and the Toronto hounds first to Eglinton Avenue and then to Aurora. A new pack was collected and a new country opened up called the Toronto and North York. The pack and the way it was hunted were both highly praised.[32] A new hunt stepped into the Toronto's vacant Eglinton country, taking over the Toronto's draghounds and fitting in with its meets. This also moved out and became the Eglinton and Caledon.

The London died in the first war; it was re-established in 1922. The Hamilton and Frontenac have been started since the second war.

The Ottawa stopped in each war, and was restarted after each. It is now the Ottawa Valley, in new country.

In British Columbia the Fraser Valley has been established.

Except on the Pacific, the Canadian climate everywhere stops hunting at Christmas or before. The Canadians can never hunt a straight-necked February or March fox except on snowshoes. Some of the hunts consequently start their seasons early: the Ottawa Valley has a few drags in June and July. The Toronto and North York runs drags in the spring to avoid the seeds. The Hamilton moved from Ontario to North Carolina from mid December to April.

The English tradition remains strong in Canadian kennels, only the Belle Rivière having any American or crossbred hounds. This is a matter of climate at least as much as of sentiment. In one regard the English tradition is defied: three of the Canadian hunts go out on Sunday.

MR THOMAS'S FRANTIC, 1920
Mr Joseph B. Thomas began assembling a pack in 1910, mostly of the very fine hounds bred by the Bywaters family. This pack was hunted by Charles Carver for Mr Daniel B. Sands in the Piedmont and Middleburg countries, then by Mr Thomas himself in the Piedmont, Mr Sands continuing, with undiminished hatred, at the Middleburg. Ill-feeling growing into open war, Mr Thomas left the area; he began to breed on a very large scale, making special use of the bloodlines of Mr Harry Worcester Smith's Grafton pack. This young reddish bitch dates from the beginning of this phase of his career. He bred on such a scale that he was able to draft extensively, which not only made possible the sortiness of his own pack, but also supplied others: thirty-two organized hunts got drafts direct from him, and dozens of others indirectly.

Second World War

During the war a milder version of the English situation was seen in several countries: much smaller fields, with ladies in a majority.[33] Wire again spread owing to more intensive food production and shortage of hunt staff for panel making.

Orthodox hunting has continued to grow since the war at its hectic pre-war rate: of the recognized packs hunting in the United States today, about forty are older than the first war, about forty were established between the wars or during the second war, and about fifty have been born since. A lot of these are in wholly new regions.

Hounds

The English hound both gained ground and lost it. Several famous hunts went from English packs to American between the wars, usually for more cry and better cold noses. A lot of people believed, with General Roger D. Williams,[34] that if English breeders had American country and American red foxes they would breed American hounds, but with more regard than Americans to conformation, levelness and pedigree.[35] But some new hunts adopted English hounds, and these included southern clubs whose climate and country might have seemed to make the American as obviously right as it was to Mr Hitchcock at Aiken. English hounds bred and entered in America were clearly more at home than imported entered hounds.

English and Irish blood had been a necessary ingredient in American hounds capable of catching red foxes. It also turned Virginia and Kentucky breeds into potential pack hounds. This principle was much extended between the wars in the creation of new crossbred packs. Welsh blood was often a factor; fell blood less often. The purpose was usually to combine the discipline and steadiness of English hounds with the nose, cry and physique of American. Crossbreds became so numerous that they got their own divisions at hound shows.

The hound of Virginia, Central Maryland and Kentucky had written and official standards before the first war. The Penn-Marydel breed acquired its name and its own quite different standards in 1934. For the first time hounds of this type were used in regions far from their places of origin: but their Old Southern lack of drive was often observed. A consequence was a new and widespread tendency to cross the Penn-Marydel and Virginian.

The Virginian hound between the wars was still to English eyes subject to enormous variation: the Rev. E. A. Milne thought judging must be impossible as no clear type was to be seen.[36] In fact, standardization did grow to a point where judging became predictable; this was the effect of the principal hound shows.

In 1924 the Riding Club of New York invited the M.F.H.A. to restart a New York hound show, which was an immediate success. The Bryn Mawr hound show joined the long-established horse show in 1914. It was held under the auspices of the M.F.H.A. and the American Foxhound Club, later joined by the Penn-Marydel Fox Hounds and the National Beagle Association. The Bryn Mawr moved to The Rose Tree, Media, in 1947 (but without changing its name) and then to the grounds of the Radnor at Malvern. The Virginia Foxhound Club had shows at Montpelier from 1934 to 1941 and from 1955 to 1960. The show moved to various places and then to Leesburg. The Leesburg show now has divisions for American, English and crossbred, the Bryn Mawr for American, English, crossbred, Penn-Marydel, beagles and basset hounds.

America : 1914 and After

Volume V of the *American F.K.S.B.* of 1931 was the first to include American and crossbred hounds. Mr Higginson's difficulty as editor was not with commercial breeders but masters of regular packs, especially in Virginia – they wanted all kinds of unpedigreed hounds registered including, in one case, a hound found in a field as a whelp.[37] Volume VI, edited by Mr Joseph J. Jones, who had been Mr Higginson's assistant, was at last representative, with credible returns from 135 packs.

Trials went on with little change (though changes were attempted) and were described by a great expert in 1948. All hounds are entered and numbered, a process lasting far into the night, and the numbers are painted on the hounds' sides. They are taken in the early morning to the casting grounds (which need extensive carparks) and the Master of Hounds calls the roll. He orders the cast as soon as the numbers can be read at fifty yards. The judges are sometimes mounted, usually on foot or in cars. The running usually ends at 10 or 11 a.m., and the meet lasts two to six days. Scoring varies widely; so does the definition of the 'Derby' for young hounds. Drinking and gambling are forbidden on the grounds, since either might influence the judges.[38]

Hill topping (mountaineering, fox racing) has continued to attract an enormous body of enthusiasts, mostly with Walkers, Triggs or wide varieties of crosses, who love the cry of hounds and the melodious toots of the cow horns. It remains true that sophisticated, literate and wealthy persons are as devoted to this sport[39] as the 'one-gallus' moonshine drinkers of Gordon Grand's more patronizing stories.

An immense advantage the hill topper and trialist has over the master of a regular pack is that his puppies are well and truly walked. 'Farming out' was introduced by Mr Higginson and the Cotesworths, and done with immense success by Mr Thomas and Charles Carver, but it remains most exceptional. The wonderful public relations of a puppy show is therefore an equal rarity. Cubhunting has always been undertaken in the same way as in England, but only partly with the same motives. The young entry is taught to hunt and go to cry, but litters are not usually meant to be scattered or weak-running cubs killed: foxes are too scarce.[40]

The odds favouring the American fox remain far longer; this is because of unstopped earths and very big coverts.

Horses and Horsemanship

On average, the horses in the American hunting field have always been quite the best in the world. English and Irish visitors have said so repeatedly.[41]

Good halfbreds have also been of great use in some countries, thanks to America's equivalent of the Premium Stallion scheme: the U.S. Army's Remount Commission, which in 1918, in collaboration with the Jockey Club, distributed thoroughbred stallions widely through America, to both individual breeders and groups, until 1946.

It also remains true, in the new countries as well as the traditional ones, that the brute power of the big halfbred is unnecessary: Americans ride to hounds over the ground, the English and Irish in it; the latter need a horse up to thirty pounds more for the same rider.[42]

The excellence of the going permits timber to be jumped at speed. It makes the second horse unnecessary. Very few American hunts have seen second horsemen out as a regular thing. It is also relevant that busy men dismount after a brisk morning's hunting and go to their offices without getting to the bottom of their horses.

The publisher and trotting-horse man Robert Bonner said about 1870 that America was far ahead of Britain in farriery,[43] a belief confirmed a little later by the startling success of American trainers in English racing, which had much to do with

UP HILL AT A CHICKEN COOP
Miss Edith Somerville made a prolonged visit to America in 1929–30; she hunted extensively and inspected a large number of hounds; fortunately she wrote and illustrated a record of her trip. She naturally devotes much space to the unfamiliar – to hill topping, to the look and comportment of American hounds, and to ingenious oddities like chicken coops. This device has not spread to Britain or Ireland, but it is hard to see why: instead of wire being replaced by post-and-rails or tiger trap, it is covered by a sort of tent made of wooden planking. This is an inviting obstacle for a horse to jump, it can be moved, and it does not involve cutting the wire and spoiling its tension.

shoeing. It was largely because of more skilful farriers that American masters went out when English would have stayed at home: caulks back and front and spiked 'neverslip' shoes were regularly changed to for ice, and patent-leather pads were put under the shoes to stop balling in the snow.[44]

The Caprilli system was more widely influential sooner in America than in Britain; big timber was jumped at the gallop with the full forward seat long before this became normal in the Shires. There were more American women than English riding cross-saddle in the 1920s, but more riding sidesaddle in recent years.

Masters and Clubs

One of the best things about American hunting is the number its history shows of very long masterships. These have made three things possible: the strict education of fields, unto the second and even the third generation; the trust and co-operation of farmers and landowners; and the sort of sustained breeding which makes possible the development of successful new crosses. One of the worst things remained the expense and exclusivity of hunt clubs. This continued between the wars to have a lot to do with people coming from elsewhere to hunt, and needing a clubhouse to stay in: Damon Runyon's 'Oriole Hunts Club', pictured as near Baltimore but feasible in many places, was as palatial as a resort hotel and a lot stricter about admission.[45] When people came to stay in a hunting country for the season they sometimes built or adapted modest hunting boxes of the English type, but more typically 'imposing Mansions' which brought revenue to the area, but not always goodwill.[46]

A phenomenon of the clubbishness of the clubs was a continued emphasis on horse shows and races, held by practically every hunt in America between the wars: and also on related activities like polo, and unrelated ones like contract bridge. Another phenomenon is the specialness of uniforms. A small minority of British hunts wear a distinctive collar with hunting scarlet, and this usually for an historical reason; almost all American and Canadian hunts have contrasting collars, often piped in still other colours, and described in such terms as 'old gold', 'robin's egg blue', and 'West Point grey'. While this may suggest an unfortunate scale of values, a really well-turned-out field – even to the point of obtrusive dressiness – is a much better ambassador for itself than some of the ragtag fields seen in England.

The American M.F.H.A. grew from surprisingly small beginnings in 1907 (considering the number of hunts then recognized by the N.S.H.A.) to a membership of more than 100 by 1933. The anomaly of recognition was put right, by affable negotiation, by Mr Henry Vaughan in 1935.[47]

Beagles and Bassets

There is no deerhunting in America, as understood in Britain. A few fox packs, however, chase hares.

Beagling has grown considerably. There were twenty-five recognized packs in 1974, mostly established since the second war but some before the first. About half are subscription packs, half private. Many are in foxhunting countries, and some, like the Fairfield County and the Ligonier, are part of a foxhunting club's establishment. The M.O.C. at The Plains, Fauquier County, is the creation of the Middleburg Orange County Pony Club. The Nantucket–Treweryn divides its season between Nantucket Island and Virginia, and the Woodfield between Ohio and Georgia. Cottontail is the most usual game; jack rabbits, swamp rabbits and hares are hunted by packs of beagles in various regions. Green is the invariable and proper uniform, with a variety of collars as rich as that of the foxhunting clubs.

There were in the same season thirteen packs of basset hounds, most of recent establishment, most private, most hunting cottontails in foxhunting country.

Semantics

America follows not Britain but continental Europe in the usual meaning she gives to 'hunting' which, like *la chasse*, means the killing of any wild animal or bird with gun or other engine.

Among orthodox foxhunting people there are enough differences of usage to cause confusion. A 'hunter' is often a person as well as a horse, even in northern Virginia.[48] Thirty-two hounds are often taken out (not sixteen couple) and kill two foxes (not a brace). Trails (rides) are cut through woods (coverts). The feed trail or night line (drag) is trailed up (hunted), and hounds sometimes lose and recover the trail (line) of their fox. Hounds are shown on the bench (flags). Panels (hunt jumps) are expensively put in to make wire jumpable, and sometimes take the form of chicken coops and Aikens.

At the same time, foxhunting is the most specifically English of any large-scale American activity, and this has unexpected side effects: entirely American writers on entirely American hunting sometimes use 'Esquire' instead of Mr for any Master of Hounds, and even adopt the English spelling of words like 'colour'.[49]

17 Europe
Nineteenth and Twentieth Centuries

'THE FIELD CHECK IN A WOOD'
The field would be unlikely to check anywhere else, since the laws of trespass forbade so much as a single hoofprint on private land outside the forest. The surviving forests were still extremely large; nearly all belonged to the king, then the republic, then the Emperor Napoleon III. From about 1830 they began to be rented to individuals, as a means of raising revenue; this became and remained the basis of nearly all aristocratic hunting. A consequence was that a pack did not have a country in the British sense, but its owner might have hunting rights in any given season in several widely distant parts of the state forests. Painting by Alfred de Dreux. From the collection of Mr and Mrs Paul Mellon.

France

In 1794, 'The game-law now established gives liberty to everyone to kill what game he may find upon his own ground, or that which he rents; and if any person, without leave, shoot on his neighbour's ground, he pays for each offence a fine of ten livres.'[1] Ever since, the rural Frenchman has made maximum use of his rights, killing tiny birds with large guns and furiously resisting trespass. 'Progress', lamented a French sportsman in 1863, 'has totally razed noble and feudal estates, and the ruin of feudality has in turn engulfed in its crash the whole apparatus of seigneurial venery, hounds and falcons, hunting and hawking establishments.'[2] *La Chasse* was translated by 'Harry Hieover' as shooting thrushes; a *chien de chasse* was a dock-tailed pointer.[3]

The pursuit of game with running hounds was therefore limited to the remaining forests. The restored monarchy of Louis XVIII and Charles X almost revived the glories of *la vénerie royale* of Louis XIV and XV. These kings and their retinue had been exiled in England. Other French noblemen hunted in England in the 1830s. Their experience did not influence French forest hunting then or later. The huntsman inspected (and sometimes ate) the *fumée*; the *limier* and relay hounds were used in the old ways; the horns blew as melodiously and as long.[4]

There were nevertheless hazards. 'The immense winding horn of the Count de Gambis [acting Master of Hounds to the duc d'Orléans], when on his shoulder, by some means or other contrived to encircle the head of a man on a pony, and the nicest management was necessary to prevent either his being pulled off his saddle, or throttled.'[5] Mr George Templer of Stover once hunted with the comte de Girardin; his instinctive who-whoop at the death, which rang over the chorus of horns, scandalized the prince de Condé.[6]

The grandest packs of staghounds in the forests near Paris were handled with all the old skill, but not the other *chasses* of the provinces; Grantley Berkeley found the hunting of the Nivernais ludicrously inept: they hunted wolf, boar, roe and fox, but 'they had not a pack of hounds able to catch any of them, unless assisted by the gun'.[7]

Hares were hunted in Normandy in open country, in the English fashion: primogeniture still operated among the Normans, and they had estates large enough and neighbours sporting enough, to ride across country.[8]

Horsemanship, hounds and above all law and opinion made English foxhunting impossible. In 1841 'The manner in which the fox is destroyed on the Continent is by the gun, or digging him with a small dog resembling our crooked-legged terriers'.[9]

By these means, 14,791 foxes were killed in France in the year ending 31 August 1837.[10] In 1880 the recommended and sporting method was to push the fox out of covert with *briquets*, and either shoot it the moment it broke, or let hounds run it very slowly in a circle which gave the *chasseur* repeated chances of a shot.[11]

Several of the small towns of the French north coast had colonies of impoverished English sportsmen; and repeated attempts were made to start foxhunting. About 1830 there were 'about twenty couples of hounds at St. Omer, which, under the management of Mr Woodbridge, so well known as a first-rate performer in Essex, had very tolerable sport, and killed a great many foxes; but it was chiefly cover hunting'.[12] There was a pack at Boulogne and one at St Malo.

A more successful and enduring attempt was made at Pau in the Pyrenees. When Sir Henry Oxenden gave up the East Kent in 1828,[13] he retired to Pau; he 'had good sport for several seasons'.[14]

The Second Republic, throughout France, made noble hunting more difficult and poaching easier. The Second Empire saw a large and costly *vénerie impériale*. Napoleon III himself had often, during his English exile, followed the Buckhounds, and he liked a gallop. He also liked to stop and talk, indulging which he often lost the hounds and so his temper.[15] The political climate was favourable to other private packs, and there were more of them than ever, hunting in leased imperial forests.

Surprisingly little was changed by the unlamented fall of the Second Empire. In 1880 red deer were hunted with full and ancient ceremony, relays only having been generally abandoned because *bâtard* (English-cross) hounds had the stamina to do without them.

The *chasseur* of this period was to breakfast on onion soup, cheese and coffee, and to take with him, for the middle of the morning, 'two hard-boiled eggs, a piece of bread, the end of a sausage, and a flask of black coffee laced with rum'. His luncheon was cold meat, more eggs and a bottle of wine. 'I forbid beer, which weighs you down.' Avoid pure water while hunting: 'You will enfeeble yourself, and expose yourself to the abundant perspirations which are often the forerunners of inflammations of the chest.' A foot bath, almost cold, was to be taken every three days, and a *grand bain*, immersing the person, once a week.[16]

In 1890 there were by the official count 271 packs of hounds in France.[17] One of the best-known packs (and most described) was that of the marquis de Valon in the Forêt d'Halattes. His hounds were, by now typically, *bâtards*, their English blood being mostly the Duke of Beaufort's; they were blue or blackish, with long unrounded ears, indifferent feet and whip sterns which were barbered. Drive was neither attained in the breeding nor sought; cry was most esteemed, and these hounds were such line hunters that they did not change to view when their stag was six feet away from them.[18] To set foot out of the forest on to farm or smallholding was as grave a matter as ever; two centimes had to be paid for each hoof print.[19] Some of the forests were very disciplined, especially Chantilly. In the Forêt d'Halattes some of the rides were actually paved. The hounds were better than their handling: 'At his best the huntsman appeared to be a mounted and picturesque master of the ceremonies, the Lord High Chamberlain of the Forest; at his worst he is a peasant or a stableman dressed up in an *opéra-comique* attire.'[20]

Entirely outside this tradition stood the *émigré* establishment at Pau. 'In France', in 1880, 'we hunt the fox very little with hounds. In the Pyrenees, in the winter, many fox hunts are organized to amuse the English who are very addicted to this sport. It sometimes even happens that the hunted fox is one taken a few days earlier

LE CHIEN DE RENARD

The Continental 'fox dog' was of two sorts: either a small scenting hound, a *basset* or *briquet*, which pushed the fox out of covert to be shot; or a terrier which went underground. These last, Robert Vyner noted with dismay, were 'in Germany called Dacks-hunden (corrupted into taxles), or badger-dogs'. The *basset d'Artois* no longer went underground, though originally bred to do so. Law and custom imposed this method of killing foxes on the French, as on New Englanders: orthodox foxhunting, involving trespass, was almost everywhere impossible.

and kept especially for the day of battle. But this fox, unbagged for the occasion, has not the stamina of a fox reared in the woods, and the hunt becomes slightly comic-opera.'[21]

Most of the masters between 1874 and 1914 were in fact American. Lord Howth was master in the late 1870s, getting Sir Reginald Graham's New Forest pack in 1878. Tom Hastings went to him as huntsman the next year, having caught pneumonia hunting in the snow with Colonel Anstruther-Thomson in Fife. He hated it. The hounds were wild (because the French shouted at them). 'The fields are not bigger than your stable-yard, and nasty rotten banks . . . I think it is very miserable work.'[22]

In 1910 Mr Frederick Prince became master, the sixth American since 1874, one of the four short-sighted brothers who had helped start the Myopia. The hounds were almost all drafts from the Duke of Buccleuch. They went very fast; thoroughbreds were ridden. The fields were mostly French, with some English and a few Americans, all well turned out and mounted. Mr Harry Worcester Smith, not a charitable observer, was pleased with all he saw.[23]

A similar pack, the Biarritz–Bayonne, was started in similar country farther east by the sea. One other English hunt was the Duke of Westminster's; in 1911 he took English foxhounds and servants to Vautrait de Mimizan, in the Landes; he hunted there and in Normandy and Brittany.

The first war had a savage effect on the *chasse à courre*. Some of the famous private packs, such as that of the duchesse d'Uzès, were successfully revived; others had a thin time because poaching had left them nothing to hunt.

[233]

There has again been a lively revival, after the still greater and more protracted devastation of the second war; the whole world of French venery is not much less numerous, and not at all less ceremonious. In the 1972–3 season, ninety *Équipages* were recognized hunting deer and boar. Harehunting is also buoyant. The subscription principle has inevitably grown. The *Société de Vénerie* is the governing body, to which has been added an *Association des Maîtres d'Équipages*. The central fascination is unchanged: it is sonorous and leisurely hound work, and has no more to do now than it ever did with the open-country gallops of English and Irish foxhunting.[24]

Belgium was considered more sporting by 'Nimrod' early in the 19th century, principally because gentlemen were more apt to live on their estates.[25] But the Belgian hunting tradition is identical to the French. Belgium is a hunting as it is a racing province of France, and the Belgian *Équipages* are recognized by the *Société de Vénerie* in Paris. Another province is Quebec, where *l'Équipage du Rallye-Kebec* was started in 1969 for wolfhunting in both crown and private forest.

The limitations which beset the ordinary sporting Frenchman confined him to small, slow hounds for the *chasse à tir*. One principal change during the 19th century was therefore the proliferation of such types. The other was the English foxhound cross, not new but far more widespread. The most important results were the *anglo* or *bâtard saintongeois* and *poitevin*. 'The vast majority of French packs', in 1880, 'are now composed of Anglo–French hounds. The drawback is that they cannot recruit from themselves.'[26] Between the wars four small packs of blue-mottled *gascon-saintongeois* were said to be the only hounds free from the contagion of English foxhound: but modern French hounds, *bâtards* as they are, are still tall, slow, sonorous line hunters for the forest.

[234]

LA CHASSE AU CERF, 1822
The restoration of the Bourbon monarchy restored royal and noble forest hunting in all its pre-Revolution forms. Much had, however, been lost. The Napoleonic Wars had occasioned the widespread destruction of forest, especially in Brittany and the west, for shipbuilding and fuel. There had also been intensive poaching, which remained a major industry throughout the 19th century, in spite of repeated laws: the urban *bourgeoisie* fully approved of a crime which filled the markets and their larders with venison. The royal forests were once again meticulously preserved, and there the glories and absurdities returned. The duc de Bourbon, a year or two after the date of this scene, had 210 couple of stag, boar and roebuck hounds at Chantilly, more than 100 hunters (and 150 other horses), and 514 servants in livery in kennels and stables alone. The lady here is no surprise, remembering the hunts of Louis XIV and XV, but the size of the hounds is.

LA CURÉE
The *fanfares* of the French chase grew in the 17th century into an interminable if pleasing ritual, but the basis of horn language was entirely practical. In the undisciplined medieval forest, *chasseurs* could not see each other, and they could neither see nor be seen by their hounds. Much communication was needed, for example to grooms holding horses and *valets* holding relay hounds. This was why it was necessary for everybody to carry a horn. *Hallali, mort* and *curée* were originally simply signals to laggard hounds, but they soon also became anthems of triumph and celebration. Today each of the *Équipages de Grande Vénerie* has its own *fanfare*. These are almost all in six-eight time; the range is an octave and a tone, from the G above middle C to the A above the treble clef. Some of the *fanfares* are modern; many are thirty bars and more. Other calls now normally used (listed, and the music printed, in the *Encyclopédie de la Vénerie Française*) are: *le volcelest, le lancé, la vue, animaux en compagnie, le relancé et bien allé, la débuché, le changement de forêt, la plaine, le bat-l'eau, la sortie de l'eau, l'hallali sur pied, l'hallali par terre ou la mort, la curée* or *l'hallali d'Orléans*, and *les honneurs du pied*.

French horsebreeding was at a low ebb throughout the 19th century. Even if horses had been a profitable product, as in England and Ireland, the tiny acreages of subdivided farms could not have supported them. Farmers who bred horses wanted heavy draught beasts, and there was no market for saddle horses. Wonderful breeds like the Barb-descended Limousin simply disappeared. Riding was ill regarded; a taste for horses 'is associated in the public mind with frivolity; the statesman, judge, barrister, physician or attorney, who ventured to appear on a well-bred hack, or driving himself in a phaeton to the Legislative Assembly, the Courts of Law, or a place of business, would endanger his reputation as a practical man and serious character.'[27]

For hunting men the answer, which had good 18th-century precedent, was to import English horses. The English saddle and English seat were learned by *émigrés* and visitors to Melton. By 1840 the nobility in the hunting field was becoming converted. But in grand circles there was still a prejudice in favour of the old style in the 1860s: Lord Ribblesdale, as a schoolboy spending holidays in Paris, saw the grave suspicion with which baron Lambert, *Lieutenant de la Vénerie*, was viewed for riding to the imperial hounds with an English saddle and double bridle.[28] What happened thereafter was that common sense separated the high school from the hunting field.

ROME, 1875
The original hounds were given by Lord Chesterfield, who brought them out as an experiment. The hunt initially needed English huntsmen as well as hounds; it also needed English horses, those of Rome being 'slow, ill-bred animals, with very high, round action in their lugubrious trot'. By 1870 hunting and racing had transformed the horses of the Campagna, by means of the importation of English thoroughbreds. The huntsman was still English, and the acting master for many years English also. This scene bears out Trollope's impression that Rome was more like a British hunt than any other outside Britain.

Italy

In the 19th century *la caccia*, like *la chasse*, was limited to the gun, with a single glorious exception.

Shortly before he became master of the Pytchley (1838) Lord Chesterfield spent a winter in Rome. He observed that the countryside was mature grazing and concluded that it could be hunted. 'He sent for fifteen or sixteen couples of draft hounds from England, and by having several sharp runs in that neighbourhood, and killing a few brace of foxes in gallant style, he quite astonished the Italians who, fond as they are of music, had never before been delighted with such harmonious melody as echoed upon that occasion through the hills and vales of that classic ground.'[29]

Lord Chesterfield went back to England, leaving his hounds, and the mastership devolved in 1837 upon principe Livio Odescalchi, master for eleven seasons. He was followed by a committee for thirty years, for which, for many years, the acting master was Mr Charles Winn Knight.

Mr Winn Knight's brother reported: 'The establishment of a pack of fox-hounds by the Earl of Chesterfield was followed by races and steeple-chases, and these produced an immediate change in the quality of the horse bred on the Roman Campagna.' The change was brought about by the importation of English thoroughbred stallions, by both noble sportsmen and rich graziers, primarily for getting racehorses but producing hunters as well. By 1870, 'The Roman horses are now fast improving. The crosses of English blood often go well over the stiff fences of the Campagna with the fox-hounds.'[30]

All the servants continued English. Everything else was English too: 'Perhaps', said Trollope, 'the nearest approach to English hunting out of England is that to be found in the Campagna.'[31]

The hunt has had a continuous theoretic life, under a succession of noble Italian masters, interrupted in fact by both world wars. After the first, marchese Camillo Casati (1919–33) found himself with no hounds. He came to England, but there were no hounds to spare. He went to Ireland and visited Mr Isaac Bell in Kilkenny; he had none to spare either. He took the marchese to County Kerry, and they bought individual Kerry beagles from farmers and tradesmen. The first they bought cost thirty-five shillings. A bush telegraph alerted the region; they ended by paying forty pounds to a cobbler for a lemon-and-white bitch. These hounds did very well in Rome.[32]

At the end of the second war, conte Ranieri di Campello made a similar revival. In this period, conte Giuseppe Cigala Fulgosi came from Rome to hunt with the Beaufort, Heythrop and Belvoir, observing how everything was managed. He became master of the *Società Romana della caccia alle volpe* in 1960. He has run the hunt, he says, in 'absolutely the most conservative British fashion'.[33]

Germany, Austria, Hungary

The Teutonic sporting tradition was of immense slaughter by the gun. In Austria in 1887: 'The number of preserves alone, not counting those in Hungary, is stated at 15,764, and on these were shot, in 1887, 32 bears, 113 wolves, 24 lynxes, 9,490 stags, 60,252 roebucks, 7,709 chamois, 2,998 wild boars, 26,411 foxes, 9,729 polecats, 1,055 otters, 2,672 badgers, 333 marmots, and no fewer than 1,439,134 hares.'[34]

The large exception to all this was Holstein. 'Nimrod's' friend Count Hahn of

Basedow had the biggest thoroughbred stud in Germany; he also had a pack each of boarhounds and foxhounds. The latter were English, and hunted and ridden to in the English fashion.

The Duke of Holstein and his brother loved England and its hunting and racing. In 1831 the duke wrote to 'Nimrod' – 'he wished me to send him a couple of young hare-hounds, and a brace of Cheshire dairy-maids'. His brother Prince Frederick hunted with Lord Anson's Atherstone: he said he was 'made for fox-hunting', and would have liked to spend every winter in England.[35] By 1840 there were several private packs of English foxhounds in North Germany.

The visits of the Empress Elizabeth of Austria to England and Ireland caused great excitement there: but they had precious little effect at home. The Empress was, in fact, in all her attitudes, specifically the friend of the Hungarians; in crossing Northamptonshire after 'Bay' Middleton, and in running after the beagles Frank Gillard found for her, she was not doing anything the aristocratic Austrians wanted to imitate.

The fox itself was nearly everywhere entirely vermin. It became more verminous when hare drives became popular. It was believed that a fox killed seventy hares a year; consequently in Mecklenburg and other places a bounty was paid for a brush. After the death of the early private packs hunting wild foxes in the north, there was a little hunting, also private, of imported bagmen.[36]

There are now several packs of draghounds in Germany. A few were started between the wars but most are recent. The packs include beagles and English foxhounds. One is a British Army hunt. There are similar draghounds in Belgium, Denmark and Holland; the last is a Royal Hunt, and H.R.H. Prince Bernhard was master for ten years, having restarted the hunt, with English hounds, in 1949.

Hungarians, like Frenchmen and Holsteiners, came to Melton in the early 19th century, especially the very popular Count Sandor, who stayed for a year with Lord Alvanley. He was once seen stuck waist-deep in a brook, his horse far away, smoking a cigar 'which he said he had lit for the purpose of keeping out the cold'.[37] But Hungarians did not need a Melton education to be horsemen and sportsmen. 'Not in Yorkshire, not in Ireland, are the gentry and commonalty more fond of a horse . . . There are several packs of fox-hounds and harriers, kept up in quite the English, or rather the rough Welsh style.'[38]

Spain, Portugal, Gibraltar

The Spaniards liked their guns. They like them still.

The Portuguese first saw English hunting under illustrious auspices. Sir Arthur Wellesley, later the Duke of Wellington, sent for a pack of hounds to divert himself and his officers. Mr (later Sir) Richard Puleston of Emral, then in Portugal, recommended as huntsman his own groom Tom Crane. 'The hounds and Tom Crane were always kept on the right of the line, whenever the army changed quarters in the Peninsula.'[39] 'Never was anything more ludicrous than our turnout: every quadruped in the army was put into requisition.'[40]

The Portuguese never forgot this English hunting, nor their old friendship with England, and late in the 19th century they embarked on the sport for themselves. Between the wars there were three hunts. They were revived, amalgamated, as the Equipagem de Santo Huberto in 1950; the hounds came from top English kennels. The huntsman and his five successors came from England too. Dress is English, though caps tend to be worn. The huntsman – the first Portuguese in the position – uses English hound language.

As well as the Commander in Chief's, there was an army hunt at Cadiz about 1814, maintained by the British garrison and called the Isla de León. There was also a 'Civil Hunt' at Gibraltar, which wore a blue uniform and kennelled its pack over the border in Spain. The Cadiz establishment was broken up at the end of the Napoleonic War, and its hounds went to Gibraltar and the officers of the 29th Regiment. Later the two packs were merged and became the Calpe Hunt of the Gibraltar garrison. The masters are recorded from 1829: all were soldiers until 1889, except one police magistrate and one naval officer. The first huntsman, from 1814 to 1835, was the Rev. Mr MacKareth. From 1842 to 1893 the huntsman was almost always an English professional. The whips were always amateur. They hunted drags and bagmen.

Scandinavia

Throughout the 19th century, northern Europe's best sport was harehunting. The hare was often hunted a long way before it was shot: this was not reluctance to kill but inability to hit. In a few places hares were also coursed. In Sweden hares were given a short close season by a law of about 1850, but the law was not widely kept. Once killed, the hare was instantly beheaded; if a pretty girl saw the whole carcase she developed a harelip.

Bears were a major scourge in the forests, killing cattle and often horses; bearhunts were therefore undertaken officially, by order of the provincial government. An area sixty miles in circumference was beaten by 1,500 men with guns. The great hazard was brandy, which caused the shooters to miss the game, even at point-blank range, but to hit each other.

Elk were hunted in the same way, but also, for sport, by an individual with a single hound. This chase, done on foot, sometimes took several days. Another method, in winter, was to hunt the elk with a pack of hounds followed on skis. Still another, widely trusted, was to lure the elk within range of a shot by means of the music of a violin.

Wolves were trapped or poisoned. In Lapland they were hunted on skis, their tracks being followed in the snow by peasants armed only with cudgels. In Sweden there were wolfhunts with hounds, which were followed on foot as the forest was too dense for horses.

The red fox was common throughout Sweden and Norway, and its pelt was an important export to Russia. There were also black foxes, and in the far north the smaller and less cunning Arctic foxes. Although continual attempts were made to shoot and trap foxes, it was found that conventional hunting with a pack of hounds, followed on foot in the forest, was the most effective way of killing them.[41]

Russia

In Russia in the 18th century, the landed nobility aped France in the hunting field as elsewhere; they had packs of hounds, *piqueurs* in scarlet coats with gold lace, full Gallic ceremony.[42]

Below this level of pretension, there was all over the Steppes an enormous squirearchy; they were addicted to hunting partly because they were genuinely sporting and partly (says Turgenev) because they had nothing else to do.[43]

'EN CHASSE, MESSIEURS!'
The lady is calling her friends from breakfast on the cover of *Figaro* in 1895. This is evidently one of the *Grandes Équipages de Vénerie*; many of these had been destroyed by the war of 1870 and the collapse of the Second Empire, but many more were born (a majority of which died in 1914). It became common at about the time of this picture for hunts to depend not on the munificence of a single owner, but on a *Société* of members, called *Boutons*, who were entitled by election and subscription to wear the livery. The *veneur* of the period was advised to drink coffee for breakfast, but one gentleman here prudently follows the contemporary English custom (see p. 148).

En Chasse, Messieurs!

A normal day's hunting very early in the 19th century is described in detail by Tolstoy. Count Rostov kept a large and typical hunting establishment, his game being wolf, fox and hare. Fifty-four hounds were brought out, with six servants and whippers-in, together with forty borzois and their eight attendants. (All these hunt servants were serfs.) In addition, the members of the party brought their own hounds, totalling a further thirty-five. The pack, hounds and borzois, thus numbered 130. There was a mounted field of twenty. Pack and field were joined by others on their way to covert, this journey being made as quickly as possible so that a neighbour did not draw it first. (Although custom delineated the 'countries' each pack hunted, local quarrels led to constant poaching.) The old count came to covert in a trap, his hunter being brought by a groom. His stirrup cup was mulled brandy in a silver goblet, followed by half a bottle of claret.

When hounds unkennelled their quarry in covert, their note revealed if it was fox or wolf. A special horn call proclaimed a wolf. As soon as it was pushed out of covert the borzois were let slip. The borzois' attendants galloped at breakneck speed to keep up with them as they coursed the game, but many borzois were frightened of wolves and reluctant to run them. The borzois were let slip in relays, the purpose being to keep the wolf out of covert; men galloped on to head it for the same reason. After a wolf had been coursed and killed, the same covert was drawn by the same hounds for a fox. The hunt took the same form and there was plenty of spirited galloping. The morning ended with a harehunt. The undergrowth was beaten and at the same time drawn; once running the hare was hunted and coursed at the same time.

The borzois were big, heavy, long-haired greyhounds – too heavy to run over deep plough – which usually lived as house dogs in the owner's home. They were highly esteemed – Ilagin paid three families of house serfs for a single bitch. This was because the course was highly competitive, the rivalry between neighbours running high.[44]

In this and the following generations, Russia was Anglophil as well as Francophil: a sophisticated landowner had French food, pictures and books, but his servants wore English livery and his hounds were English.[45] This spirit was fed by English in Russia and by Russians in England. 'The English residents at St Petersburg have a fox-hunting establishment eleven miles from the capital, and the hounds are hunting as we hunt them in England; but from the very short season allowed them by the climate, it cannot be expected that a succession of good sport can be the result.' The establishment was called the British Hunt; 'Some parts of the country hunted over are as good as the others are bad; and the game pursued has been the fox, the hare, and occasionally the wolf, but it is now [1840] confined to the fox.'[46] A lot of English hounds went to Russia, including Lord Southampton's Quorn pack, sold by Sir Harry Goodricke. Hunt servants went too. English-style hunting became part of cavalry training: but not always usefully: officers were obliged to keep behind their colonel, who was apt to be old, fat and frightened.[47]

Bear and elk were hunted as in Scandinavia, with armies of peasants driving the game towards the guns. 'In case of a scarcity of men, women and girls go out; but this is highly objectionable, as it is out of the power of the strictest disciplinarian to keep order.'[48] This was functional hunting, but it took a splendid ceremonial form too. The Czar had a fourteen-day hunt in 1890 on the lines of the grandest German *battues*. On these occasions, until the first war and the end of all such diversions, the beaters were mounted servants with French horns; the game they propelled towards the guns included fox, roe, occasional wolves and all sorts of birds.[49]

'CHASSE À COURRE WITH CARRIAGE AND PAIR'
The pair is in fact a tandem, much more difficult to drive and much more dashing than a pair, and consequently a favourite vehicle for first-flighters in England as well as France. (Jack Mytton once tried to get his leader to jump a gate.) These people are actually following hounds on wheels, something possible in some of the French forests owing to the expensive care lavished on the rides, which were almost roads, often fenced, sometimes paved. It was also feasible in relation to what French forest hunting was (and is) about: the hounds, though English cross *bâtards*, are sonorous line hunters, and the joy of the chase lies in appreciation of their work and music. Apart from the unnerving social aspects, an American hill-topper would be more at home with this philosophy of hunting than an English or Irish foxhunter. Painting by René Princeteau. From the collection of Mr and Mrs Paul Mellon.

18 English Hunting in Far Places

India

When the British got to India they found coursing of various kinds of antelope with cheetah; drives on an enormous scale, in which 40,000 men drove the game towards hides or elephants, of which 3,000 might be deployed;[1] and pig sticking. The British learned this sport from the Rajputs. They loved it. An Englishman writing from Madras about 1835 'draws a comparison between hog hunting and fox hunting, deciding in favour of the former. He says that he has seen both, and is of opinion, that were hogs as abundant in England as they used to be in India, foxes would be much neglected.'[2]

Many servants of the Honourable the East India Company were nostalgic for the sports of home. They found plentiful foxes, but they had to course them because they were practically scentless.[3] In the north west the foxes were silver with black tails; about 1820 it was great sport to course them with Arab greyhounds and Arab horses.[4] The British also found jackal, and imported hounds to hunt them; 'hunting of Jackals in Bengal' was known to Beckford in 1780 as a variant of his own sport.

Calcutta was the centre of English hunting, although the sport in 1840 was 'a bad imitation of cub-hunting'.[5] 'Nimrod's' son 'was out with the Calcutta fox-hounds: they are a capital pack, but it is devilish hot work'.[6] There were also English foxhounds at Madras, Bombay and Poona.

Hounds were a tremendous problem. Conditions required good noses, courage, stamina. It was expensive getting them out: in 1840 'the average price per couple in India is twenty guineas'.[7] Once there, 'the climate kills five hounds out of ten'. The Calcutta Hunt Club had to enter twenty-five couple annually because so many died.[8] Horses were not a problem. Arabs, Capers, Walers, English thoroughbreds and some very good countrybreds were all available for hunting as for racing, polo and pig sticking.

At the big centres of commerce and government, hunting was, like racing, largely civilian. In the 1860s and 1870s the best supported was the Madras Hunt. This had a bad period in the 1850s owing to the Mutiny and the consequent loss of sub-scriptions; it was revived in 1862 by Mr R. A. Dalyell, the son of Mr John Dalyell, master of the Forfarshire. He went out three days a week; his pack of thirteen couple came mostly from the Pytchley.[9] On 18 December 1875 the Prince of Wales hunted at Madras. The master and a few others wore scarlet; dress and horses varied widely; a few ladies were out. They had a wonderful hunt, nine miles very fast, mostly in

Left
BOAR HUNTING IN MEWAR,
ABOUT 1835
This is Maharana Jawan Singh (1828–38), head of the Sisodhyia clan of Rajputs, claiming descent from Rama, the mythical king of Ajodhya. His state was the home of the Bhils, the passionate *shikaris* described by Kipling in *The Tomb of his Ancestors*. Princes like Jawan Singh taught pig-sticking to the British, many of whom found it more exciting than any foxhunting.

Below left
PIG STICKING
Pig-sticking is extremely exciting and dangerous, not only because the 'spear' rides at top speed over rough and blind country, but also because he meets at the end a beast quite as formidable as the wild boar of Europe.

Above
OOTACAMUND, 1869
The Ootacamund hounds were established in 1835, hunting sambur, a large deer, with imported English foxhounds. Like most other Indian hunts they changed to jackal, which they have now hunted for at least 100 years. Running this leopard was probably accidental and certainly dangerous. The country is in the Nilgiri Hills, and lies between 7,000 and 7,500 feet.

paddy fields, and killed a stout jackal at the finish.[10]

In the north west there were unguessable numbers of regimental packs in the years between the Mutiny and the first war. Near Peshawar there were at least a dozen recorded packs belonging to British and Indian regiments. In 1870 the best known of all army hunts, the Peshawar Vale, was established as a station subscription pack, combining two regimental packs. For the summer, the hounds were walked 130 miles or more to the hills, moving by night. There was infinite goodwill, among Pathan chiefs as well as British officers: but there were awful difficulties. Masters changed over sometimes several times a season. Jackal became so scarce in the 1880s (as again in the 1920s) that carted black buck or nilgai were hunted, or drags laid. The condition and cost of hounds were a constant problem. There were often wars, and in the 1920s and 1930s a political atmosphere like that of Ireland in the time of the Land League. With all this went great advantages: keen people, good horses, friendly landowners, a climate in which hounds could be bred, stout jackal, amateur staff, and a country called 'the Shires of India'.[11]

There were all kinds of improvisations. When Kipling's 'Brushwood Boy' joined his regiment, one of the diversions the station offered was 'the disreputable remnants of a pack of hounds'.[12] Mr T. F. Dale was whipper-in and huntsman of a pack of three couple of English foxhounds, a spaniel, a fox terrier and a mongrel. The terrier was a necessity in the sugar cane; this covert was invaluable for jackal hunting because jackal have a sweet tooth, but the leaves cut the hounds like knives. A local problem was a tribe called the Binjaris, who, esteeming the flavour of jackal, were apt to ruin sport.[13]

Between the wars there were at least ten packs of stud-book hounds in India (and many others less well equipped); among the best known were the Peshawar

[243]

Vale, Lahore, Quetta, Mhow and Ootacamund. Sir George Meyrick hunted the last, in the Nilgiri Hills in south India, before his long and glorious mastership of the New Forest. It is the one important survivor, hunting jackal, in scarlet, in strictly conventional style.

Colonel John Cowen sold his foot beagles to Rangoon for £50; not much is known of their later history. In Ceylon, the 'Nuwera–Ellia Subscription Pack' was started in 1836; in 1839 they killed sixty-eight elks and eight wild hogs with English hounds.[14]

Australia and New Zealand

John Macarthur established Australia's first herd of Merino sheep, and in 1794 exported the first wool. He thus founded Australia's prosperity. 'With the assistance of one man and half a dozen greyhounds,' said Mr Macarthur, 'my table is constantly supplied with wild ducks and kangaroos.'[15] The younger sons who followed him to Australia came from British landed families; officers came from the American colonies, and remembered pre-Revolution Virginia and Carolina. The new life they built was transplanted from England and the Old Dominion. So were convicts. With convicts came the army. With both army and squatters came horses; English thoroughbreds began to arrive in quantity in the 1820s. They were widely distributed among the squatters, many of whom got thoroughbred mares as well as good Caper halfbreds; the result was the Waler, the splendid all-purpose Australian horse, often thoroughbred though seldom of reliable pedigree.

The squatters hunted informally, like the squires of Virginia in 1750 or England in 1700; the game was kangaroo and dingo.

In 1852 Mr George Watson of Ballydarton, County Carlow, came out to Melbourne. He brought a few couple of hounds from his father's famous kennel, established the Melbourne Hounds and began hunting kangaroo. In his first years he made a very early start with a few friends, rode out into the bush, hunted for an hour and was back in Melbourne as the rest of the world was getting up. But the

P.V.H., 1880
Peshawar was the last important military station on the road to the Khyber Pass. Owing to the chronic trouble on the North West Frontier a great many regiments were stationed there, though most only for a short time. Some had bobbery packs, some English foxhounds, depending how much money could be raised in the officers' mess. The Peshawar Vale was established from two regimental packs in 1870; it had some of the best hounds, and claimed quite the best country, in all India. The summer was impossible for hounds, who were therefore taken far into the hills, as shown here: 'the Trek through the Khyber'.

[244]

AUSTRALIA, 1850s
Even before 1800 kangaroo were being
coursed, for the pot, with greyhounds.
Horses arrived in sufficient numbers.
from South Africa and Chile, for races
to be held at Parramatta in 1810, and
a few hounds were brought from
England at about this time. Horses
and hounds enabled the squatters –
sporting younger sons and ex-officers –
to hunt kangaroo and dingo with their
friends. Kangaroo remained the game
when Mr George Watson brought out
a draft from his father's Carlow kennel
and established the Melbourne hunt
in 1852; but in Queensland, New
South Wales and remoter Victoria
kangaroo hunting remained entirely
informal. The kangaroo dog was described in 1872 as 'a large rough greyhound, that hunts both by sight and
by nose'. (This strongly suggests Scottish deerhound blood, likely enough,
since so many Scotsmen went to
Australia.)

country was rapidly becoming tamer and more settled, and within a short time the
fields were much larger and better dressed and the hunting was orthodox. Emus
were hunted as well as Kangaroos and one at least gave a famous run.[16]

In 1857 red deer were imported by the Chirnsides of Werribee to Point Cooke.
They multiplied enormously there and Mr Watson was invited to come with his
hounds to hunt them. This was a great success; one stag outran the hounds, going
twenty-five or thirty-five miles, season after season. The hinds ran just as well.
Jackal were imported from India by Colonel Roberts, the Indian Army agent for
buying remounts. Foxes were also imported; like rabbits they became a plague;
a few years later the government of Victoria paid bounty for 130,000 foxes in seven
years, which was approximately the number killed by hounds in England in the
same period.[17] One consequence was that jackal and 'corn-fed kangaroos' were no
longer needed for hunting anywhere near Melbourne; another was that there were
five packs of hounds in Victoria regularly advertising their meets.[18]

Trollope attended the opening meet of the Melbourne Hounds in 1872. 'The
country would be very rough; – so much was acknowledged, – and the fences very
big; but it was suggested to me that if I would only drink enough sherry I might see
a good deal of the run.' Two hundred horsemen were out, fifty in scarlet; there were
many ladies in carriages and a few mounted. Rumours flew as to what was to be
hunted. 'The huntsman was crabbed and uncommunicative. The master was soft
as satin, but as impregnable as plate armour.' Hounds were thrown into high
heather; they ran a drag for seven miles, and a bagged dingo which was taken alive
after another two. Trollope devised a method of waiting by each fence until someone broke the top bar, and 'perceived that there was a regular company of second-
bar men'.

In Queensland and New South Wales the sport was still kangaroo. In Queensland
Trollope went out with three others and four kangaroo dogs. 'The hounds scatter
and the men scatter, and it will often happen that a man is attempting to ride down
a kangaroo without a hound, and a hound making the same attempt without a
rider.' There was no jumping but there were very sudden turns in groves of trees.

English Hunting in Far Places

Female kangaroos jettisoned their young from their pouches as they ran, but one picked up a terrier and ran with it in its arms throughout the chase. The terrier was unhurt and unperturbed.[19]

Hunt clubs multiplied everywhere; there were several near Adelaide, Perth and Sydney as well as Melbourne. At Fremantle the Plympton Beagles became the Fremantle Hunt Club and then, about 1910, the West Australia Hunt Club. Sydney had many hunt clubs in the 1890s, but nearly all died in the first years of the 20th century as the country was developed. Such Sydney hunting as survived in 1912 was drag: there were plenty of foxes but they were killed in other ways.[20] Melbourne hunting had by this date settled to three packs: the Melbourne Hunt, of which Mr Watson was master until 1906; the Oakleigh Club; and the Findon Harriers. Everywhere the obstacles were solid timber stockfences; both horses and riders had to be top-class.

A new hunt, the Pine Lodge, was started in West Australia in 1963 by Mr David Pardoe, hunting wild foxes with stud-book hounds from Victoria and England.

Tasmania had its first settlement of convicts in 1803. With the convicts came soldiers, and with them horses and hounds. The horse population grew rapidly in a favourable climate for breeding.

In central Tasmania, between Launceston and Hobart, organized hunting started extremely early.

One of the first luminaries of what became the Midland Hunt was the Rev. Bobby Knopwood; he had lost an enormous fortune at cards in England. They hunted kangaroos and imported deer.

The first firm records date from 1842 when Mr James Lord was master of the Hutton Park Beagles at Campbell Town. The Lord family later owned the hounds again; Mr Carr Lord gave them to the newly formed Midland in 1917. Hare as well as deer have been successfully introduced; both are hunted, as well as kangaroo and wallaby, by English foxhounds.

There were other private packs. The best was probably that of Archdeacon Thomas Reiby, Prime Minister of Tasmania and later Speaker of the Legislative Council. He lived the life of a rich English squire, with a thoroughbred stud of high quality and a pack of hounds. The hounds hunted a tame stag with a ribbon round its neck.

Since the second war three other hunts have been established in Tasmania: the Northern (1953) which hunts a drag with a beagle–foxhound crossbred pack; the Bowood (1955) which hunts kangaroo with foxhounds; and the Ringwell (1967), a private pack hunting drag and hare.

Trollope makes no mention of hunting in New Zealand. He came too soon. Had he made his trip a dozen years later he would have found half a dozen or more packs.

Both the North and South Islands were seriously colonized from 1840. In both islands there is some of the best open grazing country in the world; to make full use of it red deer were introduced in 1851 and fallow in 1864; both did well, and gave the people something to hunt. The European hare was also introduced in the 1860s and multiplied enormously. Coursing was very popular and harehunting began. In Canterbury in the 1870s there were several private packs of imported harriers and beagles.

The oldest surviving formal hunt is the Pakuranga (1874), with a dairy country south of Auckland in the North Island; then the Rangitikei (1881), near Marton

NEW ZEALAND, 1891
Horses came to New Zealand the moment it was properly colonized in 1840; within a year of the foundation of Wellington and Nelson there were races at both, and within ten years at Canterbury. English thoroughbreds were imported as well as Walers, and the New Zealand horse was very good indeed. Emu was coursed, but huntable game had to be introduced. Red and fallow deer and hare were all tried, and all flourished; harehunting became the pre-eminent sport, although the growth of wire later made for some draghunting. Both North and South Islands had several thriving hunts by 1890, typically with countries of fine-scenting natural grass. The growth of New Zealand hunting, and of its railway system, makes this scene possible in 1891 anywhere between Invercargill and Auckland.

English Hunting in Far Places

200 miles to the south. There was immediately rapid growth in the South Island; the South Canterbury was formed by the amalgamation of the area's private packs in 1882, and the Otago at the same time. The Brackenfield was established just north of Christchurch in 1883, and the Birchwood, near Invercargill in the extreme south, in 1886. Nearly all growth in the next decades was in the North Island: the Hawkes Bay near Hastings in 1890, the Poverty Bay near Gisborne in 1892, the Waikato on the Bay of Plenty in 1904, the Taranaki near New Plymouth in 1905, the Manawatu near Palmerston North in 1909, and the Dannevirke, nearby to the east, in 1911.

Nearly all these new hunts chased the hare; their coats were therefore green and their hounds harriers. The obstacles were usually gorse or barberry hedges, but these were increasingly replaced by wire. Partly for this reason draghunting has grown.

Population and wealth have tended to concentrate in the North Island: so therefore has hunting. The Christchurch has been started in the South, but the Opotiki (1932), Wairapara (1947), Northland (1952) and Taupo (1962) in the North. There are also a number of unrecognized hunts, mostly in the North, some of considerable age.

Africa and the Middle East

The most important event in South Africa's sporting history was the arrival of Lord Charles Somerset as Governor in 1814. Being a younger son of the 5th Duke of Beaufort, he was a lifelong hunting man, and soon after his arrival imported a pack of hounds.

In the early 1820s: 'The fixture was about ten miles from Cape-town, where I was agreeably surprised at finding fourteen couple of well-sized and well-shaped dogs ... At eleven o'clock we met a field of about twenty gentlemen "togged" in scarlet, with one or two exceptions, and mounted in such a manner that would not have suffered much by a comparison with many English turns-out.

'After a few false alarms, owing to the dogs running the antelope, with which the country abounds, off went a noble dog-jackal, differing very slightly from our fox, making for the Blue Berg mountain, across the flats. After a splendid chase of between thirty and forty minutes, with only two checks, they ran into him in fine style, as he was getting through a hedge of aloes.'[21] The hunt has a continuous history ever since; drags are now more frequent than jackal hunts.

Johannesburg became the centre of a new breeding industry in the Rand. The goldfields brought thoroughbred racing and hunting. The Rand Hunt Club, like the Cape Hunt and Polo Club, now hunts jackal sometimes but drags usually. It has an enviable tradition of long masterships. Its very fast hounds come from the Blencathra and College Valley.

A third pack, the Hatherley Club Draghounds, grew out of a riding club at Pretoria. The pack has been bred from Rand Club hounds.

All these packs have scarlet livery; all hunt every Sunday in the season.

South Africa saw the end of the Royal Buckhounds. Disbanded in 1901, they were sent to Lord Chesham at the Cape. Captain Cape of the 18th Hussars took them out: $11\frac{1}{2}$ couple, kennelled on the deck of a transport. A lot of ice was needed to keep them cool. On arrival they were kennelled on Cape Town racecourse; they first met on 3 August at the Central Gaol. Duiker and blackbuck were the game. Captain Cape found good small coverts near Maritzburg which he drew as though

THE LIMURU

Mr H. S. Morton became master in 1965 and hunted hounds from 1968; his first whip is Mr Ndegwa Kuniara, his second Mrs Morton. The home country has become largely unhuntable, even with a drag, owing to Africanization: there is considerable building, much new wire, and fencing round certain properties of a height almost to keep out birds. The drags are now laid much farther out from Nairobi, to the north.

for foxes. They had some fine runs. But pneumonia and jaundice carried off most of the hounds and in September the rest were dispersed.[22]

The English settlers in the Kenya highlands brought with them, like the colonists of Virginia and the squatters of Australia, the tastes of their actual or alleged 'county' backgrounds. To indulge them they sent for thoroughbred horses and English foxhounds. Half a dozen packs existed before the time of the Mau Mau. Of these, only the upcountry Molo Hunt survived; the rest closed down as their supporters left the country. Their hounds went in 1952 to a new establishment, the Limuru, near Nairobi. As its country was Africanized and more European farmers left, the Molo too was disbanded in 1969; its hounds went to the Limuru. The latter hunts still, chasing a drag made of guinea-pig or buck droppings mixed with castor oil and dispensed from a paint can, and an occasional duiker or reedbuck. The whipper-in, who has sometimes hunted hounds, is Mr Ndegwa Kuniara, the only black African who has ever held such an appointment.[23]

The army and the imperial government have taken hunting to all sorts of other places, even those apparently grossly unsuitable. Kipling has a fascinating if largely imaginary account of the 'Gihon Hunt' on the banks of the Nile. The game was fox – 'No jackal, but Abu Hussein the father of cunning' – and the country a few hundred feet of intensive cultivation along 120 miles of the river. The kennels were on the governor's barge. Hounds were not always steady to newly buried corpses in shallow graves.[24]

The Arabs of the Middle East had a long and strong hunting tradition; from the nature of their scentless and treeless countries they coursed with cheetah and saluki. The former were used for various sorts of gazelle and antelope, the latter for hare and sometimes fox. The fox was eaten, like the rest, its flesh being considered medicinal.[25]

The tradition of desert hunting has deteriorated. Oil-rich sheikhs have latterly hunted from fast cars and light aircraft, using machine guns. The beautiful Arabian oryx has by these means become extinct, except for ninety which are all in captivity.[26]

British soldiers and officials brought a different sort of hunting to the Middle East, especially during and after the first war. Bobbery packs hunted jackal in Iraq. Palestine had a more formal organization, with English hounds, which was revived during the second war by the army. The hounds were described in 1943 as locally bred of good English blood; the sugar cane was usually a sure find. Early in the season hounds coursed the jackal (and sometimes hare or fox) because there was no scent; the November rains stopped coursing and produced good scenting conditions. The country round Gaza was the best, owing to smaller coverts and better going.[27] Recent events have not encouraged orthodox hunting in this area.

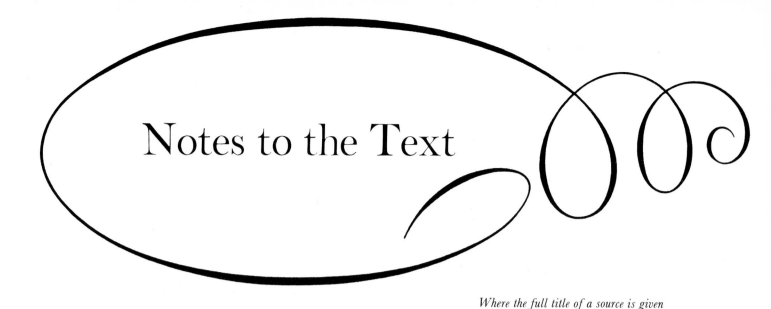

Notes to the Text

Where the full title of a source is given in the bibliography, references in these notes are to the author's name and, if necessary, to a shortened title.

1 THE ANCIENT WORLD

1 Desroches-Noblecourt, Christiane, *Tutankhamen*. London 1963
2 Wilkinson, Sir J. Gardner, *Manners and Customs of the Ancient Egyptians*, (Ed.) Birch, London 1878; Vol. II, ch. 8.
3 Anderson, J. K., Plate I.
4 Butler, ch. 6
5 Genesis, x 9
6 Proverbs, xxx 29, 31
7 Xenophon, *Cyropaedia*, I 4, IV 3
8 Yetts, W. Percival, *The Horse; A Factor in Early Chinese History*, *Eurasia Septentrionalis Antiqua* IX, 1934
9 Xenophon, *Cyropaedia*, I 2
10 Xenophon, *OEcumenicus*, IV
11 *Odyssey*, XIX
12 *Iliad* X, *Odyssey* IX, XII
13 Hesiod, *Works and Days*, 604
14 Hesiod (attr., probably wrongly), *Shield of Hercules*, I
15 Xenophon, *Horsemanship*
16 Xenophon, *Cygeneticus*, V, VI, etc
17 Plutarch, *Life of Lycurgus*
18 Aristotle, *Politics*, II v 7
19 Plato, *Republic*, III 412
20 Aristotle, *Politics*, I viii 11–13, VII ii 14
21 Xenophon, *OEcumenicus*, V
22 Cicero, *De Officiis*, XIII
23 Virgil, *Georgics*, III, 75–91, 404–13
24 Ovid, *Halieutica*
25 Horace, *Odes*, I i
26 Pliny, *Epistles*, I 6, IX 10, V 18
27 Grattius, *Cygenetica*, I
28 Oppian, *Cygeneticus*, I
29 Grattius, I; Strabo, *Geography*
30 Oppian, I
31 Oppian, IV
32 Aelian, *Characteristics of Animals*, XII 46
33 Oppian, III, IV
34 Martial, *Epistles*, X 37
35 Oppian, IV
36 Athenaeus, VII 282
37 Virgil, *Aeneid*, IV 129 sq
38 Arrian, *Cygeneticus*, I, XXIV
39 Arrian, XX, XXXIV
40 Vegetius, *De Re Militari*, VII

2 THE DARK AGES

1 Proctor, Col., *History of Italy*, 2nd ed. London 1844. Ch. I
2 Baring-Gould, Rev. S., *The Lives of the Saints*, London 1877, 'November'
3 Einhardt (Eginhard), *Vita Karoli Magni*, 19, 22
4 Gaufridus Malaterra, *De rebus gestis Roberti Guiscardi*
5 Bede, *Ecclesiastical History of England*, III 9, '14, 22, etc
6 Asser, *Life of King Alfred the Great*
7 Malmesbury, William of, *De Gestibus Regum Anglorum*, Rolls Series, 90, i (1887) Vol. I
8 Tyrrell, James, *The General History of England*, Vol. I, book 6.
9 Malmesbury, *loc. cit.*
10 Maxwell, Sir Herbert, *Memories of the Months*, Edinburgh 1897
11 Joyce, P. W., *Social History of Ancient Ireland*, London 1903. Vol. II
12 *Táin Bó Cúalnge (Saga of Cuchulain)*.
13 Major, Johannes, *History of Greater Britain*, 1521
14 *Oisin in Tirnanoge*
15 *Acallamh na Seanórach*
16 *Book of Aicill*; Rennes MS
17 Brehon Laws
18 Qu. Joyce, *op. cit.*

3 EARLY MIDDLE AGES

1 Lambert d'Ardres, *c.* AD 1000, *Revum Gallicarum et Francicarum Scriptous*
2 Contemps. qu. Buchanan-Jardine
3 Geoffrey of Monmouth, *Historia Britorum*, and others
4 Qu. Evans, Joan, *Life in Medieval France*, London 1925
5 (Ed.) Dryden, Alice, as Appendix to her ed. of Twici
6 *Anglo-Saxon Chronicle*, AD 1087
7 Hume, David, *History of England*, London 1831
8 Manwood, under 'Forest'
9 *Charta Foresta*, art. 6
10 Matthew Paris, *Historia Anglorum*, I
11 Qu. Stenton, D. M., *English Society in the Early Middle Ages*, London 1951
12 9 Henry III
13 Fitz Nigel, Richard, *Dialogus*
14 Fougères, Etienne de, *Livre des Manières*, 1178
15 Household Accounts, qu. Stenton, *op. cit.*
16 Brakelond, Jocelyn of, *De rebus gestis Samsonis Abbatis Monasterii Sancti Edmundi*
17 6 Edward I, 20
18 Wardrobe Accounts, 1299
19 Albertus Magnus, *De Animalibus*, Lib. VIII, Tract. II, Ch. I, II; Lib. XXII, Tract. II, Ch. 18
20 Joinville, *Histoire de Saint Louis*, XCIX 507; XCVI 494
21 Qu. Chenevix-Trench
22 Polo, Marco, *Concerning the Kingdoms and Marvels of the East*, tr. Yule, Col. Henry. III, 36
23 Macnab of Macnab, A. C., *Unto the Third and Fourth Generation* (unpub. MS)
24 Yule, Col. Henry, notes to Polo, II, 3, 30
25 Polo, I 61, II 3, 17, 18, 19, 20
26 Mandeville, Sir John, *The Voiage and Trauaile of Syr Iohn Maundeville*, journey begun 1322; account printed 1499, 22, 23

4 LATER MIDDLE AGES

1 *Roy Modus*, folios 13, 67, 75
2 Gaston Phébus; also miniature illustrations in Bibliothèque Nationale
3 *Paston Letters*
4 Chaucer, Geoffrey, *Canterbury Tales: Wife of Bath's Tale*
5 13 Richard II, ch. 13; 22 Edward IV, ch. 7
6 Poggio Bracciolini, *De Nobilitate*, 1437
7 York, Duke of, *Master of Game*
8 Chaucer, Geoffrey, *Nun's Priest's Tale*
9 Froissart, *Chronicles*, I, ch. 210
10 Fabyan, Robert, *Chronicles of England and France*
11 Malory, Sir Thomas, *Le Morte Darthur*, 1470, 1st ed. Caxton 1485; III 5–7; IV 6; VI 14, 16; etc
12 Buchanan-Jardine
13 Correspondance qu. Ferrière, *Valois*
14 *Livro da Montaria*

5 THE SIXTEENTH CENTURY

1 Erasmus, *In Praise of Folly*
2 Fleurange, *Histoire des Choses Memorables de 1499 à 1521*
3 Budé, intro.
4 Le Roy, intro.
5 Diplomatic papers qu. Ferrière, *Valois*
6 Monteil, Alexis, *Histoire des français des divers états*, Vol. VI
7 Cavendish, George, *Life of Wolsey*, c. 1530, pub. 1641
8 Saint Foix, Germain François Poullain de
9 Brézé, letters
10 Contarini, Venetian ambassador, qu. Ferrière
11 Throckmorton to Queen Elizabeth, 27 December 1559
12 Brézé to René de Savoie, 10 January 1524
13 Charles IX, ch. 8, 27–28
14 Prince Charles Alexandre de Croy to Henry Prince of Wales, 8 August 1609.
15 Fouilloux, ch. 61
16 Castlenau to Henri III, 11 September 1584
17 Rowland Whyte to Sir Robert Sidney, 12 September 1600
18 Pace, Richard, *De Fructu*, 1525
19 Jonson, Ben, *Everyman in his Humour*, I, 1
20 Bacon, Francis, *Of Kingdoms*
21 Cockaine
22 Gascoigne (or Turberville)
23 Sidney, Sir Philip, *Arcadia*
24 Kingsley, Charles, *Westward Ho!* ch. 3
25 Elyot, Sir Thomas, *Governour*, 1531
26 Shakespeare, *Venus and Adonis*, 674 sq
27 Gascoigne (or Turberville)
28 Markham, *Country Contentments*, I, 4
29 Blundeville
30 Gascoigne (or Turberville), ch. 64, 65, 70
31 Elyot, *op. cit.*
32 Markham, *Country Contentments*, I, 1
33 E.g. by Gascoigne, ch. 10, 13
34 Markham, *Country Contentments*, I, 3
35 Gascoigne, ch. 63
36 Bacon, Francis, *Apothegms*, 74
37 Harrison, William, *Description of Britaine* in his ed. of Holinshed, Raphael, *Chronicles, now newlie augmented to the yeare 1586*
38 *Archaeologia*, Vol. III
39 Qu. Sidney, ch. 2
40 Blundeville
41 Prospero d'Osma to Earl of Leicester
42 Wyatt, Sir Thomas, *Satire* 1
43 Markham, *How to Chuse* etc
44 Letter of Peter Martyr
45 Burckhardt, Jacob, *The Civilization of the Renaissance in Italy*
46 Letters Catherine de' Medici to Leonora de' Medici, qu. Ferrière
47 Ferey to Catherine de' Medici, qu. *ibid*
48 Gascoigne, ch. 1
49 More, Thomas, *Utopia*, Book II

6 EUROPE: SEVENTEENTH AND EIGHTEENTH CENTURIES

1 Salnove, Part III, sec. 4, ch. 1, 2
2 *Traitté*, Vol. II, Book 4, ch. 18
3 Chambers, *History of France*
4 Dampière, *Recueil*
5 *Journal des voyages de deux jeunes Hollandais*, 11 February 1657
6 Dangeau, *Journal*, 12 November 1686
7 Saint Simon, 28 June 1713
8 Bath, Earl of, *The World*, Vol. I, no. 17, 1753
9 Egan, *Book of Sports*, no. 9
10 *Traitté*, Vol. I, preface, 3; Book I, ch. 1; Vol. II, Book 4 ch. 1 sq
11 See Buchanan-Jardine
12 'Nassau Senior', Charles, Prince of Nassau-Siegin,
correspondence 1784–89
13 *Traitté*, Vol. II, Book 4 ch. 5, 18
14 Couterie, Le Verrier de la
15 Horace Walpole to George Montagu, 17 May 1763, etc
16 Mercy-Agenteau, comte de, to Empress Marie Thérèse, letters February to November 1776
17 Illus. *Coburg Hunting Chronicle*,
gouache series by Wolff Pickner
18 Illus. paintings by Philip Ferdinand von Hammilton for Charles VI
19 Raimondi, *Delle Caccie*, 1621
20 Castellamonte, Amadeo di, *Venaria Reale*, 1672
21 Beckford, *Thoughts*, Letters 1, 12

7 BRITAIN: 1600–1750

1 Burton, Robert, *Anatomy of Melancholy*, II, 2, 4
2 Nichols, John, *Progresses, processions, & festivities of James I*, 1828
3 James I, King, *A Kinge's Christian Dutie towards God*, 1603
4 Vlitius, *Venatio Nov-Antiqua*, 1644
5 Walton, Izaak, *The Compleat Angler*
6 Dorothy Osborne to Sir William Temple, Letter 28, 1653
7 Pepys, Samuel, *Diary*, 11 August 1661
8 Evelyn, John, *Diary*, 21 February 1689
9 Swift, Jonathan, *Letters to Stella*
10 *Grub Street Journal*, 19 August 1734
11 Bacon, *Apothegms*, 7
12 Brathwaite, Richard, *English Gentleman and English Gentlewoman*, 1630
13 Defoe, Daniel, *Memoirs of a Cavalier*
14 Fielding, Henry, *Tom Jones*, IV 5; V 12; VI 9, VII 2; etc
15 Bacon, *Apothegms*, 27
16 Defoe, *Extracts from a Plan of the English commerce*
17 Shaftesbury, Earl of, qu. Gilpin, Vol. II
18 Duke of Buckingham to Lord Rochester, 1674
19 Descr. Dixon, W. S., *North Countree*, appendix
20 Evidence cited Dixon, W. S., *Olden Days*, ch. 10
21 Qu. *Ibid.* ch. 7
22 Descr. Fawcett, *Turf, Chase and Paddock*
23 Descr. Dixon, W. S., *North Countree*, appendix
24 Qu. Kent, *Charlton*
25 Alexander Pope to Joseph Addison, 19 November 1712
26 Qu. Kent
27 Hound list qu. Bathurst, *Charlton & Raby*, ch. 2
28 Qu. Kent
29 Qu. Dixon, W. S., *Olden Days*
30 Lord Delawarr to Duke of Richmond, 10 September 1734
31 'Curious Manuscript account at Ashdean House' descr. and qu. Kent
32 Lists qu. Bathurst, *Charlton & Raby*, ch. 2
33 Map displayed Burton Tricentenary Exhibition,
Norwich, March 1873
34 Hardwicke, Earl of, *Walpoliana*
35 Yarborough, Earl of, intro. to Cook, *Observations*
36 Sir William Pelham to Sir Edward Conway 1623
37 Memorandum of 20 April 1713
38 Lord Arundell to 'Nimrod', 1833
39 Throsby, John, *Excursions in Leicestershire in the year 1790*
40 Lists qu. Bathurst, *Charlton & Raby*, intro.
41 Shadwell, Thomas, *Bury Fair*
42 *Spectator*, 12 July 1711
43 De Mandeville, Bernard, *Fable of the Bees*, 1714
44 Deed qu. Berkeley, *Life*, I, 1
45 Lists qu. Bathurst, *Charlton & Raby*
46 Lord Monson to Lord Charles Bentinck, qu. Bentinck, Ld. C.
47 Duke of Richmond's hound lists, qu. Bathurst, *Charlton & Raby*
48 Chafin, *Cranborne Chase*
49 'The Druid', *Scott & Sebright*, ch. 5
50 Recollections of an old man, qu. Reynard, *Holderness*, ch. 2
51 Kennel book qu. Prior, C. M. *The Aldby Foxhounds, Country Life*, 16 November 1935
52 Thomas Bright to Sir Henry Slingsby, 18 November 1738
53 Sir Robert Walpole to Earl of Carlisle, 14 July 1730
54 Preamble to Articles of Association, 13 November 1722
55 *Victoria County History: Hertfordshire*, I
56 Hone, Vol. III
57 Beaufort, 3rd Duke of, *Diary*
58 *Spectator*, 12 July 1711
59 Walton, Izaak, *The Compleat Angler*
60 Cox, Part I
61 Dixon, W. S., *Olden Days*, ch. 6
62 Newcastle, *La Méthode et Invention Nouvelle*, Antwerp 1657; English ed. 1666
63 De Grey, Epistle Dedicatory; Book i, ch. 4
64 'Curious manuscript account,' qu. Kent
65 *Spectator*, no. 55, 1711
66 Fielding, Henry, *Tom Jones*, v, 3

8 BRITAIN: THE MEYNELLIAN PERIOD 1750–1800

1 Qu. Cook, *Observations*
2 Qu. Delmé Radcliffe, ch. 9
3 Hawkes, *Meynellian System*
4 'Nimrod', *Life of a Sportsman*, ch. 4
5 Hawkes
6 Hawkes
7 Guerinière, François Robichon de la, *École de Cavalerie*. Paris 1751
8 Qu. Sidney, ch. 19
9 'Nimrod', *Life of a Sportsman*, ch. 2

Notes to the Text

10 Qu. Burrows
11 Dick Christian, qu. 'The Druid', *Post & Paddock*, 'lecture'
12 'Nimrod', *Life of a Sportsman*, ch. 2
13 By Dick Christian, qu. 'The Druid', *Silk & Scarlet*, 1
14 Established by hound-lists qu. Bathurst, *Spencer & Warde*. *Baily* confuses two Lord Lonsdales
15 Nethercote, ch. 1
16 'The Druid', *Post & Paddock*, ch. 14
17 'Nimrod', *Life of a Sportsman*, ch. 2
18 'The Druid', *Post & Paddock*, ch. 14
19 Different accounts in Cook, 'Scrutator', and 'The Druid'
20 'The Druid', *Post & Paddock*, ch. 14
21 Heber's *Calender*, 1763
22 Qu. Egerton Warburton, *Annals*
23 'Nimrod' *Life & Times*, preface
24 'The Druid', *Scott & Sebright*, ch. 5
25 Egan, no. 6
26 'Nimrod', *Condition of Hunters*, Letter 1
27 Randall, John, *Old Sports*
28 'Nimrod', *Life & Times*, ch. 15
29 'The Druid', *Post & Paddock*, ch. 14
30 'Nimrod', *Life of a Sportsman*, ch. 14
31 This pedigree follows 'Venator' and 'Nimrod'; it is doubted by Cook and

'Scrutator'.
32 View expressed e.g. by Cook; 'The Druid', *Post & Paddock*, ch. 14; 'Nimrod', *Life of a Sportsman*, ch. 14
33 Beckford, *Thoughts*, letter 3
34 Cook
35 'Scrutator', *Hunting & Sporting*, ch. 15
36 'Nimrod', *Chase, Turf & Road*, 1
37 Warde, Charles, *Hunting Diary*, 24 February 1780, 13 November 1789
38 MS qu. *North Cotswold*
39 These dates are disputed; Lord Bathurst, *Spencer & Warde*, appears to have established them from hound-lists
40 'Nimrod', *Life of a Sportsman*, preface; ch. 5
41 *Ibid.*, preface
42 'The Druid', *Post & Paddock*, ch. 14
43 Listed 'Aesop', ch. 1; and Austen-Leigh, letter 1 sq
44 Austen-Leigh, letter 6
45 'Nimrod', *Life of a Sportsman*, ch. 15
46 Cook, *Observations*
47 Qu. 'Aesop', ch. 1
48 Sam Nicoll, qu. 'The Druid', *Silk & Scarlet*, 4
49 'Aesop', ch. 1; Kent, *Charlton*
50 'Aesop', ch. 1
51 Loder Symonds, ch. 3
52 Southey, *Common-place Book*, 4th series
53 Qu. Prior, *Aldby*. (See note 51, ch. 7)
54 *Yorkshire Courant*, various issues

55 'The Druid', *Scott & Sebright*, ch. 5
56 'The Druid', *Silk & Scarlet*, ch. 4
57 Pick's *Callender*, 1776
58 Two ballads, qu. Dixon, W. S., *Olden Days*, ch. 6
59 Cowen, ch. 1
60 *Sporting Magazine*, November 1794
61 'The Druid', *Post & Paddock*, ch. 14
62 'Harry Hieover', *Hunting Field*, ch. 1
63 Raikes, Thomas, *Diary and Reminiscences of Social Life, from 1831 to 1847*
64 *Sporting Magazine*, February 1795
65 Egan, no. 13
66 Kent, *Charlton*; Bathurst, *Charlton & Raby*, ch. 2
67 Qu. Kent
68 Date conjectural: Taylor, ch. 1
69 Lord Stawell, qu. Austen-Leigh, letter 2
70 Diary qu. Greaves, *Lady Curre's Hounds*
71 Judd, *Scotland*
72 Minutes qu. Murray; *Baily* wrongly suggests two distinct packs
73 Hunt accounts qu. Babington
74 Sidney, ch. 19
75 'The Druid', *Scott & Sebright*, ch. 4
76 Many accounts, e.g. by Fanny Burney (Mme d'Arblay)
77 Qu. Russell, Lord John, *Memoirs of Charles James Fox*
78 'The Druid', *Scott & Sebright*, ch. 4

79 'Nimrod', *Life of a Sportsman*, ch. 1 etc
80 *Sportsman's Dictionary*, 'Coursing with Grey-Hounds'
81 Blaine, 'Greyhounds'
82 Daniel, Vol. 1
83 'Nimrod', *Life of a Sportsman*, ch. 3
84 *Sportsman's Dictionary*, 'Otter-hunting'
85 *Ibid.*, 'Badger'
86 *Ibid.*, 'Hunting-matches', 'Wild-Goose-Chase'
87 Lawrence, *Horse*, sec. 34
88 Paintings of Francis Barlow, d. 1702, and John Wootton, d. 1765
89 Beckford, *Thoughts*, letter 5
90 Lawrence, sec. 34
91 'Nimrod', *Chace, Road & Turf*, 1.
92 Lawrence, sec. 34
93 Sidney, ch. 3
94 *Sportsman's Dictionary*, 'Hunting-Horse'
95 Berenger, Vol. 1
96 Lawrence, sec. 34
97 Sidney, ch. 23
98 Lawrence, sec. 28
99 Lennox, *Merrie England*
100 *Sportsman's Dictionary*, 'Forests'
101 Gilpin, Vol. 1
102 Petrie, Sir Charles, *The Four Georges*, London 1935
103 *Torrington Diaries*, Vol 1
104 Warner, Rev. Richard, *A Walk through some of the Western Counties of England*
105 Beckford, *Thoughts*, letter 23

9 BRITAIN: THE GOLDEN AGE 1800–1850

1 Sidney, ch. 11
2 'Nimrod', *Chace, Turf & Road*, 1
3 'The Druid', *Silk & Scarlet*, 1
4 *Ibid*
5 Creevey; 'Nimrod' *Tours*
6 Egan, no. 13
7 Osbaldeston, ch. 3
8 Qu. Blew, *Quorn*, IV, 1
9 'Cecil', *F.K.S.B.*
10 Cook, *Obervations*; 'Nimrod', *Chace, Turf & Road*, 1
11 'Nimrod', *Tours*
12 Evidence in Ellis, ch. 3
13 'Nimrod', *Life of a Sportsman*, ch. 11, and elsewhere
14 Wilson, Harriette, *Memoirs*, ch. 20
15 Dick Christian, qu. 'The Druid', *Silk & Scarlet*, 1; Eardley Wilmot, appendix
16 Mills, John, *Sporting Life*
17 'Gelert', *Fores's Guide*
18 'The Druid', *Silk & Scarlet*, 1
19 Eardley Wilmot, ch. 7
20 Date uncertain. Lord Bathurst's conclusion here followed
21 'Nimrod', *Life of a Sportsman*, preface
22 'The Druid', *Silk & Scarlet*, 2

23 'Nimrod', *Life of a Sportsman*, preface
24 Nethercote, ch. 3
25 The two creations confused 'The Druid' and confuse *Baily* still.
26 G. S. Foljambe, qu. Bentinck, Lord C.
27 'The Druid', *Silk & Scarlet*, 1
28 Osbaldeston, ch. 3
29 'The Druid', *Silk & Scarlet*, ch. 1
30 E.g. 'Nimrod', 'Scrutator', 'Gelert', 'Cecil'
31 Bentinck, Lord H., *Goodall's Practice*
32 'The Druid', *Post & Paddock*, ch. 13
33 Qu. extensively, Goodall, D. M.
34 Osbaldeston, ch. 3
35 G. S. Foljambe to Lord George Bentinck, qu. Bentinck, Lord C.
36 Lists in full in Bentinck, Lord C.
37 Collins, *Farming and Fox-Hunting*, 1, 2, 3
38 G. S. Foljambe to Lord George Bentinck, qu. Bentinck, Lord C.

39 Qu. 'The Druid', *Silk & Scarlet*, 4
40 Bathurst, *Foxhounds*, ch. 4
41 'Gelert', *Fores's Guide*
42 'The Druid', *Post & Paddock*, ch. 14
43 Goodall, William, *Diary*, 11 April 1855
44 Bentinck, Lord H., *Goodall's Practice*
45 'Nimrod', *Life of a Sportsman*, ch. 11
46 Osbaldeston, ch. 4
47 G. S. Foljambe to Lord George Bentinck, February 1823
48 Bentinck, Lord H., *Goodall's Practice*
49 Whyte Melville, *Riding Recollections*, ch. 6
50 Capt. Percy Williams, qu. 'Gelert', *Fores's Guide*
51 Surtees, *Town & Country Papers*
52 Smith, Tom, *Life of a Fox*, 'Warwick'
53 Osbaldeston, ch. 33; Surtees, *New Sporting Magazine*, March 1832; 'Venator'; 'Nimrod', *Tours*
54 Vyner, *Notitia Venatica*

55 'The Druid', *Post & Paddock*, ch. 13
56 Pitt, Frances, ch. 1
57 'Gelert', *Fores's Guide*; 'Cecil', *North Warwickshire*
58 'The Druid', *Post & Paddock*, ch. 13; *Silk & Scarlet*, 4
59 'Nimrod', *Life of a Sportsman*, ch. 16
60 'Nimrod', *Life of a Sportsman*, ch. 13; *Life & Times*, ch. 15
61 'The Druid', *Post & Paddock*, ch. 14
62 Surtees, *Town & Country Papers*, 'Mr Jorrocks'
63 Berkeley, *Life*, II, 7
64 Berkeley, *Reminiscences*, 6
65 Berkeley, *Life*, I, 7
66 'Scrutator', *Recollections*, ch. 5
67 Bathurst, *V.W.H.*, ch. 2
68 'Gelert', *Fores's Guide*
69 'Nimrod', *The Chace etc.*, 1
70 Jem Hills, qu. 'The Druid', *Scott & Sebright*, ch. 5
71 'Nimrod', *Life & Times*, ch. 15
72 Surtees, *Sponge*, ch. 37
73 8th Duke of Beaufort, qu. Bathurst, Earl, 'Gloucestershire' in Lonsdale Library *Fox Hunting*
74 Qu. 'The Druid', *Scott &*

Sebright, ch. 5
75 Loder Symonds, ch. 1
76 Eardley Wilmot, ch. 2
77 Marsh, the 'sporting shoemaker', qu. Eardley-Wilmot, ch. 8
78 Lyon, William, *Chronicles of Finchampstead*, 1895
79 Surtees, *New Sporting Magazine*, 1831
80 'Nimrod', *Life of a Sportsman*, ch. 16
81 Qu. 'Aesop', ch. 2
82 Letter qu. Dalling, Lord, *Life of Lord Palmerston*, Vol. III
83 'Aesop', ch. 2; Delmé-Radcliffe
84 Jorn Warde, qu. 'The Druid', *Scott & Sebright*, ch. 5
85 'Nimrod', *Tours*
86 'Harry Hieover', *Stable Talk*, I
87 Delmé Radcliffe, ch. 13
88 *George Carter*, ch. 5
89 Smith, Tom, *Life of a Fox*, 'Wiley'
90 Berkeley, *Reminiscences*, ch. 5
91 'Scrutator', *Management*, letters 6, 9, 11; *Recollections*, ch. 1
92 E.g. descriptions of adjacent hunts in *The Master of the Hounds*
93 *Sporting Magazine*, November 1822
94 'Nimrod', *Tours*
95 Fully described, Davies, *Russell*, ch. 5
96 Smith, Tom, *Life of a Fox*, 'Devonshire'; Davies, *Russell*
97 Local bard qu. 'Nimrod', *Tours*
98 Davies, *Russell*
99 'Nimrod', *Tours*
100 'Sylvanus', *The Bye-Lanes and Downs of England*, 1850
101 Vyner, *Notitia Venatica*
102 Dixon, W. S., *North Countree*, ch. 3
103 'Nimrod', *Tours*
104 Accounts qu. Pease, *Cleveland*
105 'The Druid', *Scott & Sebright*, ch. 5
106 'Nimrod', *Northern Tour*, 24 March
107 Machell, ch. 5
108 'The Druid', *Saddle & Sirloin*, ch. 2
109 *Ibid*
110 'The Druid', *Post & Paddock*, ch. 14; Berkeley, *Reminiscences*, ch. 5
111 Russell, Lord C.

112 Berkeley, *Life*, II, 9
113 'Nimrod', *Life of a Sportsman*, ch. 6
114 Delmé Radcliffe, ch. 12
115 Tom Grant, huntsman, qu. Kent, *Charlton*
116 Taylor, ch. 1
117 Surtees, *Town and Country Papers*, 'Jorrocks'; *Handley Cross*; passim
118 'The Druid', *Post & Paddock*, ch. 13
119 'Scrutator', *Recollections*, ch. 19
120 'The Druid', *Post & Paddock*, ch. 13
121 Cook, *Observations*
122 Rev. John Russell, qu. Davies, ch. 12
123 'Nimrod', *Northern Tour*, 23 November
124 'Nimrod', *Northern Tour*, 25 November; Smith, Tom, *Life of a Fox*, 'Sandy'.
125 'Nimrod', *Northern Tour*, 6 December
126 Babington, *Fife*
127 Sidney, Lennox, Ribblesdale etc.
128 All descr. 'The Druid', *Scott & Sebright*, ch. 4
129 Carleton, *Sporting Sketchbook*, 1842
130 Sidney, ch. 19
131 Delmé Radcliffe, ch. 6
132 Sidney, ch. 19
133 Johnson, *Hunting Directory*
134 Apperley, N. W., *Diary*, 7 August 1869
135 'Nimrod', *The Horse and the Hound*, 'Hunting'
136 Cook, *Observations*
137 *Ibid*
138 Vyner, *Notitia Venatica*
139 'Nimrod', *The Horse and the Hound*, 'The Hound'
140 Sidney, ch. 22
141 'Nimrod', *loc. cit.*
142 See e.g. Delmé Radcliffe, Vyner
143 Delmé Radcliffe, ch. 10; Smith, Tom, *Extracts*
144 'Scrutator', *Recollections*, ch. 13
145 'The Druid', *Silk & Scarlet*, I
146 'Nimrod', *The Horse and the Hound*, 'The Hunter'
147 Egan, no. 13
148 'Nimrod', *loc. cit.*
149 Lawrence, sec. 34
150 'The Druid', *Post & Paddock*, ch. 12
151 'Harry Hieover', *Stable Talk*, II
152 Youatt, William, *The Horse*

153 'The Druid', *Post & Paddock*, ch. 13
154 'Nimrod', *loc. cit.*
155 Sidney, ch. 5
156 'Nimrod', *loc. cit.*
157 Prior, C. M. *History of the Racing Calender & Stud Book*
158 'Nimrod', *Condition of Hunters*, letter 5
159 'Nimrod', *Chace, Turf & Road*, 13
160 'Harry Hieover', *Stable Talk*, II
161 'Scrutator', *Horse & Hounds*, ch. 7
162 'Nimrod', *Condition of Hunters*, letters 13, 16
163 'Harry Hieover', *Stable Talk*, I
164 Lawrence, sec. 17
165 Delmé Radcliffe, ch. 7
166 Surtees, *Analysis*
167 Surtees, *Facey Romford*, ch. 6
168 'Nimrod', *Condition of Hunters*, letter 18
169 'The Druid', *Post & Paddock*, ch. 13
170 Smith, Tom, *Extracts*, ch. 3
171 'Harry Hieover', *Hunting Field*, ch. 5
172 Sidney, ch. 23
173 *Ibid*. ch. 14
174 Adams, Vol. III, 'Hunting Seat'
175 Paraphrased by Sidney, ch. 13
176 Many quotations, *ibid*.
177 'Harry Hieover', *Stable Talk*, II
178 'The Druid', *Post & Paddock*, ch. 13
179 Lawrence, sec. 25
180 'Nimrod', *The Horse & The Hound*, 'Horsemanship'
181 Whyte Melville, *Riding Recollections*, ch. 2, 3
182 'Scrutator', *Science*, ch. 22
183 'Harry Hieover', *Stable Talk*, I
184 Alken, *National Sports*, ch. 13
185 'Scrutator', *Science*, ch. 22
186 Lawrence, sec. 16
187 Cook, *Observations*; Surtees, *Hunting Tours, Analysis*
188 'Nimrod', *The Horse & the Hound*, 'The Hackney'
189 Trollope, *The American Senator*, ch. 1
190 'Harry Hieover', *Bipeds and Quadrupeds*
191 Surtees, *Facey Romford*, ch. 6
192 'Nimrod', *Life of a Sportsman*, ch. 2
193 Sidney, ch. 23
194 Delmé Radcliffe, ch. 8; 'Cecil', *Records*, ch. 14
195 Delmé Radcliffe, ch. 8

196 E.g. Illustrations to *Facey Romford*
197 Surtees, *Town & Country Papers*, 'Past & Present'
198 Delmé Radcliffe, ch. 8
199 *Ibid*.
200 Surtees, Handley Cross, ch. 27
201 Sidney, ch. 23
202 Wilson, Harriette, Memoirs, ch. 20
203 Surtees, *Handley Cross*, ch. 3
204 'Nimrod', *Sporting Magazine*, January 1825
205 Cook, *Obervations*
206 *Ibid*.
207 Lawrence, sec. 36
208 Delmé Radcliffe, ch. 11
209 E.g. Sidney, Surtees
210 Osbaldeston, ch. 3
211 Lord Kintore to 'Nimrod', 15 June 1834
212 'Scrutator', *Management*, letter 2
213 Trollope, *British Sports*, 'Hunting'
214 E.g. Lawrence, sec. 34
215 Surtees, *Town & Country Papers*
216 Surtees, *Analysis*
217 Cook, *Observations*
218 Surtees, *Sponge*, ch. 36
219 'The Druid', *Silk & Scarlet*, IV
220 Lawrence, sec. 35
221 Surtees, *Town & Country Papers*, 'Nimrod', 2
222 *Ibid*, 'Mr Jorrocks', 1
223 Surtees, *Handley Cross*, ch. 42, 44, 45
224 Surtees, *Town & Country Papers*, 'Nimrod', 1
225 Lawley, *Druid*, ch. 10
226 E.g. 'Nimrod', *Sporting*
227 Disraeli, *Sybil*
228 Delmé Radcliffe, ch. 8
229 Surtees, *Handley Cross*, ch. 7
230 Disraeli, *Sybil*
231 Carlyle, Thomas, *Past & Present*, 1
232 Eliot, George, *Middlemarch*
233 Cook, *Observations*
234 E.g. 'Scrutator', *Management*, letter 12
235 Smith, Tom, *Life of a Fox*, 'Chester'
236 'Scrutator', *Management*, letter 21
237 'Scrutator' and 'Nimrod', both repeatedly
238 Smith, Tom, *Extracts*, ch. 1
239 Smith, Tom, *Life of a Fox*, 'Wily'

10 BRITAIN: VICTORIAN AND EDWARDIAN 1850–1914

1 Corbet, *Tales & Traits*, 'The Banished Maid'
2 Paget, Guy, *Rum 'uns*, 1
3 Qu. Anstruther Thomson, *Hints*
4 *The Field*, April 1894
5 'Brooksby', *Best Season*
6 Davenport, *Memories*, ch. 8
7 'Brooksby', *Best of the Fun*, ch. 64
8 'Brooksby', *Cream of Leicestershire*, 'Billesdon'

9 E.g. Dale, *Fox*, ch. 2
10 Paget, Guy, *Rum 'uns*, ch. 2; Higginson, *Try Back*, ch. 7
11 Whyte Melville to John Anstruther Thomson, 26 February 1864
12 Anstruther Thomson, *Three Great Runs*
13 Whyte Melville, *Riding Recollections*, ch. 14
14 Bentley, H. Cumberland, *Dimple, a Memory of 1894*

15 'Brooksby', *Best of the Fun*, ch. 64
16 Henry Chaplin, qu. Londonderry, *Chaplin*, ch. 7
17 Higginson, *Try Back*, ch. 7
18 Will Goodall to Lord Forester, 24 July 1855
19 'Brooksby', *Hunting Countries*, 1
20 Lord Lonsdale to Sam Gillson, 24 May 1908
21 Qu. Dixon, W. S. *Hunting Year*, 1

22 Bradley, *Foxhound*, intro.
23 'Brooksby', *Hunting Countries*, 1
24 Londonderry, *Chaplin*, ch. 4
25 Frank Gillard, qu. Bradley, *Gillard*, ch. 1; Graham, Sir R., ch. 3
26 'Brooksby', *Hunting Countries*, 1; Collins, *Farming & Foxhunting*, IV, 3
27 'Brooksby', *Hunting Countries*, 1
28 *Ibid*.
29 Bell, ch. 10

Notes to the Text

30 Qu. Bradley, *Gillard*, ch. 1
31 Musters, *Great Run*
32 'Brooksby', *Hunting Countries*, I
33 Sidney, ch. 19
34 'Brooksby', *Hunting Countries*, I
35 Anstruther Thomson to 'Brooksby', 6 March 1895
36 Sassoon, *Foxhunting Man*, VIII, 2
37 Randall, James, I, 25
38 'Brooksby', *Hunting Countries*, I
39 Gerald Hardy, qu. Higginson, *Try Back*, ch. 7
40 Bradley, *Foxhound*, ch. 6
41 Qu. Higginson, *Try Back*, ch. 7
42 'Cecil', *Records*
43 'Brooksby', *Hunting Countries*, II
44 *Ibid.* I
45 'Scrutator', *Hunting & Sporting*, ch. 9
46 Andrews, *Reminiscences*
47 *Ibid.*; 'Brooksby', *Hunting Countries*, II
48 Andrews, *Reminiscences*
49 Andrews, *Horse, Hound etc.*; 'Brooksby', *Hunting Countries*, II
50 'Brooksby', *loc. cit.*
51 'The Druid', *Saddle & Sirloin*, ch. 15
52 'Brooksby', *loc. cit.*
53 Tom Rance, qu. 'The Druid', *Scott & Sebright*, ch. 5
54 Letters qu. Bathurst, *V.W.H.*, ch. 3
55 Robert Worrall to Sir William Throckmorton, 14 June 1916
56 Qu. Bathurst, *V.W.H.*, ch. 6
57 Blair-Oliphant, P. Kington, qu. Anstruther Thomson, *Three Great Runs*; Lowe, G. S. in de Trafford.
58 Whyte Melville, *Riding Recollections*, ch. 11
59 Cripps, Col. Fred., *Life's a Gamble*, 1957, ch. 8
60 Bradley, *Foxhound*, ch. 10
61 Higginson, *Try Back*, ch. 6
62 Watson, *Sketches*, 'The M.F.H.'
63 Bell, ch. 18
64 Loder Symonds, ch. 11
65 'Brooksby', *Hunting Countries*, I
66 Charles Kingsley to Thomas Hughes, November 1857
67 'Brooksby', *Hunting Countries*, I
68 *Ibid.*
69 Aldin, *Time I Was Dead*, ch. 4
70 'Brooksby', *Hunting Countries*, I
71 Graham, Sir R., ch. 1
72 Local farmer, qu. Higginson, *Try Back*, ch. 6
73 'Brooksby', *Hunting Countries*, I
74 'Scrutator', *Hunting & Sporting*, ch. 9
75 'Brooksby', *op. cit.* II
76 Back, ch. 1
77 Aubrey Wallis, qu. Bradley, *Foxhound*, ch. 12
78 Apperley, N. W., *Diary*,

79 'Brooksby', *op. cit.* II
80 Apperley, N. W., *Diary*, II, 15 January 1872
81 Qu. Fawcett, *Turf, Chace & Paddock*
82 'Brooksby', *op. cit.*, II
83 Dixon, W. S., *Bramham Moor*, ch. 9
84 'Brooksby', *loc. cit.*; Dixon, W. S., *Hunting Year*, ch. 9
85 Dixon, W. S., *Men, Horses & Hunting*, ch. 14
86 Bradley, *Foxhound*, ch. 5
87 'Brooksby', *Hunting Countries*, I
88 *Ibid.*, II
89 Apperley, N. W., *Diary*, 20 October, 4 November 1870, 24, 27 February 1871, 1 January, 19 September 1872, etc
90 *Ibid.*, 3 April 1875, 22 February 1876; Bradley, *Foxhound*, ch. 4
91 Beach-Thomas, ch. 7
92 'The Druid', *Saddle & Sirloin*, ch. 2
93 Fothergill
94 'Brooksby', *Best of the Fun*, ch. 7
95 'Brooksby', *Hunting Countries*, I
96 'Scrutator', *Hunting & Sporting*, ch. 2
97 Davenport (eye-witness), ch. 8
98 Taylor, ch. 12
99 Molyneux, ch. 2
100 Sassoon, *Foxhunting Man*
101 'Brooksby', *Hunting Countries*, I
102 Price, *Wales*, appendix
103 Anderson, T. Scott, ch. 1 etc.; Dixon, W. S., *Men, Horses & Hunting*, ch. 19
104 Barstow, *Lothians*, 1, 2, 4
105 Trollope, *The Eustace Diamonds*, ch. 37, 38
106 Tom Firr, qu. letter Lord Lonsdale to Arthur Thatcher, 1 January 1904
107 Graham, Sir R., ch. 2
108 Maxwell, Sir Herbert, intro. to 1897 ed. of Berkeley, *Reminiscences*
109 'Gelert', *Fores's Guide*
110 'Aesop', *Hampshire*, 1861
111 Bryden, *Hare Hunting*, in Aflalo
112 Lists qu. Bathurst, *Foxhound*, ch. 9
113 'Brooksby', *Hunting Countries*, I
114 Bradley, *Foxhound*, ch. 3
115 Corbet, *Tales and Traits*
116 Bathurst, *Foxhound*, ch. 6
117 'Cecil', letter of 11 January 1873
118 'Brooksby', *Hunting Countries*, repeatedly
119 Lord Calthorpe, qu. Anon, pamphlet *On the Deterioration of the British Horse*, 1878

120 Corbet, *Tales and Traits*
121 *Ibid.*
122 Prior, F. M., *Horse and Hound*, 20 May 1938
123 Andrews, *Reminiscences*
124 Whyte Melville, *Market Harborough*, ch. 6
125 *Ibid.*, ch. 17
126 Corbet, *Tales & Traits*
127 Whyte Melville, *Riding Recollections*, ch. 3
128 *Ibid.*, ch. 6
129 Sidney, ch. 14
130 *Ibid.*
131 *Ibid.*
132 Bentinck, Lord H., *Fox-hunting*
133 Whyte Melville, *Market Harborough*, ch. 1
134 Trollope, *Hunting Sketches*, 'Hunting Farmers'.
135 'Scrutator', *Science*, ch. 22
136 Whyte Melville, *Market Harborough*, ch. 8
137 *Ibid.* ch. 1
138 Sidney, ch. 23
139 Anstruther Thomson, *Hints*
140 Whyte Melville, *Market Harborough*, ch. 17
141 'Aesop', ch. 4
142 Geen, Philip, *Days Stolen for Sport*, ch. 1
143 Trollope, *Hunting Sketches*, 'The Lady'
144 Paget, Guy, *Rum 'uns*, ch. 1
145 Sidney, ch. 21
146 *Ibid.* ch. 15
147 Trollope, *loc. cit.*
148 'Scrutator', *Science*, ch. 47
149 Watson, *Sketches*, 'A Young Hunting Lady'
150 Whyte Melville, *Riding Recollections*, ch. 7
151 'A Lady', *Hints to Ladies*, in Bentinck, Lord H., *Foxhunting*
152 Collins, *Tales of Pink and Silk*, 'The Fair Horse-Breaker'
153 Trollope, *American Senator*, ch. 37
154 Trollope, *Hunting Sketches*, 'The Lady'
155 Sidney, ch. 15
156 Whyte Melville, *Market Harborough*, ch. 1
157 Sidney, ch. 22, 23
158 Mason, Finch, *Sporting Recollections*
159 Dixon, W. S., *Hunting Year*, ch. 5
160 Andrews, *Reminiscences*
161 Dixon, W. S., *Hunting Year*, ch. 12
162 Whyte Melville, *Market Harborough*, ch. 13
163 'Aesop', ch. 4
164 Watson, *Sketches*, 'The First Meet'

165 Williams, *Point to Point*, ch. 2
166 Quarrell, T. R., *The Worcestershire Hunt*, 1929
167 Trollope, *Hunting Sketches*, 'The Hunting Parson'
168 Trollope, *British Sport*, 'Past'
169 Sidney, ch. 18
170 Whyte Melville, *Riding Recollections*, ch. 5
171 Sidney, ch. 23
172 *Ibid.*, 22
173 'Brooksby', *Hunting Countries*, I
174 Trollope, *American Senator*, ch. 2, 10
175 Aldin, *Scarlet to M.F.H.*
176 Trollope, *Hunting Sketches*, 'The Master'
177 'Scrutator', *Recollections*, ch. 14, 18
178 Trollope, *loc. cit.*
179 Sidney, ch. 22
180 Trollope, *British Sports*, 'Hunting'
181 Sidney, ch. 22
182 'Scrutator', *Science*, ch. 46
183 Russell, Fox, *Sporting Sorrows*, 'M.F.H.'
184 Qu. North, *Hunting*, 'General Notes'
185 Trollope, *Hunting Sketches*, 'The Master'
186 Collins, *Tales of Pink and Silk*, 'A Distinguished Stranger'
187 Trollope, *American Senator*, ch. 80
188 'Scrutator', *Hunting & Sporting*, ch. 6
189 Sidney, ch. 22
190 Robert Worrall to Sir William Throckmorton, 14 June 1916
191 Sidney, ch. 23
192 Dixon, W. S., *Hunting Year*, ch. 9
193 Sidney, ch. 22
194 'The Druid', *Silk & Scarlet*, II
195 'Brooksby', *Hunting Countries*, I
196 Trollope, *British Sport*, 'Hunting'
197 Trollope, *Hunting Sketches*, 'The Man Who Hunts and Doesn't Like it'
198 Sidney, ch. 21
199 Russell, Fox, *Sporting Sorrows*, 'The M.F.H.'
200 Dixon, W. S., *Hunting Year*, ch. 10
201 Nethercote, ch. 1
202 Sidney, ch. 22
203 Bentinck, Lord H., *Foxhunting*
204 Andrews, *Reminiscences*
205 'Brooksby', *Hunting Countries*, II
206 Kipling, Rudyard, *My Son's Wife*, 1913, in *A Diversity of Creatures*
207 Underhill, G. F., in Aflalo
208 'Brooksby', *Cream of Leicestershire*, 1872–3
209 Trollope, *American Senator*

11 IRELAND: TO 1914

1 Stringer, *Experienc'd Huntsman*, 1714
2 Paper of 1792 qu. 'Maintop' in Coaten
3 Fitzpatrick, ch. 1
4 E.g. Fitzpatrick, ch. 8
5 Fitzpatrick, ch. 1
6 'Harry Hieover', *Stable Talk*, II
7 All forms are used in various sources
8 Somerville & Ross, *Mount Music*, ch. 1
9 Lever, Charles, *Charles O'Malley*, many chapters
10 Vyner, *Notitia Venatica*
11 'Maintop' in Coaten

12 Whyte Melville, *Riding Recollections*, ch. 13
13 Bell, ch. 22
14 Eye-witness qu. Fitzpatrick, ch. 2
15 *Ibid.*, ch. 11
16 Trollope, *Landleaguers*, ch. 9
17 *Kilkenny*, ch. 17; conclusion
18 Fitzpatrick, ch. 13
19 *Ibid.*, ch. 5
20 Whyte Melville, *Riding Recollections*, ch. 8

21 Bell, ch. 40
22 Eye-witness account, Conyers, *Reminiscences*, ch. 1
23 Trollope, *Landleaguers*, ch. 10
24 'Maintop' in Coaten
25 Winthrop Astor Chanler to his wife, 13 November 1902
26 Smith, H. W., *Sporting Tour*, 1, ch. 12
27 Bell, ch. 37
28 *Ibid.* ch. 19
29 'Dalesman', *Horse and Hound*,

5 April 1974
30 Buchanan-Jardine
31 Kennel book, 24 February 1812
32 Trollope, *Phineas Finn*, ch. 17, 19; *Kellys and O'Kellys*, ch. 21, 22
33 Trollope, *Landleaguers*, ch. 10
34 Bell, ch. 38
35 Somerville & Ross, *Further Experiences*, ch. 12
36 Morris, *Hibernia Hippica*, ch. 22

37 Whyte Melville, *Riding Recollections*, ch. 9
38 *Ibid.*, ch. 8
39 'Harry Hieover', *Stable Talk*, 11
40 'Nimrod', *Nimrod Abroad*, 11
41 Corbet, *Tales & Traits*
42 Morris, *Hibernia Hippica*, ch. 9
43 *Ibid.*, ch. 17, 20, 21
44 Underhill, G. F., in Aflalo
45 Morris, *Hibernia Hippica*, ch. 12
46 Somerville & Ross, *Dan Russell the Fox*

12 AMERICA: COLONIAL TIMES TO CIVIL WAR

1 Smith, Captain John, *A Map of Virginia*, London 1612
2 Hakluyt, *Voyages*, 111, *Travels of Job Hartop*
3 *Ibid.*, 11, *Voyage of John Davis to the North West Passage*
4 Bradford, William, *Of Plimouth Plantation*, c. 1650
5 Cooper, J. F., *The Last of the Mohicans*
6 Clayton, Rev. John, of Jamestown: letter to the Royal Society, 1688
7 Beverley, Robert, *The History and Present State of Virginia*, 1705, Book IV, part 2
8 Court records, qu. van Urk, *American Foxhunting*, 1, 2
9 *Virginia Gazette*, 3 December 1736
10 Letter to England, 1739
11 Lord Fairfax to George Fairfax, 6 April 1746
12 Qu. 'Nimrod', *Nimrod Abroad*, 11
13 Contemp. qu, van Urk, *American Foxhunting*, 1, 4
14 Washington, *Diary*, 12

December 1785
15 Washington to Lafayette, 1 September 1785
16 Washington, *Diary*, 1 February 1789
17 Bishop Meade, qu. Parton, James, *Life of Thomas Jefferson*, 1882
18 Scharf, J. T., *History of Maryland*, Baltimore 1897, Vol. 11
19 Hiltzheimer, Jacob, *Diary*, 23, 27 December 1765
20 Rules qu. Milnor, *Gloucester*
21 Letters qu. van Urk, *American Foxhunting*, 1, 2, 5
22 Qu. *Turf, Field & Farm*, 13 January 1882
23 Dale, *Fox*, ch. 9
24 Kalm, Peter, *Travels into North America*, 1750
25 Cooper, J. F., *The Last of the Mohicans*
26 Qu. van Urk, *American Foxhunting*, 1, 1
27 Herbert, W. H., *Field Sports*, intro.
28 *Cabinet*, 1832

29 *A.T.R.*, February 1830
30 *Spirit of the Times*, 6 December 1856
31 Letter to *A.T.R.*, March 1834
32 *Spirit of the Times*, 6 December 1856
33 Taney, R. B., *Memoir*, Baltimore 1872
34 *A.T.R.*, February 1837
35 *A.T.R.*, December 1829
36 Skinner, Col. Fred., *Turf, Field & Farm*, October 1874
37 *Ibid.*, November 1881
38 *A.T.R.*, January 1834
39 Skinner, Col. Fred., *Turf, Field & Farm*, September 1887
40 Skinner, Col. Fred., *Cincinatti Daily Times*, 27 August 1879
41 Scharf, *op. cit.*, 11
42 Maynadier, Col., qu. *A.T.R.*, September 1829
43 *A.T.R.*, February 1837
44 Milnor, *Gloucester*
45 *Aurora General Advertiser*, 1803 sq.
46 Taylor, Bayard, *The Story of Kennett*, 1866

47 Cobbett, William, *A Year's Residence in the United States of America*, 1828
48 Darlington, *Rose Tree*, ch. 4 sq.
49 Legend qu. van Urk, *Rolling Rock*, ch. 3
50 *Cabinet*, 1829
51 *Turf, Field & Farm*, 13 January 1882
52 *Spirit of the Times*, 18 October 1856
53 Lowell, James Russell, *New England Two Centuries Ago*, 1865
54 Dwight, Rev. Timothy, *Greenfield Hill*
55 Elliott, *Carolina*
56 Garrett, ch. 33
57 Webber, C. W., *The Hunter Naturalist*, Philadelphia 1852
58 Garrett, ch. 33; Trigg, ch. 3
59 Article 7, qu. *A.T.R.*, June 1835
60 'Nimrod', *Nimrod Abroad*, 11
61 Cooper, J. I., *Montreal*, ch. 1 sq.
62 *New Sporting Magazine*, June 1836

13 AMERICA: CIVIL WAR TO 1914

1 Skinner, Col. Fred., *Turf, Field & Farm*, 1873
2 Assheton, Capt. W. qu. Mackay-Smith, ch. 10
3 Higginson & Chamberlain, 11
4 Higginson, *Country Gentleman*, 1911
5 Qu. Mackay-Smith, ch. 18
6 McClary, J. McI., *Horse & Hound*, 27 February 1974
7 Indeed the whole circumstances are the subject of widely different accounts
8 Higginson & Chamberlain, 1
9 Potts, Mrs Allan, qu. Higginson & Chamberlain, 11
10 Trollope, *British Sports*, 'Hunting'
11 Higginson & Chamberlain, 1; Stewart, Redmond C., *Diary*, 14 November 1909
12 Stewart, Redmond C., *The Foxhound*, April 1912
13 *Outing*, October 1891
14 *Daily Evening Telegraph*,

Philadelphia, 22 March 1877
15 Higginson, *Country Gentleman*, 1911
16 Cody, Col. William F., *Buffalo Bill's Life Story*
17 Mather, Charles E., letter to A. H. Higginson
18 Mather, *Radnor*, intro.
19 Dohan, Joseph M. (brother of M.F.H.) to A. H. Higginson
20 Qu. Whitney & Martin, Part 1
21 Riddle, Samuel D., letter to A. H. Higginson
22 Knott, O'Malley, *Gone Away*
23 Griswold, *Hounds & Horses*
24 *Harper's Weekly*, 14 October 1882
25 'Brooksby', *Best of the Fun*, ch. 20
26 *Harper's Weekly*, 14 October 1882
27 Knott, ch. 21
28 Higginson, *Country Gentleman*, 1911
29 *The Field*, 19 January 1895

30 'Brooksby', *Best of the Fun*, ch. 65
31 Diary, qu. van Urk, *American Foxhunting*, 11, 7
32 *American Field*, 9 November 1895
33 Stephens, ch. 1, 3, 7
34 Price, F. H., qu. Forbes, Allan, *Norfolk County*
35 *Boston Herald*, 30 November, 2 December 1883; 19 October, 21 December 1884
36 Report qu. Forbes, *Norfolk County*, ch. 30
37 Descr. Garrett, ch. 21; Gingery, Lewis, in Connett.
38 *Rider & Driver*, 1904
39 E.g. Higginson (in history, autobiography and fiction); H. W. Smith (unpublished autobiography); Potts, Allan; Mrs Potts; Mackay-Smith; van Urk.
40 Potts, ch. 10
41 Higginson, *Perfect Follower*, ch. 5

42 Skinner, Col. Fred., *Turf, Field & Farm*, 6 December 1889
43 Harris, Joel Chandler, *Scribner's*, 1893; letter to J. M. Henry, 29 September 1905
44 Trigg, ch. 2
45 Williams, Gen. R. D., *Foxhound*, ch. 1, 3
46 Robert Cotesworth, qu. Higginson & Chamberlain, 11
47 Garrett, ch. 3
48 Breese, foreword
49 *Ibid.*
50 Smith, H. W., unpublished autobiography qu. Mackay-Smith, ch. 15
51 Irving, Washington, *Sketchbook*
52 Stowe, Harriet Becher, *Sunny Memories*
53 Trollope, *American Senator*, ch. 10

Notes to the Text

14 BRITAIN: 1914 AND AFTER

1 Higginson, *Try Back*, ch. 9
2 Dixon, W. S., *20th Century*, Part II, ch. 10
3 Record issued with Brock, *Hunting by Ear*
4 Higginson, *Try Back*, ch. 6; Bathurst, *Foxhound*
5 Berry, *More Hunting*, ch. 8
6 Higginson, *Letters*, 10
7 Collins, *Farming & Foxhunting*, ch. 7
8 Acton, *Hounds. Modern Foxhound*; Higginson concurs –
marginal note in his copy
9 E.g. tribute by Sir Peter Farquhar, *Horse & Hound*, 2 November 1973
10 Higginson, *Try Back* and elsewhere
11 Clapham, Richard, *Foxhunting in Lakeland*, in Lonsdale Library, *Foxhunting*
12 Clapham, *Foxes, Foxhounds*, ch. 15
13 Andrews, *Horse, Hound etc.*, ch. 2
14 Sir Edward Curre, qu. Higginson, *Try Back*, ch. 12
15 Bell, ch. 19
16 Higginson, *Two Centuries*, ch. 9
17 Bathurst, *Foxhound*, ch. 3
18 Paget, J. Otho, *Hunting Reflections*
19 Bathurst, *Foxhound*, ch. 9
20 Farquhar, *loc. cit.*
21 Fawcett, *Turf, Chase & Paddock*
22 *Horse & Hound*, 14 December 1973
23 Richardson, *Many Countries*, ch. 9
24 Barrow, *Hunting the Fox*
25 Frederick, Sir Charles, *Manners & Customs*, in Lonsdale Library, *Foxhunting*
26 Somerset & Apsley, *Goddess*, ch. 3
27 Pollard, *Riding & Hunting*, ch. 1
28 Wallace, Capt. R. E., *Horse & Hound*, 2 November 1973

15 IRELAND: 1914 AND AFTER

1 Bell, ch. 43
2 Bowen, 'Tipperary'
3 Lanier, *Foxhunting Abroad*
4 'Dalesman', *Horse & Hound*, 15 December 1972, 30 March 1973, 5 April 1974
5 Armitage, *A Long Way to Go*

16 AMERICA: 1914 AND AFTER

1 Sands, D. C., letter qu. Higginson & Chamberlain, II
2 Somerville, E., *States*, ch. 11
3 Higginson, *Try Back*, ch. 9; and elsewhere
4 McClary, J. McI., *Horse & Hound*, 27 February 1974
5 Tribute qu. Mackay-Smith, ch. 18
6 Thomas, ch. 4
7 Qu. van Urk, *American Foxhunting*, II, 15
8 McClary, *Portion*
9 Somerville, E., *States*, ch. 10
10 Higginson, *Try Back*, ch. 11
11 James R. Kerr, Jr. to J. B. van Urk, 8 August 1940
12 Compare Reeve, *Recollections*, 22 November 1922; Higginson, *Try Back*, ch. 10; Somerville,
E., *States*, ch. 21
13 Newbold Ely, qu. Mackay-Smith, ch. 23
14 W. B. Watkins, qu. *Ibid.* ch. 20
15 Somerville, E., *States*, ch. 21
16 Reeve, *Diary*, 6 February 1932
17 Harding, Minette, *Horse & Hound*, 3 November 1972
18 van Urk, *Rolling Rock*
19 H. I. Nicholas, qu. Higginson, *Two Centuries*, ch. 6
20 Crawford, ch. 9
21 Marquand, J. P., *Point of No Return*, I, 7
22 Wooldridge, Sam, *The Chase*, June 1926
23 Crawford, ch. 9
24 van Urk, J. B., *Middleburg Chronicle*, 9 December 1938
25 Updike, John, *Couples*, 1, 9
26 Somerville, E., *States*, ch. 2
27 Crawford, ch. 9
28 Streatfield, G. H., *Horse & Hound*, 22 December 1972
29 Grant, *Arapahoe*
30 *New York Times*, 3 April 1972
31 Cooper, J. I., *Montreal*
32 E.g. *The Chronicle*, 17 November 1939
33 Reeve, *Journal*, 1944–5
34 Williams, Gen. R. D., *Foxhound*
35 E.g. Graham, J. A. A., *Sporting Dog*
36 Qu. Higginson, *Try Back*, ch. 13
37 Higginson, *Perfect Follower*, ch. 6
38 Gingery, L. F., *Foxhound Field*
Trials, in Connett.
39 E.g. Henry, S. J.
40 Higginson, *Letters*, 10
41 E.g. 'Brooksby' and Edith Somerville
42 Charles McNeill, qu. Higginson, *Letters*, 6
43 'Vera', *Our American Cousins at Home*, 1873
44 Higginson, *Letters*, 26
45 Runyon, Damon, *Money from Home*
46 Jenks, *Huntsman*
47 Crawford, ch. 9
48 McClary, *Portion*
49 E.g. van Urk, *American Foxhunting*

17 EUROPE: NINETEENTH AND TWENTIETH CENTURIES

1 Tench, Capt. Watkin, *Letters Written in France to a Friend in London*, 1796
2 Toussenel
3 'Harry Hieover', *Stable Talk*, II
4 O'Connor, *Field Sports*, II, 1
5 'Nimrod', *Nimrod Abroad*, II
6 D'Ewes, ch. 8
7 Berkeley, *Life*, II, 13
8 O'Connor, II, 8
9 Vyner, *Notitia Venatica*
10 *Journal des Haras*, 1837
11 Diguet
12 Vyner, *Notitia Venatica*
13 A disputed date: some accounts say 1832
14 Vyner, *Notitia Venatica*
15 Ribblesdale, ch. 15
16 Diguet
17 Couteulx de Canteleu
18 Ribblesdale, ch. 15
19 Aldin, *Time I Was Dead*, ch. 3
20 Ribblesdale, ch. 15
21 Diguet
22 Thomas Hastings to Col. J. Anstruther Thomson, April 1879
23 Smith, H. W., *Sporting Tour*, II, ch. 17
24 Dauchez, Alain, Secrétaire Général de la Societé de la Vénerie, *Baily* 1972–3
25 'Nimrod', *Nimrod Abroad*, I
26 Diguet
27 Etreilles, baron d', *Le pur sang en France*, 1873
28 Ribblesdale, ch. 15
29 Vyner
30 Wynn Knight, Col. Frederick, letters qu. Sidney, ch. 6
31 Trollope, *British Sports*, 'Hunting'
32 Bell, ch. 49
33 Cigala, conte, qu. Gardiner, Leslie, *Horse & Hound*, 3 November 1972
34 *Evening Standard*, 18 August 1888
35 'Nimrod', *Nimrod Abroad*, I
36 Dale, *Fox*, ch. 5
37 'Nimrod', *Nimrod Abroad*, II
38 Sidney, ch. 6
39 'The Druid', *Scott & Sebright*, ch. 5
40 Lever, Charles, *Charles O'Malley*, ch. 97
41 Lloyd, L., *Field Sports*, ch. 10, 16, 17
42 Turgenev, *Sportsman's Sketches*, 6
43 Turgenev, *Three Portraits*
44 Tolstoy, *War & Peace*, IV, 3
45 Turgenev, *Sportsman's Sketches*, 10; *Nest of Gentlefolk*, 11
46 'Nimrod', *Nimrod Abroad*, II
47 Hayes, Capt. H., *Among Horses in Russia*, 1900
48 'Nimrod', *Nimrod Abroad*, II
49 Cripps, Col. F., *Life's a Gamble*, 1957, ch. 10

18 ENGLISH HUNTING IN FAR PLACES

1 Williamson, Capt. Thomas, *Oriental Field Sports*
2 Letter qu. 'Nimrod', *Nimrod Abroad*, II
3 Dale, *Fox*, I
4 D'Ewes, *Sporting*
5 Qu. Vyner, *Notitia*
6 Qu. 'Nimrod', *Nimrod Abroad*, II
7 Vyner, *Notitia*
8 'Nimrod', *Nimrod Abroad*, II
9 Babington, *Fife*
10 'Brooksby', *Foxhound, Forest and Prairie*
11 Hurst, *P.V.H.*
12 Kipling, Rudyard, *The Brushwood Boy*
13 Dale, *Fox*, 8
14 Qu. 'Nimrod', *Nimrod Abroad*, II
15 Qu. Huxley, Elspeth, *Their Shining Eldorado*, London 1967
16 Inglis, ch. 5
17 Dale, *Fox*, 4
18 Fitzpatrick, ch. 8
19 Trollope, *Australia & New Zealand*, II, ch. 18
20 Inglis, ch. 5, 6
21 Letter qu. 'Nimrod', *Nimrod Abroad*, II
22 Cape, *Buckhounds*
23 *Observer*, 23 January 1972
24 Kipling, Rudyard, *Little Foxes*, from *Actions & Reactions*
25 Doughty, Charles M., *Wanderings in Arabia*, London 1908
26 *Sunday Times*, 17 December 1972
27 Morrison, E., ch. 6

Bibliography

Acton, C. R., *The Modern Foxhound*. London 1935
Sports & Sportsmen of the New Forest. London 1936
Hounds. London 1939
The Fox-hound of the Future. London 1953
Adams, John, *An Analysis of Horsemanship*. 3 vols. London 1805
'Aesop' (Heysham, W. Nunez), *Sporting Reminiscences of Hampshire from 1745 to 1862*. London 1864
Aflalo, F. G., (Ed.) *The Sports of the World*. London 1905
Aldin, Cecil, *Ratcatcher to Scarlet*. London 1921
Scarlet to M.F.H. London 1926
Time I was Dead. London 1934
(with Barrow, A. S. ['Sabretache']), *Hunting Scenes*. London 1936
Alken, Henry, *The National Sports of Great Britain*. London 1825
Allison, Benjamin R., *The Rockaway Hunting Club*, Pvt. 1950
Allison, William, *Memories of Men and Horses*. London 1922
American Farmer, various issues
American Field, various issues
American Turf Register and Sporting Magazine, various issues
Anderson, J. K., *Ancient Greek Horsemanship*. Oklahoma 1961
Anderson, T. Scott, *Hound and Horn in Jedforest*. Jedburgh 1909
Andrews, Tom ('Gin and Beer'), *Fox Hunting Reminiscences*. London 1930
Horse, Hound, Hoof and Turf. Worcester 1934
Anstruther Thomson, Col. John, *Three Great Runs*. London 1889
Hints to Huntsmen. London 1891
Eighty Years' Reminiscences. 2 vols. London 1894
Apperley, C. J., see 'Nimrod'
Apperley, Newton Wynne, *North Country Hunting Half a Century Ago*. Darlington 1924
A Hunting Diary. (Ed.) Cuming, C. E. London 1926
Armitage, Marigold, *A Long Way to Go*. London 1952
A Motley to the View. London 1961
Arrian, *Cygeneticus*
Auden, J. E., *A Short History of the Albrighton Hunt*. London 1905
Austen-Leigh, J. E., *Recollections of the Early Days of the Vine Hunt*. London 1865
Babington, Lt. Col. John, *Records of the Fife Fox-Hounds*. Edinburgh 1883
Back, Philip, *From Terrier Boy to Field Master*. Plymouth 1938
Badminton Library, *Hunting*. London 1885
Baily's Hunting Directory, various editions

Ball, R. D., and Gilbey, Tresham, *The Essex Foxhounds*. London 1896
Baret (or Barrett), Michael, *Hipponomania, or the Vineyard of Horsemanship*. London 1618
Barrow, A. S. ('Sabretache'), *Hunting the Fox*. London 1926
Shires and Provinces. London 1926
Barstow, C. M., *Days with the Lothian Hounds*. Edinburgh 1872
Bathurst, Earl, *The Breeding of Foxhounds*. London 1926
The Earl Spencer's and Mr. John Warde's Hounds. 3rd ed. Cirencester 1932
A History of the V.W.H. Country. London 1936
The Charlton and Raby Hunts. London 1938
Beach Thomas, Sir William, *Hunting England*. London 1936
Beard, John, *A Diary of Fifteen Years' Hunting, viz., From 1796 to 1811*. Bath 1813
Beckford, Peter, *Thoughts on Hunting*. Salisbury 1781
Bell, Isaac, *A Huntsman's Log Book*. London 1947
Bentinck, Lord Charles, *Lord Henry Bentinck's Foxhounds*. London n.d.
Bentinck, Lord Henry, *Goodall's Practice*. London 1871
Foxhunting: What to do . . . and What not to do. London n.d.
Berenger, Richard, *History and Art of Horsemanship*. London 1771
Berners, Dame Juliana (ascr.), *The Boke of St Albans*. 1486
Berkeley, Grantley, *Reminiscences of a Huntsman*. London 1854
My Life and Recollections. 2 vols. London 1865
Berry, Michael, F., *Foxhunting from The Times*. London 1933
More Foxhunting from The Times. London 1937
A History of the Puckeridge Hunt. London 1950
Birdsong, Col. G. L. F., *Sporting Sketches*. Georgia 1863–4
Blagg, Charles J., *A History of the North Staffordshire Hounds and Country 1700–1901*. London 1902
Blaine, Delabere P., *An Encyclopaedia of Rural Sports*. London 1840
Blew, W. C. A., *The Quorn Hunt and its Masters*. London 1899
Blundeville, Thomas, *The fower chiefest offices belonging to Horsemanshippe, That is to saye, the office of the Breeder, of the Rider, of the Keeper, and of the Ferrer*. London 1565 sq.
Bovill, E. W., *The England of Nimrod and Surtees*. Oxford 1959
Bowen, Muriel, *Irish Hunting*. Tralee 1955

Bradley, Cuthbert, *The Reminiscences of Frank Gillard with the Belvoir Hounds 1860–1896*. London 1898
The Foxhound of the Twentieth Century. London 1914
Brander, Michael, *Hunting and Shooting*. London 1971
Breese, Louis V., *Some Unwritten Laws of Organized Foxhunting*. New York 1909
Brezé, Louis de, *Les Chasses de François Premier*, Letters 1514–30, (Ed.) Ferrière, comte Hector de la. Paris 1869
Brock, D. W. E., *Hunting by Ear*. London 1960
Bromley-Davenport, William, *Sport*. New ed. London 1868
Bruce, Brig. Gen. C. D., *The Essex Foxhounds and Adjacent Hunts*. London n.d.
'Brooksby' (Pennell-Elmhirst, Capt. E.), *The Hunting Countries of England*. 2 vols. London 1882, 1883
The Cream of Leicestershire. London 1883
The Best Season on Record. London 1884
Fox-hound, Forest and Prairie. London 1892
The Best of the Fun. London 1903
Buchanan-Jardine, Sir John, *Hounds of the World*. 2nd ed. London 1937
Buckland, Harry, *A Master of Hounds; being the life story of Harry Buckland of Ashford, by One Who Knows Him*. London 1931
Budé, Gillaume (Budaeus), *De Venatione*. Paris c. 1530
Burrows, George T., *Gentleman Charles: A History of Foxhunting*. London 1951
Butler, A. J., *Sport in Classic Times*. London 1930
Cape, Col. H. A., *The Closing Chapter of the Royal Buckhounds*. Windsor 1946
Carleton, J. W., (Ed.), *The Sporting Sketch Book*. London 1842
Carlisle, R. H., *Fox-Hunting Past and Present*. London 1908
Carter, George, *Hound and Horn: or, the Life and Recollections of George Carter, by 'I.H.G.'* London 1885
'Cecil' (Tongue, Cornelius), *The Fox-Hunter's Guide*. London 1849
The Stud Farm. London 1851
Stable Practice. London 1852
Records of the Chase. London 1854
Hunting Tours. London 1864
The Kennel Stud Book. Vol. 1. Wolverhampton 1866
The Belvoir Hunt. London n.d.
The Billesdon Hunt. London n.d.
The North Warwickshire Hunt. London n.d.
The Quorn Hunt. London n.d.
Chace dou Serf, la, c. 1250, (Ed.) Dryden, Alice. Northampton 1908
Chafin, Rev. William, *Anecdotes and History*

Bibliography

of Cranborne Chase. 2nd ed. London 1818

Chalmers, Patrick, *The History of Hunting*. London 1936

Chapman, Capt. F., *Reminiscences of the Wensleydale Hounds 1686 to 1907*. Eastbourne *c.* 1909

Charles IX, King of France, *Traité de la Chasse au cerf*, (Ed.) Neufville, Nicholas de. Paris 1625

Chenevix-Trench, Charles, *A History of Horsemanship*. London 1970

Clapham, Richard, *Foxhunting on the Lakeland Fells*. London 1920
Foxes, Foxhounds and Fox-hunting. London 1922

Coaten, A. W. (Ed.), *British Hunting: a Complete History of the National Sport of Great Britain and Ireland from Earliest Records*. London 1910

Cockaine, Sir Thomas, *A Short Treatise on Hunting*. 1591

Collins, George E. ('Nimrod Junior'), *History of the Brocklesby Hounds 1700–1901*. London 1902
Farming and Fox-Hunting. London 1935
(fiction) *Tales of Pink and Silk*. London 1900

Collyns, Charles Palk, *Notes on the Chase of the Wild Red Deer*. London 1902

Connett, Eugene V. (Ed.), *American Sporting Dogs*. New York 1948

Conyers, Dorothea, *Sporting Reminiscences*. New York 1920
(fiction) *The Straying of Sandy*, 1908; *The Boy, Some Horses and a Girl*, 1914; *Follow Elizabeth*, 1929; *The Scratch Pack*, n.d.; etc.

Cook, Col. John, *Obsevations on Fox-Hunting*. London 1826

Cooper, John ('Venator'), *The Warwickshire Hunt from 1795 to 1836*. London 1837

Cooper, John Irwin, *The History of the Montreal Hunt*. Montreal 1953

Cooper, Leonard, *R. S. Surtees*. London 1952

Corbet, Henry, *Tales and Traits of Sporting Life*. London 1864

Country Gentleman, various issues

Country Life, various issues

Couterie, la Verrier de la, *École de la Chasse aux Chiens Courants*. 1778

Couteulx de Canteleu, comte de, *Manuel de Vénerie Française*. Paris 1863

Cowen, G. A., *The Braes of Derwent Hunt*. Northumberland 1955

Cox (or Coxe), Nicholas, *The Gentleman's Recreation: In Four Parts, viz. Hunting, Hawking, Fowling, Fishing*. London 1674
The Huntsman. London *c.* 1680

Craft of Venery. Anon, *c.* 1450, (Ed.) Dryden, Alice. Northampton 1908

Crawford, Everett L., *Let's Ride to Hounds*. New York 1929

Crossing, William, *A Hundred Years on Dartmoor*. 3rd ed. Plymouth 1901

Cuming, E. D., *British Sport past and present*. 1909

Cummins, Geraldine, *Dr. E. Œ. Somerville*. London 1952

Dale, T. F., *The History of the Belvoir Hunt*. London 1899
The Eighth Duke of Beaufort and the Badminton Hunt. London 1901
Fox Hunting in the Shires. London 1903
The Fox. London 1906

Dampière, marquis de, *Recueil de fanfares pour la Chasse*. Paris 1770

Daniel, Rev. Wm. B., *Rural Sports*. 3 vols. London 1807; Supplement 1813

Darlington, Geo. E., *Fox Hunting in Delaware County, Penn., and Origin and History of the Rose Tree Fox Hunting Club*. Philadelphia 1901

Davenport, Henry S., *Memories at Random: Melton and Harborough*. London 1926

Davies, Rev. E. W. L., *Memoir of the Rev. John Russell*. London 1878; and see 'Gelert'

Dease, Edmund F., *A Complete History of the Westmeath Hunt*. Dublin 1898

de Costobadie, F. Palliser, *Annals of the Billesdon Hunt 1856–1913*. Leicester 1914

De Grey, Thomas, *The Compleat Horse-man; and Expert Ferrier*. 5th ed. 1684

Delmé Radcliffe, F. P., *The Noble Science*. London 1839

de Trafford, Sir Humphrey (Ed.), *The Foxhounds of Great Britain and Ireland*. London 1906

D'Ewes, J., *Sporting in Both Hemispheres*. London 1858

Diguet, Charles, *Le Livre du Chasseur*. Paris 1880

Dixon, H. H., see 'The Druid'

Dixon, William Scarth, *In the North Countree*. London 1889
A History of the Bramham Moor Hunt. Leeds 1898
The Hunting Year. London 1912
Hunting in the Olden Days. London 1912
The Cattistock Hunt. London 1921
Fox-Hunting in the Twentieth Century. London 1925
Men, Horses and Hunting. London 1931

'Druid, The' (Dixon, H. H.), *The Post and the Paddock*. 'Hunting ed.' London 1857
Silk and Scarlet. London 1859
Scott and Sebright. London 1862
Saddle and Sirloin. London 1870

Eardley-Wilmot, Sir John, *Reminiscences of Thomas Assheton Smith, Esq*. London 1860

Eeles, Henry S., *The Eridge Hunt*. Tunbridge Wells 1936

Egan, Pierce, *Book of Sports*. London 1832

Egerton-Warburton, R. E., *Short Account of the Tarporley Hunt Club 1762–1869*. Intro. to *Hunting Songs*. London 1870

Elliott, Col. William, *Carolina Sports by Land and Water*. New ed. London 1867

Ellis, C. D. B., *Leicestershire and the Quorn Hunt*. Leicester 1951

Fairfax-Blakeborough, J. *Short Histories* of various hunts

Fawcett, William, *Hunting in Northumbria*. London 1927
Turf, Chase & Paddock. London 1932
The Cattistock Hunt. London 1933

Ferrière, comte Hector de la, *La Chasse sous les Valois*. Paris 1869

Field, The, various issues

Fitzpatrick, B. M., *Irish Sports and Sportsmen*. Dublin 1878

Forbes, Allan, *Sport in Norfolk County*. Boston 1938

Forbes, Comm. W. B. ('Maintop'), *Hounds, Gentlemen Please!* London 1910

Fores's Guide, see 'Gelert'

Fores's Sporting Notes and Sketches, various issues

'Forester, Frank', see Herbert, W. H.

Fothergill, George A., *Hound Trailing – Past and Present*. Kendal 1924

Fouilloux, Jacques de, *La Vénerie*. Paris 1561

Foxhound, The, various issues

Gascoigne, George (ascr.), *In the Commendation of the Noble Art of Venery or Hunting*. London 1576. See Turberville, George

Gaston III, 'Phébus', comte de Foix, *Livre de la Chasse*, 1387. (Ed.) Lavalle, Joseph. Paris 1854.

Garrett, George J., *Fifty Years with Fox and Hounds*. Midland, Ga. 1938

'Gelert' (perhaps Davies, Rev. E. W. L.), *Fores's Guide to the Foxhounds and Staghounds of England*. London 1850

Gilby, Sir Walter, *Hounds in Old Days*. London 1913

Gilpin, Rev. William, *Remarks on Forest Scenery*. 2 vols. 3rd ed. London 1808

'Gin and Beer', see Andrews, Tom

Goodall, Daphne Machin, *Huntsmen of a Golden Age*. London 1956

Graham, Joseph A., *The Sporting Dog*. New York 1904

Graham, Sir Reginald, *Foxhunting Recollections*. London 1908

Grand, Gordon, *Redmond C. Stewart: Foxhunter & Gentleman of Maryland*. New York 1938
(fiction) *Colonel Weatherford and His Friends; Colonel Weatherford's Young Entry; The Silver Horn; The Millbeck Hounds; Old Man;* etc.

Grant, William W., *A Quarter Century of the Arapahoe Hunt*. 1954

Grattius, *Cygenetica*

Greaves, Ralph, *High Days and Bye Days*. London 1931
Short Histories of various hunts

Griswold, Frank Gray, *Hounds and Horses*. New York 1926
Sport on Land and Water. 7 vols. Pvt. 1914 sq.

Harper, Fletcher, *Orange County Hunt*, 1900–1947. Pvt. n.d.

Hawkes, John, *The Meynellian Science, or Fox Hunting upon System*. Pvt. *c.* 1810

Hayes, Capt. M. H., *Riding and Hunting*. London 1912

'Heathen, Dick', see Paget, Guy

Henry, Samuel J., *Foxhunting is Different*. New York 1938

Herbery, Henry W. ('Forester, Frank'), *Field Sports in the United States*. 2 vols. New York 1848

Heysham, W. Nunez, see 'Aesop'
'Hieover, Harry', *Stable Talk and Table Talk*. 2 vols. 2nd ed. London 1846
The Hunting Field. London 1850
Bipeds and Quadrupeds. London 1853
Higginson, A. Henry, *Foxhunting in America*. New York 1911
Letters from an Old Sportsman to a Young One. New York 1929
As Hounds Ran: Four Centuries of Foxhunting. New York 1930
Try Back: A Huntsman's Reminiscences. London 1932
The Meynell of the West: Being a Biography of James John Farquharson, Esq. London 1936
Peter Beckford Esquire: a Biography. London 1937
A Tale of Two Brushes. London 1943
Two Centuries of Foxhunting. London 1946
Foxhunting Theory and Practice. London 1948
(fiction) *The Perfect Follower*. London 1944
(with Chamberlain, J. I.), *The Hunts of the United States and Canada*. Boston 1908
Hunting in the United States and Canada. New York 1928
Hobson, Maj. E. S. C., *An Introduction to Fox-Hunting*. London 1911
Hope, Brig. Gen. J. F. R., *A History of Hunting in Hampshire*. Winchester 1950
Horlock, K. W., see 'Scrutator'
Horse and Hound, various issues
Hull, Denison B., *Thoughts on American Fox-Hunting*. New York 1958
Hurst, Capt. G. S. *The P.V.H. (Peshawar Vale Hunt)*. Aldershot 1934
Hutchinson, G. T., *The Heythrop Hunt*. London 1935
Inglis, Gordon, *Sport and Pastime in Australia*. London 1912
Jenks, Almet, *The Huntsman at the Gate*. London 1953
Johnson, T. B., *The Hunting Dictionary*. London 1830
Judd, Harry ('Tantivy'), *The Lanarkshire and Renfrewshire Hunt*. Glasgow 1900.
Scottish Hunts. Glasgow 1902
Jusserand, J. J., *Les Sports et Jeux d'Exercise dans l'Ancienne France*. Paris 1901
Kent, John, *History of the Charlton Hunt*: in *Records and Reminiscences of Goodwood and the Dukes of Richmond*. London 1896
Kilkenny, *Memoirs of the Kilkenny Hunt, by 'One of its Members.'* Dublin 1897
Knott, M. O'Malley, *Gone Away with O'Malley*. New York 1944
Langlois, M., *Dictionnaire de Chasses*. Paris 1739
Lanier, Charles D., *We Go Foxhunting Abroad*. Pvt. 1924
More Foxhunting in England. Pvt. 1927
Lawley, Francis, *Life and Times of 'The Druid'*. London 1895
Lawrence, John, *The Horse in all his Varieties and Uses*. London 1829

Le Masson, Edmond, *La Nouvelle Vénerie Normande*. Avranches 1841
Lennox, Lord William, *Merrie England, its Sports and Pastimes*. London 1858
Le Roy, Loys (Regius), *Traitté de la Vénerie*. 1572. (Ed.) Chevreul, Henri. Paris 1861
Lloyd, J. Ivester, *Hounds*. London 1934
Come Hunting! London 1952
Beagling. London 1954
Lloyd, Capt. L., *Field Sports of the North of Europe*. New ed. London 1885
Loder Symonds, F. C. & Percy Crowdy, E., *A History of the Old Berks Hunt from 1760 to 1904*. London 1905
Londonderry, Marchioness of, *Henry Chaplin, A Memoir*. London 1926
Longrigg, Roger. *The History of Horse Racing*. London 1972
Lonsdale Library, *Fox Hunting*. London 1930
The History of Hunting. London 1936
Machell, Hugh, *John Peel, Famous in Sport and Song*. London 1926
Mackay-Smith, Alexander, *The American Foxhound 1747–1967*. Millwood, Va. 1968
American Foxhunting. Millwood, Va. 1970
McLary, Jane McIlvaine, *A Portion for Foxes*. New York 1972
McNeill, C. F. P., *The Unwritten Laws of Foxhunting*. 2nd ed. London 1911
Madden, D. H., *A Chapter in Medieval History: the Fathers of the Literature of Field Sports and Horses*. London 1924
Manwood, John, *Treatise of the Forest Laws*. c. 1580
Markham, Gervase, *How to Chuse, Ride, Train and Diet both Hunting Horses and Running Horses*. 1599
Country Contentments. new ed. 1631
Mason, Finch, *Sporting Recollections*. London 1885
Flowers of the Hunt. London 1889
Mather, Charles, *Master of Radnor*. Pvt. 1947
Mayo, Earl of, and Boulton, W. B., *A History of the Kildare Hunt*. London 1913
Mills, John, *The Sportsman's Library*. London 1845
The Life of a Foxhound. London 1848
The Flyers of the Hunt. London 1859
The Sporting Life of England. New ed. n.d.
Milnor, W. Jr, *Memoirs of the Gloucester Fox Hunting Club*. Philadelphia 1830
Molyneux, Jack, *Thirty Years a Hunt Servant*. London 1935
Moore, Daphne, *Short History of the Carmarthenshire Foxhounds*. n.d.
Mordaunt, Sir Charles, and Verney, Rev. W. R., *Annals of the Warwickshire Hunt 1795–1895* London 1896
Morris, M. O'Connor, *Triviata, or Crossroads Chronicles*. London 1877
Hibernia Hippica. London 1900
Morrison, Eric, *Fox and Hare in Leicestershire*. London 1954
Murray, James, *Runs with the Lanarkshire and Renfrewshire Foxhounds*. Glasgow 1874

Musters, John Chaworth, *The Great Run with John Chaworth Musters' Foxhounds*. London c. 1876
Neale, Douglas, *Nearly All Hunting*. London 1950
Nethercote, H. O., *The Pytchley Hunt; Past and Present*. London 1888
Neufville, Nicholas de, see Charles ix
Newcastle, Duke of, *A General System of Horsemanship*. London 1666
New Sporting Magazine, various issues
'Nimrod' (Apperley, C. J.), *The Condition of Hunters*. London 1825
Hunting Tours. New ed. London 1835
Memoirs of the Late John Mytton Esq. London 1835
The Chace, the Turf, and the Road. London 1837
Northern Tour. London 1838
My Life and Times. London 1842. New ed. Edinburgh 1927
Life of a Sportsman. London 1842
The Horse and the Hound. London 1842
Nimrod Abroad. 2 vols. London 1843
(with others), *Sporting*. London 1838
North, Lord, *A Century of Hunting with the Warwickshire Hounds*. London 1891
Hunting. London 1910
North Cotswold Hunting, From 1772 to 1921. Evesham 1923
O'Connor, Roderic, *The Field Sports of France*. 2nd ed. Paris 1847
Oppian, *Cygeneticus*
Organized Foxhunting in America. New York, n.d.
Osbaldeston, George, *Autobiography*. (Ed.) Cuming, E. D. London 1936
Paget, Major Guy, *Rum 'uns to Follow: Memoirs of Seventy Years in the Shires, by 'Dick Heathen, A Melton Roughrider.'* London 1924
Life of Frank Freeman, Huntsman. Leicester 1948
Paget, J. Otho, *Hunting*. London 1900
Memories of the Shires. London 1920
Hunting Reflections. London n.d.
Pease, Sir Alfred, *The Cleveland Hounds as a Trencher-fed Pack*. London 1887
Hunting Reminiscences. London 1898
Half a Century of Sport. London 1932
Peer, Frank Sherman, *Cross Country with Horse and Hound*. New York 1902
Pennell-Elmhirst, Capt. E., see 'Brooksby'
Pitt, Frances, *Hounds, Horses and Hunting*. London 1948
Perrin, Olivier (Ed.), *Encyclopédie de la Vénerie Française*. Paris n.d.
Pollard, Hugh B. C., *Riding and Hunting*. London 1931
The Mystery of Scent. London 1937
Potts, Allan, *Fox Hunting in America*. Washington 1912
Price, Edwin W., *Horn and Hound in Wales*. Cardiff c. 1890
Proctor, Frank, *Fox Hunting in Canada and Some Men Who Made It*. Toronto 1929
Under Six Sovereigns: Fox Hunting in Canada. Toronto 1955
Randall, James L., *A History of the Meynell*

Bibliography

Hounds and Country. 2 vols. London 1901

Randall, John, *Old Sports and Sportsmen, Or, the Willey Country*. London 1873

Random Recollections of the Belvoir Hunt, by 'A Sportsman.' London 1897

Reeve, J. Stanley, *Radnor Reminiscences*. Boston 1921
Foxhunting Recollections. Philadelphia 1928
Red Coats in Chester County. New York 1940
A Foxhunter's Journal. Philadelphia 1952
Great Runs with the Cheshire. Pvt., n.d.

Reynard, Frank H., *The Bedale Hounds 1832–1908*. Darlington 1908
Hunting Notes from Holderness 1726–1914. Pvt., n.d.

Ribblesdale, Lord, *The Queen's Hounds*. London 1897

Richardson, Charles ('Shotley'), *The Complete Foxhunter*. London 1908
Hunting in Many Countries. London 1922

Richardson, Mary E., *The Life of a Great Sportsman*. London 1919

Ridgeway, Prof. Wm, *Origin and Influence of the Thoroughbred Horse*. Cambridge 1905

Rowan Hamilton, Gawin, *Annals of the Downe Hunt*. Belfast 1903

'Roy Modus', *Le Livre du Roy Modus et de la Royne Racio. c.* 1338. (Ed.) Blaze, Elzéar. Paris 1834

Russell, Lord Charles, *Some Recollections of the Chase*. Bedford *c.* 1879

Russell, Fox, *Cross Country Reminiscences*. London 1887
In Scarlet and Silk. London 1896
Sporting Sorrows. London 1901
(Ed.) *Sporting Society*. 2 vols. London 1897
(fiction) *The Haughtyshire Hunt*, 1897; *Colonel Botcherby M.S.H.*, 1899; *Outridden*, 3rd ed. 1901

Rutherford, James H., *The History of the Linlithgow and Stirlingshire Hunt 1775–1910*. Edinburgh 1911

Salnove, Robert de, *La Vénerie Royale*, 1655. (Ed.) Favre, L. Paris 1888

Sandford Evans, Major W., *The Pembrokeshire Hunt*. n.d.

Sassoon, Siegfried, *Memoirs of a Fox-Hunting Man*. London 1928

Scott, W. H., *British Field Sports*. London 1818

'Scrutator' (Horlock, K. W.), *Letters on the Management of Hounds*. London 1852
Horses and Hounds: A Practical Treatise on their Management. New ed. London 1858
Recollections of a Fox-Hunter. London 1861
Practical Lessons on Hunting and Sporting. London 1865
The Science of Foxhunting and Management of the Kennel. London 1868
(fiction) *The Master of the Hounds; Lord Fitzwarine*; n.d.

'Sabretache', see Barrow, A. S.

Sidney, S., *The Book of the Horse*. London 1875

Sitwell, Sacheverell, *The Hunters and the Hunted*. London 1947

Skelton, W. C., *Reminiscences of Joe Bowman and the Ullswater Foxhounds*. Kendal 1921

Smith, Harry Worcester, *A Sporting Tour Through Ireland, England, Wales and France*. 2 vols. Columbia, S.C. 1925
Life and Sport in Aiken, and Those Who Made It. New York 1935
A Sporting Family of the Old South. Albany, N.Y. 1936

Smith, Thomas, *Extracts from the Diary of a Huntsman*. London 1838
The Life of a Fox. London 1843
Sporting Incidents in the Life of Another Tom Smith. London 1867

Somerset, Lady Diana, and Apsley, Lady, *To Whom the Goddess . . .* London 1932

Somerville, E. Œ., and 'Ross, Martin', *Irish Memories*. London 1917
The States Through Irish Eyes. Boston 1930
The Sweet Cry of Hounds. London 1936
(fiction) *An Irish Cousin*, 1889; *Some Experiences of an Irish R.M.*, 1899; *The Silver Fox*, 1902; *Further Experiences of an Irish R.M.*, 1908; *Dan Russell the Fox*, 1911; *In Mr. Knox's Country*, 1915; *Mount Music*, 1920; *An Enthusiast*, 1921; *French Leave*, 1928; etc.

Somerville, William, *The Chace*. London 1730

Sparrow, Geoffrey, *The Crawley and Horsham Hunt*. London 1931

Spirit of the Times, The, various issues

Sporting Magazine, The, various issues

Sportsman's Dictionary or Gentleman's Companion for Town and Country. London 1778

Stephens, C. A., *Fox-Hunting*. Philadelphia 1872

Stretton, Charles, *Sport and Sportsmen*. London 1866

Stringer, Arthur, *The Experienc'd Huntsman*. Belfast 1714

Strutt, Joseph, *Sports and Pastimes of the People of England*. London 1801

Surtees, R. S., *Hunting Tours*, (Ed.) Cuming, E. D. Edinburgh 1927
Town and Country Papers. (Ed.) Cuming, E. D. Edinburgh 1929
Analysis of the Hunting Field. London 1846
(fiction) *Handley Cross*, 1843; *Mr. Sponge's Sporting Tour*, 1852; *Mr. Facey Romford's Hounds*, 1865; etc.

Sutherland, Douglas, *The Yellow Earl*. London 1965

Symonds, Henry, *Runs and Sporting Notes from Dorsetshire*. Blandford 1899

'Tantivy', see Judd, Harry

Taplin, William, *The Sporting Dictionary and Rural Repository*. 2 vols. London 1803

Taylor, Humphrey R., *The Old Surrey Fox Hounds*. London 1906

Thomas, Joseph B., *Hounds and Hunting through the Ages*. New York 1928

'Thormanby', *Kings of the Hunting-Field*. London 1899

Thornton, Col. Thomas, *A Sporting Tour through Various Parts of France in the Year 1802*. 2 vols. London 1806

Tongue, Cornelius, see 'Cecil'

Toussenel, A., *Tristia; Histoire des Misères et des Fléaux de la Chasse en France*. Paris 1863

Tozer, E. J. F., *The South Devon Hunt*. Teignmouth 1916

Traitté de Toute Sorte de Chasse et de Pêche. Amsterdam 1714

Trigg, Col. Haiden C., *The American Fox-Hound*. n.d.

Trollope, Anthony, (Ed) *British Sports and Pastimes*. London 1868
Australia and New Zealand. 2 vols. London 1873
Hunting Sketches. New ed. n.d.
(fiction) *The Kellys and the O'Kellys; Phineas Finn; The Eustace Diamonds; The American Senator; The Landleaguers*; etc.

Turberville, George (ascr.) *The Noble Art of Venery or Hunting*. 1576

Turf, Field and Farm, various issues

Twici, William, *Le Art de Vénerie*, etc. *c.* 1328, (Ed.) Dryden, Alice, Northampton 1908

Underhill, G. F., *The Helterskelter Hounds*. London 1894
A Century of English Fox-Hunting. London 1900
The Master of Hounds. London 1903

Uséz, duchesse d', *La Chasse à Courre*. Paris 1912

van Urk, J. Blan, *The Story of American Foxhunting*. 2 vols. New York 1940
The Horse, the Valley, and the Chagrin Valley Hunt. New York 1947
The Story of Rolling Rock. New York 1950

'Venator', see Cooper, John

Vyner, Robert, *Notitia Venatica*. London 1841

Watson, Alfred E. T., *Sketches in the Hunting Field*. London 1880

Webster, P. C. G., *Fox-Hunting in Staffordshire*. Lichfield 1876

Welby, John, *Memoirs of the Belvoir Hounds*. Grantham 1867

Whitney, C. W., and Martin, E. S., *Hunt Clubs and Country Clubs in America*. Boston 1928

Whyte Melville, George, *Riding Recollections*. London 1878
(fiction) *Market Harborough*. London 1857

Williams, L. H. W., *History of the Glamorgan Hunt*. London 1973

Williams, Michael, *The Continuing Story of Point to Point Racing*. London 1970

Williams, Gen. Roger D., *Horse and Hound*. Lexington, Ky. 1905
The Foxhound. New York 1914

Willoughby de Broke, 18th Lord, *Advice on Fox-Hunting*. London 1906

Willoughby de Broke, 19th Lord, *Hunting the Fox*. London 1920
The Sport of Our Ancestors. London 1921
The Passing Years. London 1924

Wilton, Earl of, *Sports and Pastimes of the English*. London 1868

Xenophon, *Art of Horsemanship Cygeneticus*

York, Edward Plantagenet, Duke of, *The Master of Game*, 1410. (Ed.) Baillie-Grohman, W. A. and F. London 1909

Youatt, William, *The Dog*. London 1845

Illustration Acknowledgments

Sources not acknowledged below are acknowledged in the captions

page

Endpapers reproduced by gracious permission
of Her Majesty The Queen
2 Bibliothèque Nationale, Paris
10 *Top* by courtesy of The Hon. Robert Erskine
Bottom by courtesy of the Oriental Institute,
University of Chicago
12 *Top* British Museum
Bottom by courtesy of J. K. Anderson, author of
Ancient Greek Horsemanship, University of
California Press, 1961
13 The Metropolitan Museum of Art. The
Cesnola Collection; purchased by
subscription, 1874–76
15 Seattle Art Museum. Norman Davis
Collection
16 British Museum
18 National Gallery, London
19 From *The Sports and Pastimes of the People of
England* by Joseph Strutt, London, 1867
20 George Rainbird Ltd
22 British Museum
24 Weidenfeld and Nicolson Ltd
25 From *The Sports and Pastimes of the People of
England* by Joseph Strutt, London, 1867
28 Bibliothèque Nationale, Paris
30 Bibliothèque Nationale, Paris
31 Victoria and Albert Museum
33 Bibliothèque Nationale, Paris
34 SCALA
36 George Rainbird Ltd. Photo Jeremy Whittaker
39 Mansell Collection
42 British Museum
45 Ashmolean Museum
46 Kunsthistorisches Museum, Vienna
48 From Diderot's *Encyclopédie*. Radio Times
Hulton Picture Library
49 Museo del Prado
51 Reproduced by gracious permission of
Her Majesty The Queen
54 National Gallery, London
Top National Galleries of Scotland
Bottom reproduced by gracious permission of
Her Majesty The Queen
56 Reproduced by gracious permission of
Her Majesty The Queen
58 Mansell Collection
63 Tate Gallery

65 Tate Gallery
66 British Museum
68 The National Trust
78 Mansell Collection
83 Mansell Collection
89 City of Birmingham Museum and Art Gallery
93 Private Collection
94 Mansell Collection
100 From *Memoirs of the Life of the late John
Mytton Esq* by 'Nimrod', London, 1835
103 Tate Gallery
125 Mansell Collection
129 Mansell Collection
131 Mansell Collection
140 *Top* Mansell Collection
Bottom from *Handley Cross* by R. S. Surtees,
London (n.d.)
141 Mary Evans Picture Library
142–3 From *Handley Cross* by R. S. Surtees,
London (n.d.)
146 Mary Evans Picture Library
149 From *The Badminton Library: Hunting* by
His Grace the 8th Duke of Beaufort and
Mowbray Morris, London, 1901
150 Mary Evans Picture Library
159 From *A Complete History of The Westmeath Hunt*
by Edmund F. Dease, Dublin, 1898
163 National Gallery of Ireland
165 Mary Evans Picture Library
167 *Top* from *Charles O'Malley the Irish Dragoon*
by Charles Lever, Dublin, 1842
170 The Sons of the Revolution, Fraunces Tavern,
New York. By courtesy of Alexander
Mackay-Smith
172–3 Colonel Gwynne Tayloe. By courtesy of
Alexander Mackay-Smith
175 Library of Congress
177 By courtesy of The Henry Francis du Pont
Winterthur Museum
179 From *The American Turf Register and Sporting
Magazine*, Vol. 3, 1831–32
180 By courtesy of J. Blan Van Urk
183 By courtesy of J. Blan Van Urk
185 National Gallery of Art, Washington. Gift of
William and Bernice Chrysler Garbisch,
1953
186 *Both* National Sporting Library, Middleburg

188–9 By courtesy of J. Blan Van Urk
189 By courtesy of J. Blan Van Urk
190 Mansell Collection
191 Mansell Collection
192 *Both* from *The Hunts of the United States and
Canada* by A. Henry Higginson and
Julian Ingersoll Chamberlain, Boston,
1908
193 By courtesy of Alexander Mackay-Smith
194 By courtesy of Alexander Mackay-Smith
196 Mary Evans Picture Library
200–1 Graphic Photo Union
204 Photo Jim Meads
206 Photo R. Clapperton
208 Photo Jim Meads
209 Photo Jim Meads
210 Photo Jim Meads
211 Photo Jim Meads
214 Photo Jim Meads
216 By courtesy of Alexander Mackay-Smith
218 By courtesy of J. Blan Van Urk
219 By courtesy of Alexander Mackay-Smith
221 Photo Allen Studio, Middleburg
222 Photo Jim Meads
224 Photo Marshall P. Hawkins. By courtesy of
Gilbert Humphrey
227 From *Hounds and Hunting Through the Ages*
by Joseph B. Thomas, Derrydale Press,
New York, 1928
229 From *The States Through Irish Eyes* by Edith
Somerville and Martin Ross, Houghton
Mifflin, Boston, 1930
233 Mansell Collection
234 Mary Evans Picture Library
235 *Top* photo VLOO
Bottom Mary Evans Picture Library
240 Mansell Collection
242 *Top* Mansell Collection
Bottom Victoria and Albert Museum.
Photo George Rainbird Ltd
243 Mary Evans Picture Library
244 From *The Peshawar Vale Hunt* by Captain and
Major G. S. Hurst, illustrated by Snaffles,
printed by Gale & Polden Ltd, Aldershot,
1934
245 Mary Evans Picture Library
247 Mary Evans Picture Library

Index

References to illustrations are in parentheses; references to captions in italics.
Hunts and hunt clubs, and their packs and countries, are in capitals; Hounds are in italics.

Index

Index

Index

Index